# The national integration of Italian return migration, 1870–1929

DINO CINEL

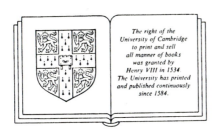

*The right of the
University of Cambridge
to print and sell
all manner of books
was granted by
Henry VIII in 1534.
The University has printed
and published continuously
since 1584.*

CAMBRIDGE UNIVERSITY PRESS

*Cambridge*

*New York   Port Chester   Melbourne   Sydney*

PUBLISHED BY THE PRESS SYNDICATE OF THE UNIVERSITY OF CAMBRIDGE
The Pitt Building, Trumpington Street, Cambridge, United Kingdom

CAMBRIDGE UNIVERSITY PRESS
The Edinburgh Building, Cambridge CB2 2RU, UK
40 West 20th Street, New York NY 10011–4211, USA
477 Williamstown Road, Port Melbourne, VIC 3207, Australia
Ruiz de Alarcón 13, 28014 Madrid, Spain
Dock House, The Waterfront, Cape Town 8001, South Africa

http://www.cambridge.org

First published 1991
First paperback edition 2002

*A catalogue record for this book is available from the British Library*

*Library of Congress Cataloguing in Publication data*
Cinel, Dino.
The national integration of Italian return migration, 1870–1929 /
Dino Cinel.
   p.       cm. – (Interdisciplinary perspectives on modern history)
ISBN 0 521 40058 9
1. Return migration – Italy – history.   2. Italy – Emigration and
immigration – History.   3. United States – Emigration and immigration –
History.   I. Title.   II. Series.
JV8132.C56   1991
304.8′0945–dc20   91-6989   CIP

ISBN 0 521 40058 9  hardback
ISBN 0 521 52118 1  paperback

This book examines the return migration to Italy from the United States from 1870–1929. A large number of Italians did not intend to settle permanently in the United States. Rather, they emigrated temporarily to the United States to make money in order to buy land in Italy. The book documents the flow back to Italy of individuals and remittances and discusses the strategies used by returnees in investing American savings.

Interdisciplinary perspectives on modern history

Editors
Robert Fogel and Stephan Thernstrom

**The national integration of Italian
return migration, 1870–1929**

# Contents

v

# Acknowledgments

Although a number of individuals, organizations, and events made possible the writing and production of this book, the writer alone carries the full responsibility for its success or failure as a work.

The research for this book was conducted in Italy and in the United States, in large and small institutions. Perhaps the richest sources of information are those in Rome, in the Banca d'Italia, and other bank archives in Italy. The readers of this book will recognize the vital importance of these bank archives.

The people who helped me with their solicited and unsolicited advice are many, and they all have my thanks. Two institutions – the National Endowment for the Humanities and Tulane University – are thanked for their financial support. My colleagues in the history profession, especially members of the Immigration History Society, have given good advice and have saved me from errors.

Thanks go also to Frank Smith at Cambridge University Press for encouragement and belief in my work, and to Herbert Gilbert for editing the manuscript.

As this book was taking shape my life was reshaped by the arrival at Tulane University of Linda Pollock, a British historian. Linda is now my wife. Sophia, our young daughter, with her Italian-British heritage, is commencing her assimilation into the extremely complex American culture. I cannot help but think that my understanding of the historical migrations to America has been enhanced because of my own experience and associations in America.

# Introduction: Emigration and the process of national integration

Return migration is today a worldwide phenomenon. According to an estimate by the United Nations, as many as one hundred million people engage every year in seasonal migrations. The phenomenon affects virtually every nation that has significant emigration or immigration. In Europe, for instance, return migration is today a mass phenomenon in Italy, Spain, Portugal, and Spain. For several decades West Germany, France, Switzerland, and the Scandinavian countries have been nations of immigration. In absolute numbers, Italy is the largest participant in the phenomenon. From 1945 to 1983 about eight million Italians left the country and five million returned. Within Italy, the south and the Veneto in the northeast are the regions most deeply affected by the phenomenon. Germany and Switzerland have been the preferred destinations of Italians.[1]

Individuals engaging in temporary international emigrations fall into two categories: seasonal migrants and temporary emigrants. Seasonal migrants relocate abroad for one season and return home at the end of it. In most cases the same individuals engage in seasonal migrations year after year. Immigration policies of countries of immigration are mostly responsible for seasonal migrations. For instance, Switzerland attracts tens of thousands of foreign workers every year and forces them to leave at the end of each season, the intention being to prevent these immigrants from becoming permanent residents of the Confederacy. More rarely, seasonal migrations are the result of personal choices by individuals unwilling to uproot their families from the home environment. Temporary emigrants, on the other hand, are individuals seeking employment in foreign countries for a number of years, then returning to home communities with savings. These individuals typically engage in a migration lasting several years, either to provide an income to families back home or to save money to achieve specific goals such as the purchase of land, the opening of a small business, or providing an elaborate wedding for a son or a daughter.[2]

1

Economists, political scientists, politicians, and social operators have been studying the impact of return migrations both in the sending and receiving countries.[3] Individuals return to native communities for many reasons, such as changes in political and economic conditions at home, undesirable changes in the countries of immigration, fulfillment of original goals, unwillingness to keep paying the high personal costs attached to seasonal and temporary emigrations, problems of adjustment in the host countries, and reassessment of the original needs that prompted emigration.[4] Regardless of the reasons advanced to go home, returnees and their savings have an impact on home communities. Individual returnees, especially if successful abroad, improve their economic conditions at home, or so they perceive upon their return. But does society in general and, specifically, do sending communities benefit economically and socially from return migration? On the surface it seems obvious that people returning with money, new skills, and broader mental horizons should become a social and economic asset. In reality returnees and their savings create a variety of social and economic problems. Inflation, decline in economic activities abandoned by temporary emigrants, discontent because of a less-than-satisfactory experience abroad, and difficulties in readjusting to life in home communities are only a few of the recurrent problems lamented by the countries reporting mass return migration.

There are two reasons why the debate as to whether return migration is a benefit or a liability for sending countries will persist for a long time. First, scholars disagree as to the very criteria to be used in assessing the social and economic impact of return migration. Second, return migrations occur in such a variety of national settings and stages of economic development that the elaboration of one model seems to be quite problematic.[5]

This book discusses return migration to Italy in the half century 1875–1925. The focus is principally on the return migration from the United States to southern Italy, although return migration from other countries and to the Italian north will be investigated at times to make comparisons. Although accurate indicators are not available, we know that millions of Italians engaged in return migration. For instance, in the period 1905–15 about two million Italians returned to Italy from overseas, two-thirds of them from the United States.[6] In percentages, other immigrant groups in the United States showed higher rates of returns than Italians did. But, in absolute numbers, more Italians returned from the United States than any other national group. The obvious question is why. Perhaps they departed from Italy with the determination to return. Or, they discovered that America was not the land of opportunity they had been led to believe it was. If we move from the subjective to the objective study of return migration, we wonder whether Italian returnees were successful or unsuccessful individuals. Were they returnees of failure? And, once back in Italy, did these returnees succeed in establishing themselves with American money? Of course this mass phenomenon did not go unnoticed. Did Italian society at large and the Italian government in particular encourage Italians to return? Or was their coming back opposed? Did the nation at large discuss a possible integration of mass emigration and return migration in the national economy? Most importantly, the return of so many individuals with American savings was bound to have a substantial impact on local economies, especially in small towns. And they seemingly did. But was such an impact profound and lasting or superficial and ephemeral? Remittances and returnees became two of the most important topics in the Italian national discourse at the turn of the century.

In Italy the public discourse on remittances and returnees was shaped by broader concerns raised by national events. After two decades of wars and diplomatic negotiations, Italy became one nation in 1870 with Rome as capital. During the following decades, national life was characterized by more or less successful efforts at creating a national economy and at integrating the vastly different regions and cultures within a national system. Italy was not the only nation trying to emerge from narrow regionalisms and foster economic and social integrations at a national level. Most Western nations were engaged in the same process, although in different ways. But Italy soon discovered a major stumbling block in the process of national integration. Southern Italy had so many social and economic problems that the integration of that region within the nation seemed to be virtually impossible. Only a few years after political unification, the *questione meridionale* (southern problem) had become the most intractable topic in the national agenda. A number of programs were legislated and set in place to help the south catch up with the rest of the nation. But, by the turn of the century, and three decades into the national experience, the questione meridionale seemed to be more difficult than ever.

Emigration, return migration and remittances entered the public discourse at this stage. Emigration started for a number of interrelated reasons. Certainly the social and economic dislocations caused by the forced absorption of the southern regional economy into the national economy greatly contributed to the rise of the mass phenomenon. Initially, official Italy opposed the mass exodus on grounds of national security, social stability, need for manpower at home, and even prestige to be maintained abroad. After all, mass emigration was an indication that Italy was less than successful in its program of national integration and economic modernization. And because the south was the region most affected by emigration, the national discourse focused on emigration as a subtopic of the southern question.

Progressively, as the programs set in place to help the south failed one by one, the topic of emigration, return migration, and remittances moved to central stage. Perhaps, some educated Italians argued, emigration was not the destabilizing force Italians said it was. Possibly, emigration was the last best hope the south had. Where the government had failed, emigration would succeed. The evidence was there for everybody to see: Returnees with American money were changing the south. From 1900 to World War I emigration and return migration as the solution of the southern questions became the preferred topic in the national discourse. For this reason I have chosen to study emigration and remittances as Italians saw them at the turn of the century: as dynamics of last resort to bring about the integration of the south within the nation and to expedite the modernization of the southern economy.

Two broad questions inspired this study. The first has to do with individual goals, strategies, and accomplishments. Italians who embraced emigration as a temporary emergency wanted to achieve some specific goals. And they embraced a set of strategies to achieve those goals. The success was assessed differently by returnees and by outsiders. Individual returnees often considered highly successful an outcome that outsiders regarded either as very modest or even counterproductive. The sad reality of the story was that many returnees became disenchanted with their return and a large number of them eventually resettled permanently in the United States. These individuals abandoned the original strategy of return migration and remittances in favor of a permanent overseas emigration only after one or more unsuccessful attempts at relocating in Italy and, most importantly, with the conviction that they had failed and wasted a number of years in the process. The second question deals with Italian society at large and with efforts made by the government and the private sector to direct the public discourse and to set in place political measures to protect remittances and returnees. In general, after an initial period of opposition to emigration, remittances and returnees were considered national assets to be integrated into the national purpose. But, of course, opinions varied as to the best course of action to be taken for such purpose. On their part, returnees seem to have been unconcerned about the large social and economic issues the nation was attaching to their experiment. Their goals were strictly personal, and they pursued them with traditional fierce individualism.

Although perhaps of some interest in itself, such study seems to have little to do with Italian immigrants in the United States. In the larger scenario of mass return migration from 1875 to 1925, the United States was like a peripheral place, where Italians went, made money, and in the end left without regrets and without substantial personal change. In reality my contention is that we cannot understand the Italian experience in the United States without some knowledge of mass return migration to Italy, its ambivalent outcome, and the lasting legacy of such experience in those who finally settled permanently in the United States. A closer look shows that the legacy of return migration and the lasting impact of that experience have become an integral part of the total experience of Italians in the United States. Ironically, Italian experience still haunts Italians in the United States. Native Italians and Italian Americans might have conveniently forgotten past experiences. Unfortunately this lack of awareness makes the interaction between Italian Americans and American society more ambivalent.

The literature on the Italian experience in the United States is puzzling, especially the literature authored by Italian Americans. On the one hand, one such body of literature argues that Italian Americans today are successfully integrated into American society. Discrimination and prejudice did not spare the first generation, and they have not altogether disappeared. But most Italian Americans today have entered the mainstream of American life. The main reason for the Italian-American success, such literature argues, is because Italian immigrants, although poor, arrived in the United States with a set of attitudes that prepared for success in a capitalistic and democratic society.[7] On the other hand, another body of literature points out that Italian Americans are still marginal and suffer discrimination in the United States. Although many Italian Americans enjoy a degree of economic success, Americans are still uncomfortable with Italian Americans. Moreover there exists a vague suspicion that there might be a connection between every Italian American, especially if successful, and the Mafia. The conflict goes deeper, according to this interpretation. And it has to do with the fact that the Italian culture, rich in family and communal values, has not been welcomed in the United States. In October 1981, for instance, I was a participant at the American Italian Historical Association annual meeting in Saint Paul, Minnesota. Robert Viscusi, one of the speakers, argued that whereas British settlers had been able to inscribe their names all over

America, Italians were denied any meaningful part in the American experience. Viscusi concluded that Italians are still excluded from American society. The audience assented. I realized that virtually all listeners – they were educated Italian Americans – shared a common sense of alienation from American society.[8]

Can we reconcile these two interpretations? More importantly, can we determine their origins? There is no doubt that many Italian Americans have achieved a considerable degree of material success – especially in comparison with Italians who did not emigrate – and of social integration. The income of Italian Americans has been above the national average. Avoiding conspicuous consumption, they invested in real estate or a family business. Being self-reliant, they generally refused to take government benefits, even when legitimately entitled. Their allegiance to the Old World faded away rapidly, and they became confident Americans. In the last two decades a number of Italians have achieved political power and national recognition. These are no small achievements in a country in which economic success, self-reliance, patriotism, and public service are highly valued. And if the achievements of Italian Americans are compared to the poverty of the immigrant generation of eighty years ago, one should conclude that in general the Italian experience in the United States is a stunning success. Yet a number of Italian Americans, especially if educated, feel differently. They complain about the demise of their culture and tradition. They blame American society for unabated discrimination. They feel marginal and alienated. Richard Gambino's passionate account of alienation in *Blood of My Blood* might overstate the case. But he is not the only one to report a malaise.

The complaints of alienation felt by Italian Americans can be interpreted within the frame of reference of the general alienation of many intellectuals in America. American society has become highly integrated, industrialized, urban, and bureaucratic. To many, there is little room for personal freedom and individual creativity in modern America. Perhaps Italian Americans voicing alienation are simply using their ethnic past as a vehicle to react to impersonal America. They surmise that, had they been able to preserve their traditions of family and community values, they would not have felt alienated at all. In such an interpretation, the ethnic past of Italian Americans is simply an artificial construction used to express a contrast between a distasteful present and an idyllic past. But I believe that the complaints of Italian Americans are specific. And such complaints should be understood within the total experience of emigration and immigration, which embraces both Italy and the United States. In the total picture the experience of return migration played a pivotal role.

Whether in Italy before emigration, upon returning from the United States, or in the United States after permanent relocation, Italians tried to break away from their marginal status to claim a larger role in society. In societies based on market economies such transition requires a certain degree of control over economic resources. Italians tried to achieve such control initially in Italy through temporary emigration to the United States and return migration to Italy, and later through permanent relocation in the United States. But the success in Italy upon returning from the United States was at best limited. Many Italians who tried temporary emigration and return and in the end resettled permanently in the United States abandoned Italy with a sense of failure. Their efforts to become part of Italian society through temporary emigration and American savings had failed. And that sense of failure was so deep and lasted so long that it affected their American experience. It is not unlikely that the alienation of Italian Americans toward the United States is also a carry-over of the alienation they experienced because of their failed return. Perhaps, on a larger scale, the alienation of Italian Americans from American society is the transference of the deepest ancestral alienation of Italian peasants toward their past, alienation they unsuccessfully tried to overcome through temporary emigration and return migration.

At this point we can introduce an interpretive model of the experience of Italian emigrants and immigrants. Whether in Italy before the first departure, in Italy upon returning from the United States, or in the United States after final settlement there, Italians tried to break away from marginal status to claim a larger role in society by improving their financial condition. Both in Italy and the United States Italians had to face similar problems. Although in different ways, both countries were affected by the rise of large-scale capitalism, the demise of regional economies, and the shifting demands for manpower by rapidly changing production cycles. In both countries individuals experienced accelerated changes, estrangement, and alienation, as they were compelled to change old habits and assume new attitudes. In dealing with such changes, immigrants and returnees, however, were not substantially different from individuals who never embraced emigration. They simply had to cope with two societies, instead of one. And what they experienced in one society was likely to affect their experience in the other. And because Italian returnees were rather unsuccessful in their resettlement in Italy, they carried with them a deep-seated disappointment, which conditioned their American experience.

This experience of Italians was not exceptional, however. Other immigrant groups experienced America through a set of mental images and expectations carried over from the old country. Irish immigrants, for instance, experienced America as a place of exile. But as historian Kerby Miller convincingly argues, the Irish sensed themselves as exiles even in Ireland before leaving. "Historians often claim," Miller wrote, "that Irish in North America saw themselves as unhappy exiles . . . That image might derive at least as much from the Irish heritage as from the American experience."[9] The Irish developed a sense of exile in Ireland because of well-known political and social adversities. Immigration further exacerbated that sense of exile and created a tension "between past and present, ideology and reality," with mixed results. In the end, however, "both the exile motif and the world view that sustained it assured the survival identity and nationalism in the New World."

The impact of attitudes developed in the Old World explains the contrast between what seems to be a successful adjustment of Italians and Irish in America and the experience of alienation among Italians and exile among Irish. The alienation of Italians and the exile motif among Irish sprang from sources more profound than the poverty and prejudice they experienced in the New World. Alienation and exile were experiences already in place before the two groups set foot on American soil. In fact, Italian and Irish made a relatively successful adjustment to American life in the span of two generations. But that success was not profound enough to dispel deep-seated perceptions carried over from Europe. The Italian experience, especially that connected with return migration, became an integral part of the Italian experience in the United States. Obviously this shows that the history of immigration is much more than the process of change from one national identity to another. It is a different way of looking at the larger process of modernization in Europe or in the United States, whereby individuals were forced to break away from old identities and forge new ones. But each stage was deeply influenced by previous stages. Without the history of return migration, the Italian experience in the United States remains partly unexplained.

These general ideas determined the argument, the logic, and the organization of this book. Chapters 1 and 2 deal with the political unification of Italy, the efforts made by the national government to integrate the south – the most disadvantaged section of the country – into the national economy, and the increasing realization among Italians that all the programs to help the south were seemingly failing. Chapter 3 discusses the main cultural characteristics of the Italian south. In facing the challenges of modernization and change, the southern ethos was both a help and a hindrance. Chapter 4 follows the growing national debate on emigration, return migration, and the impact the phenomenon was expected to have on the south specifically and the nation at large generally. By the early 1900s many Italians had accepted the conclusion that return migration and remittances were changing the south, a result that had eluded all governmental programs. The remaining chapters discuss return migration and remittances in the south and the impact they had. Chapter 5 traces the intensity of return migration from the 1870s to 1929 through statistical indicators and other literary evidence. Chapter 6 is dedicated to remittances: how they were channeled to Italy, how they were regarded by the public and private sectors, and the fight over the control of the process. Chapter 7 explains how returnees invested the money made in America. Chapter 8 describes and illustrates regional differences in investments of American money. Chapter 9 deals with those immigrants who equated return with retirement. In addition, the chapter discusses whether the failure of return migration might have been caused by discriminating economic policies by the central government. The Conclusion attempts to synthesize how return migration and remittances should be interpreted within the larger frame of reference of Italian immigration in the United States.

This book deals almost exclusively with Italy, but it is written for Americans, and it is intended to be a contribution to the study of Italian immigration in the United States. Perhaps this study will give Americans a better understanding of the millions of Italians who in the end, by choice or by default, settled permanently in the United States. The subject is naturally of special interest to Italian Americans. I know for a fact that many immigrants were unwilling to discuss with children and grandchildren the vicissitudes of their return migration. As a matter of fact some children of immigrants discovered only after the death of their parents that the parents had owned property in Italy, a fact never discussed with the children. In many cases those properties had been bought with American savings, before the final resettlement in the United States. In this story many third- and fourth-generation Italian Americans will learn of another aspect of the tormented process that ended up with the permanent settlement of their ancestors in the United States. Italian Americans will also learn why their immigrant ancestors were so ambivalent about America and why perhaps they themselves do not feel totally at home in the United States.

# 1  *The difficult task of national integration*

*The goal of national integration*

From 1848 to 1870 the populations of the Italian peninsula experienced the *Risorgimento Nazionale*, the political integration of the Kingdom of the Two Sicilies (Italian south and the island of Sicily), the Papal States (central Italy), the Grand Duchy of Tuscany (the region around Florence), and the Austro-Hungarian Lombardo-Veneto (the northeast) with a handful of minor states into the Kingdom of Italy. The leadership of the movement was provided by the Kingdom of Sardinia (Piedmont and the island of Sardinia) and its king, Victor Emmanuel II. The capital, originally in Turin, moved south to Florence, and finally to Rome, when in 1870 Italian troops forced the pope to surrender his state and his sovereignty over the city.[1]

The political integration of Italy mirrored other processes of national integrations occurring in the major countries of the Western world in the nineteenth century. Regional cultures and economies were progressively absorbed into national cultures and economies. The several independent German states, for instance, found their economic, political and, to a degree, cultural integration into a unified Germany. The American Civil War too was fought over the issue of regional (state) versus national (federal) integration. France and Great Britain, of course, had been politically unified for centuries. Both nations, however, embraced major programs of economic and political integration of their still heterogeneous populations and economies.[2]

For educated people in the nineteenth century, national integration seemed an eminently desirable goal The architects of the Italian process envisioned only positive results. Social reform would follow political unification. Trade barriers would be abolished. A national economy would replace inefficient and uselessly competitive regional economies. Individual freedom would stimulate entrepreneurial abilities. Administrative equalization would contribute to break down long-standing regional animosities. The school and the army would

10

join in the crusade. In the end, Italy would be stronger and more respected. In reality the process was tormented, ambivalent, and only partially successful. The resistances were many. Old political and economic structures were slow to disappear. Individuals and communities clung to local and regional loyalties with tenacity. Tradition was the most sacrosanct word among the peasantry; the new national state announced its advent with secular rituals that scared the still religious peasants.

In Italy it was clear from the beginning of the national experience that the south would be ill-equipped and reluctant to join the rest of the nation. Geography and history had burdened the region with handicaps so serious that the integration of the south within the new nation seemed virtually impossible. We begin our story with the events leading to national integration in Italy, and the progressive discovery of the disabilities of the south. Emigration, return migration, and remittances were direct results of the process of national integration. Initially they were considered undesirable events. Eventually, and perhaps because no other program seemed to work in the south, the national discourse focused on these dynamics as the best resources the south had to join the rest of Italy.

In Italy national integration had strong supporters among northern industrial operators and southern large landowners. Most peasants initially reacted with indifference and often with open hostility. Isolated communities remained unaware for years that political unification had occurred, until the new tax collectors showed up in different uniforms. In the Italian northeast, for instance, farmers and peasants openly fought to maintain their allegiance to the Austro-Hungarian Empire. Most Veneti and Lombards were willing to forgo greater political independence to enjoy the benefits of the Austrian administration. Because of lack of popular support, the Lombardy region had to be conquered with military help from France. The south was claimed by Giuseppe Garibaldi with a handful of venture soldiers against the opposition of the rural masses who feared the anticlericalism of the northerners.[3] Sicilians, traditionally opposed to political integration, were convinced to join the Kingdom of Italy only with the promise that they would be granted ample regional autonomy.[4] Peasants in the Papal States acquiesced to the occupation by Italian troops because they were convinced that no government would be worse than the papal government.[5]

In general the peasants' opposition stemmed from inability to understand the goals and accordingly the benefits to be derived from the creation of a modern state. Besides, peasants and farmers regarded the change as an obscure threat to their regional loyalties. Accustomed to lives defined by regional cultures, where a mountain range, a river, a specific dialect, a unique religious ritual determined the boundaries of one's world, peasants could not grasp the benefits to be derived from removing regional barriers and centralizing power. After all, regional loyalties had provided security for centuries.[6] Writing three decades after the political unification of Italy, an observer remarked that regional loyalties opposed the process of national integration: "In no country of Europe," Pasquale Villari wrote, "are local loyalties still so marked as they are in Italy."[7]

To the promoters of political unification, the opposition of the peasants did not come as a surprise. After all, Italian peasants had traditionally lived at the margins of any political process occurring in Italian states and had been ignored for centuries. But the promoters were also aware of the destructive potential of peasant upheavals. True to their past, peasants staged violent upheavals during and immediately after political unification. In Calabria, for instance, Garibaldi's troops opened the prisons, setting free both political prisoners and common criminals. Some criminals became leaders of gangs of brigands, who terrorized Calabria for years.[8] Peasant discontent flared up in open rebellion in Sicily, Puglie, Abbruzzi and Molise, and Emilia Romagna.[9] The regions not affected by peasant violence were the exception to the rule. But these episodes which occurred in the 1860s did not arrest the process of national integration, although at times the survival of the nation seemed at stake.[10] In due course, however, the promoters of the new Italy awoke to the realization that in a democratic or semidemocratic society national integration could not occur without some form of popular support. Whatever their previous allegiance, peasants had to be persuaded that the new nation could give them a better future than the old sovereigns had.[11]

But, if peasants generally opposed the new state, other groups strongly supported national integration. Educated elites, northern entrepreneurs and southern landowners had political and economic reasons to back the movement. Educated Italians had been influenced by the liberal ideas spread by the French Revolution about the need for national integration and social reform. Italy, these people argued, could not take its place in Europe, nor could it compete in world markets, without being politically united. The economy would become the major beneficiary with the progressive elimination of trade barriers, the rationalization of the economy, and finally a strong nation ready to compete with other European and American economies. The road to political and economic integration was hazardous and long. But the supporters of the new state were confident that Italy had the economic and human resources to bring about its national integration, as other Western nations were doing at that time.[12]

Economic indicators seemingly corroborated the confidence that the country had a bright future. Cotton growing largely expanded, especially in the south, during the 1860s, mostly because of the decline in imports from the American Confederacy.[13] The war between France and Germany in 1870–1 increased the demand for Italian agrarian products, especially wheat. In the Italian south alone, wheat production swelled from 12 to 20 million hectoliters per year, wine from 2 to 8 million, and olive oil from 600,000 to one million and a half hectoliters from 1860 to 1870.[14] Because of increased world demand, prices of agrarian commodities rose. In Campania, for instance, wheat prices escalated from 17 lire per quintal in 1850 to over 37 in 1868. Olive oil and citrus fruit prices increased by about 40 percent. Wine prices topped the list with a sevenfold increase, mostly because of the greatly enlarged demand from France, whose vines had been ravaged by the phylloxera.[15] Independence from foreign domination, political unification, and a certain degree of social and economic reform, so the architects of Italian political unification argued, would greatly help this rapidly expanding economy.

### The emergence of a national problem: The south

The Italian south was to play a key role in the new national economy. After all, the south was rich. This was a common assumption in the Italian north. To realize its full potential, the south needed political freedom. And freedom was exactly what northerners came to offer. Gioacchino Pepoli, the first Italian Minister of the National Economy, expressed a sentiment common among northerners, in a speech delivered in Naples in 1862: "This fertile land blessed by God above all others lacked only one thing to be the richest and happiest in the world: freedom."[16] Even Camillo Benso di Cavour, the promoter of Italian unification, argued in 1860 that within twenty years the south would be the richest region in Italy.[17]

The honeymoon between unrealistic northern assumptions and southern realities ended soon. The Chamber of Deputies in Rome provided the forum for the unhappy confrontation. Southern representatives like Napoleone Colajanni, Ettore Ciccotti, and Giustino Fortunato revealed to northern colleagues the sad reality of the south. Fortunato, for instance, told his northern colleagues that the south was so removed from their expectations that they, the northerners, could not begin to fathom the problems of the south. "We southerners," he told them, "were still in the Middle Ages, and all of a sudden you northerners pushed us into the modern world. Gunshots were the most powerful argument you had to convince us not to oppose national unification."[18] With bitter disappointment, southerners began to suspect that national unification had been in reality a military and economic takeover. Northerners, on their part, developed misgivings about bringing the south into the new nation. "Had we known then – before political unification – what we know now," a northern representative retorted to Giustino Fortunato, "we would not have fought for political unification. That was an honest mistake on our part, stemming from a set of erroneous assumptions about the true situation of the south and the alleged desire of southerners to join Italy."[19] The discovery of these differences, the bitterness of the south, the disappointment of the north, and the economic dislocations caused by the wars pushed the two sections of the country to the brink of civil war.[20]

It took several decades before the country could have a reliable profile of the Italian south.[21] By the turn of the century, however, a sizable literature documented the handicaps that nature and history had heaped on the south. Beginning in the early 1870s, social scientists headed by Sidney Sonnino and Leopoldo Franchetti conducted surveys in the south and made their findings available.[22] The government itself conducted an extensive investigation of the conditions of the agrarian economy and of the peasants in the late 1870s, the most comprehensive such study ever undertaken in Italy.[23] Educated southerners too, like Pasquale Villari, Arcuri De Viti De Marco, Francesco Saverio Nitti, Ettore Ciccotti, and Giustino Fortunato, among others, contributed to this revelation.[24] Slowly a consensus emerged. The south was different from the rest of the nation. And that difference stood in the way to national integration. Northerners came to believe they had married a corpse. With self-denigration, southerners themselves accepted the conclusion that the south was a "savage Italy" (*Italia barbara*).[25] Northerners and southerners concurred that the south was the major challenge for the new nation. The national debate on the "southern question" (*la questione meridionale*) had started.

## The natural environment

The few visitors who ventured off the beaten track discovered that romantic Naples and glittering Palermo were exceptions. Most southern regions were neither beautiful nor fertile. For instance, the Basilicata plateau, most of Calabria, and the hinterland of Sicily were clay soil which, during the rainy season, turned into mud, likely to cause mudslides. In fact, in 1885 309 families from Basento in Basilicata were buried under such a mudslide. The whole Apulia region soil was mostly limestone, covered only by a few inches of topsoil. Hot summers and infrequent rains made wheat growing virtually impossible. Artificial irrigation was out of the question, for lack of perennial rivers. The output per acre showed the southern disadvantage; at the turn of the century, for instance, in Basilicata the output of wheat per acre was one-third of the national average.[26]

Visitors noticed also the marked differences between northern and southern communities. Geographical isolation was the rule in southern towns. In the Italian north people lived either directly on the land they farmed or in small communities close to the farmland. In the south people lived almost exclusively in large communities, ordinarily located on mountaintops. It was the rule for many southern peasants to walk two hours or more to go to work. Families living on the land were the exception.[27] Progressively visitors became aware that the concentration on large settlements was the result of geography, history, and economy. Although not uncommon in central and northern Italy, malaria had been the rule in the flatlands since the fifteenth century. Hilltops and mountains were the only livable places. Moreover, hilltops were the only safe areas: Southern Italy had been for centuries the target of hostile incursions by many peoples living around the Mediterranean.[28] The organization of the southern economy too had fostered the creation of nucleated communities. In general southern renters and sharecroppers worked several tracts of land located apart from each other. Moreover, given the intense competition to secure the most favorable land contracts, farmers seldom worked the same tract of land for a number of years. In many instance they entered into new contracts every year. These circumstances prevented them from settling anywhere in the countryside. Moreover, day laborers had to be available to work anywhere and therefore often were willing to relocate to estates in neighboring towns. Obviously, the best arrangement was to reside in a centrally located community.[29]

By the early nineteenth century, geography, history, and economics had locked southerners into large towns, isolated from each other by long distances. A survey taken in the early twentieth century, for instance, revealed that in the region of Basilicata only 9 percent of the population resided in the countryside. In Sicily the percentage was 10, in Calabria 18.[30] The Bari province, in Apulia, had the lowest percentage of people living on the land: only one out of every one hundred.[31] Land values were obviously affected: properties adjacent to towns sold at a higher price than distant properties. The time wasted in going to and coming from work was not the only reason.

Security was another reason. In distant farms it was difficult and virtually impossible to protect crops from night thieves. Finally effective farming in distant plots was made more expensive by commuting time.[32]

Visitors to the south were surprised by the differences between the geographical and human landscapes of the north and south. But they were even more startled by the poverty, and the intellectual and social backwardness of southerners. After all, the south northerners had come to know through their reading of classical literature was a place of beauty, economic prosperity, and cultural refinement. Visitors realized that their reading of the classics had to be updated through the study of history. Northerners who preached the gospel of national integration were startled when southerners argued: "To you northerners, national integration and social reform are desirable and attainable goals. They are not to us. History made us different."[33]

Visitors willing to understand the south were forced to become amateur historians. Through history they entered a territory even more unfamiliar than the human landscape they could see. The history of the south since the fall of the Western Roman Empire had been a maze of foreign dominations: Byzantines, Greeks, Lombards, Arabs, Hohenstaufens, Normans, and finally French and Spanish took turns in exploiting or developing a region that, until the time of the Crusades and the discovery of America by Columbus, was the center of world trade. On balance, the south had mostly a history of exploitation, which left it economically dependent, socially disintegrated, and morally dejected.[34] Three historical events had a major impact in shaping the south: first, the hegemony of the Florentine banks in the economy of the south, established through services provided to the House of Anjou in the thirteenth century; second, the effective removal of the landed aristocracy from the management of the land in the sixteenth century; third, the emergence of a preindustrial proletariat in Naples and Palermo in the eighteenth century.

## The economic hegemony of the Florentine banks

The Florentine banks established the economic dependency of the south in the thirteenth century; that dependency has never been terminated. The banks moved into the south by lending money to Charles of Anjou in his first expedition to southern Italy and Sicily in the early 1270s. In 1282, after the Sicilians ousted the French, to reconquer the island, Charles asked for additional loans from the banks. In an agreement signed in 1282, the banks were to provide the capital needed to field an army. King Charles, on his part, granted the banks the franchise to collect taxes, coin money, the administration of the salt works, the monopoly on the sale of salt, the franchise on maritime trade, the rents of all state-owned lands in Apulia, and finally the most lucrative franchise to control the export of wheat.[35]

Aware that these advantages might not last long, the Florentine banks, owned by the powerful families Bardi, Peruzzi, and Acciaiuoli, setting aside any long term plans for the economic development of the region, concentrated on extracting money as quickly as possible.[36] The hatred of southerners did not deter Florentine bankers from unrelenting exploitation.[37] The impact on the southern economy was devastating. Wheat production rapidly declined, mostly because Florentine banks offered local producers low prices. Increased rents on state-owned land in Apulia depressed cattle raising. Local and international commerce fell into the hands of foreign merchants. The Tyrrenian trade was controlled by Florentine merchants and a handful of commercial houses from Pisa. The commerce in the Adriatic was monopolized by Venetian merchants.

With the death of Robert of Anjou, the last in the dynasty, in 1343, the Florentine banks lost their privileges; some even failed. But the south had no resources of its own to shake its economic dependency. On the one hand, by the close of the first half of the fourteenth century, the powerful city-states of Florence, Pisa, Genoa, Milan, and a handful of smaller cities, like Lucca, Volterra, Bergamo, and Brescia, had developed powerful local economies with commercial ties to European and Eastern countries.[38] On the other hand, through a series of informal arrangements validated by the new Spanish rulers of the south, northern commercial houses kept control of the southern economy.[39] The fall of Constantinople in 1453, followed by the exclusion of Europeans from eastern Mediterranean ports, the discoveries of America in 1492 and of a new route to the Indies in 1498 diverted international trade to the north and the east. These events sealed the economic dependency of the south.[40]

The Spanish domination which started in 1503 further aggravated the situation.[41] For the Spanish crown the goal was not the economic well-being of southern Italy; rather the advantage of the imperial capital through the collection of taxes. The outcome was disastrous. A tax on silk exports, for example, reduced production by four-fifths in twenty years.[42] Duties were collected also on commodities carried from region to region, although within the kingdom. The government promoted the export of nonprocessed materials from the south to the north, such as wheat, olive oil, and textiles, and imported finished products, only to collect additional taxes.[43] Lacking adequate capital, southerners were forced to abandon whatever internal trade they had previously controlled.[44] Impressed by the organizational efficiency of northern Italian and foreign merchants, the crown granted them the franchise to collect taxes.[45] Because of high taxes, local production declined and the crown had to sell state land to generate income. Genoese and Florentine merchants stepped in and bought, thus increasing their economic power in the south.[46]

## The disengagement from the land

The Bourbons implemented another policy that had the most profound impact on the south: the disengagement of the aristocracy from the management of the land. Until the late seventeenth century, the south was like most of Europe: a feudal society with local lords managing their estates with a high degree of autonomy from the crown. By the early eighteenth century, an increasing number of lords were leaving their estates and moving to Naples and Palermo. By the mid-eighteenth century, the lords managing their estates directly were the exception. The rule was for them to live at the court while managing their estates through middlemen. One of the reasons for leaving seems to have been the spreading of malaria.[47] Available evidence, in fact, shows that the infection did not spare mountain communities and estates of lords. The major reason for leaving, however, was political. The Bourbons, like other enlightened monarchs of the time, increased their power and centralized the decision-making process by undermining the authority and the autonomy of the local gentry.[48]

The Bourbons pursued their goal by making the direct management of the land burdensome, and by making court life irresistibly attractive. To implement their strategy, the Bourbons reviewed the feudal land titles granted by previous rulers. The review process often ended in court. This forced the landed aristocrats to live in Naples, often for years, until their cases were solved. Moreover, the fiscal policies of the crown and the ruthlessness of tax collectors did not spare nobles. When landed aristocrats presented their complaints to the king, the crown promised to take quick action. In reality the king purposely avoided making any decision in order to force nobles to be away from their estates. Finally increased taxation and the low prices foreign merchants were willing to pay for wheat rendered the management of the land an unwelcome chore. Unwilling or unable to confront these problems, many bailed out: they hired middlemen to manage their estates. The court provided not only culture and entertainment, but also careers to satisfy ambitions and to provide extra income. By the late eighteenth century only a handful of southern estates had resident owners.[49]

This estrangement became contagious. Owners of medium and, even, small properties, hoping to be able to live on rents, increasingly abandoned the management of their properties and rented them to peasants.[50] Free from the responsibility of land management, medium and small owners pursued other careers. But opportunities were limited. Individuals with a law degree could practice law, which demanded moving to the provincial capital because legal services were not needed in small communities. Eventually an oversupply of lawyers made the legal profession unprofitable. Individuals with a classical education found jobs as tutors for children of wealthy families, mostly in Naples and Palermo. But in this field too opportunities were limited and relocation a requirement many were unwilling to face. There were no jobs in industries: unlike central and northern European nations the south had not yet been affected by incipient industrialization.[51]

Disengaged from the management of the land and unwilling or unable to enter other useful occupations, owners of small and medium properties engaged in politics. In a region where land was the almost exclusive economic resource, the office of the mayor carried awesome power: he appointed municipal officers, determined the use of commercial land, assessed property values and taxation, managed local charities, and arbitrated litigations among peasants. On account of such vast powers, landowning families engaged in the political process to control the office of the mayor.

The departure of the landed gentry and the disengagement of medium and small landowners from the management of the land had a lasting impact on the south. Renters and sharecroppers had no interest in making improvements on the plots they rented. Moreover, renters and sharecroppers had little or no experience in land management. Thus productivity declined. More importantly, however, the dissociation between management and ownership created a set of expectations that became a lasting legacy in the south. Land was the basis of social prestige and the source of family income. The management of the land, however, was spurned as unbecoming. Hence, the exploitation of the land was less important than the rents and the social prestige it generated. This frame of mind affected propertyless peasants too. Their greatest dream was to own land to rent it out, not to farm it. The actual exploitation of natural resources was the task of second-class citizens, the peasants, who had little knowledge of farming techniques, no managerial skills, and virtually no interest in land improvement. A gentleman's proper occupation was leisure and politics.

The southern social fabric was obviously affected by the dissociation between ownership and management. A gentleman's claim to social status was not based on tested abilities to exploit natural resources, but on land ownership. Interactions among groups was not cemented by economic interests, but rather on power and prestige stemming from land ownership. Power in southern Italy had been effectively severed from its economic basis. The road to the abuse of power was wide open.

### The emergence of a preindustrial proletariat

The emergence of a preindustrial proletariat in Naples and Palermo was the third historical event to shape the south. In northern Europe the rise of an urban proletariat was the result of dislocations generated by industrialization and the consolidation of farming. In the Italian south, it was a unique phenomenon brought about by the decline of the agrarian economy and the absence of industrialization. Throughout the eighteenth century a number of southern peasants left the countryside for the cities of Naples and Palermo for several reasons. The spreading of malaria forced some to abandon unsafe towns. Others followed their masters when they took up residence in Naples and Palermo. High rents and burdensome sharecropping contracts led others to see no future in farming. Finally the fiscal policies of the crown made it impossible for many to live off their wages. In fact, to make the south competitive, the Bourbons supported cutting wages to reduce the cost of wheat production. Under the circumstances, country laborers could no longer make ends meet, and many left for Naples or Palermo without any plan for making a living.

Naples and Palermo were not geared to absorb the incoming masses. Some newcomers found jobs as servants in noble families. A very few, especially the youngest, learned a trade and found steady employment. Most newcomers, however, remained permanently unemployed, desperately searching and fighting for food and shelter. Landed aristocrats, who had previously relocated in Naples and Palermo from country estates, provided protection and, when possible, food and shelter. In return, this army of unemployed supplied their protectors with services, ranging from legitimate to criminal activities. Thanks to these unemployed, the underworld of the *Camorra* in Naples, the Mafia in western Sicily, and the *'ndragheta* in Calabria eventually flourished and created social ties the government found impossible to break.[52]

By the early nineteenth century the social fabric of Naples and Palermo showed unique characteristics. Social interactions were not based on a sound economy of production and services, but on sheer patronage. The urban proletariat was ready to volunteer any service to patrons, in exchange for protection, shelter and food. Disengaged from the management of the land, landed aristocrats living in Naples and Palermo came to regard their elevated social status as a license to exercise personal power in any way they saw fit. After all, in a society lacking the basic elements of economic integration, there are very few objective restrictions to the use and abuse of personal power.

Landed aristocrats used their power to act not necessarily against the law, but certainly outside the law. Each became a law unto himself, with a band of retainers to enforce it. These individuals in time provided the rank and file of the Mafia in and around Palermo and of the Camorra in Naples and surrounding territory. Mafia and Camorra were not organizations as we envision them today; rather they described commonly accepted behavior. A mafioso was an honorable man, in the common parlance. Mafiosi were not necessarily criminals; rather they were individuals determined to defend their rights and those of their group by using personal power. They did not rely on the power of the state or on an objective system of law for protection.[53] Unfortunately Naples and Palermo were not the exception. On a smaller scale, the same dynamics were at work in provincial capitals, medium-size towns, and small villages. Virtually everywhere, landed families living on rents indulged in the arbitrary use of power. Willingly or unwillingly, peasants accepted it, as long as they were given food and protection. The idea of a state based on an objective legal order was out of place virtually everywhere in the south. In the end, southern society was left without an objective basis for viable social interactions. These, in fact, are not established in a vacuum. Rather, they are the result of ways in which individuals regard property, and the personal and social use of it.[54]

*The nineteenth century*

Efforts made throughout the nineteenth century to change the south generally failed. On paper feudal rights were abrogated in 1808 in the Italian south, and in 1812 in Sicily. To implement the new socioeconomic order, the Napoleonic rulers in the south and the Sicilian Bourbons pressed by the British government engaged in a program of land reform. But those changes were short-lived. The restoration mandated by the Council of Vienna in 1815 reestablished the economic and social control of southern landowners.[55] Although the Bourbon crown, under pressure from Great Britain, supported the termination of feudal entails and some sort of land reform, large landowners in the end sabotaged every attempt.[56] When the south became part of a unified Italy, the central government made some feeble attempts to enact a program of land reform. But by the end of the century it was obvious that the program was going nowhere. Large landowners not only retained control of their old estates, but often enlarged them by buying additional properties. To implement its reforms, the government carved out of estates previously owned by Italian states and the church small properties and placed them on the market to give peasants the opportunity to become landowners. The intent of the government was to increase the number of landowners, because, according to the wisdom of the time, only a broadly based "rural democracy" assured a broad base of political support. Besides, the sale of land provided some immediate benefits. The profits were to be used to offset the national debt and subsidize national improvements. Unfortunately the land reform program was to be implemented by local administrations. Landowners mastered enough power to bribe local administrators and buy land put on the market. When bribes did not suffice, landowners used intimidation. In many cases neither bribes nor intimidation were needed. After all, local administrations were generally controlled by landowners.

A few peasants purchased small properties by borrowing money from local moneylenders, who were the local large landowners. Of course, these properties were not the most desirable in the area. Lack of managerial skills, high interest rates, low yields, and increasing taxation forced many new small landowners out of the market within a few years. Large landowners promptly stepped in to buy at very low prices, often as a repayment of loans. In the end, land reform reached the opposite effect than the one intended by legislators. Peasants who had some money or borrowed it to buy properties were once again virtually destitute, while large landowners had enlarged their estates.[57]

The increased power of southern landowners spelled further degradation for peasants. The end of feudal entails deprived peasants of the common rights they had enjoyed in feudal days. In the new market economy, which replaced the old feudal system, peasants had to fend for themselves, the former protections of the lords being no longer available. The increased destitution of peasants had two consequences. First, it increased the social and economic control of landowners and their managers. Second, it provided new ammunition to existing social and economic groups of protest: brigands, Mafia and Camorra.[58]

*Brigandage, Mafia, Camorra*

Brigandage was predominantly a rural phenomenon. Brigands were former peasants, angry at the broken promises of land redistribution made by the government. When they realized that political unification would not terminate their social and economic disfranchisement, they left their families and sought refuge in the mountains. Descending from their mountain refuges, they stole cattle, robbed travelers, and entered towns at night to offer protection and demand extortion.[59] The brigands' victims were not the powerless, but landowners and wealthy merchants. Apparently, peasants supported brigands: they were the vindicators of peasants' rights.[60]

Political developments following national unification provided political legitimacy to brigands. After the fall of the Kingdom of the Two Sicilies, Ferdinand II sought refuge in Rome at the papal court to organize his return to Naples. Of course, he needed the support of some of his former subjects. Brigands and Ferdinand became allies as they discovered that they had a common enemy in the northern Italians who had occupied the south. To Ferdinand, northerners were the usurpers of his throne. To brigands they were deceptive individuals unwilling to keep their promises of land reform. Ferdinand and brigands became overnight allies. Ferdinand offered them money and a new public image: brigands were no longer common criminals, rather defenders of the rights of the Bourbon dynasty. The new goal was to bring back to Naples Ferdinand and push out of the south the invading Piedmontese. The Vatican enhanced the image of the brigands by validating the claims of Ferdinand to his throne and the action of the brigands to defeat Victor Emmanuel, a king excommunicated by the church.

The pope's support for Ferdinand was also a warning to Italy. The Italian government openly stated that the ultimate goal was the integration of all Italian states, the papal included, into one nation. The pope reacted by threatening excommunication on anybody who would dare to jeopardize the papal domains. In 1870 Italy carried out its plans, notwithstanding the opposition of many European nations. The king and the government were excommunicated. Overnight, the pope became the second ally of the brigands who added to their agenda the return of the pope to his states. To cope with the threat of the brigands, the government had to field an army twice as large as that assembled to force the Austrians out of the northeast, at staggering financial cost. After two decades of guerrilla warfare, brigands were defeated. But the social damage caused by brigands survived long after the last of them were either apprehended and executed, or escaped to America. Brigandage was the sign that the discontent of many southerners could not find a legitimate voice in Italy. Peasants had to continue to exist outside society.[61]

Peasants were not the only group disgruntled by the policies of the new government. Landowners quickly discovered that the government was less tolerant of local autonomies than the Bourbons had been. After the fall and departure of the Bourbons from Naples, a number of absentee landowners returned to their estates. But they were the minority. Most remained in Naples or Palermo, determined to keep their power and patronage. Of course, the Piedmontese government was equally determined to force a rational and bureaucratic government in the south. Southern nobles, however, were not deterred: nobody knew the region and its traditions better than they did. Among the best of southern traditions, nobles counted the Mafia in Sicily and the Camorra in Naples. To oppose the power of the state, southern nobles reinforced their power and patronage by expanding the roles of Mafia and Camorra.

By the second half of the nineteenth century, the Camorra was the most powerful institution in and around Naples. Through emissaries, landowners openly committed crimes, counting on police protection and the traditional *omertà* (secrecy) of peasants.[62] Children were trained in the ways of the Camorra from an early age: they started with theft, then advanced to carrying out extortion, and finally graduated to physical violence and murder. Political offices in and around Naples were controlled by the Camorra. In 1880 a city councilman in Naples remarked that the city was clean for the first time in history, thanks to the Camorra, which had secured the franchise for garbage collection. The police force and the courts were controlled by the Camorra.

The Mafia originated in the rural areas of the province of Palermo in the early nineteenth century and progressively moved into the city itself. Like the Camorra, the Mafia rejected the authority of the modern state and vindicated the use of arbitrary personal power as the ultimate form of social control. Most Western societies, to break the opposition of arbitrary personal power resisting the authority of the state, monopolized the means and use of physical force. The private armies of ex-feudal lords were disallowed and replaced with national armies under the command of generals directly accountable to the central government. The armies' stated purpose was the preservation of the national territory; equally important, however, was the use of the national armies to put down organized opposition to governmental policies. This process encountered resistance every-

where. The Mafia and the Camorra were two outstanding examples
of successful opposition, as they are to this very day.[63]

The Mafia dons were generally large landowners who recruited
their informal armies from the ranks of lesser landowners and peasants. The major goal of the mafiosi was the control of land contracts.
Owners of medium and small properties were forcefully instructed
as to how much they could charge for rent. Renters were instructed
about their obligations. And both owners and renters were forced to
pay for protection. Owners and renters who preferred established
legal channels soon discovered that their properties and lives were
in danger. Often by the time they realized the danger they were in,
it was too late. In 1875 a magistrate from Palermo resigned from the
bench, declaring that it was useless to try to enforce an officially
established code of law when the accepted law of the region, revered
by virtually everybody, was the unwritten code of the Mafia.[64]

It is historically inaccurate to conclude that Mafia, Camorra, and
brigandage were the norm in the south. It would be equally erroneous, however, to consider them social aberrations in an otherwise
sound society. In reality Mafia, Camorra, and brigandage were the
three most visible indicators of a social ethos southerners shared. The
basic assumption was that social relations were not based on objective
criteria, legally established, socially verifiable, and enforceable in the
court of law. Rather, society was cemented by personal relations of
a patron-client type, in which the power of the patron was disengaged
from objective criteria and controls. The exercise of that power did
not require social justifications and certainly refused legal and objective constraints.[65]

### The modern state moves in

The impulse toward the integration of all Italian states in one nation
originated in the Kingdom of Sardinia, which had implemented social
and economic reforms since the French Revolution. After the annex-
ation of the south to Italy in 1860, the Piedmontese extended their
legal and administrative system to the rest of Italy. The Piedmontese
had no doubts that the south would benefit from becoming part of a
modern state. After all, they argued, the south was rich and through
independence it would prosper even more. Soon enough, however,
the Piedmontese realized that the south lacked the human, economic,
and social resources to make the transition.[66]

A few examples will suffice to give an idea of the conflict between
north and south. The Piedmontese judicial system, based on individual freedom and social equality, was unacceptable to southerners. To

them personal freedom was much less important than client dependency, and social equality less relevant than patronage. The jury system introduced from the north was ridiculed by southern magistrates. It was unheard of that a group of ordinary citizens would pass a verdict on the behavior of a gentleman. A gentleman was not to be questioned or judged by anybody, a magistrate included.[67] The economic policies introduced by the Piedmontese baffled southerners. For instance, the suppression of the *Monti Frumentari*, primitive farmers' cooperatives, providing individuals with seeds in the fall to be returned at harvesting time at nominal interest, and their replacement with modern savings and loan associations confused small farmers, renters, and sharecroppers. To them a cash economy was a mystery. The new taxation system too created havoc in the south, where tax evasion was the rule. And unfortunately the south was poor, contrary to what northern Italians had been led to believe.[68]

In the debate over national priorities in economic matters, the central government was forced to adopt policies less favorable to the south. In fact, to compete with other European nations, the Italian government had to favor northern manufactures. Southern farmers felt left out.[69] The abrogation of internal tariffs, and the opening up of the Italian economy to imports from other European countries found the south totally unprepared. Several southern industries were forced to close.[70] National integration deprived the south even of its exterior splendor, its bureaucracy, its army, and especially its king. Naples ceased to be the capital of a kingdom and residence of a court, only to become a provincial capital. The old local bureaucracy too disappeared, to make room for northern administrators who descended upon the south armed with the determination to replace the southern chronic clientelism with a scientific administration. The Bourbon army was disbanded, as well as many local police forces, whose alliance to the new government was, at the very best, dubious. These ex-soldiers and ex-policemen increased the rank and file of the urban semiemployed or unemployed, when they did not join the armed opposition of the brigands.[71]

The Italian Risorgimento, however, was not an unmitigated disaster for the south. Rather, political unification forced the north to come to terms with the geographical and historical circumstances that had created the southern problem. Besides, the south was forced to face its predicament in the unavoidable comparison with the north. Both northerners and southerners developed misgivings about their abilities to deal with the demands national integration created. Northerners realized that the socioeconomic structures of the south provided only dim hopes that southerners could be integrated into a modern state. Southerners became progressively aware that they had derived few benefits from joining the new nation. Accordingly, both sides began to entertain serious doubts as to whether national integration was desirable.

Few thoughtful individuals, however, came to the conclusion that the best course of action would be the creation of two Italies. Such a solution would translate for northerners into a public confession of political inability; for southerners, it implied a proclamation to the world that they were stepchildren in Italy, perennially alienated from the modern world. For all Italians, the creation of two Italies would force the ultimate recognition that Metternich was right when he called Italy a "purely geographical expression." It was obvious that there could be no Italy without the south, and that the south could never be Italian without some form of national integration. The southern problem (*la questione meridionale*) became one of the most important national issues. From 1860 to the present the integration of the south into the nation became perhaps the most discussed topic in Italy. The secular marginality of southerners had to come to an end. But the story of those efforts further revealed the true face of the south as well as the limited choices available to the Italian government. The south had to be integrated into the new nation. But seemingly the task was nearly impossible.[72]

# 2   *A blueprint for change*

*The role of the national government*

The national debate on how to integrate the south into a politically unified Italy started in the early nineteenth century. Before political unification occurred, it was the mandatory topic of conversation among educated Italians. After 1860 it became one of the major concerns of the national government and the source of endless accusations and recriminations. For example, when the northern socialist Enrico Ferri, rather untactfully, claimed that although northern Italy had small enclaves of crime the south had just a few small oases of honesty, the Chamber of Deputies had to be adjourned in a hurry as southern newspapers demanded an apology.[1] The southern rebuttal, voiced by the Sicilian socialist Napoleone Colajanni, was that the north had created the southern problem. After all, there was no southern problem before the south was dragged into the new nation.[2] Northerners started indulging in negative stereotypes of southerners, contemptuously called *terroni* and *cafoni*, while southerners engaged in an orgy of accusations toward an oppressive north, as they blamed the government for their unfortunate predicament.

Parliamentary rhetoric and popular prejudices did not prevent thoughtful Italians from addressing the problem in a realistic way. From the initial variety of opinions, a broad consensus slowly emerged. First, because of geography and history the south had unique problems requiring special legislation and preferential treatment. Second, the special legislation was to be phased out as soon as the south caught up with the rest of Italy. This consensus was based on the assumption that it was within the power of the government to set in place a number of programs in favor of the south. This was the hope. Events were to show that the ability of the government to set in motion substantial changes in the south was limited indeed.

This chapter deals with governmental efforts to integrate the south into the new nation. In reviewing the record, southerners argue that

28

their region was left out on purpose, while the industrializing north received preferential treatment. Available evidence shows that the south was not left out intentionally and with malice. Rather, the Italian political classes failed in their efforts both because of monumental errors and because the realities of international politics and economics reduced the range of political options. Moreover, southerners too contributed to their increased misery by claiming that most of their problems stemmed from their having become part of Italy. Like other groups facing similar circumstances in other nations, they argued that political independence from Italy would place them in control of their destiny and put an end to their unfortunate dependency upon the north. But regardless of the solutions proposed either by southerners or by the Italian government, the dynamics that increased the economic disfranchisement of the south were the result of larger processes so pervasive as to seem intractable.

The study of the failed attempts at integrating the south within the nation is important in order to understand emigration, return migration, and the impact of remittances. In fact, by the end of the century – after three decades of national life – it became obvious that a variety of governmental programs set in place to modernize and integrate the south with the rest of Italy had failed. The south seemingly could not be helped. The nation at large and the government in particular were at a loss. It was exactly at that time that emigration, return migration, and remittances became mass phenomena. Single-handedly, these new dynamics, which the nation had originally regarded as negative events, seemed to bring about those changes that decades of governmental interventions and special programs had been unable to set in motion. Of course, the attention of the nation focused on these new phenomena with eager anticipation. The promoters of political unification and national integration had discussed a variety of dynamics to bring the south in line with the rest of the nation. But emigration and return migration were not among them. But by the end of the century they came to occupy central stage. And to an extent it was the failure of governmental programs that enhanced the importance the nation attached to emigration, return migration, and remittances as dynamics of last resort.

*Federalism versus centralization*

The early debate addressed the issue of the best model to be used to integrate the Italian states into one nation. Leading Western nations provided the models of federalism and centralization. Should Italy become like the United States of America, a federation of different regions, or a centralized nation like France, with a high degree of integration?[3] The debate did not end with the political unification of Italy. Rather, the debate became part of the ongoing political discourse to this very day. Every time a centralized government was set in place, like during fascism, advocates of regional autonomy lamented the demise of cultural and social differences and condemned the disregard for the rights of minorities. On the other hand, when regional autonomy was protected, fervent nationalists predicted the advent of anarchy. For instance, the new constitution approved in 1947 was a sharp departure from centralization toward regionalism, which had reemerged during World War II as a reaction to fascism. Yet, the implementation of the 1947 constitution is still very much debated in Italy. Nationalists point out the dangers of regionalism; while minorities in South Tyrol, Val d'Aosta, Sicily, and Sardinia complain that regional autonomy is simply given lip service.[4]

Sharp regional differences were and are, to a degree, common features in European nations. Politicians were cognizant, however, that the Italian situation was unique. Unlike other Europeans who had regional loyalties, Italians knew only local loyalties, ordinarily referred to as *campanilismo*.[5] It was this fierce loyalty to the commune, exclusive of any other loyalty, that kept Florence and Leghorn fighting for centuries, Venice against Treviso, Naples against the Neapolitan provinces, and Genoa against Turin. The list could go on almost indefinitely.[6] Under the circumstances both centralization and federalism seemed inadequate for Italy. A strong central government patterned on the French model with provincial *prefetti* would necessarily give a large degree of autonomy to each town. In the south such a system would preserve the power of patronage of large landowners. This outcome was unacceptable, because the new government had committed itself to the creation of a "rural democracy" of small farmers loyal to the new state and not to old landowners. A federal system with a weak central authority and powerful regional governments was likely to curb the power of patronage of large landowners, but it would preserve regional differences and animosities. The south would remain as insular and isolated as ever.[7]

A federation of largely autonomous Italian regions presented other problems as well. Profound social and cultural differences and often secular animosities divided populations within the same region. But, even in the hypothesis that effective regional government could be set up, how would they be integrated into a national federation? By 1860 only 3 percent of the Italian population spoke Italian, and to many, especially in Sicily, Sardinia, and in the Italian northeast, the Italian language was incomprehensible. The very word Italy and the recent event of political unification were unknown. History had created regional differences so profound that a federation of Italian states could not survive.[8]

Popular upheavals occurring in the south immediately after unification made northerners aware that the south would be a reluctant partner in the national adventure. In 1860–1 Naples and Palermo staged open insurrections, which only the army could put down. In 1866 Sicily was again up in arms because the government was unwilling to grant all the autonomies Sicilians wanted.[9] Popular upheavals occurred even in the north. But they quickly subsided. In the south they developed almost into full-fledged civil war.[10]

It was Camillo Benso of Cavour, the chief promoter of the political unification, who decided in favor of centralization, reversing his previous stand on the issue. Early in his political career he had excluded a centralized government for Italians, claiming that Italy would never be truly liberal until Italians learned self-government at the local level. Even as prime minister, he stated his preference for the federal system. In practice, Cavour never gave federalism and regionalism a chance. After the Kingdom of Sardinia annexed Lombardy in 1859, Cavour convinced the king to extend the Piedmontese centralized system of government to that region, without consultation with the people or political leaders. The opposition of the Lombards was appeased with the assurance that the Chamber of Deputies would decide in favor of federalism or centralization as soon as the war would come to an end. The centralized system was subsequently applied to Emilia-Romagna, Umbria, Marche, the Neapolitan provinces, and Sicily, and finally to Tuscany, Veneto, and the Papal States, always by royal decree, without popular vote. In each instance, people were assured that the Chamber of Deputies would make the final decision. But that day never came, as Cavour made sure that the debate of centralization versus federalism would never reach the floor.[11]

In the end, centralization became the political model for Italy. Events following political unification led Cavour to fear the disruptive potential of regionalism and to question the readiness of most Italians for self-government. He came to suspect, for instance, that the "feeble Etruscan race" (Tuscans) would never amount to anything if left on their own. His contempt for southerners knew no bounds. He was horrified when he learned that in Naples regionalism was about to blossom into anarchy, while some southerners talked about secession from Italy. As for Sicilians, Cavour confessed that he had always been unable to understand their culture, especially their legal system. True to his word, he never traveled south of Florence, and even when in Florence on business, he confined himself to his hotel room.[12]

But even after Cavour died, the issue of federalism versus centralization was never debated in the Chamber of Deputies. Politicians feared that decentralization and federalism would endanger the fragile political unity. Besides, political leaders were determined to present to the world the image of a centralized, efficient and highly integrated Italy. The purpose was to attract foreign capital. The nation did not have the money to create those infrastructures, like railroads, needed for the take-off of a modern economy. Finally enlightened southerners acknowledged that a centralized government could be more beneficial than a federal system for the south. They nourished high hopes that centralization would finally terminate the power and patronage of large landowners, the major stumbling block in the emancipation of southern populations.[13]

But these high hopes foundered on the rocks of political expediency. Individuals running for national office in southern districts quickly learned that the support of large landowners was essential to their political success. After all, because deference was one of the main traits of southern culture, large landowners controlled large blocks of peasant votes. And landowners were willing to deliver those votes to individuals who promised not to interfere in local affairs. In the end, the centralization set in place to create a rural democracy of small farmers independent of the power and patronage of large landowners failed. In the south it was business as usual, even after political unification.[14]

## Playing the great power

Soon after political unification some Italian nationalists argued that the modernization of the south and its integration into a national economy could be achieved through a vigorous program of national expansion, a result that Great Britain and France had already achieved.[15] Disregarding the endemic weaknesses of the south, these nationalists argued that if Italians had been able to achieve the seemingly impossible goal of national unification, they were also ready to become a colonial power. In the process, nationalists concluded, Italians would be forced to set aside regional differences and work toward national integration as a prerequisite for a vigorous foreign policy.

Nationalists disregarded the recent abysmal performances of the Italian army and the problems of the national economy. They were single-mindedly committed to bringing back the old glories of the Italian Renaissance and of the Roman Empire. They chose to ignore the fact that the Italian army and navy had collapsed in the two embarrassing defeats at Custoza and Lissa in 1866. They overlooked the fact that the unification of the country had been made possible by a sequence of fortuitous international events, the weakness of the Bourbon army, and the military help from France in the northern campaigns against Austria. Moreover, they ignored warnings from more sober minds that the new nation had to face so many political and economic problems at home, especially in the south, that it was suicidal to embark on a program of colonial expansion.[16]

Paradoxically, it was among southerners that the mirage of colonial expansion found its most ardent supporters. Some observers argued that the southern support was an escape from poverty and powerlessness into an imaginary wonderland. This might have been the case. One of the components of powerlessness seems to be the inability to discern how to get out of it. But seemingly there were good reasons for southerners to support colonial adventures. An Italian presence in northern Africa would sever the ties of dependency of the south from the north. The south would become the geographical center of colonial Italy and the ideal geographical location for new industries. Moreover, the colonies could become the destinations for the surplus Italian population. In time, colonies would become a source of profit for the nation at large.[17]

Not surprisingly, it was Francesco Crispi, a Sicilian, who committed the nation to a disastrous colonial program in Africa. The major failures of the program were not the military defeats, but the social and economic burdens imperialism forced on the south. In the end, the dependency of the south from the north worsened. For a successful African campaign, the new nation had to shoulder two additional economic burdens: the creation of infrastructures to favor war industries and the logistic services needed to support the army in a foreign continent. Obviously, the government increased taxes and the south had to share the burden. In 1860 the tax burden of the south was 170 million lire. By 1896 it had escalated to 414 million, an increase of almost 250 percent. Northerners were convinced that the south could shoulder the burden, because they believed that there was much idle cash in the south. In reality the south had very little idle cash and increased taxation crippled the already precarious economy of the region. Ironically, most tax money collected in the south ended in northern coffers. In fact, almost all war contracts were awarded to northern industries, because the south was ill equipped for large-scale industrial production.[18]

In the end, the African adventure left the south poorer and increasingly separated from the rest of the nation. Southerners eventually realized that their ardent support for colonial expansion had been the result of their monumental political immaturity. Increased taxation deprived them of much needed cash, which could have been invested more profitably in economic improvements. Because of war contracts, the industrializing north came out of the war in a stronger position. The gap between the north and the south had widened. For the south, the colonial adventure had been an unmitigated disaster.

### The state entrepreneur

Social and political reforms attempted in the last quarter of the nineteenth century equally failed to close the gap between north and south. Rather, those reforms created a new type of dependency in the south. By the late nineteenth century, most Western nations had embraced the principle that government should play a role in promoting economic development and social reform. Classical economic liberalism had preached that the function of the state was the preservation of freedom. Labor commotions, demands for political reforms, social dislocations caused by industrialization, and the very increasing complexity of a society affected by a variety of social, political, and economic dynamics demanded that governments take a lead. Each nation, of course, experienced the transition in a particular way, determined by historical traditions and present necessities. Italy was no different.

The political leaders of the two decades after political unification belonged to the *Destra*. They were affected by nostalgia for the heroic times of the Risorgimento and committed to overseas expansion as a way to keep the heroic times alive.[19] The generation that followed was different. They were pragmatic politicians eager to prove that they could be as effective in reshaping the country as their fathers had been in putting it together. Riding the crest of the popular discontent that set in when the high expectations of reforms raised by political unification did not materialize, these new politicians, called the *Sinistra*, promised to undertake a program of economic and social reconstruction. To secure popular support the men of the *Sinistra* took a schizophrenic posture: on the one hand, they promised to lower taxes; on the other they committed the country to social reforms and national improvements.[20]

The program of public works undertaken by the Left pushed north and south further apart. The drainage program can be cited as an example. Drainage was a pressing national need after roads and railroads, both to reclaim land for farming and to make farming safe from malaria, especially in several southern regions. The two major target areas were the Po delta in the northeast and several sections of the south, where malaria was rampant. In the northeast drainage proceeded expeditiously. The area to be drained was flat and a number of existing infrastructures created by the Austro-Hungarian Empire facilitated the process. In the south drainage, as an observer put it, was "an endeavor worthy of pioneers." It had to be implemented in remote areas with no roads and it could count on very few infrastructures already in place. Thus drainage was successfully brought to an end in very few places of the south. There malaria remained public enemy number one until fascism.[21]

The implementation of the drainage program emphasized a difference between north and south. In the northeast the private sector took advantage of the new opportunities and of the availability of additional farmland. Borrowing money from local banks, northerners purchased the reclaimed land from the government, introduced improvements and in the end they became self-sufficient farmers. In the south the private sector did not, and perhaps could not, take advantage of the opportunity. Capital was scarce, banks virtually nonexistent, interest rates prohibitively high, transportation inadequate or nonexistent, managerial skills and willingness to take risks in short supply. In the end, contrary to expectations, the drainage program, although expensive, failed to stimulate the private sector in the south.[22]

The failure of the drainage and similar programs in the south alerted government officials that more vigorous efforts were needed to stimulate the southern economy. The increasingly accepted political wisdom in Italy and elsewhere in the Western world was that governments had to play a larger role in stimulating and perhaps even regulating the economy. The final responsibility for the economic soundness of a society, however, was the private sector's. But in the case of the Italian south, the government was forced to go far beyond the subsidiary role and to undertake programs that even the most liberal economists and social scientists of the time considered hardly acceptable. Specifically, the government offered special incentives and bonuses to the private sector, and played a major role in establishing banks and promoting land improvements.[23]

The increased governmental intervention had several unintended consequences. First, to implement the programs, the government was forced to recruit managers in the north, for lack of trained personnel in the south. The presence of northern managers fostered among southerners an already pervasive suspicion that the government was actively promoting the dependency of the south. Second, the increased governmental role reinforced other already unrealistic expectations among southerners that social and economic problems in the region had to be solved by the government. Third, every failure or

delay in implementation was blamed on the inefficiency of governmental programs. The reinforcement of such attitudes among southerners made them almost incapable of realizing that governmental
programs in their region could ever succeed without the partnership
of the private sector. Finally legislators who had initially selected the
south as the beneficiary of governmental programs eventually realized
that it was politically more advantageous to implement them in the
north rather than the south. A governmental program in the north
was ordinarily brought about in a shorter period of time, and its
impact was more readily apparent. These measurable accomplishments provided much needed political ammunition at election time.
In addition, northern voters outnumbered southerners two to one.
Moreover, politicians were well aware that northerners more often
than southerners checked the records of individuals running for national office. Failed or delayed governmental programs in the south
were likely to become an embarrassment rather than an asset in national elections.[24]

In the end, the program of national improvements with its emphasis
on the south further enhanced dependency of the south and its alienation from the rest of the nation. The increased taxation to support
the programs drained capital from the south. The urge of politicians
to bring about quick results made the government less willing to invest
in the south. Funds were diverted to the north. Not without some
reason, southerners felt that their taxes were subsidizing the north.
Finally the enlarged presence of the national government in the south
fostered a new type of patron-client relationship between national
government and southern masses. As in the old days, large landowners were expected to take care of peasants as patrons do with
clients; in the new Italy southerners assigned the central government
the role of patron, with the task of satisfying all their needs. The
southern passion for dependency had not been broken; it was only
directed to a more powerful patron.[25]

*Avoiding the larger world*

The unpreparedness and resistance to change of southerners was not
the most formidable obstacle in the intergration of the south. The
dependency of Italy from foreign capital limited what the government
could effectively do for the south. Italian politicians came to this
realization only slowly and painfully, because most of them were
quite unprepared and perhaps unwilling to understand the dynamics
of the international economy and its impact on political choices. In
the end, they painfully resigned to the realization that Italy could not

survive without foreign capital and that decisions made in London and Paris affected the south more profoundly than legislation passed in Rome.

The promoters of political unification shared the faith that Italy had a bright economic future. They believed that Italy had abundant natural resources, especially in the south, and that independence would release free enterprise. After all, the long history of Italy seemed to support this assumption. Italy had been economically prosperous when independent and impoverished under foreign domination.[26] But this faith faded within a few years. The alleged abundance of natural resources proved to be a fallacy. From 1862 to 1864 scores of small companies surrendered franchises granted by the government for the exploration of mineral resources. Scientific surveys had shown that the resources for which the government had granted franchises did not exist. Independence failed to bring about economic glories. Rather, political independence had proven to be very costly. By 1861 war expenses and war reparations to the Austro-Hungarian Empire amounted to 1,482 million lire. The debt of the new nation was 2,446 million lire. In the next four years the national debt increased by an additional 2,187 million, while total state revenues from 1861 to 1865 totaled 2,842 million. By the end of 1865, serious observers in Italy and abroad questioned whether the new nation, burdened by seemingly unsolvable economic problems, would survive.[27]

But Italy did survive, and was able to honor its obligations. Burdened with war debts and staggering yearly deficits, the government borrowed from citizens and foreign investors. But there was little money available in Italy. Contrary to the assumption entertained by northerners, the south was poor and capital formation was slow in the nation at large. In 1860, for example, only the city of Turin had a viable banking system, with two banks and two savings institutions with combined assets of 50 million lire. Foreign capital assured the survival of the fledgling country. In 1865, for instance, Italy paid 85 million lire in interest on government bonds to foreigners, while foreign investments in national bonds totaled 1,170 million lire, one-third of the national debt.[28]

Foreign capital played an even larger role in the capitalization of major Italian banks. The Banca Anglo Italiana was established exclusively with foreign capital. The Società Generale di Credito Mobiliare opened with 50 percent foreign capital. Foreign capital invested in Italian banks reached the sum of 100 million lire in 1865.[29] Moreover, foreign capital provided 70 percent of the money to build the railroad system. According to an 1860 estimate by the government, Italy needed 6,000 kilometers of railroads by 1870 at a cost of 1,500 million lire, which neither the Italian government nor the private sector could put together. Foreign capital moved in. For instance, the Sudbahn, a corporation operating in the Italian south had headquarters in Vienna and operated exclusively with French capital. The Società Vittorio Emmanuele, with the franchise for northwestern railroads, used French capital exclusively. The Società delle Strade Ferrate Romane, with the franchise for railroads in central Italy, was controlled by financiers in Paris.[30]

Foreign investments assured the survival of the new nations and a modest degree of economic development. But foreign investments created obligations and dependencies that in the long run were more costly than the dividends the state paid annually to foreign investors. Italian politicians soon discovered that the range of their choices was limited by the demands of foreign investors doing business in Italy. This economic dependency from foreign capital created for Italy a much broader and unpalatable political dependency from France and England. Accordingly, the Italian government was forced to revise internal policies when they did not meet the approval of foreign capital. More specifically, several programs in favor of the south had to be set aside when foreign investors voiced strong disapproval. Concerned with immediate returns, foreign investors saw few advantages by investing in the south with prospects of poor and slow returns, when quicker and larger profits could be had in the north.

But there was one positive outcome in this encounter between foreign capital and Italians. Politicians and economic operators were forced to compare Italy with more advanced nations. The naive assumption of vast natural resources and the belief in the abundance of idle cash, especially in the south, were replaced by the realization that Italy was short in cash and poorly equipped to compete in European markets. In 1860, when Italy had but a few hundred kilometers of railroads, France, Germany, and Great Britain had more than 20,000 each. These three nations were accomplishing the transition from local production and distribution to mass production and national distribution. Agriculture was being rationalized and mechanized to respond to the demands of new urban markets, which in turn had expanded through industrialization. The need for large capital to subsidize industrial production had led financiers to replace traditional banking practices with new approaches to saving, lending, and investing.[31]

Forced to reassess their narrow and unfounded assumptions about their economic potential, Italians realized that the nation was ill prepared to compete in European markets. For instance, in 1860 the south was still cut off from the rest of Italy and Europe for lack of railroads.

Agriculture was carried out with premodern techniques. In most regions land tenure was still feudal for all practical purposes, although on paper feudalism had been terminated. Only the cities of Milan, Turin, and Genoa had industries that could stand comparison with those in central and northern Europe. In the rest of the nation, cottage industry was the rule. And these were not the most alarming indicators of Italy's unfortunate predicament. As the economist Francesco Ferrara pointed out in 1866, the worst indicator was that southerners did not even feel the need to change. "Italy," Ferrara wrote, "is buried in its past and does not want to be awaken."[32] Resistance to change within the nation and in the south especially, and constraints from foreign capital placed Italian politicians in an undesirable predicament. The confidence the Left had shown in assuming power in 1877 had all but disappeared by the late 1880s.

## An unexpected competitor: The United States

But the unpleasant discoveries of dependency were not to stop here. In their survey of the international scene, politicians soon discovered a more ominous threat: the arrival of American products in European markets. The American competition spread so fast that Europeans were caught by surprise. By the end of the American Civil War the presence of American goods in European markets was negligible. Ten years later the impact was so profound that fact-finding commissions were sent from Great Britain and France to assess what had fueled such an astonishing economic development. American goods affected Italian markets later than other European markets. The lack of a national network of transportation made it quite difficult for American goods to reach remote Italian villages. But as soon as the national network of railroads was in place, Italy became an outstanding casualty of American competition. Among the Italian economists and social scientists who crossed the Atlantic to research the American phenomenon was Egisto Rossi.[33]

The first reactions of Europeans were disbelief and denial. A German observer remarked that Europeans had nothing to fear: American farmers were only European outcasts, lacking perseverance. An Italian commentator wrote: "Europe has nothing to fear from the United States. Europe is and always will be rich and the center of the world economy. Europe will always produce enough to overpower any American competition. Our land is fertile; and our farmers are the best in the world." And an Italian politician assured the business community that "the economic advantage of the United States is a fallacy that time will dissipate."[34] Seemingly Italians based their optimism on the reassuring economic indicators of the early 1870s, when Italian exports soared because of the demand created by the Franco-Prussian War and other world events.

More attentive observers, however, realized that the European economy was likely to become, and in a short time, a dependency of the American economy.[35] After a year in the United States, Egisto Rossi outlined the secret of the American success: abundance of fertile land, mechanization, efficient and relatively inexpensive transportation, willingness to experiment, a tax system promoting the accumulation of capital, and the absence of a large army.[36] In addition, Rossi pointed out that the American advancement rested on a wisely protective tariff for American manufactures, still ill equipped to compete with Great Britain, and a work ethic alien to most Europeans, especially southerners.[37] A comparison between European and American economies indicated that the United States had technological advantages, especially in transportation, that Europeans had not yet set in place. Accordingly, production and transportation costs dropped in the United States. For example, Americans managed to move a ton of wheat from Chicago to Liverpool (5,000 kilometers apart), for less money than it cost Europeans to transport a ton of wheat from Reichenbach to Trieste (1,000 kilometers apart). Rossi predicted two major consequences: a flow of capital from Europe to the United States, prompted by better and safer investment opportunities in America and social unrest in Europe; and the progressive decline of small properties in Europe. Also, capital would flow from Europe to the United States in the form of payments for imports of farm products. Small properties would be unable to compete with large-scale agrarian capitalism. The center of gravity of world economics was rapidly moving West, while the survival of small-scale capitalism was in doubt.[38]

The decline in farm commodities prices and the trade imbalance in Italy showed the depth of the Italian dependency on other economies. By 1887 Italy became an importer of wheat after several centuries as an exporter. Wheat imports soared from 700,000 tons in 1892 to over one million in 1901.[39] The price of wheat declined from 39 lire per quintal in 1874 to 34 in 1880, to 23 in 1887, to 20 in 1894. The price of corn dropped from 23 lire in 1873 to 13 in 1894. Competition from Europe affected other Italian commodities. Wine dropped from 85 lire per hectoliter in 1880 to 59 in 1890; olive oil from 159 lire per hectoliter in 1884 to 115 in 1891.[40]

It was questionable whether Europe, and especially Italy, could avoid becoming an economic dependency of the United States. The dynamics of the international market were rapidly changing. The

Italian south, for example, was turning from an exporter to an importer of wheat. To cope with these changes, Rossi suggested that Italy set in place tariffs on agrarian imports to keep out American wheat, raise wages to increase both spending and savings, and decrease local and state taxes.[41] But the implementation of these recommendations proved to be impossible. The mounting national deficit, the program of national improvements, the financial obligations to foreigners, and the colonial adventure in Africa resulted in higher taxes. In 1906 Sidney Sonnino argued that the Italian tax system was so burdensome as to prevent most citizens from saving any money. And without savings, the national economy could never take off.[42] Notwithstanding mass emigration and the decrease in the labor market supply, wages did not increase significantly by the turn of the century.[43] And the protective tariff ended in disaster. It alienated France, Italy's best trade partner, and it failed to keep American wheat from reaching Italian markets.[44] It was obvious, by the early 1890s, that the Italian economy was peripheral at best in the North Atlantic system. And progressively the economic dependency of Italy on the United States was deepening.[45]

*A marginal economy*

As the process of internationalization of the North Atlantic markets accelerated its pace from 1880 to 1900, Italian politicians progressively discovered their powerlessness to help the south. Tariff legislation created additional problems for the south. The banking system almost collapsed because of reckless investments and, in the end, foreign investors came to disregard the south as one of the soft spots in the North Atlantic economic system. The precipitous decline in the prices of farm commodities from 1878 to 1885 alerted economic operators that the south would collapse without some form of protection. State expropriations of land properties for tax insolvency escalated at an alarming rate in the south. The earning power of landowners, renters, and sharecroppers declined. After much debate the government set in place a new tariff in 1887: it was strongly protective of the textile and iron industries and mildly protective of agriculture. The tariff on imported wheat, for example, was raised from 1.40 lire per quintal to 3, and the following year to 5.[46]

The new tariff, however, did not ingratiate Italy to France, its best trade partner, which had traditionally absorbed the largest share of Italian exports, especially wine, raw silk, and vegetables. In 1886 France requested that Italy abide by a commercial treaty signed in 1881, with lower tariffs for France. Italy insisted that the 1881 trade agreement had to be renegotiated.[47] France refused to accept the Italian terms and imposed war tariffs on all Italian exports to France. Trade between the two nations came to a virtual standstill. Italy was forced to undertake the costly task of opening new markets in Germany and other European countries. From 1881 to 1887, yearly exports to France had totaled 444 million lire and imports 307. In 1888 imports from France declined to 164 million lire and exports to 165. The impact on Italian foreign trade was devastating. In 1887 Italy's exports totaled 2,607 million lire; the following year they declined to 2,067 with a loss of 540 million. The decline registered in 1888 continued with only minor fluctuations during the following five years. Wine exports to France declined from 2.6 million hectoliters in 1887 to 1.8 million the following year. The south, as a major producer of wine and vegetables, was devastated.[48]

The loss of the French market was the result of an enormous miscalculation. But, unfortunately, that was not the only error. Overconfident about the soundness of the Italian economy, Italian financiers engaged in speculation in real estate, especially in the cities of Rome, Florence, Palermo, and Naples, where the demand for housing by incoming immigrants was greatest. And for a while the profits were high. The Banca Tiberina of Rome, for example, with a capital of only 30 million lire, made a profit of almost 5 million in 1887 by speculating in real estate in Rome. By the end of that year, however, it was obvious that the Banca Tiberina had overextended itself. Other financial institutions, like the Società Generale di Credito Mobiliare and the Banca Generale were in trouble for excessive speculation in real estate. Financial troubles increased when French investors began to withdraw their funds from Italian banks. Prime Minister Francesco Crispi tried to salvage the situation by asking Bismarck to pressure German financiers to support Italian stocks. The efforts were ineffective. Eventually both the Società Generale di Credito Mobiliare and the Banca Generale failed. By 1893 the Italian banking system was in disarray. A good number of Italian banks failed. Credit was available only through savings and loans institutions and popular banks with limited capital. Italy was virtually cut off from the international financial market.[49]

The reaction of European financiers to the opening of the Suez Canal can be used as an example of the misgivings of foreigners about the soundness of the Italian economy. When the canal opened in 1870, the most direct line of communication between England and India via Egypt and the Suez Canal was through the Calais–Brindisi railroad; 1,300 kilometers of that railroad were in Italian territory. Seemingly Brindisi was destined to become one of the busiest European ports. Italian railroads were to derive a major benefit and the south experience an economic recovery. These were the hopes. The reality was quite different. Skeptical about the reliability of Italian railroads and quite aware that the port of Brindisi was not deep enough for large ships, European merchants preferred to trade with the Orient through the ports of Marseilles, Genoa, and Trieste.[50] Accordingly, foreign financiers declined to make investments in the port of Brindisi or the railroad line between Calais and Brindisi.

There is little evidence that a northern conspiracy was responsible for making the Italian south a dependency of the north, as several southerners have argued for some decades now.[51] After all, some of the most prominent prime ministers were southerners. Moreover, to accept the conspiracy theory implies to attribute to Italian politicians planning abilities and a degree of sophistication that can hardly be documented. The evidence shows that Italian politicians were surprisingly ignorant of the economic assets and liabilities of the country as well as almost totally unaware of the economic strength of the central and northern European countries and of the United States.[52]

International financial dynamics as well as political choices in Italy exacerbated the southern problem and increased the differences between that region and the rest of the nation. The administrative centralization set in place in the 1860s preserved virtually unscathed the hold of the landed aristocracy and thus made impossible social and economic changes in the south. The hope of modernizing and integrating the south through a colonial expansion in Africa foundered on the rocks of increased taxation, growth of the northern Italian economy, and a lack of funds to modernize southern agriculture. The program of national improvements undertaken by the Left in the south had to be revised in the light of pressures exercised by foreign investors, invariably reluctant to invest in the south. Eventually the government was forced to expand its role in the south beyond what was considered politically acceptable, with the result of negative reactions from the north. Contrary to expectations, the private sector did not respond to governmental programs. In the end, the government was forced into the role of patron of the south. Southerners developed the expectation that the government owed it to them to bring about single-handedly the modernization of the region.

The dependency of the Italian economy on foreign capital greatly restricted the range of choices available to politicians. Foreign capital was essential for the economic survival of Italy. When depressions struck the Atlantic economic system, Italian economic operators discovered the depth of the dependency of the Italian economy. In the end, the specific programs in favor of the south had to be set aside.

By the end of the century the south was an economic dependency of the north to a higher degree than in 1860. But the north too was far from being economically self-sufficient. It was itself a dependency of stronger European and American economies. The south was a dependency within a dependency. The pageant of modernization was a celebration the south could observe from afar, not join.

The repeated failure of governmental programs in integrating the south with the rest of the nation, the reluctance of southerners to embrace change, and the general persistence of the so-called southern problem led many educated Italians to ask themselves why the south was so different and whether some other approach should be found to integrate the region with the rest of the nation and with Western economies. Debates in the Italian Chamber of Deputies and Senate progressively revealed that southern representatives shared a cultural past vastly different from northern counterparts. To what extent, many asked, was the southern Italian culture receptive to the new message of national integration and economic development? Had the various efforts to integrate the south with the rest of the nation failed mostly because the north had paid little or no attention to the cultural peculiarities of the south? Eventually northerners realized that they had a poor and often erroneous knowledge of southern culture. Were southerners, some argued, prisoners of a cultural past that made it very difficult for them to relate to modern values?

# 3   *The southern ethos*

*The puzzling south*

Italians have been fascinated and puzzled by the south for a long time. Northerners do not consider their education completed until they take the grand tour of the south. The early investigators of the 1860s and 1870s, like Leopoldo Franchetti and Sidney Sonnino, have been followed by cohorts of scholars, graduate students, and politically committed individuals.[1] The south has the unique fascination of being geographically so close to the north, yet psychologically so distant and almost as mysterious as are primitive cultures.[2] The best profile of the south, however, emerges not from the writings of scholars, but from those of fiction writers. In the nineteenth century, the Sicilian Giovanni Verga captured the imagination of Italians with his accounts of Sicilian life in *I Malavoglia* (1881) and *Mastro Don Gesualdo* (1889). In this century, Corrado Alvaro, a native of Calabria, scrutinized the soul of his region in a series of short stories.[3] Tommaso di Lampedusa's *Il Gattopardo* revealed the secrets of Sicilian high society more intimately than hundreds of scholarly publications.[4] But it was Carlo Levi, an outsider confined for years in a small town of Basilicata by the fascist regime, who wrote, in my opinion, the most insightful book on the south.[5]

Foreign scholars are surprised by the elusive nature of southern culture. Constance Cronin, for example, after studying the structure of southern families for years, remained baffled and concluded: "The basic cause of the entire problem is the intricacy of the Italian social organization, which is designed to keep things hidden, and has very effectively done so. The southern Italian skill at confusing the issue is nowhere better illustrated."[6] Perhaps Cronin was wrong. Southerners do not engage in a conspiracy to keep outsiders confused. Their culture is unique because their history was unique, as other scholars pointed out. Some of them spent years in the south, and especially in Sicily, to make sense of a culture that seems to be so

45

elusive. Their conclusions are divergent in many respects; but they all concur that the study of southern culture presents unique challenges. This chapter deals with southern culture as a prerequisite to understand the way in which southerners embraced emigration and return migration.[7]

But, is it relevant or useful to study southern culture? Does it explain the unfortunate predicament of the south and the alienation of its inhabitants? Scholars espouse different points of view. Some argue that culture explains everything; others that it is merely a reflection of the economy. The more traditional attitude is that culture explains almost everything. This approach, best exemplified by Edward Banfield, is based on some form of cultural determinism. It links economic underdevelopment to the reactionary and traditional qualities of peasant culture. Such culture makes social change and economic development virtually impossible. Banfield, an American scientist, argues that a culture of "amoral familism" explains the backwardness of the Italian south.[8] The British historian Dennis Mack Smith concludes that mutual distrust and inability to take collective action prevented Sicilians from embracing modern social and economic values.[9] "Present-orientation," unwillingness to embrace long-term projects, extreme individualism, distrust of organized government, the instinctive preference for monopoly over competition are other cultural traits traditionally quoted to explain the failure of economic development in the south.[10] Many scholars argue that the south was doomed to failure by these reactionary and to a degree self-destructive habits.

Some modern scholars have discarded the role of culture and emphasized the importance of economic dynamics. The Schneiders, for example, argue "that Sicily has not developed economically has nothing to do with its culture." The specific nature of the Sicilian economy and the trade arrangements between Sicily and northern European countries, which monopolized the Sicilian resources, explain the economic underdevelopment of Sicily in modern times. Culture, the Schneiders maintain, "does not determine a society's place in a world system; rather it reflects the various roles which society has played in the past."[11] Thus the study of economic world systems and specifically the dependent role of the Italian south from more developed northern regions, rather than the study of culture, the Schneiders conclude, will provide the key to the understanding of the south.

This chapter explores southern culture at the turn of the century and the economic dynamics that shaped it. The purpose is to assess the personal and collective tools southerners had in coping with the demands and the changes imposed by the larger society. In the end, the responses of southerners to the process of national integration in

Italy, the decision to embrace temporary emigration and return migration, as well as to send remittances back to Italy to be invested stemmed from the culture southerners shared, and from their understanding of the opportunities surrounding them. In general, southern culture was a complex system of beliefs and practices stemming from a rather static view of life and society. But that culture had room also for change and adaptability. And southerners were forced at the end of the century to explore alternative strategies of survival, especially when traditional goals and practices proved to be obsolete. Ironically, the search for alternative ways to pursue traditional goals slowly and almost unnoticeably changed the original goals themselves. And southerners, with much surprise, found themselves in a new world.

### Citizens and pagans

To modern minds, the most puzzling aspect of southern culture is the resistance of traditional values to unavoidable changes. Modern technology has left its imprints in the south: new houses, especially along the coast, highways, railroads, resort areas, and expanding cities have been changing the southern landscape since unification. Naples and Palermo are modern metropolises. Life in the south is as comfortable as in most of Europe. Yet, the visitor familiar with Franchetti's report of the 1870s, with Coletti's observations of half a century later, or with Carlo Levi's descriptions of the 1930s realizes that the south of today is only slightly different from that of one hundred years ago. This resistance to change has been reported many times over the decades. Coletti talked about the "transcendent resistance to change of southerners"; Senator Stefano Jacini commented on the despair of politicians trying to introduce changes in the south. Agriculturalists dispatched to the south in the 1870s and 1880s to teach peasants better farming techniques gave up in despair. One of them wrote: "I think that the ancient Romans practiced more advanced farming techniques than our peasants do today. There is nothing one can do to induce peasants to change. I believe that resistance to change is in the very blood of southerners."[12] Today's visitors are likely to reach the same conclusion. An American observer, for instance, remarked: "People tell me that everything in the south had changed. What they mean is that everything looks different."[13]

Resistance to change is a common characteristic in traditional societies. But in the Italian south such resistance seems to have survived longer than anywhere else. How can we explain this? Carlo Levi advanced an intriguing interpretation, based on the history of the south, which has saddled the region with an almost endemic sense of powerlessness. Levi argues that southerners cannot relate to change because they lack a sense of history. A sense of history implies that a group believes itself to have some form of control over its destiny. Southerners do not, Levi observes, because past events killed that faith in them. They see themselves as part of the natural cycle, which cannot be altered. They are one with the earth, the sun, the seasons, and their cattle. "They cannot have an individual conscience, since everything in nature is essentially linked to everything else, humans included. They live immersed in a world where history has no place."[14] Southerners are pagans. The only gods they recognize are those of nature. Those gods have total control over humans. Citizens, on the other hand, believe in gods who allow humans to shape their destinies in freedom. But these gods, Levi concludes, never reached the south. Christ, the god of citizens, stopped at Eboli.[15]

This view allows little room for social organization and political action. The very idea of the state makes little sense, because it stems from a belief in collective control over events and confidence that individuals can bring about positive changes. "To southern peasants," Levi remarks, "the state is more distant than the sky. It does not matter what kind of state it is, its statutes, its programs. Peasants cannot relate to it, because it does not fit in their mental universe."[16] Soon after political unification, the government was stunned in realizing that southerners preferred brigands, Mafia, and Camorra to the services provided by the state. In reality southerners did not have to choose. The state with its organization and its potential for change was not a viable alternative.

Eventually southerners were forced to deal with the state. Taxes and military service were unpleasant realities that did not spare the south. In dealing with the state, southerners elaborated two contradictory responses. On the one hand, they saw the state as a necessary evil, not different from the adverse powers of nature, like hail, malaria, or death itself. Resignation was the only appropriate response. On the other hand, they regarded the state as a power with discretionary control of mysterious energies, not unlike nature itself, capable of bringing about desirable changes. The belief that the state was evil prevented southerners from understanding its functions and from giving any allegiance to it. The conviction that the state had magic powers made them blame the state for all the misery in their lives. The former attitude was rooted in traditional peasant fatalism, fostered by centuries of oppressive governments; the latter stemmed from the assumption that any positive change was beyond their control.

These deep-seated perceptions are still common among southerners, educated and uneducated alike. For uneducated southerners, the state is mostly an evil force. Their supreme ambition is to fool the state by a stroke of luck.[17] Of course, peasants in general are ill equipped to fight against the state. But the privileged few who succeed become popular heroes overnight. Levi met one such hero in Gagliano, a small town in Basilicata. His nick-name was "Faccialorda" (dirty face). He became a hero in New York, and his fame reached Gagliano even before he returned. While working in construction he injured himself. He fully recovered, but maintained that he had lost his hearing. American doctors insisted that Faccialorda's hearing was perfect. But he kept denying it for two years, until the company offered him two thousand dollars in compensation. He promptly crossed the Atlantic to enjoy the fruits of his American fortune and to bask in the newly acquired fame. By a strike of luck, Faccialorda "had fought and won against the powerful institution of the state."

Faccialorda was the only such hero in Gagliano. Peasants, of course, needed more than one story to include in their epic narratives of peasant triumphs. Eventually southerners assembled a core of such popular tales. One such story was that of Saracino, a man who left Italy to avoid the draft. He emigrated to Great Britain, where he made a small fortune. His two children pursued professional careers: one became a lawyer, the other a doctor. When World War I broke out in 1914, he sent his children back to Italy to avoid the draft. The following year, when Italy too entered the war, Saracino's children left for Spain. Nobody in the Saracino family was going to serve any king, any state, anywhere. To southerners, Saracino and his children were not draft evaders, but heroes granted honorary citizenship in every southern town.

Only individuals could overpower the state, but only through a stroke of luck, and only for one brief moment. Groups could not. History had taught southerners that painful lesson in the two decades following political unification, when the Italian government dispatched the army to defeat the brigands. The story of the brigands was, and still is, popular among southerners. It fired the imagination of writers for a century and offered peasants a sense of tragic pride like nothing else. To southerners, brigandage was the desperate and, in the end, futile effort to fight the evil state. Brigandage was finally eradicated. Its legacy continued in occasional outbursts of violence, in the burning of city halls and police and customs officers' barracks. These episodes invariably ended with the execution or imprisonment of leading agitators. Corrado Alvaro beautifully immortalized the saga of the brigands in the story of Antonello, a brigand committed to helping the poor. He was captured by Italian soldiers. Antonello's ultimate goal was to tell his side of the story to the local magistrate. But he was aware that he would not be granted even such a small satisfaction by the state.[18]

Educated southerners are more likely to believe that the state has the power of bringing about spectacular changes. Seemingly this faith has little in common with the opposite belief that the state is evil. In reality the two beliefs are a variation of one theme. Both posit that the state is all powerful: in a negative sense for peasants, in a positive sense for educated individuals. Unfortunately the Italian government, educated individuals argue, never used its power to solve the southern problem. Even eminent southerners, like Napoleone Colajanni, Ettore Ciccotti, and Giustino Fortunato shared this belief.[19] Contemporary scholars concur. Francesco Cerase, for example, argues, although wrongly, that north and south were virtually on the same economic footing at the time of political unification. The economic dependency of the south was the result of biased governmental policies that favored the industrial north at the expense of the agrarian south he points out. In Cerase's mind the failure was the result of planned and almost conspiratorial policies determined by powerful northern lobbies. The state had the resources to transform the south. The failure shows that the government did not will it.[20]

### The origin of the alienation of southerners

Why this alienation from the state? Ignorance can explain, at least in part, the peasants' attitude. But what about educated southerners? Even today's visitors to the south cannot avoid being puzzled by the almost total distrust for people in position of power and leadership, even among educated southerners. According to southerners, power is corrupted and corrupting, and invariably used for devious purposes. Leaders are never concerned with the public good. Rather, their only interest is personal and family aggrandizement. But, if southerners are so distrustful of the power of the state, and if the state is something to be feared and avoided, how do southerners construe their personal identities and structure their social interactions? After all, in most Western societies the idea of the state as an organized society is central to the construction of personal identities and to the organization of social and economic functions.

What shaped the culture of the south? Of course, the three events mentioned in Chapter 1 – the hegemony of the Florentine banks, the disengagement of the southern nobility from the direct management of the land, and the creation of an urban proletariat in Naples and

Palermo – were lasting negative legacies. They created a dependency on foreign economic interests and social attitudes and cleavages within the south that made most difficult the acceptance of the ideals and organization of the modern state. Here I will add another set of economic and political events that occurred in the seventeenth and eighteenth centuries under the Neapolitan Bourbons. These events further reinforced the dependency of the south on outside economic operators and indirectly affected the internal structures of the region itself and its culture.[21]

With the discovery of America in 1492, the south lost its commercial advantage. The routes of trade moved from the Mediterranean to the Atlantic and from the south to central and northern Europe. In the new North Atlantic economy, the south found its dependent role as exporter of wheat. The central characters in the new economy were rural entrepreneurs, who have been described as broker capitalists. They differed from merchant, industrial, and financial capitalists in several ways. They exported exclusively for distant markets. They controlled only marginal assets. They did not determine the final destination of their products. They were at the mercy of outside entrepreneurs and of foreign markets. And they engaged only in short term speculative investments.[22] They were the merchants supplying central and northern European markets with southern Italian wheat.

This market oriented economy had two major characteristics: lack of integration within the south, and dependency on foreign interests. And the two characteristics were interrelated. Obviously, foreign interests determined both production and marketing. But, more importantly, foreign interests dealt with each southern town separately. This prevented the formation of a solid, although dependent, south with common interests. The south was reduced to an economic dependency without any internal cohesion and with no power to work out an agenda of its own.

This economic dependency from outside and the lack of internal cohesion had a lasting impact on the south in four areas. The first area was a duality of power between viceroy and nobles, with the nobles having the upper hand most of the time. The power of the nobility stemmed from their control of the economic resources of the region – wheat – marketed in central and northern Europe. Because the real economic interests of the south were outside the region, the power of the state was irrelevant. In addition, Spain had no theory of empire. It did not provide positive control, but had almost a total lack of governance. In exchange for their financial support of the empire, southern nobles were allowed to operate with the highest degree of independence, as the Bourbon viceroys found out. One of them, the count of Olivares, commented in the sixteenth century: "With the barons I am everything; without them I am nothing."[23] Southern nobles never contemplated rebelling against Spain; revolt was unnecessary. Of course, when in the eighteenth and nineteenth centuries the more advanced nations of the North Atlantic system engaged in political centralization as a better way to respond to the demand of growing national economies, southerners did not follow suit. They failed to respond both because no integrated regional economy was emerging in the south and because a well-established tradition of opposition to centralization rejected the new approach.

The second element was the ineffectiveness of state bureaucracies, which allowed individual bureaucrats to pursue their interests at the expenses of the state. The centralization of state bureaucracies occurred in Europe in the seventeenth century. The ultimate goal of such change was to make individuals accountable to the state directly and to curtail the power and autonomy of local lords. The process required the training of new bureaucratic officers loyal to the central government and the recruitment of professional armies to enforce the policies of the state and to overpower the private armies of local lords. The loyalty of the bureaucrats to the state was assured through the prebendal system. The bureaucrat kept for himself all the tax returns beyond a predetermined amount to be forwarded to the state. Of course, bureaucrats assigned to southern Italy had very few reasons to be loyal to the ineffective central government of Spain. Accordingly, they vindicated the same degree of autonomy from the central government that nobles had vindicated for centuries. The Spanish crown, which excluded southern Italians from official positions at the court, allowed Spanish bureaucrats to operate with a high degree of independence. Thus bureaucratic service turned into "legalized robbery" with "free enterprise" pervading all administrative levels. In the end, the private use of public resources by bureaucrats at all levels became endemic in the south.[24]

The third element was the isolation of one town from another. The disappearance of regional markets severed the ties among communities and, eventually, even the roads connecting one town with another disappeared, absorbed by adjacent land properties. Eventually the old structures, whereby cities, towns, and villages were integrated through bureaucratic and commercial hierarchies, disappeared. Each community turned into a self-contained world, with exclusive ties to the distant foreign markets through rural entrepreneurs exporting wheat. The lack of economic diversification fostered stagnation and the lack of roads isolated communities from each other. People were born, married, and died within self-contained communities. The attachment to one's world became fierce, not because foreign ideas were threatening, but because no other world was available.[25]

The fourth element was the insecurity of life in the countryside. That insecurity forced people to live in densely nucleated settlements and made travel difficult and dangerous. Southern towns were surrounded by enormous farming areas ranging from seventy-four square kilometers per town in Sicily to forty-two in the Neapolitan provinces.[26] The uninhabited countryside and mountain ranges provided the ideal refuge for bandits. Bandits were casualties of the political and economic process who, turned loose from the social order, compensated for their losses through theft and extortion, supported by violence. Fear of bandits, the danger of isolation and long distances between towns discouraged the creation of small settlements. The only relatively safe roads were those used by the rural entrepreneurs who transported wheat from the hinterland to the coast with mule trains.[27]

These social and political arrangements shaped a culture that survived well into the twentieth century. By the time of political unification in 1870, the south had no viable economy of its own. Rather, it was a dependency of distant markets, as a supplier of wheat. The imports were confined to the bare necessities of life and to the rural implements needed for farming. Each community was geographically isolated from the others, both because of distances and lack of roads. The only real connection was with the distant foreign market. But those markets were so remote that they could not provide cultural sustenance and very little economic support. Communities were also isolated from the center of power, because nobles and rural entrepreneurs vindicated an almost total autonomy in managing their estates and conducting their business. Bureaucracies did not provide links with the centers of power either. Neither were bureaucrats capable or willing to enforce the law. Rather, they were the first to either evade it or break it. The power of the state was more apparent than real; that of merchants and nobles virtually unbounded. In the end, each town was almost totally isolated from the others. Individuals with power recognized no outside authority. Those without power had no protection. Land was the discriminating element between the former and the latter.[28]

In such a society producing for foreign markets, those who controlled land had all the power. Those who did not own land could not even count on the state for the protection of basic rights. The state was virtually powerless in dealing with large landholders and local nobles. Under the circumstances, the chasm between peasants and landowners turned into hatred and resentment on the part of peasants and arrogance on the part of landowners. In the end, peasants became totally distrustful of any person in position of power and authority. The topic of the conflict between landowners and peasants was one of the most discussed in the nineteenth century. Giuseppe Alongi, a state employee, wrote that "gabelotti consider peasants as second rate animals. Horses and cows are certainly more important than peasants to all gabellotti."[29] Napoleone Colajanni observed that anybody who was somebody regarded peasants either as nothing or something less.[30] Sidney Sonnino remarked that Sicilian barons considered their inherent right to use violence toward peasants with assurance of impunity.[31] Northern judges and magistrates sent to the south were puzzled by the reaction of southern gentlemen to the jury system. Gentlemen found it unacceptable to have to testify in court and to be tried by a jury. Equally they objected to spending money to try a peasant. As a Sicilian baron put it, if a peasant was suspected of a crime, he was punished without further ado.[32]

Reports sent to the Minister of the Interior in Rome by local prefetti and chiefs of police stated repeatedly that there was no hope of building some form of social solidarity in the south as long as peasants were not granted basic human rights. For instance, the chief of police of Palermo argued that "gentlemen should not be allowed to treat peasants like enemies and slaves."[33] The prefetto of Cosenza commented that peasants had been abused for so long that it would take decades before anybody could convince them that there was a role for them in southern society.[34] The daily La Sicilia Agricola reasoned that peasants should not be compared to, and treated like, animals. After all, their contribution to the general welfare was obvious.[35]

The experience of powerlessness was common among peasants of premodern societies. The puzzling element about southerners is that it persisted well into the twentieth century, and still is a large element in southern culture. Giustino Fortunato used to tell his colleagues in Rome: "I am the representative of nothingness." Even the language expresses to this very day powerlessness. To the question: "What did you eat today?" a southerner will answer: "Nothing." If asked: "What do you want?" a southerner will shrug his shoulders and answer: "Nothing." If a problem arises and someone asks: "What can we do?" the most likely answer is: "Nothing." The protracted experience of powerlessness created self-contempt. "We are not men," a southerner said recently. "We talk, but we do not understand what we say and our words disappear like in the depth of the sea."[36] Powerlessness and self-contempt led to further distrust of others and isolation. Any other person, in such a society, becomes a potential enemy. The greatest social virtue is privatism. Southerners call this "to be social." As one of them put it recently: "Being social means most of all not getting involved with others, staying at home, and never listening to conversations about other peoples' lives."[37] Obviously, within such a culture, the achievement of some form of social solidarity is a most difficult goal.

### The geographical isolation of southern towns

This all-pervasive isolation is perhaps the most damaging legacy in southern culture. Isolation is almost tangible in the very location of southern towns. It permeates all social interactions at the local and regional levels. It characterizes southern culture and the peasants' world view. And, most importantly, it is the very key to understanding the intricate mechanisms of family interactions. The geographical isolation is still noticeable. It was much more apparent at the time of mass emigration. After political unification, the government started to build a national network of roads to integrate the south. Limited funds made it impossible to provide any southern town with at least one road. Towns and cities located on the flatlands and along valleys were the most fortunate. But communities located on the top of mountains were bypassed and remained isolated until recent years. Fascism and World War II terminated the isolation of many southern communities; they were finally connected with the outside world through a road. Yet, isolation is still pervasive. People without personal transportation have to rely on public transportation to go to other towns or to the railroad station. In most cases distances are long, and transportation is provided only once or twice a day. It is not uncommon to meet older people who have left the native town only on rare occasions.

Southern towns are isolated not only from the larger world but also from each other, even within their immediate region. Two neighboring towns might have one main road linking each of them to a provincial or national road and to a commonly shared railroad station; but no road linking the two directly. In the late nineteenth century, the isolation of towns from each other was virtually total. Visitors, if well accepted, are properly warned not to associate with people from other towns. In 1975, for instance, when I was doing research in Verbicaro, a hill town in the province of Cosenza, I was warned not to go to neighboring Orsomarso, because those people had never been properly civilized, I was told, and still displayed traces of barbarism.

Isolated from the country at large and from neighboring towns, each southern town was like a world into its own. Writing at the turn of the century Pasquale Villari observed: "In no country of Europe are local differences so marked as they are in Italy."[38] And an American observer remarked: "Italian towns are unlike in everything, except the fact that they are different."[39] It fostered *campanilismo*, which has survived to this day. World War II initiated a process of change. But, as Carlo Levi reported for the years immediately before World War II, people from small southern towns regard individuals from neighboring towns as enemies. And, unfortunately, it is still true. Geographical isolation and *campanilismo* increased powerlessness. Individuals confined within the narrow horizons of their own towns could not tap other resources but those available in town to solve problems. Social and economic experiments conducted elsewhere went unknown. Social tensions emerging in the community had to find their solution or explosion within the community itself. Virtually nobody had friends in other villages: it was practically impossible and socially suspicious. And this is true even today. As an American reported: "Life in a southern village is exclusive of all other life. Distances are great and transportation expensive and difficult. No one seems to have friends in other villages, and cities are places to go when you need a permit or a special medical examination . . . As long as I stayed," this American concluded, "I was committed to a very particular, circumscribed life."[40]

## Social isolation

Geographical isolation could have fostered social solidarity among inhabitants of each town. It did not. Social isolation within each town was as pervasive as geographical isolation among towns. The competition over the scarce economic resources available prevented southerners living within a given community from establishing social solidarity, as every individual came to regard others as potential or actual enemies. This assertion is flatly rejected by some historians. Donna Gabaccia, for instance, in a study of western Sicily concluded: "All over western Sicily people shared one set of ideas about class, occupation, cooperation and conflict; all over the region artisans enjoyed a unified and strong tradition of occupational identification and voluntary association. From this set of shared ideas and experiences, Sicilians created many traditions as they moved through space and time."[41] This is a moving statement and a wonderful tribute to western Sicilians. Unfortunately it is based, in my opinion, on a selective reading of some evidence. I came across few cases of social solidarity. Leadership, organizational techniques and the setting of realistic goals are prerequisites for social solidarity, all three badly lacking among southerners at the time of mass emigration. Even the short-lived movement of the Fasci Siciliani, which flourished in 1893–4, showed a level of class consciousness but a low degree of social solidarity. The Fascianti were, to use Hobsbawm's expression, "primitive rebels" rather than organized laborers. The world of southern peasants was by and large characterized by social isolation.

Social isolation was the result of land tenure. History had created a variety of land tenures in the south, all of which could be reduced to two: large estates and minute properties. In large estates farming was carried out either by sharefarmers or by gang laborers. Sharefarmers were individuals working a section in a latifondo, with a sharefarming agreement. A sharefarmer often farmed two or more plots in two or more latifundia. Contracts between owners and sharefarmers were of one year's duration. Contracts were verbal and owners had total discretion over the terms of the contract until harvest time. Sharefarmers were in constant competition both to secure the most lucrative contracts and to force competitors out of the market, because the demand for plots far exceeded the availability of land. Gang laborers were individuals hired from the marketplace daily by landowners or their agents. In an oversupplied labor market, the competition was fierce. Often, it set father against son, as the young and robust son was more likely to be hired than the aging father.[42]

The competition among owners of minute properties was equally intense. Through the process of inheritance and partition, many properties had become too small to be profitable. To make ends meet, owners of minute properties tried either to secure a sharefarming contract or, more preferably, to buy more land. In the former case, they encountered the opposition of other sharefarmers. In the latter case, they aroused the animosities of other small farmers in trouble, who felt threatened by rising small landowners.[43] The Italian government too contributed to this tension. Beginning in 1861, the government placed on the market almost 30,000 small plots carved out from large properties previously owned by the church and former Italian states. It was an unprecedented opportunity for many propertyless peasants to join the class of landowners. The competition among potential buyers was intense because cash was in short supply, the quality of the land for sale vastly different, and the integrity of the personnel in charge of the sale highly questionable. And the competition did not let up even after the purchase, because many new landowners had no previous experience in running farms independently. Some new owners lost their properties for tax delinquency, others for defaulting in their payments.[44]

Competition among sharefarmers and laborers made class solidarity and economic cooperation virtually impossible, as visitors reported. The prefetto of Palermo noted that peasants were so suspicious of each other as to refuse any form of cooperation.[45] The prefetto of Cosenza, requested to report on farmers' associations in the province, answered that cooperation was still an unknown word among peasants.[46] The writers of the Inchiesta Jacini in the 1870s unanimously stressed that adamant resistance to any form of cooperation was the major stumbling block in the modernization of the southern economy. Over the years, the situation did not improve noticeably. In 1910, for instance, a writer from Cosenza remarked that some peasants had joined societies promoted by students or labor leaders. But, notwithstanding high-sounding statements in official declarations, most members had no idea what economic cooperation and social solidarity were all about. Peasants, the writer concluded, although willing to join organizations with recreational or social goals, resisted the idea of economic cooperation like the plague.[47] Statistics indicators gathered by the government on mutual aid societies revealed that the south lagged behind the north, with many southern towns reporting no voluntary organizations.[48] Even today southern peasants seemingly do not see the potential of social solidarity and economic cooperation. The common wisdom is that to be social an individual has to avoid getting involved with others. As a Sicilian peasant put it not long ago: "In the south, if you bring two individuals or two families together, they will kill each other. The wise man never gets involved with others."[49]

Only a small minority of southern peasants were ever affected by organizations and militancy. Leadership was generally provided either by outsiders, or intellectuals and students with little or no understanding of the peasants' demands.[50] Peasant organizations were short-lived, even when governmental repression did not terminate them. Their goals were mostly restricted to some forms of recreational interaction. Their achievements were hardly meaningful and lasting, and certainly not profound enough to change significantly the conditions of the peasants. Although commendable, the portrait of southern peasants as class conscious and as organized laborers is, in my opinion, inaccurate. Sporadic rebellions did not end the social isolation of southerners. And the legacy of social isolation is still a great part of southern culture.

*Cultural isolation*

Cultural isolation was, and still is to a degree, as visible and pervasive in the south as geographic and social isolation. Illiteracy or semiliteracy kept southern peasants mentally isolated from the national culture. Although strongly resisted, compulsory education increased the percentage of young people attending school, even in the south. For instance, in the early 1870s, only 33 percent of the children of school age attended school in the south. After thirty years and endless governmental efforts, the percentage had increased to 60.[51] This was certainly an improvement. But 40 percent of the children who should have been attending school were not doing so in the early twentieth century. Unfortunately regardless of how we read these statistics compulsory education and school attendance did not break the cycle of illiteracy and cultural isolation. With the exception of some urban areas, children attended school for three years only. By age nine, boys followed their fathers to work and girls helped their mothers at home. Thus literacy for most was limited to the ability to sign one's name and to read a few words. For all practical purposes most southerners were illiterate. Increased governmental efforts to foster public education in the twentieth century have not achieved impressive results. As late as 1950 three out of every four southerners were considered functionally illiterate.[52] An American observer wrote recently: "Women know how to sign their own name; but in any practical sense they are illiterate."[53] These functionally illiterate peasants are isolated from the national culture and from any knowledge transmitted through the printed word.

Gentlemen took pride in the fact that, unlike peasants, they were literate. Most prominent families had traditionally hired a tutor to give an education to their children. Although literate, however, southern gentlemen too lived in a mentally circumscribed world, and were generally unaware of the changes occurring in the Western world. Their main interests were law and literature. Over the years, their preferences have not changed. Even today, the two most popular majors at the University of Naples are law and belles lettres. The keen interest in natural and social science as well as in technology, so prevalent in modern societies, was virtually absent in the late nineteenth century and it is questionable whether it has been granted citizenship to this very day. Steeped in the world of classical literature, rhetoric, and law, gentlemen were cut off from technical and social sciences.

Of course, southerners enjoyed and still enjoy a rich popular culture, which anthropologists and visitors found and still find fascinating. That culture, however, offered a poor escape from isolation. Proverbs, songs, and festivals emphasized the fatalistic and pessimistic worldview of peasants. The world was and remains a cruel place where freedom of action was limited or nonexistent. Even the most cherished human experience, love, was deceptive, as a Calabrian proverb put it: "Get married and for a short time you will experience the sweetness of honey which will soon turn into poison."[54] In such a cruel place there was no reason to expand one's knowledge or to go beyond the narrow boundaries of one's fragile stability. The language itself increased social isolation. Rich in concrete words and images, southern dialects remain inadequate to convey emotional and intellectual messages of a certain complexity. This cultural isolation was noticed with frustration by visitors. Northern Italians especially expressed frustration because, although speaking the same language, they were unable to establish meaningful communications. In 1887, for instance, the prefetto of Cosenza wrote: "Those who have been in school for a number of years can understand and speak Italian. But I am left with the feeling that there is a wall between them and myself."[55]

### A culture of coping

Fatalism about human existence in general and personal isolation in southern communities specifically were the two harsh realities of life. To cope, southerners developed a culture centered on four elements: escape, family, honor, and friendship. Because present and future were immutable, southerners found a happy refuge in the past. The mythical past offered a world without exploitation and hunger, a world of miraculous events and personal victories, a wonderful escape from the present. Nobody questioned the objectivity of that mythical past. It was the constant assertion of countless traditions handed down from generation to generation that made it true. Every community counted a number of storytellers who perpetuated these myths without fear of contradiction. It was relatively unimportant that the past had not been what peasants wanted to believe. The crucial element was the importance of their historical perception.

Religion and history provided in different ways the raw material for the creation of the mythical past. Religion offered the solace of a past characterized by social equality, moral retribution and divine help against the evil forces of nature. History buttressed the perception of uniqueness and importance in each community. Over the centuries, southerners created a rich anthology of stories, proverbs, allegories, and popular plays to transmit the mythical past from generation to generation. It was only recently that this wealth of rural traditions appeared in print. Seemingly it was in Sicily and Calabria that the richest anthologies were created.[56]

Religion proclaimed that there had been a golden age, when social relations were based on love, not greed. As a Sicilian proverb put it: "Adam was the root, we are the branches. The foundation of true human nobility is good moral behavior."[57] Greed entered the world through Cain, who, according to southern folklore, was a successful businessman. After him, greed ruled the world through the powerful. Punishment in an afterlife awaited individuals whose lives had been ruled by greed. A colorful Sicilian proverb provided a long list of all classes of people to be found in hell: "Hell overflows with tax collectors, public prosecutors, judges, public notaries, and physicians. But the largest group is made up of monks and priests. This occurs because in this world the poor who catches a flea is sentenced to prison, whereas the powerful who steals an estate is publicly praised."[58]

But in every age God had sent his saints to redeem society from greed and reestablish the correct hierarchy of values. Unfortunately only the poor were willing to listen. One such saint was St. Gerlando. A victim of oppression, St. Gerlando left his family one day and with a handful of companions retreated to a mountain pass. Wealthy landowners and merchants, guilty of oppressing peasants, were forced to pay a handsome sum to cross the pass. The money was distributed among the poor. So pleased was God with Gerlando that he granted him the power to perform miracles. The people, aware that God had selected Gerlando, built a chapel for him by the pass. There Gerlando spent his days in prayer, healing sick people and taking time off only to set the toll wealthy travelers had to pay. In the end, social equality was restored.[59]

Another story emphasized God's predilection for the poor. In ancient times, in a society ridden with injustice, God sent a good king to restore order. He held court every day. When individuals appeared to plead their cases, the king paid little attention to them. Instead, he observed their hands closely. People with delicate hands were quickly dismissed and thrown in jail. People with callous hands were granted what they wanted in addition to land. To the attendants surprised by such behavior the king explained: "At the beginning God blessed those who work and so do I. But God cannot stand those who live in idleness. And neither do I."[60] Obviously even in the mythical past, society was not perfect; yet God had constantly been on the side of the oppressed. And that was no small consolation to powerless and oppressed southerners.

History provided an escape from isolation by redeeming the desolate present through a glorious past. In many southern villages the creation of a mythical past began with the search for links with ancient Rome. Some towns traced their origins to the Greeks or Etruscans. Because the south had been invaded frequently by foreigners, the stories emphasized either the heroic resistance to invaders or shrewdness in evading enemy occupation. Towns that could not link themselves directly to an old origin or to some heroic events created imaginary connections with nearby towns with such a documented past. For instance, the people of Castel San Giorgio, near Naples, claim that it was a Greek settlement. But history does not record any significant event occurring there. However, Titus Livy describes the heroic resistance of nearby Lucera to Hannibal's attack in 216 B.C. and its deep fidelity to Rome even after homes were sacked and burned. The citizens of Castel San Giorgio promptly created a role for themselves. Their story was that they avoided occupation both because of *fortuna* (fate) and of political savvy. They appeased Hannibal by convincing him that he had nothing to fear from them. This glorious or inglorious past seemingly still provides inspiration for present decisions. On Sept. 8, 1943, when German troops occupied the town, local officials reminded the Castelsangiorgesi to use toward Germans the same savvy their ancestors had displayed toward Hannibal. And later, in 1945, citizens were told to repeat the performance with entering American and British troops. Because both occupations occurred in September, Castelsangiorgesi showed their good will by offering Germans first and Allies later platters of newly harvested grapes.[61]

Towns unable to assert direct links with antiquity struggled to create a mythological past while blaming their present isolation and misfortune on the lack of such a past. In some cases, to correct the unfortunate situation, some towns even dropped the traditional patron saint in favor of a more palatable protector. The story of Nissoria, in Sicily, illustrates these points. Founded in 1746 by the prince of Paternò, Nissoria had no link with antiquity. But oral legends, later allegedly corroborated by archeological findings, claimed that Nissoria was the site of the ancient city of Imakara, mentioned by Cicero. Some stories even alleged that as early as 900 B.C. Greeks had founded on the same site the settlement of Piknos, later destroyed in the wars between Syracuse and Carthage.

But regardless of any possible link with antiquity, Nissoria's past was irrelevant in comparison with that of neighboring Assoro, a Greek settlement. In 440 B.C. Assoro had shared with Syracuse a victory over Carthage. Assoro's success in the old days explains, in popular accounts, why it dominates surrounding cities even today. When the railroad between Palermo and Catania was built, for instance, Assoro was granted a connection. Nissoria was denied. Recently the highway Catania Palermo bypassed Nissoria in favor of Assoro. Seemingly even a change of saints did not help Nissoria. In the early 1850s the

Nissorini decided to drop their patron, St. Gregory of Armenia. He had been ineffective to halt epidemics in the 1840s. Besides, he had become a bishop by attaching himself to petty nobility, a class betrayal the Nissorini were not ready to forgive. Saint Joseph was selected as a replacement; he had impeccable credentials as protector of manual labor and he was certainly powerful. In 1854 the prince of Paterno was granted permission by the Vatican to rededicate the church of Nissoria to St. Joseph. But the change did not alter Nissoria's fortune, as the cases of the railroad and highway indicated. As the Nissorini argue today, their bad luck is the result of an evil spell on their town by Assoro.[62]

Family life was another way to escape isolation. Among southerners, the family was the center of life. It provided relief from fate and isolation. Within the family, an individual experienced some form of power, although birth, death, and life cycles remained out of human control. More importantly, families provided a refuge from the burden of isolation. A Sicilian proverb illustrated the importance of the family: "An unmarried adult is like a nobody mixed with nothing."[63] An individual without a family was incomprehensible, although many adults could not, in fact, get married. Family life and the obligations it created were a man's primary responsibility: politics, work, economy, religion, and even love were secondary. The education of boys and girls, courtship and marriage, and family roles were protected by rituals and traditions emphasizing personal responsibility to family solidarity. Richard Gambino, who experienced such family solidarity in this country, wrote: "All obligations, feelings or rights of individuality were repressed by any father, mother, daughter or son."[64] Daily life was centered on family solidarity. The most coveted commendation for a father was that his family was his whole life, a praise often inscribed in tombstones. Fathers were protective and jealous of their wives and willing to endure endless hardship for their children. Real women, as Sicilians put it, were "exclusively home and church." Children were loved and spoiled, but they were expected to be obedient to parents and take care of them in old age.[65]

Because families were so central to individual life, individuals engaged in outside activities mainly for the sake of their families. Conflict among competing individuals, of course, was likely to arise, especially in the south, where the economic resources were scarce. Southerners resolved their conflicts by maintaining that each individual had to pursue his own interests and his family's even, if necessary, at the detriment of others. In this struggle without rules, the shrewd and cunning was the *furbo*. He used his astuteness to manipulate others, without alienating them if possible. The immediate goals were personal and family advancement. The individual who was taken advantage of was called *fesso*. Southerners had little sympathy for him. Southerners did not attach any moral connotation to *furberia* and *fesseria*. They were simply facts of life. However, the individual who engaged in any sort of social and economic activity without being aware that others would try to make him *fesso* was considered a real fool. To avoid becoming a *fesso* was a personal moral obligation, not the obligation of the *furbo*. Obviously, every southerner considered himself a *furbo*, constantly ready to prove himself and defend his family by making everybody else a *fesso*.

But what happened when an individual discovered that he had been made a *fesso*? It was intolerable, because it was a direct insult to one's dignity and freedom of action, and an indirect insult to one's family. Honor dictated that an offense against the person, the patrimony and the family had to be vindicated. The wrong had to be rectified, with blood if necessary. This sense of honor among southerners seemed to be an artificially inflated sentiment to outsiders. However, if we consider that families were the only social units in which southerners had some form of control, we can understand why retaliation was often so violent. An offense to the self or the family was perceived as the ultimate disgrace, because, without the family, the individual was nothing. Family property, family prestige, and the integrity of the women being part of the family were the three areas in which honor had to be preserved at all costs. Property, defined as every material possession of the family, was crucial to independence. Prestige entitled families to social respect in the community and ranked them according to the behavior and success of the members. A lack of success of a member or a disreputable action, real or perceived, affected all members of the family. Women were considered the vulnerable members of the family. Loss of virginity by a daughter or an extramarital affair by a married woman spelled family failure in two ways. The woman was suspected of treason to her family. The usurper, by successfully attacking the woman, had proclaimed his disregard for the honor and dignity of the men in the family. Because the family was so central to one's experience, the defense of family honor was the primary responsibility of adult males.[66]

To defend their honor and achieve the limited goals possible in a precarious economy, families needed friends. The procurement of friends was the fourth mechanism of coping among southerners. In southern society, friendship was never a personal endeavor. It was a family affair. Individuals did not befriend individuals. Only families did befriend other families to achieve mutually desirable goals. And friendships were cemented with lavish rituals, like banquets, to show to the whole community that in the future the two families would act as a unit. Friendships created mutual obligations that were almost as sacred as those within families. The betrayal of friends was punished almost as severely as the betrayal of family members. And the reconciliation of two hostile families followed a patterned ritual even more lavish than the creation of new friendships. In southern communities, where opportunities were limited, competition fierce and isolation rampant, the management of family friendships was a most difficult task. The endless turnover of friendships created a constant strife and much anguish and bloodshed.[67]

## Troubled southern families

The topic of families as the most valuable assets of southerners needs further exploration. Seemingly families provided a refuge from fate and isolation. But did they really? The celebration of family closeness and stability has been a constant in the literature about the south.[68] Historians of Italian immigration in the United States equally emphasized that strong family loyalties smoothed the transition of southern Italians from the Old World to the New World.[69] But there are those who disagree. A study conducted in the 1950s in Sicily concludes that "feelings of inadequacy are strong and insulate individuals even within families."[70] Another study conducted in Calabria argues that families are social units of last resort, unable, however, to offer meaningful escape from isolation and powerlessness.[71] And an American observer reported: "They (couples) are together; but they share little."[72] Because families were so central in the experience of southerners, it is important to explore this topic further.

Evidence available from the turn of the century shows that many families experienced a high degree of distress. Stability and closeness were difficult goals to achieve and maintain. A survey of housing in the city of Cosenza in 1908 revealed that as many as 15 percent of the households had been abandoned by the breadwinner.[73] Emigration too became "a silent divorce court."[74] Southern prefetti reported that many families never heard from fathers after they left for overseas.[75] Visitors to Calabria noted that family desertions were common. Moreover, in discussing the impact of emigration, they reported: "It is not difficult to understand what happens to families in a province where about 50,000 wives do not live with their husbands to whom they have been married for only a short time."[76] Rates of illegitimacy were twice as high in the south as in the north. In 1902, for instance, 45 per 1,000 newborns in Cosenza were illegitimate; in contrast, the rate was 28 in the northern province of Genoa.[77] No divorce statistics are available, of course, because divorce was not legalized until 1976. Available evidence, however, shows that family stability was not a common experience. Rather, southern families experienced stress and instability, even before mass emigration.[78]

Other evidence shows that family closeness and solidarity were difficult goals. Abele Damiani, a Sicilian, commented: "Love is a scarce commodity in most families. There are fathers actively promoting the prostitution of their sons and daughters. Incest, prostitution and illegitimacy have reached startling proportions."[79] The prefetto of Palermo added that concubinage, adultery, and prostitution were quite common among peasants. He remarked that the control of fathers over their families was more apparent than real, because fathers were out of the house from sunrise to sunset. A judge in Palermo commented that "there is no love, no affection, no family life in Sicily." Damiani concluded that some people were concerned that the Sicilian family as an institution was coming to an end.[80] Sicily was not the exception. In the early 1900s the state prosecutor in Calabria sounded the alarm that something had to be done to save local families from disintegration. A local magistrate added that family stability and solidarity were in jeopardy and that society could no longer count on families for the education of children. He pointed out that desertions, prostitution, illegitimacy were increasing every year. Emigration only contributed to making a bad situation worse.[81]

How should we explain this evidence? Perhaps there was a degree of bias in reports from prefetti and magistrates, who were ordinarily northerners not familiar with family behavior in the south. Southerners too voiced the same concerns. Some of them made excuses for the too common family problems, like Francesco Angarano who blamed the "highly passionate temperament" as the root of family instability.[82] But he did not deny that southern families were in trouble. Perhaps the evidence has to be read in a comparative perspective. A degree of family instability has to be expected in every society. But insofar as rates of illegitimacy are indicative of family life, the south, with rates twice as high as those in the north, seemed to have experienced more serious family problems. Perhaps there was a dichotomy between prescribed and actual behavior in family matters. A northern magistrate assigned to Sicily reported his astonishment at the discovery of the contrast between public and private behavior of women. In public, they had to cover even their faces, and they were forbidden to engage in conversation with any men outside the immediate family. In private, their sexual behavior was quite free. Adultery was quite common and tolerated. Men would openly keep concubines and engage in extramarital affairs well known to wives and children.[83] If this assessment is accurate, then the stable and united family of the south was an ideal more than a reality. Perhaps, the seemingly stable and united family was the result of inner family dynamics controlled by women, as an American observer speculated. Men were jealous and possessive of their women. Besides, they considered them inferior and excluded them from men's gatherings. Women accepted the inferior role to boost the ego of their men who could not experience power and control anywhere else but in the family.[84]

But regardless of the explanation we can find for the discrepancy between prescribed and actual family behavior, we can draw some conclusions. First, fate and isolation circumscribed the lives and determined the range of possibilities of southerners. Optimism was a rare commodity, notwithstanding the festive attitude of southerners. Time has not changed the outlook substantially. As an observer remarked: "The southern expects nothing, not from the land, not from his neighbors or government, perhaps least from the government."[85] It was the same attitude Mario Puzo observed in his immigrant parents: "Bent on survival, they narrowed their minds to the narrowest line of existence."[86] Even today the fight is the same: to eat and stay alive. Under the circumstances, why should southerners not hope for change? The fear is that change might bring about a future more painful than the present.[87] Visitors marveled at the ability of southern peasants to endure the unendurable, because, as one put it, "they live like beasts whose sense of dignity has died centuries ago."[88]

### Adjustment to change: Emigration and return

Many will object to this negative assessment of southern culture. After all, visitors to the Italian south are impressed by the genuine warmth of the people, their friendliness, their willingness to help, and by the generally festive attitude of southerners. And I have been captivated myself by that culture to which I return almost every year. Yet, if one lives in the Italian south for a protracted period of time and especially if one engages in any activity (other than being a tourist), one is likely to discover a vast dichotomy between a glittering folklore and a harsh reality. Life in the south, even in cities, is hard and perhaps harder than in most other European regions. One does not necessarily need to conclude, as Constance Cronin did, that there is a conspiracy among southerners to deceive outsiders. But one must be aware of the existence of a puzzling cultural dichotomy, which visitors and scholars alike have pointed out for several centuries.

If we compare the main characteristics of southern Italian culture, on the one hand, with the goals of national integration and economic modernization promoted in Italy at the turn of the century, on the other, we realize why southern Italians were ill prepared to join a modern or modernizing nation. The process of national integration required a commitment to the organization of the state and a shared belief in the power of collective action to bring about favorable changes. But the ability to embrace those beliefs was in short supply in the south. Besides, the economic dependency of the south on foreign markets and the social and cultural characteristics that such dependency had set in place had undermined the confidence of southerners in any large-scale organization. In addition, the endemic geographical isolation of southern communities, coupled with the social and cultural isolation of its inhabitants, had created a culture of fierce individualism, which rendered southerners unreceptive to the gospel of social solidarity. The core of the southern culture was the family, whose interest and honor every individual was expected to place ahead of any personal goal. But even the family was a troubled institution, at least at the turn of the century. After all, a precarious economy adversely affects family life too. To reinforce their fragile families, southerners sought friends. Family, honor, and friends were the cultural universe of southerners. It was a confined and precarious universe. But it was the only one they had.

Suddenly, this fragile cultural universe was forced to cope with even bigger challenges unleashed by the process of national integration and economic modernization of Italy. Southerners were forced out of their region to make a living. In the process they had to deal with more advanced nations than Italy was at the turn of the century. Economic changes forced their departure. And southerners relied on their culture to cope with the change. The new economic dynamic was a new and unexpected dependency of the south. By the late 1880s, in fact, the south ceased to export wheat and turned into an importer of wheat. In addition, olive oil and wine, the two other cash crops of the south, were losing ground in international markets because of the competition from Greece and Spain. Moreover, at the end of the nineteenth century, the prices of food commodities were dropping drastically. To compound the southern problem, the region became the target of manufactured exports arriving from central and northern Europe and the United States as well. And of course, southerners were not immune to the seduction of the new material things. Southerners, to generate the money to buy in the new dependent market, had to emigrate to the same regions that were sending them the goods to buy.

Like other emigrants, southerners could have decided to relocate permanently in nations with jobs for them. They did not. Their decision in favor of temporary emigration and return was prompted by their culture and their economy. Similarly, southern culture determined also the other characteristics of emigration and return migration. A permanent relocation in another country was a monumental change, which southerners in general rejected. Their fatalism, their "transcendent resistance to change," the fear that drastic changes might create even larger problems than the present ones prevented them from embracing permanent emigration. Besides, the availability of land in many southern communities led them to believe that what they needed most was cash to buy land. Temporary emigration was certainly a change, especially for those heading for overseas. But southerners were not opposed to some degree of change, especially if embraced to preserve the essential of family life so important to them. Southerners embraced temporary emigration and return as strictly individual choices, for the sake of their families and relying on a network of friendships. Geographical, social, and cultural isolation prevented them from embracing emigration as a large-scale enterprise, organized and directed by the state, or even by their regions. Each town selected its destinations, friendship and family ties provided the link between immigrants abroad and families in Italy, and the goals to be achieved were strictly confined to the welfare of the family. Of all the characteristics of southern emigration, the lack of coordination by any agency and the independence of each town in engaging in the process are perhaps the best indications of the uniqueness of the southern Italian culture.

In the end, the conservative southern culture was overpowered and finally changed by economic dynamics. Southerners embraced temporary emigration and return migration to generate the cash they needed to preserve the traditional life, now threatened by the new economic dependency of their region. But in the process of pursuing rather conservative goals through temporary emigration and return, southerners were progressively seduced by their experience as immigrants and at the same time disenchanted by the original goals they had so eagerly embraced. Emigration and return migration unleashed economic dynamics of such magnitude that even the conservative southern culture could not arrest. The southern ethos determined the parameters of Italian emigration, return migration and remittances for a number of decades. But, economic dynamics, in the end, overcame cultural resistances, at least for a large number of Italians.

# 4    *The national debate*

*The challenges of the new state*

When European emigration started in the 1870s, Italians largely ignored it. The new country had to face so many challenges that the
departure of a few thousand people seemed irrelevant. Soon enough,
however, emigration became a mass phenomenon that could not be
ignored. The debate on emigration engaged Italians at virtually all
levels. Popular writers made Italians aware of the event, its pitfalls
and rewards. Social scientists discussed its causes, assessed the potential for the nation, and made recommendations. Politicians debated
the responsibilities of the government and of the private sector as
well as how emigration could be channeled to achieve larger goals.
And interest groups struggled to promote, discourage, or direct the
phenomenon, according to their own private agendas.

This chapter deals with the national debate on emigration from the
1870s to World War I. Initially the national debate focused on the
large national problems of political integration, economic development, and the special needs of the south, as Chapters 1 and 2 describe.
Part of the national debate was also concerned with the effort to
understand southern culture as the only way to deal effectively with
the region. The debate on emigration was marginal at best. Emigration
was considered a nuisance, perhaps serving as a safety valve at times,
a means to be rid of undesirable and disgruntled Italians. Progressively the debates about the south and emigration converged, as more
and more people realized that not only southerners were emigrating
in large numbers but also that the southern problem could perhaps
be solved through return migration and remittances. By the beginning
of the century, the national debate on the integration of the south
had focused on emigration, return migration, and remittances as the
most important dynamics for a southern renaissance.

The reader should be aware from the beginning, however, that the
public discourse never reached a consensus. This chapter will reveal

the variety of political postures within the country. It will especially emphasize the discrepancy between those in favor of a traditional society and those open to change and experimentatiòn. It will show the concern and also the indifference of the nation toward those who left. It will outline the transition from a disengaged state, to a government taking an active role in protecting emigration and return migration, only to reverse itself and return to a hands-off policy in matters dealing with emigration and return migration. It will emphasize how different groups tried to use the phenomenon to their ends, which they invariably labeled as "national goals." Throughout all these debates there is a strange absence or silence. Emigrants, immigrants, and returnees never make an appearance. Ironically, at the end of a long debate, the national government removes itself from the southern question. The argument concluded: nothing could be done for the south by the government that the south could not do better by itself.

The thrust of the debate was national integration, a concern Italians shared with many other nations in the Western world. The economic dynamics at work in industrializing nations in the late nineteenth century demanded an acceleration in the processes of social and economic integration within nations. The creation of national markets made possible by railroads, the rapid introduction of industrial production through technological advances, the appearance of large corporations with their need for large capital and supporting services, and finally the rapid growth of cities, which forced political leaders to experiment with new political and organizational techniques, were all unprecedented phenomena that demanded a degree of social and economic integration untested in Western nations. National prosperity was linked not only to the availability of national resources, but also to the collective will to set aside narrow loyalties and clannish traditions in favor of larger national loyalties and standardized behavior.

The transition from the old to the new order brought about structural dislocations and demanded difficult personal readjustments. Small-scale farming was replaced by commercial farming and cottage production by industrial production. Small farmers were forced out of their plots, unable to compete with commercial farmers, as farm commodities prices dropped drastically. Cottage industries came to an end as technology and large-scale capital made possible industrial production for national markets. The released manpower was forced either to retrain itself for the new economy or to look for work elsewhere.[1] Structural dislocations and personal readjustments had to be reconciled with the new order. And emigrants were among the individuals most deeply affected by the transition. The debate on national integration could not ignore them, because they were the living indications that something was not working in the process. In Italy the debate still goes on.

## The liberal state

The debate started in 1869, before the occupation of Rome, in the Italian Chamber of Deputies, then meeting in Florence, the temporary capital of the new nation. Ercole Lualdi pointed out to his colleagues that beginning in 1864 emigration from his district of Busto Arsizio, not far from Milan, had been on the increase and had reached the alarming figure of one thousand departures in 1867. Lualdi asked: "What causes the departure of so many people?" After all, he added, "people did not leave because of spirit of adventure; they departed unwilling and cursing landowners and government." If the government fails to act, he concluded, in the near future Italy will register a shortage of manpower. In his answer Prime Minister Luigi Menabrea stressed the classical position of the liberal state. It was not the responsibility of the public sector to deal with mass emigration. Landowners and industry operators were to blame. It was the obligation of those exploiting the economic resources in the district, he concluded, to find a job for every resident. Lualdi's follow-up could not be but polemic. As the representative of one of the wealthiest districts in the nation, he wanted to shift the blame to the public sector. The government, Lualdi stated, could not expect landowners and industry operators to solve every problem. After all, they were doing the best they could under the adverse circumstances created by the new government. How could landowners and industry operators expand their operations and thus create new jobs, when the government had increased taxation to the point of making further investments virtually impossible?[2]

The Lualdi-Menabrea exchange revealed the existence of a dichotomy in Italy. On the one hand, the government had undertaken a major program of national improvements for the development of a modern economy, the national railroad system being the first priority. The program could be implemented only by increasing taxation, a burden that made difficult further investments by the private sector. On the other hand, landowners and industry operators were held responsible for the economic dislocations forcing people to leave, and were asked to be more aggressive in bringing about a solution. It was obvious from the debate that the government was unwilling to take any blame or to implement any measure to deal with emigration.

Another debate occurred in 1872 between Guglielmo Tocci, the representative from Cosenza in the south, and Giovanni Lanza, then minister of the interior and prime minister. Tocci argued that emigration from his district was on the increase. People blamed their departure on government and landowners. Moreover, Tocci concluded, it was obvious that emigration was a loss of manpower the nation could not endure. Lanza replied that emigration was not necessarily a loss for the nation or an indicator of poverty and economic dislocation. He observed that emigration from Germany was not caused by poverty. Rather it was the result of better opportunities across the Atlantic. Moreover, he quoted the traditional emigration from the Italian province of Genoa, certainly prompted by aggressiveness and personal courage, not poverty. But, regardless of how one could assess the phenomenon, the minister concluded that landowners and industry operators were responsible for providing full employment. After all, the government was carrying its fair share of the economic burden by funding transportation and education. Citizens could not reasonably expect more.[3]

In reality notwithstanding the disclaimers of the prime minister, the government was alarmed. While proclaiming its faith in economic liberalism, in practice the government regarded emigration as a public enemy. As early as 1868, the Minister of the Interior issued an instruction urging the prefects to discourage and if necessary to oppose emigration. Police departments were directed to release visas for expatriation only "to people who already have a secure job in the country where they intend to go, or enough money to be self-supporting for a time."[4] Years later another instruction urged mayors to increase their efforts to discourage emigration and to deny visas to indigent people, because they were likely to ask for repatriation at government expense.[5] Instructions were generally disregarded. Prefects and mayors had more pressing business to attend to; after all, the new state was still recruiting personnel for key administrative positions in the 1870s. The departure from a province of a few thousand poor people, potential troublemakers, was likely to be considered a blessing. Among other things, it relieved some potentially explosive social situations.

*Public awareness*

Public opinion eventually took notice of emigrants. Daily columnists, fiction writers, reporters, and even poets could not ignore a phenomenon involving thousands of people and virtually every Italian province. The popular reaction was astonishment, sympathy, and finally a resigned surrender to incomprehensible events. Neither emigrants nor writers understood the reasons why so many people had to leave, nor did they feel that emigrants had any control over their destiny. Emigration was a monumental disruption of the traditional order. Seemingly emigration had no redeeming features. There was a great deal of fatalism in this popular literature on emigration. Antonio Marazzi, for instance, in a three-volume novel on the emigration of two Italians to Argentina, portrayed the powerlessness of his characters toward landowners in Italy, emigration agents, natural forces at sea, and the unfamiliar environment in South America.[6] Nicola Marcone took a similar approach in a volume on Italian emigration to Brazil.[7] In a poem written in 1865, the popular Giacomo Zanella described the painful departure of a father from his family, pain mitigated only by the emigrant's surrender to God's will.[8] Another poet, Edmondo De Amicis, aware of the hardships that Italians would have to endure abroad, portrayed the throngs of emigrants boarding a ship as a crowd pushed to premature death. De Amicis's reaction was a strong sympathy for this "outpouring of all human tragedies."[9] Other writers, like Giovanni Florenzano and Antonio Caccianiga, expressed indignation at the countless exploitations of uneducated emigrants by emigration agents, shipping companies, and industry operators in the countries of immigration.[10]

Italian economists too took notice of the phenomenon. Obviously, they did not share the sense of powerlessness of popular writers. They believed that they could understand the causes of mass emigration, although their opinions diverged as to how to deal with it. In general, however, they struggled to interpret the phenomenon in reference to the national interest. For some, it was a tragic occurrence; for others, it was an unprecedented opportunity. European economists generally assumed that the human resources of a given nation were its most valuable capital. The departure of so many citizens was a loss for the nation, many Italian economists argued. As emigration increased, some leading economists questioned this assumption. Francesco Ferrara, for instance, argued that unused capital was no capital at all. Accordingly, unemployed Italians leaving the country did not subtract valuable capital. On the contrary, their departure was a national relief. Besides, emigration was potentially beneficial to the nation through remittances and returnees with improved skills. Ferrara concluded that the future of Europe was going to be brighter, mostly because of the 60,000 Europeans leaving the Continent every year, most of whom returned with money and skills.[11] Gerolamo Boccardo, another economist, envisioned mass emigration as a way of opening foreign countries to Italian exports.[12] Some leading Italian politicians agreed. Two prime ministers, Camillo Benso di Cavour and Marco Minghetti, maintained that emigration should not be interfered with, because in the long run, it would result in the creation of new markets for Italy.[13]

But, if some scientists were willing to point out the long-term positive impacts of emigration, others were ready to show that the phenomenon was a destabilizing force in Italian society and that governmental intervention was needed to prevent further disruption. The Marchese di Cosentino, for instance, argued that emigration was a drain of capital, a threat to family stability and to local economies, a loss of political prestige abroad, and an escape for debtors and criminals.[14] To minimize the disruption, the government had to regulate emigration by selecting the destinations and by making it mandatory that every emigrant travel on Italian ships. Di Cosentino went so far as to advocate the suspension of individual freedoms. After all, he argued, nations had the right to suspend individual liberties in times of war. Emigration was a national emergency to be equated to a war.[15]

Progressively the debate focused on the role the government was expected to play, both to minimize the destabilization of national life and to maximize the benefits to be derived by return migration and remittances. Leone Carpi, for instance, argued that mass emigration was the ominous indicator that some far-reaching social and economic changes were occurring in the country. Undoubtedly he maintained, emigration had some actual or potential benefits, like releasing the pressure from the Italian labor markets, decreasing the number of poor people, increasing commerce between Italy and other countries, and, most importantly, channeling much needed capital to Italy through remittances. Although the carrier of all these benefits, emigration was still a social ill, he observed. It was the government's responsibility to discipline emigration by removing the reasons compelling people to leave. That was the ultimate goal. And as long as emigration remained a necessity, the government had to discipline the phenomenon in the national interest. And because emigration was going to be a mass phenomenon for at least a couple of decades, Carpi concluded, the government should urge Italians to go to South America, where Italians would feel more at home than in the United States, and the Italian nation could foster its economic interests through an increased Italian presence.[16]

Some economists speaking for special-interest groups emphasized the positive aspects of emigration, using the successful emigrations of British and Germans as examples. Jacopo Vigilio, for instance, a Genoese with strong ties to local shipping companies, engaged in the emigration trade, stated that emigration had to be encouraged, not opposed. After all, emigration would reestablish the demographic balance in Italy, decrease the pressure on local labor markets, increase the bargaining power of Italian workers at home, expand trade between Italy and the countries of destination, promote the growth of the national merchant marine, and finally enlarge the numbers of small landowners through the wise investment of savings from abroad.[17] By the early 1870s, the debate had produced a variety of positions ranging from outright condemnation because of the destabilizing power of emigration to enthusiastic support for its potential benefits.

## The new obligations of the modern state

The tempo of the debate increased in 1874, following two widely publicized events. In New York an Italian ship unloaded in 1876 several hundred emigrants who had been assured a passage to Brazil. In Genoa, an agent, to whom about fifty departing families had entrusted tickets and savings, disappeared leaving the families stranded. In reporting the two events, columnists lamented that there were no satisfactory statistics on emigration available in Italy, a failure that precluded any serious debate on the phenomenon and its potential impact on the nation. Writers argued that the government had to protect emigrants, at least to the extent of shielding them from exploitation at the ports of embarkation. Reporters concluded that the two events widely publicized in Italy were only the tip of the iceberg. For every major scandal brought to the public attention, they concluded, hundreds went unreported.

Educated Italians began to debate emigration and its implications at professional meetings. The first congress of Italian economists, which occurred in Milan in 1875, could no longer ignore emigration. The congress, organized by young economists, was determined to denounce traditional economic liberalism and argue in favor of a more active role by the government in the national economy. The model, of course, was Germany and, to a lesser degree, Great Britain. In the minds of the organizers of the congress, emigration was not meant to be a major topic of discussion. Eventually it became one of the central issues after a presentation made by the economist Luigi Luzzatti. He argued that Italy was the only large European nation in which emigration was dealt with exclusively as a matter of national security. The Italian government had not awakened yet to the social and economic implications of mass emigration, Luzzatti concluded. He recommended that Italy do what more enlightened European nations had already done: keep accurate statistics of the phenomenon, establish emigration offices, and pass legislation to protect emigrants during the journey from native towns to countries of destination.

The congress produced some results. In 1876 the Minister of Agriculture, Industry and Commerce began the regular publication of yearly emigration statistics, and Senator Torelli launched the Società di Patronato (Protective Society), a privately funded organization to assist emigrants in the journey from their villages to the ports of embarkation. The Società had virtually no funds, and no personnel to implement its program. Although largely ineffective, the Società provided the first indication of an emerging social awareness. Moreover, it marked the first step toward the acceptance of the principle that emigration was a phenomenon requiring some degree of social and economic planning.[18] The same year Gaspare Finali, then minister of agriculture, introduced a bill in the Chamber of Deputies to regulate emigration, but no action was taken on the bill because the government had fallen a few weeks later. But it had become clear that the government could no longer afford the luxury of ignoring the phenomenon.

## The conservative reaction

As emigration developed into a mass phenomenon, large landowners sensed the disruptive potential for their economic interests and social status. The departure of thousands of peasants was going to force wages up. Landowners, who were already struggling with the economic changes forced on them by national unification, by the internationalization of markets, and by increased taxation argued that mass emigration and consequent wage escalation would jeopardize the survival of the agrarian economy. Moreover, landowners were concerned that mass emigration, followed by mass return, would progressively destabilize the traditional values that had served Italy so well for centuries. By living abroad for a number of years, landowners argued, emigrants were likely to absorb new ideas and perhaps return with the hope of altering the existing social order and stir up rebellion among the still submissive Italian peasantry. After all, landowners concluded, rebellious peasants had already written the most infamous pages of Italian history.

Some educated landowners introduced their concerns into the public discourse on emigration for the dual purpose of influencing public opinion and minimizing the negative impact of mass emigration. Antonio Caccianiga, for instance, argued that large landowners were not to blame for mass emigration. On the contrary, Italian peasants had never been as prosperous, well paid, and generally happy as in the 1870s. Emigration was a phenomenon artificially stimulated by agents who allured peasants with the illusion of a better life somewhere else. After all, Caccianiga added, peasants could not complain. Landowners were taking good care of peasants directly and indirectly: directly, by giving them decent wages; indirectly by paying taxes to support state services available to all, peasants included. In addition, nobody ever starved in Italy. Municipalities had traditionally taken care of individuals unable to fend for themselves. And, even under the worst circumstances, Italy was still the most wonderful place in the world, which no individual in his right mind would ever want to abandon. "In Italy," he concluded, "the sun shines for the poor too. The beautiful Italian climate allows the poor to tour their villages, asking for alms. And in Italy an individual does not need much to get by. God has given us the best climate in the world."[19]

Caccianiga's paternalistic attitude was shared, at least to a degree, by most landowners. Antonio Mina, for instance, openly argued that unchecked emigration would eventually destabilize the traditional social order. In fact, emigrants claimed the right to move about freely, seeking higher wages and better living conditions. Obviously, Mina concluded, allowing uneducated peasants to decide for themselves was the surest recipe for social disaster.[20] The writers of the 1870s Inchiesta Jacini, all of them wealthy landowners, unanimously explained mass emigration as the result of peasants' greed and restlessness. Landowners had traditionally been kind to peasants and intended to be so in the future.[21] One of these writers blamed the press for presenting landowners in an unfavorable light, then legitimizing the peasants' discontent and restlessness.[22] The report for the province of Genoa lamented "the spreading evil of emigration supported by the new dangerous idea that people are free to go wherever they please."[23] And the writer for the region of Tuscany condemned "the immorality of the young generation which claims the right to abandon land and family, to pursue personal fulfillment."[24] It was obvious that many large landowners perceived mass emigration to be a serious threat to their social and economic power, which they identified with social stability.

But this posture was not shared unanimously. Some more perceptive landowners agreed that emigration was the result of political and economic failures. Politically, the process of national unification had failed to include peasants, who, accordingly, felt no allegiance to the new state and its agenda. Economically, most peasants lived in conditions of such poverty and powerlessness that emigration was the only way out. Slowly, a series of publications unveiled the appalling poverty of peasants and indirectly denounced the callous paternalism of landowners. In 1875, for instance, Pasquale Villari observed: "The social and economic conditions of millions of peasants are incredibly poor and totally unknown to educated Italians."[25] In a report on northern peasants, Sidney Sonnino remarked: "Our peasants live lives unfit for humans. Peasants work from sunrise to sunset seven days a week. Regardless of how hard they try, they will never be able to get out of abject poverty." And in the south conditions were even worse: "Our peasants are worse off than the serfs of the Middle Ages. Peasants live like beasts. Their sense of dignity seems to have died long ago."[26] And Giustino Fortunato vividly described how one could almost "touch the sadness of the physical and social landscape of the south and the tragic reality of southern peasants who live for months and years without ever seeing a happy face."[27] These writers had no problems in finding evidence to support their claims. Even in the relatively prosperous province of Genoa there were cases of thirty families sharing one large hut. In the city of Cosenza, of 1,400 dwellings surveyed in 1881, 400 housed more than six people per room, and another 400 from four to six. In the province of Palermo, it was "common for ten to fifteen people to share one room and one bed." And these were the lucky people. Thousands lived on the streets for lack of shelter.[28]

These reports had a profound impact on the consciousness of educated Italians and altered the direction of the public discourse on emigration. Many Italians became progressively aware that the traditional social order, which larger landowners wanted to preserve, rested on social and economic inequities no longer acceptable. But, regardless of the ethical conclusions to be derived from social and economic inequities, political wisdom advised that some solution should be found to avoid social unrest and possibly a social revolution. The first step toward a solution was a frank admission that Italian agriculture was anachronistic, irrational, and certainly noncompetitive in the Western world. Besides, Italian peasants were so uneducated that any change would be most difficult. The economist Francesco Zanelli, among many others, compiled in 1877 a long list of the liabilities of the Italian economy. Lack of capital and outdated farming techniques opened the list. Moreover, the expanding textile and manufacturing industries of north and central Italy were attracting whatever new capital was becoming available in the nation. In addition, like many other peasants in Europe at that time, Italian peasants too were demanding, sometimes forcibly, higher wages and better living conditions. In order to satisfy these legitimate demands, landowners would have to pay higher wages and in the end be left with less capital to implement changes. Zanelli concluded that the Italian agricultural economy was like an old, irrational, and perhaps unchangeable system. The private sector could never reform it; only the government could.[29]

Very few educated Italians could disagree with these premises. But many disagreed with the conclusion. There were those who believed that the private sector could indeed reform the Italian agrarian economy. For instance, absentee landowners could be enticed to come back to their estates and manage them directly. Their presence and direct management could help overcome what Francesco Coletti had called the "transcendent resistance to change" of Italian peasants, especially in the south. But landowners resisted the suggestion. Life in cities was more exciting than life in the country. Besides, in the south, land management was considered unbecoming for a gentleman. Another route to reform was to offer incentives. The Marchese di Cosentino, for example, suggested that the government could lower the taxes of landowners who resided on, and managed, their estates.[30] Change could be promoted also by rewriting inheritance laws. According to long-established tradition, Italian children came into ownership of land only upon the death of their parents. But by that time most children were too advanced in age to engage in experimentation and change. New legislation should be set in place, it was proposed, to have children inherit the land at a younger age, when individuals were more likely to embrace change.[31]

The suggestion accepted by most economists was that in order to modernize Italian agriculture large estates should be broken up and small properties created instead. The argument advanced was that large estates had been the ruin of Italy throughout history. Large estates had created an abject peasantry totally disaffected from the land and from the political process. Large estates had also created a narrow-minded, antiquated, and arrogant landed elite. The bond between land and farmers could be reestablished only by giving as many farmers as possible small farms to own and run on their own. Seemingly the historical argument was compelling. It was certainly subscribed to by most Italian economists at the turn of the century. But the economic reality was different. Nations more advanced than Italy were moving in exactly the opposite direction: from small and independent farms to large and consolidated properties to rationalize production in order to supply the needs of large urban markets.[32]

Progressively, and as a result of a larger national debate, the national discourse focused on the Italian south. Initially, some observers, like Pasquale Villari, had argued that southern agriculture would change, thanks to the economic liberalism set in place by the new government. In time, it became obvious that southern landowners had effectively sealed themselves off from the national agenda. Searching for a solution, several scientists, like Sidney Sonnino and Leopoldo Franchetti, pointed out that no change was possible without a revision of the existing agrarian contracts. Traditionally, southern landowners had exercised total discretion in setting up the terms of the contracts. The suggestion that a revision was in order to give peasants a stake in the land and some sense of power encountered strong and unanimous adverse reactions. Landowners argued that the state, its increased taxation, was to be blamed for the backwardness of the southern agrarian economy and the poor conditions of the peasants. In addition, southern landowners knew that they did not have to be too vocal in expressing their disapproval of the suggestion. In Rome they mastered enough political power to prevent any discussion about southern contracts from reaching the floor of the Chamber of Deputies.

All these arguments became almost irrelevant in the 1880s. A sequence of events, followed by some political decisions, changed the direction of the national discourse. The rapid decline of farm commodities prices in international markets rendered small farming almost obsolete and certainly noncompetitive. In setting national priorities, the Italian government chose to favor industrial over agricultural productions in order to make Italy a modern industrial nation. Southern landowners, traditionally opposed to any governmental interference, did not object to a course of action that, in the end, left them in control of the south. Their only demand, readily granted by the national government, was a substantial protective tariff, especially on wheat. Some educated and embittered southerners pointed out that the government decision to protect industries implied that the nation had given up both on the modernization of southern agriculture and on the integration of the south within the national economy. But these embittered souls found very few listeners. Anthropological theories increasingly popular at the end of the century had gained many converts to the idea that southerners were inferior. It was simply unrealistic to expect that southerners could function in a modern society. Their destiny was to live in an outdated past.[33]

Peasants, of course, were unaware of the issues discussed in the national debate that centered on them. Although unaware of the national debate, however, peasants were experiencing a mounting frustration for two reasons. First, the process of national integration had increased their expectations of social reform and better living conditions. But those expectations had remained unfulfilled. Second, the new nation seemed to be even less attentive to the plight of peasants than the former Italian states had been. Some observers, especially in the south, alerted educated Italians to the impending danger that peasant disaffection would become revolt if no reform were set in place. The government rejected these warnings and demands for reform, and the peasants staged several revolts. The bloodiest occurred in Sicily in 1893. It failed. Martial law was imposed, the leaders were executed or sentenced to jail, and the peasants returned to work. But not all of them did so. Some concluded that because neither reform nor revolt would succeed, they would emigrate.[34]

In the end, conservative minds, and especially large landowners, were successful in interjecting their agenda in the national debate. Not only were they skillful in equating their interests with the national interest and with social stability, they were also capable of neutralizing any effort to alter the existing social order. While promoting their image, they pointed out both the shortcomings of the new liberal state and the lack of preparation of peasants to play any role toward the modernization of the nation. Notwithstanding the number of participants and the arguments advanced, conservative minds contributed virtually nothing new to the debate on national integration.

## Emigration and nationalism

As conservative landowners articulated their position in the debate in order to keep peasants out of the center of national interests, nationalists endeavored to bring peasants in through the backdoor of colonialism. The debate on whether Italy should become a colonial power started as soon as the wars for national independence finished. Objectively, there seemed to be no reasons for colonial adventures: agriculture produced barely enough to feed the country, industry was in its infancy, and certainly it was unprepared to compete in international markets; the armed forces had proven to be an international embarrassment and, most importantly, capital was in very short supply. But, as the nationalists argued, the leading European nations were one and all colonial powers. And Italy, the most recently arrived European power, could be no less.

In mass emigration nationalists found the justification for Italian colonialism. Italy needed colonies as settlements for its surplus population, they argued. Nationalists differed as to how Italy would carry out its colonial destiny. Cristoforo Negri, for instance, argued that mass emigration to Brazil and Argentina would eventually make Italians the largest national group in both countries, at which point Italy was entitled to take over. Negri was never clear as to how the takeover would occur.[35] Other writers used nationalism to support private interests. Jacopo Virgilio, for instance, an individual with strong ties to Genoese shipping companies, supported economic colonialism and condemned military expansion. Private companies, not the government, Virgilio added, should engineer the process. The government's major responsibility was to provide legitimacy and to offer protection against foreign governments pressing immigrants to give their allegiance to Italy. The economic achievements of the Genoese shipping companies in Latin America on behalf of Italy was obvious, Virgilio concluded. There was no reason to alter that course of action by direct government intervention.[36]

But, in the national debate, Virgilio was voicing a minority position. Most nationalists, true to the climate of opinion of the times and eager to recapture the heroic times of the wars for independence, argued in favor of military colonialism. After all, nationalists pointed out, how could Italy resettle citizens in territories not under total Italian control? Obviously, some, like Leone Carpi, readily admitted that economic colonization had to go hand in hand with military imperialism. The task was monumental, but, as Gerolamo Boccardo argued, "Italians should not fear the glorious challenge of colonization."[37] After all, Italians had been the best colonizers in history, as Cesare Correnti and Emilio Cerruti pointed out.[38] There was no reason to argue that Italians of the nineteenth century could not revive the glories of the past. More sober minds, however, like Luigi Luzzatti, deplored that Italians were so unrealistic as to think that military imperialism was in the national interest. The nation was struggling through monumental internal problems. There were no resources, Luzzatti concluded, to embark on overseas expansion.[39]

As emigration increased, nationalists stepped up the tempo of the debate. Some voiced opposition to the departure of so many young people for international destinations. Others pointed out that emigrants would be better off financially and socially if they could relocate in countries controlled by the Italian government. The *Rassegna Nazionale*, a liberal journal started in the early 1880s, became the new forum for the national debate on Italian nationalism. But regardless of the disagreements among nationalists, all of them generally agreed that the national government had to engage in colonization to channel emigration. But individuals in government were not easily convinced. The government had no financial resources to invest for the purpose, they replied. Besides, the political wisdom of the time was that the government's task was to protect freedom and avoid even the appearance of social and economic planning, especially in regard to emigration.[40] In the end, however, Italy engaged in colonialism in

North Africa. But the African colonies failed to become the preferred destination of emigrants. Nationalists had engaged the attention of the nation for a number of years. The possible link between colonialism and emigration made many converts, especially among educated Catholics. But in the end the debate produced next to nothing. Or, to be more precise, it was one of the biggest disappointments in the national debate on emigration.[41]

### Changing governmental roles

Seemingly the debate on emigration and national integration was going nowhere. But, among the many conflicting opinions, one could detect the formulation of a broad question. Should not the government play a larger role in social matters as it was already doing in the economy? Conservative politicians readily answered in the negative. In 1883, for instance, Prime Minister Agostino De Pretis argued against a request made by Diomede Pantaleoni that Italy occupy Libia to provide an easy outlet for departing Italians. Emigration, the prime minister remarked, was the result of complex dynamics which governments should not perturb. And he concluded that "nobody should entertain the idea that the government has the right and the power to bring about change."[42] With uncommon logic, however, the prime minister argued that the private sector had an obligation to do something about these social dynamics which the government was unable to deal with. De Pretis restated his position in regard to another interrogation by Sidney Sonnino, who asked why the government was unwilling to prosecute emigration agents preying on emigrants. In his answer, De Pretis became even eloquent by quoting Charles Darwin and Herbert Spencer and the survival of the fittest. And he concluded: "The government will not interfere with emigration, neither will Italy stop any citizen who intends to leave the country from doing so."[43]

Political realities, however, forced De Pretis to reconsider his political philosophy and his Spencerian assumptions. Peasants who had never heard of Darwin were becoming increasingly vocal in expressing dissatisfaction and bitterness. The social and economic changes promised at the time of independence had never materialized. Callously, the government had even silenced Garibaldi, who had sided with the peasants. Mass emigration, many emigrants had come to conclude, was the result of the abysmal failure of the government. Popular writers gave voice to the disappointment of the peasants. Edmondo De Amicis, for instance, argued that the real Italy of the 1880s did not resemble in any way the Italy politicians had promised

during the wars for independence.[44] Land redistribution, the corner-
stone of the promised reform, had never been attempted.[45] The disaffection of the peasants was so profound, Ada Negri commented,
that they had not even tried to stage a rebellion. The only protest
peasants were able to express was in their departure, Mario Rapisardi
reported. As many observers noted, emigrants departed cursing landowners and government and swearing revenge upon returning.[46] And
public opinion was increasingly sympathetic to the cause of the peasants. Many writers expressed admiration at the courage of illiterate
peasants braving the crossing of the ocean. The government was
obviously the main target of the blame.[47]

The peasants' demand for governmental intervention found support among many groups. The Italian bureau of statistics, which had
been publishing yearly data on emigration since 1876, openly criticized the inaction of the government.[48] Luigi Bodio, its director,
launched a scathing attack on virtually all Italian prefects for their
lack of concern for departing Italians.[49] The Italian Geographical Society, the National Council of Industry and Commerce, and the Su-
perior Council of Statistics supported some form of governmental
action in favor of emigrants.[50] Visitors returning to Italy from Italian
communities in North and South America recounted horror stories
of exploitation and poverty, which only governmental intervention
could mitigate. Obviously, the national debate was shifting in favor
of governmental action, and moving away from the cherished objec-
tion that emigration would depopulate the country, create labor shortage and make impossible internal colonization.[51]

Eventually these pressures forced the introduction of a bill in the
Chamber of Deputies in 1887. It was Francesco Crispi, a Sicilian, who
voiced the new philosophy of the government. Emigration was no
longer considered a problem of national security and social order. It
was a political problem and as such it belonged in the national political
discourse. "The government," Crispi stated, "must protect emigrants,
direct them to nations where they will find work, and assist them
while they work in foreign countries."[52] The introduction of the Crispi
bill increased the tempo of the national debate and divided politicians
in two camps. Supporters of traditional policies argued that the bill
was a step in the wrong direction: Italy could not march toward
socialism with impunity. The supporters of the bill skillfully elaborated on the potential benefits the country would derive from legislation protecting emigrants: remittances, returnees with more skills,
and, most importantly, the unshakable loyalty of emigrants to Italy.
To his colleagues Crispi reported with alarm that countless numbers
of Italians who had already given up their Italian citizenship, sworn

loyalty to other nations and resettled permanently overseas. Should such a trend continue, Crispi concluded, Italy would deprive itself permanently of the immense benefits emigration could bring about. Assisted emigration was a national necessity in order to bring about important national goals. The national purpose was not different from the goals individual immigrants were pursuing.[53]

The projected impact of remittances and returnees affected the national debate and enlarged the number of supporters for the new bill. One of the most articulate supporters was Francesco Saverio Nitti, then a young scientist and a politician, who had been observing emigration for a number of years. Personal energy, entrepreneurial spirit and the determination to improve economically were the new compelling reasons for many Italians to leave. Unfortunately, Nitti concluded, the Crispi bill did not go far enough in protecting emigrants. And that was unfortunate for the country. The sad political reality was that "the great electors of the south," as he called them, mastered enough power in Rome to kill a more liberal bill. The southern electors were concerned that mass emigration would eventually force wages up and decrease the labor supply. Nitti was eloquent; but his attack of the southern electors did not win him many friends in the south or in Rome. And the bill was passed as Crispi had originally presented it.[54]

The bill, passed into law in 1889, was obviously an unsatisfactory compromise. Although stating that the protection of emigration was a national obligation, the law made virtually no provisions for enforcement. For instance, the law made several provisions to protect emigrants at the ports of embarkation from exploitation by emigration agents. These were individuals who recruited emigrants in Italian towns, channeled them to the ports of departure, provided them with room and board as they waited in Genoa or Naples, purchased tickets and exchanged money. The potential for abuses was obviously immense and agents took full advantage of the emigrants' innocence. The national press ran daily stories of abuses by agents who in the end left entire families stranded in Naples or Genoa. To end the abuses, the law mandated that every agent be licensed and spelled out penalties for various types of abuses. However, according to the law, no agent could be brought to court until the abused emigrants had departed. Moreover, no enforcement agency was set in place in Rome to reconcile regional differences in the interpretation of the law.[55]

By 1890 the national debate had focused almost exclusively on the inadequacy of the 1889 law. From Genoa, Pietro Maldotti, a priest, documented for the national press that the legal provisions of the

1889 law were systematically disregarded not only by agents but by courts as well. For example, Italians leaving for Brazil were made to pay for their tickets, although the Brazilian government had already paid for all Italians directed to that country.[56] The young political writer Luigi Einaudi showed that the numbers of abuses by agents was increasing because it had become obvious that the law could not be enforced.[57] Giovanni Battista Scalabrini, the bishop of Piacenza, called on voluntary organizations to assist departing Italians, because the government had proven its inability or unwillingness to do so.[58] The Italian Geographic Society proposed to set up employment agencies abroad.[59] The need for such agencies was immense, Egisto Rossi, a commissioner of emigration, remarked in 1892. Only two such agencies existed in New York and in Boston allegedly servicing several hundred thousand Italians.[60] Obviously, by the early 1890s the national debate had expanded. Theoretically, most Italians had come to agree that the government had to play a role in protecting emigrants. In practice, political compromises and bureaucratic inefficiency made it very difficult to enforce protective legislation. The call was for the private sector to step in.

## Nationalism: The refurbished argument

As the national debate focused on remittances, returnees, and the benefits that Italy would derive from emigration, nationalists seized the opportunity to present a refurbished argument. Military occupations of foreign territories were rejected, mostly on practical grounds. The abysmal failure of Italian troops in Africa had convinced even the most ardent nationalists that military glories were out of reach, at least for a time. The new argument was based on demographic colonization. Italian emigrants would flock to a specific destination until they would become the numerical majority. At that point, according to the shared wisdom of the time, Italy was entitled to take over that country and annex it to the national territory. Of course, there were disagreements as to the preferred destinations. Some, like the economist Diomede Pantaleoni, opted for northern Africa on the grounds of geographical proximity and historical ties dating back to the Roman Empire.[61] A large number argued in favor of South America both because of the Latin environment familiar to Italians and because of the expected and predicted disappearance of the inferior races of blacks, Indians, and mulattoes in the competition for survival.[62] The supporters of Italian settlements in Brazil and Argentina, like Gerolamo Boccardo, disregarded that South American nations were full-fledged states, entitled to the same sovereignty of other Western nations. Rather, he considered them as territories still open to a takeover from outside. More sober minds retorted that nationalism was as rampant in South America as it was in Europe and the United States. Accordingly, Brazil and Argentina would never acquiesce to a foreign takeover. The alternative, promoted, among others, by Leopoldo Franchetti, was to channel Italian emigration to African nations like Eritrea, where a political takeover could be both possible and justifiable.[63] But some economists, like Luigi Bodio, observed that mass emigration to a northern African country required large capital, which Italy did not have.[64] Eventually the plans for northern Africa were set aside, mostly on racial grounds. Nationalists finally directed their attention to South America.[65]

By the turn of the century the nationalists had elaborated a new plan for Latin America, buttressed with historical arguments. As in the old days, the growing population of Greece had created a Magna Graecia in southern Italy, so in modern times the growing population of Italy would establish a Greater Italy in South America. Some nationalists, like Giovanni Bovio and Lelio Bonin, readily pointed out that Italians could become the dominant group in South America in a couple of decades.[66] Nitti corroborated this optimistic outlook by pointing out that the emigrants of the 1890s were quite different from those of the previous decades. Initially, poverty had pushed Italians out of the country. Now, adventurousness and courage were impelling them to go. Pride in Italy and its future, not the old desperation, were the driving forces.[67] And Luigi Einaudi poetically portrayed the new emigrants as individuals led by a prince merchant, in the fashion of the Italian Renaissance.[68]

The nationalists were unable to monopolize the national debate. To the glorious rise of a Greater Italy in Latin America, more realistic minds opposed the true reality of Italian emigration in that continent. There was no greater Italy across the ocean; only a number of little Italies, inhabited by uneducated, unskilled, bewildered, and socially marginal Italians. There was no prince merchant leading them. Rather, there were plenty of agents, bosses, and padroni exploiting them. And discouraging accounts by visitors to North and South America entered the national debate. Giuseppe Giacosa, for instance, shocked the nation with his stories of appalling poverty among Italians in New York and Chicago.[69] Some argued that, of course, Italians in the United States were poor. But that was the result of their lack of ability to compete in an Anglo-Saxon country. Latin America was going to be different. But visitors to that continent retorted that poverty was the common condition of virtually all Italians in South America too. Paolo Barbera, for instance, wrote: "In Buenos Aires, capital is English, management French and menial labor Italian."[70] And there were no indicators that the situation would change any time soon.

Nationalists failed to sway public opinion and national government to support plans for a Greater Italy in Latin America. But they increased the tempo of the national debate on the role that the government should play in emigration matters. This heightened concern, together with the increasing dissatisfaction over the ineffectiveness of the 1889 law, prompted the need for another bill in 1901, presented to the Chamber of Deputies by Luigi Luzzatti. Those who opposed governmental intervention had not disappeared altogether, as Maffeo Pantaleoni made manifest in his speech on the Senate floor in defense of classical political liberalism. But, after three decades of national debate on emigration, most legislators were willing to engage the government in the process. The new law mandated the creation of a Commissariato dell'Emigrazione to coordinate all activities on behalf of emigrants, set guidelines for transatlantic fares, and set up labor offices in the major American destinations.[71] Lack of funds largely curtailed the effectiveness of the law. It became obvious to every observer, however, that after the turn of the century the government was actively engaged in regulating mass emigration and, to a degree, even in assisting it. The 1901 legislation remained virtually unchanged, with minor modifications, until the advent of fascism. By that time World War I had created social and economic dislocations of such magnitude that the traditional national debate on emigration had moved in totally new directions. Fascism maintained that Italy needed all its manpower for the creation of its "third empire."[72] Emigration was rejected as unpatriotic.

### The southern problem

As the national debate focused on the role of the government, mass emigration became an increasingly southern phenomenon. Before the end of the century, northern emigrants outnumbered southerners. After 1900, southerners made up the overwhelming majority of the overseas emigrants. Obviously, the debate could not avoid establishing a link between the tormented southern problem and emigration. The government had already adopted a general policy of preferential legislation for the south until such a time when the region could catch up with the north. Should the government, and this was the new question introduced in the national debate, pass special legislation to protect emigration and return migration in the south? The variety of responses witnessed to the number of interest groups and disagreements about fundamental policies. Large landowners, like Antonio

Di Vito Di Marco, agreed that the private sector was better equipped than the public to bring about the desired changes in the south. Of course, the south was a disadvantaged region; but the problems of the south should not be magnified, Di Marco pointed out. After all, the north had its set of problems too, and mass emigration from the south was an endemic phenomenon not to be dramatized. Others, like Nitti, were less sanguine. History had made the south different; and only governmental intervention and political will could obliterate the differences and make the south like the north. As Nitti argued, immediately after political unification, the government had thrown its support behind the industrializing north and forgotten the south. It was about time to reverse the trend. Nitti was one of the strongest supporters of the 1904 special legislation to create new industries in Naples.[73]

The seriousness of the southern problem impelled some to advocate radical changes. Ettore Ciccotti, for instance, a socialist representative from the south, argued that "the underdevelopment of the south was a casualty of the northern capitalist growth." Only prudential reasons kept Ciccotti from advocating revolution: the cycle of capitalistic growth in the north, Ciccotti argued as a good Marxist, was not yet advanced enough to warrant a social revolution. Besides, the southern masses were unprepared to achieve political power. Ciccotti's pessimism about the southern masses ran deep: he shared some of the ideas quite common in those days that southerners were racially inferior to northerners. Others were less pessimistic about the political abilities of southerners and more willing to advocate reform instead of revolution. Gaetano Salvemini, for instance, argued that the root of the southern problem was the lack of a middle class. In modern or modernizing nations the middle class had provided the momentum for change. The social and economic stagnation of the south could be corrected only by promoting the growth of a southern middle class, a difficult, although not impossible, task, Salvemini concluded. Moreover, Salvemini added, one should not despair of southern peasants, as Ciccotti had done. They were more capable of political action than social scientists had given them credit for.

The social and economic disabilities and potential of the southern masses moved increasingly to the center of the national debate. It was obvious that without some form of mass mobilization the south could not be changed. But could southern peasants be politically mobilized? Antonio Gramsci agonized for years over this question. To him the south was an amorphous society lacking any form of social integration. The *latifondo* had created such a society, with a handful of families having all the power and masses of peasants lacking social solidarity and incapable of organized action. Gramsci was seriously criticized for his negativism about the south. His critics argued that the monolithic powerless south depicted by Gramsci never existed. There were endless social and economic varieties within the south, ranging from the Puglie with a large scale capitalistic economy to the pastoral economy of Sardinia.[74] Moreover, the critics contended, the south was experiencing an economic renaissance of a sort, at least in some areas like Naples with textiles and Palermo with shipping. But Gramsci retorted that those rare pockets of development were artificially induced cases to buy the support of the southern masses for the government. Southerners had been led to believe that the industrialization of the south was only a question of time. In reality Gramsci concluded, the government had made a clear choice in favor of the north and abandoned the south. But the government did not want southerners to know this.

The argument that the government had abandoned the south did not go unchallenged. The commitment of the government to the region could not be questioned, supporters of the government remarked. In 1901, for instance, the government had set in place a commission to attract industries to Naples and the surrounding territory. In 1902 Prime Minister Giuseppe Zanardelli signed a law providing special assistance to the region of Basilicata. In 1906 the Chamber of Deputies passed special legislation in favor of Calabria after the earthquake of Messina. Another bill provided incentives for southern industries, like sulphur mining in Sicily.[75] Finally the government took the unprecedented step of recommending the revision and reform of all agrarian contracts, the most sacred cow in the south. The proposal had been made another time before. Without such a reform, the government asserted, the south was doomed to stagnation. But the outcry of southern landowners was so loud that Rome could not ignore it. The proposed bill was tabled and a commission set in place to survey the conditions of southern peasants and to assess the changes that had occurred in the south since the first national survey in the 1870s. The results of the survey provided much needed political ammunition for one of the most spectacular turnabouts in the national debate on emigration.[76]

## The liquidation of the south

The publication of the findings of the survey and their interpretation marked the most dramatic turning point in the national debate on emigration. Nitti, by then a much respected scholar, synthesized the conclusions commonly shared by the several writers of the survey.

Emigration was no longer considered a destabilizing event. Rather, it was a powerful and welcome social and economic revolution set in motion by southerners. They, through emigration, return migration, and remittances, were "creating a new rural democracy based on work."[77] By rural democracy Nitti meant a society with large numbers of small landowners, the result of American remittances. Under the circumstances, governmental programs in favor of the south were either superfluous or counterproductive.[78] Contrary to what social scientists had been arguing in the previous two decades, Nitti concluded that "the invisible hand of the free market" was bringing about the modernization of the south. Even such an authority as Francesco Coletti, the leading expert on Italian agriculture and emigration, accepted the conclusions of the survey after some initial misgivings.[79]

And the writers of the survey had eight volumes of evidence to introduce as supportive evidence for their conclusions. Ernesto Marenghi, the technical consultant for the survey, pointed out that in the debate over the integration of Italian society, emigration was no longer considered a destabilizing force, as the writers of the 1870s survey had unanimously argued. Emigration, he remarked, "has brought about a true peaceful revolution without subverting the institutions of the state. Returnees have helped change ideas and attitudes. Savings are inundating the south." Emigration and return migration were finally accomplishing what the Risorgimento had been unable to set in place. Return migration was "the greatest and most profound change the south had ever known."[80] Even the aging Leopoldo Franchetti, an earlier foe of mass emigration, joined the chorus of those singing the praises of emigration and humorously confessed: "As we were busy writing books and passing legislation to modernize and integrate Italian society, southern peasants who emigrated to the Americas and returned proved to be the true agents of change."[81]

The writers of the Inchiesta did not fabricate the evidence they submitted to the national debate. By the early 1900s hundreds of visitors to the south pointed out that the region was changing, thanks to remittances and returnees. American visitors were impressed too. One of them, Antonio Mangano, reported to Americans that the entire south was being rebuilt with American money.[82] America was becoming a household name even in the most remote Italian villages.[83] Italians observers showed that savings and returnees were bringing about unprecedented personal and structural changes. The most important structural change was the arrival of American capital, an event which would perhaps have to continue for a couple of decades, they argued. After such time, the south would be well on its way to modernization and independence from foreign help, remittances included.

Besides remittances, emigration was promoting change by transforming the emigrants themselves. Returnees were individuals with new ideas and attitudes which, in the long run, would transform the south, as most observers eagerly believed. New money and new men: the south did not need anything else to move into the modern world and become an integral part of the Italian nation.

Seemingly returnees were new men. The old deferences had disappeared, replaced by a sense of individual dignity. Landowners complained that the *Americani* no longer displayed the traditional signs of deference, like taking off their hats and bowing to superiors. Priests too lamented the disappearance of old-fashioned piety and respect for the clergy, replaced after the American experience by a secular vision of life. Returnees themselves were aware that they had changed, as one of them pointed out: "When we left, we felt guilty. We were told that we were not free to choose to go. Now we know differently and nobody will ever tell us again where we should go and what we should do."[84] Observers noted that these new men had an impact on southern society in two areas especially: education and voluntary organizations.

The creation of public schools in the south had been a tormented chapter of national history since independence. New school buildings were sacked and burned down. Teachers were regarded as dangerous individuals and forced to leave through intimidation. Local administrations systematically disregarded instructions from the central government on mandatory schooling. Peasants opposed schools on practical and ideological grounds. Boys were expected to follow their fathers to the fields by the age of eight. To pursue an education was generally considered a class betrayal, because in the south only the gentry and clergy were educated.[85] Of course, a variety of dynamics contributed to overcome the opposition of southerners to mandatory schooling. But returnees figured prominently in the change. In the province of Cosenza, for instance, one observer reported that several illiterate returnees went back to school, thus setting an example for those who had never emigrated.[86] Similar reports were sent to Rome by other prefects. The impact was dramatic: illiteracy in the south declined from 70 percent in 1871 to 33 percent in 1921.[87]

Returnees helped overcome also individualism and distrust among southerners. And they promoted voluntary organizations. Obviously, in this case too, a variety of dynamics contributed to the change; but returnees figured prominently in the equation. For instance, immediately after political unification, efforts by agrarian societies and labor organizations from the north to set up voluntary organizations in the south encountered profound resistance. Social solidarity, as a prefect put it, was hard to find in the south. Two decades later, voluntary organizations were appearing everywhere in the south. The impact of returnees was spelled out by an observer from Calabria: "Returnees are having a great impact on the growth of voluntary organizations. Where they exist, they make them stronger. Where they do not exist, they create them."[88] As a prefect pointed out, it was only a question of time before southerners would realize that social solidarity was one of the necessary ingredients toward the social and economic modernization of the region.

These personal dynamics, however important, were eclipsed by a brighter structural change: capital. Italians, southerners included, had traditionally relied on temporary emigrations to balance family budgets, as a report from the Department of Agriculture pointed out in the early 1870s. But the savings generated by internal temporary emigration were never large enough to make investments possible. Overseas emigrations were making available unprecedented sums of money southerners would eventually invest. Although objectively modest, remittances seemed very large to southerners. Even local prefects pointed out that they had never seen so much cash in their regions. American savings eventually became almost an inebriating concept to southerners. It was only a question of time before the south would own capital large enough to bring about the modernization of local economies. The national debate on emigration could not have ended on a more positive note. Southerners, not their government, were going to bring about the integration of their region within Italy.[89]

Seldom did the south experience so much optimism as in the early twentieth century. Observers unanimously remarked that mass emigration would end sooner than expected, because remittances were coming in at such a rapid rate. Life was changing dramatically, as a southerner pointed out: "The Americani have radically transformed these previously god-forsaken regions."[90] Prefetti wrote that returnees and remittances were breaking down the cycle of poverty, fatalism, and powerlessness that had burdened the south for centuries. Popular writers joined in the celebration of the new golden age.[91] As the prefetto of Palermo wrote in 1907 in a report to Rome: "These Americani give us hope that one day Sicily too will be able to join the civilized world."[92] It was a change of unprecedented magnitude.

From the early 1870s to the late 1920s the national debate had come full circle. Initially, emigration was considered a marginal phenomenon, not to be included in the equation of national integration. Progressively, pressures from interest groups, emigrants included, and a change in political philosophy as to the role of the government in social and economic matters forced the issue of emigration into the national debate. As the debate evolved, a variety of solutions were proposed, most of them the result of efforts by interest groups to equate their agenda with the national agenda. The variety of solutions proposed evidenced that only the national government could integrate emigration, remittances, and return migration in the national agenda. Notwithstanding the 1888 and 1901 laws, however, emigration, remittances and return migration seemed to evade efforts made to integrate them into a national goal. The recovery of the south seemed to be more elusive than the central government had anticipated. And in the end, official Italy itself recognized that emigrants themselves were the best agents the south could find for its integration into the national economy and society. Emigration, return migration, and remittances were the dynamics to be observed and fostered in order to expedite the changes affecting the south.

# 5  *Return migration*

The national debate on emigration was based on the assumption that the phenomenon would be temporary and that virtually all emigrants would return to Italy. But when consuls began to send reports to Rome that increasing numbers of Italians were becoming citizens of Western Hemisphere nations and relinquishing the idea of returning, the government became alarmed and tried to prevent temporary emigration from becoming permanent through legislative measures. Even the language used by the Italian Bureau of Statistics in elaborating its data shows that emigrants were expected to return. According to the bureau, there were two types of emigration: temporary and permanent. Temporary was the emigration of less than one-year duration; permanent was the emigration of several years. But there was no category to classify individuals relocating abroad permanently.[1]

The return of Italians from international destinations and especially from overseas is important for several reasons. First, the popular assumption, especially among Americans, is that the transatlantic emigration of Europeans was a one-way movement. The popular mythology linked to the image of America as a nation of immigrants, the ideology of American exceptionalism and its corollary that every person who set foot on American soil believed himself so fortunate that returning to the native country was unthinkable, and the need to celebrate the advancement of ethnics in America were reasons for focusing on permanent immigrants. Historical accuracy, however, and a more balanced view of the transatlantic movement as a process of mutual enrichment between the United States and Europe compel us to pay attention also to the millions of Europeans who returned. Second, in Europe, and especially in those nations where emigrants were expected to return, return migration was attentively observed and assessed for the dynamics it was expected to unleash in home societies. Of course, not all returnees were greeted with open arms. Emigrants rejected at Ellis Island for health reasons or because of criminal records, and returnees with incurable diseases created serious problems for national and local governments. Besides, these unfortunate returnees were regarded as an embarrassment by relatives and friends. But even returnees with money, although welcomed because of their savings, did not escape the scrutiny of their townspeople, often followed by negative assessments for some less desirable influences they eventually introduced in home societies. Third, the integration of returnees in home communities was identified by many as a significant problem in national affairs. And the debate on the integration of returnees in the social and economic life of the nation is still going on in the Italian south, as well as in many other nations where return migration is a mass phenomenon. Scholars are far from a consensus as to whether return migration has a lasting negative or positive impact on home societies. The ongoing debate indicates that the dynamics generated by emigration and return migration are as complex as the process of modernization and as such they are perceived today as ambivalent dynamics.

This chapter addresses two major issues. The first has to do with the very fact of return migration: how data were gathered, how Italy and the United States assessed the phenomenon, and how some external forces influenced the way in which return migration occurred. The second deals with typologies of returnees. Of course, the decision to emigrate was not taken lightly in the first place. But neither was the decision to return embraced without considerations for alternatives. Who was more likely to return? And what did returnees have in mind when they resettled in Italy? The answer to these questions is important, not only for the study of return migration, but for the history of the Italian south in general. In fact, by the turn of the century educated Italians came to regard return migration and remittances as the most effective dynamics the south had been given to change and join the rest of the nation.

## The intensity of return migration

Return migration from the Americas to Europe was a common phenomenon at the turn of the century. The only notable exception was the Jewish group. Perhaps as many as 40 percent of all Europeans heading for the United States eventually returned to Europe.[2] Statistics for South America are less reliable; but return migration from South America, although less common, was a mass phenomenon too. It was only at the turn of the century that countries on both sides of the Atlantic began to gather reliable data on return migration. But the fact of return migration was noticed both in Europe and the United States as early as the second half of the nineteenth century.

Return migration was an unprecedented feature of the so-called new immigration. Americans were not enchanted by it, both for patriotic and economic reasons. Among new immigrants, returning Italians were the major targets of American resentment. Their refusal of resettling permanently in the United States was interpreted as a gross disregard for the uniqueness and superiority of America. In addition, the frugal habits of Italians in the United States and the substantial savings they were channeling to Italy were regarded as detrimental to the national economy. Money had to be spent in the nation where it was made, Americans argued. Italian visitors could not but notice the resentment of Americans toward returning Italians. One of them reported to Italy the typical reaction of most Americans: "Italians come in the spring to escape poverty in Italy. They complete against our workers by accepting minimal wages and when winter comes they leave like birds of passage."[3] Americans found such behavior intolerable and one of them reported with horror that he had met Italians who had crossed the Atlantic several times. After all, if all Europeans had found in the United States the El Dorado they had been looking for, why should Italians be different and spurn the United States?[4]

Some Americans and Italians alike concluded that Italians returned from the United States because they found life in an Anglo-Saxon country difficult, and acceptance and assimilation virtually impossible. However, these observers were puzzled when they realized that Italians were returning in large numbers, even from Latin America, allegedly a continent where Italians had a clear cultural advantage in terms of acceptance and assimilation. In Argentina, for instance, Italians were known as *golondrinas,* to the dismay of the local government in desperate need of permanent settlers. As an observer put it: "The Italian in Argentina is no colonist; he has no house, he will not make a homestead; he has nothing: his sack is his patrimony, fatigue purchases his sustenance, and his only hope is a modest saving."[5] This was not the whole picture. Many Italians settled permanently in Argentina. But an even larger number crossed the Atlantic every year because of the inversion of seasons between Italy and Argentina. Brazil was no different as a destination for Italians. More people emigrated permanently and with families to Brazil than to the United States and Argentina. But return migration from Brazil was a mass phenomenon, as many prefects reported. Of course, Italian consuls in Argentina, Brazil, and the United States approved of return migration and opposed naturalization. The return of the immigrants was an indication, according to consuls, that Italians were unwilling to sever the sacred bond to their home country.[6]

In Italy, emigrants were expected to return as a matter of course. Tradition had established the pattern. Many Italian regions had developed a tradition of temporary emigrations within Italy since the eighteenth century. And in those migrations, individuals invariably returned to home societies at the end of the season. When international emigration started, Italians did not change their outlook: distances were longer, but emigrants were expected to return. That was the rule. And nobody seemed to question it. When some individuals departing for the Americas manifested the intention of settling permanently there, public opinion stigmatized them on moral grounds. The writers of the Inchiesta Jacini of the 1870s, for instance, unanimously denounced emigrants intending to leave the country for good. It was a menace, they wrote, to traditional social stability.[7] The church too added its condemnation. Emigration could be tolerated only as a temporary emergency to cope with a serious financial problem. But, priests argued, family stability and traditional moral values required that individuals return.[8] The Civiltà Cattolica, a magazine published by the Jesuits, took an even harder posture. Emigration had to be discouraged, except in rare cases, because it fostered the dangerous principle that an individual had the freedom to choose where to live.[9] Emigrants themselves, at least initially, had ambivalent feelings about their departure and certainly were determined to return. For instance, when a government inspector visited a ship about to depart from Genoa to South America, some emigrants aboard approached him to assure him that they would return as soon as they had made enough money to pay their debts. Obviously, the conventional Italian morality of the time demanded that emigration be embraced as an exceptional device for a limited period of time.[10]

When emigration evolved into a mass phenomenon, educated Italians discussed ways to lessen the temptation of emigrants to abandon their loyalty to Italy and relocate permanently in foreign countries. Some writers argued that consular services should be increased to keep the bond between immigrants and the mother country alive. Others discussed ways to create incentives in Italy to make returning more profitable. And finally some presented a more elaborate plan. First, the Italian government should support and promote the establishment of Italian enclaves in selected American cities, where immigrants would be protected from the seduction of the new society. Second, after three to five years, immigrants should return, to be replaced with new emigrants from Italy. Thus the settlements would

be permanent, but individual immigrants should join them on a ro-
tating basis.[11] The general public and educated observers alike shared
the assumption that emigration was a social and economic dynamic
that had to end where it started, in Italy.

Reality matched the expectations. Government officials, popular
accounts, personal letters, and testimonies by observers concurred
that most emigrants returned after two to ten years. And that was
obvious since the early 1870s. The prefects, for instance, unanimously
reported that, after a number of years, virtually all emigrants returned,
as expected. The only exceptions were the young males evading the
draft.[12] The prefect of Cosenza voiced a common sentiment, when he
wrote: "Opportunities attract them overseas; but filial piety and ancestral traditions bring them back to families and communities."[13] The
same prefect reported in 1881 that even when entire families left, they
did not sell their land if they had any. Rather, they entrusted the
family farm to relatives until the day of their return.[14] Privately conducted surveys corroborated the prefects' reports.[15] Even American
consuls in Italy noticed with surprise that most Italians migrating to
the United states eventually returned. The consul in Genoa wrote to
Washington: "With few exceptions, peasants go overseas to make
money, and once they have reached their goal, they go back to spend
the balance of their lives in a quiet, frugal way."[16] The popular literature had a new image to use for new stories: that of the American
returnee with shining shoes, a new suit, straw hat, and, in the best
scenario, a cane and a golden watch. Italians had never seen the like
of such men, especially peasants.

It was only at the turn of the century that both Italy and the United
States began to gather data on return migration, although for different
purposes. The Italian government was pressed to do so by a shift in
the national debate on emigration, return migration and the problems
connected with integrating returnees into home communities. Any
assessment in this regard had to rely on indicators of return migration.
It was obvious that returnees and remittances were having a major
impact in the economy and in society. Small groups voiced the concern that without reliable indicators there was no way of planning
how best to channel returnees and savings in productive directions.
The American government, for its part, was increasingly concerned
over savings channeled to Europe by immigrants. Because commercial
banks refused to handle the small accounts of immigrants, many sent
their savings back to Europe, thus depriving the American economy
of millions of dollars. Moreover, return migration was an unprecedented occurrence in the United States, and public opinion did not
regard it favorably. Statistical indicators could become the first step

toward a policy directed at keeping immigrant savings in the United States.[17]

*Gathering the data*

The Italian government began to gather data on emigration in 1876, as a response to pressures from Italian economists and other groups which claimed that, without reliable indicators, it was impossible to assess the impact of the phenomenon. From 1876 to 1904, indicators for emigration were derived from *nulla osta*, a statement from local mayors that an individual had no criminal record, and thus he was entitled to have a passport. After 1904 indicators were derived from the passports themselves. Although fairly accurate, the two systems had shortcomings. For instance, there was no way of documenting whether the release of a *nulla osta* by a mayor was followed by the release of a passport. Moreover, even if the passport was released, we cannot ascertain whether the individual used the passport and in effect left for the declared destination. After all, because these procedures took a long time, individuals could change their minds: they could decide not to go or to leave for another destination than the intended one. Moreover, a passport was valid for three years. Any crossing of the Atlantic within the three-year period went unreported. In addition, if an individual required a new passport after the three-year period, he was counted as a new emigrant, like an individual who had never left. Finally, many emigrants changed their minds as to the intended destination between the time they applied for a *nulla osta* or a passport and the actual departure. Efforts made by the Commissariato Generale dell' Emigrazione to gather more reliable data by tallying all people traveling by railroad to Genoa, Naples, and Palermo in third class and by asking captains of ships departing from these ports to compile logs of all passengers in third class had only limited results.[18] Obviously Italian indicators on emigration have some limitations. But some of them have been, at least in part, corrected by modern statisticians, like Massimo Livi–Bacci.[19]

As for return migration, since 1866 the Italian department of the navy gathered data on the numbers of individuals arriving at Italian ports without discriminating as to the nationality or the purpose of their visit to Italy. Beginning in 1901 the Commissariato Generale dell'Emigrazione requested all captains of ships arriving in Genoa, Palermo, Naples, and Messina to provide lists of passengers, with the nationality and intended destination in Italy for each passenger. Of course, individuals entering Italy through other ports as well as returnees from European countries, or returnees arriving at French and German ports and proceeding to Italy by train were not counted. Beginning in 1906, captains were further requested to provide the province of origin of each individual returnee. Captains were less than eager to comply with these instructions. Some avoided altogether to ask passengers their final destination and gave the port of arrival as the final destination of all their passengers. Other captains did not ask passengers the province of origin. And some simply provided the Commissariato with a list of names with no further annotations. Although incomplete, these passenger lists document the intensity of return migration and regional differences.

Italian registers of population provide an additional source of data on return migration. Individuals leaving home towns for a period of over one year were canceled from registers of population; returnees intending to reside in home communities at least one year were reregistered. Both procedures were based, of course, on statements of intentions. Only 20 percent of the emigrants requested to be canceled. The other 80 percent implicitly stated that they would return within a year.[20] The low rates of cancellations is to be explained either through sentimental attachment or self-protection. In case of failure or forced return within a year, a returnee could save face by documenting that he did not intend to stay abroad for more than one year. Reregistration rates were high. For instance, in the two years 1908–9, for every hundred cancellations there were sixty-four reregistrations.[21] Reregistration rates provide only approximate indicators, however. Returnees for a period shorter than one year could not reregister. Yet we know that many immigrants returned to Italy only for a few months, either during the winter or during the summer, if coming from the Southern Hemisphere.[22] Other returnees reregistered, intending to resettle in Italy permanently or for a period of over a year. Subsequently many changed their minds and left again, this time without asking for a cancellation.[23] Most importantly, many emigrants did not bother to ask for a cancellation or a reregistration. These bureaucratic procedures must have seemed irrelevant to many people embracing international migration.[24]

In Italy the most accurate data on return migration were collected by the Commissariato Generale dell' Emigrazione in the years 1905–6. They were the result of a special survey mandated by the Italian government to have more accurate data on return migration, a topic that was moving to central stage in the national debate at the beginning of the century. The survey designed by the Commissariato contemplated that every ship captain calling at the ports of Genoa, Naples, Messina, and Palermo be provided with forms requesting detailed information ranging from sex to occupation for every individual entering Italy either temporarily or permanently. In addition the government requested the Commissariato to compare rates of return with rates of emigration. To comply the Commissariato compared the 1905–6 data on returns with the 1901–5 data on emigration already available. The reason for the selection of the 1901–5 period was that most emigrants stayed overseas from two to five years. Thus the returnees of the 1905–6 period were likely to have departed sometime between 1901 and 1905. Unfortunately the survey left out returnees entering Italy through other ports or by railroads. Besides, several captains neglected to comply with the request of the Commissariato and turned in the passengers list without any annotation. Notwithstanding all these limitations, the 1905–6 survey provides the most complete indicators on Italian return migration.[25]

In the United States, data on return migration were gathered by the Commissioner of Immigration. The commissioner devised a simple classification. Individuals leaving the United States for a permanent relocation elsewhere were called emigrant aliens; those entering the United States with the intention of establishing a permanent domicile were classified as immigrant aliens. Persons entering the United States for a temporary visit were defined as nonimmigrant aliens; immigrants domiciled in the United States leaving for a temporary visit abroad were categorized as nonemigrant aliens.[26] A comparison between the data gathered by the Commissioner of Immigration and other available data shows considerable variance, mostly the result of individuals who declared that they were returning to Europe only for a visit but in the end did not come back to the United States.[27] Notwithstanding the limitations of American and Italian data, available indicators show that return migration from the United States to Italy was a mass phenomenon until World War I.

*The intensity of return migration*

The combined use of American and Italian indicators yields a varied profile of return migration. Although American data allow comparisons between Italians and other immigrants, Italian data show regional differences among returning Italians. American immigration authorities, following the provisions of the law of Feb. 20, 1908, began to keep official records of the outward movement of aliens only on July 1 of that same year. However, records of the Trans-Atlantic Passenger Association for the period 1899–1910 show that during that time thirty-seven steerage passengers were carried from the United States to European ports for every hundred such passengers brought from Europe to the United States. These percentages are corroborated by other sources as well.[28] In the years 1908–10, 823,311 aliens departed from the United States with the intention of settling permanently abroad, a larger number, as the Dillingham commission pointed out, than the total immigration to the United States in any year prior to 1903 and considerably larger than the total number of immigrants admitted to the United States from 1820 to 1840. The number for the year 1908 is larger than those for the previous years, since many aliens departed because of the severe economic depression of 1907. But the 1909 and 1910 indicators were equally unexpectedly high.[29]

In American data, Italians appear as the group most actively engaged in return migrations. Of the 823,311 returnees of the 1908–10 period, 308,900 were Italians, that is 37.5 percent of all returnees. The second largest group were Poles, with 82,901 individuals, that is 10.1 percent of the total, followed by Magyars with 51,319 (6.2 percent), Croatians and Slovenians with 44,736 (5.4 percent), and Slovaks with 41,726 (5.1 percent), each of the other groups showing less than 5 percent of the total. Southern Italians largely outnumbered northern Italians: 259,381 southerners against 49,596 northerners. A comparison between emigrant aliens departing and immigrant aliens admitted shows that during the same period 548,000 Italians were admitted into the United States as immigrant aliens out of a total immigrant population of 2,576,226 individuals. In percentages, Italians were 21.3 of the total immigrant population, followed by Poles with 10.6 percent, Jews with 9.5, English with 5.5, each of the other groups sharing a percentage below 5. Obviously, Italians were both the largest immigrant and returning group, a fact that the Dillingham commission reported with regrets.[30]

Although Italians were the largest group of emigrant aliens departing in absolute numbers, other groups showed higher rates of returns in relative numbers. For instance, computations made by J.S. Gould indicate that 69 percent of the immigrants from Bulgaria, Serbia, and Montenegro and 63 percent of those from Greece departed as emigrant aliens. Italians returning as emigrant aliens were 58 percent of the incoming number of Italians, followed by Austro-Hungarians with 34 percent, Germans with 22, Russians with 16 and British with 12.[31] American public opinion, however, paid little attention to the return of Slavs and Greeks, because both groups were relatively small. For instance, in the period 1908–10, the total immigrant aliens admitted from Bulgaria, Serbia, and Montenegro was less than 40,000 individuals and the Greeks 88,000. Italians with over 300,000 arrivals in the same period could not escape the attention and the scrutiny of American public opinion.[32]

The profile of emigrant alien Italians shows that returnees were predominantly males (90 percent), of working age (between 14 and 44), and unskilled. Four out of five returnees had been in the United States for a period shorter than five years; the balance had been in the country for less than ten years. Italians returning after a period longer than ten years were slightly over 1 percent of all returnees. Nine out of ten returnees were classified as common laborers, and only 5 percent reported having exercised a skilled occupation in the United States. Those with professional skills were less than 1 percent. Other groups with large percentages of emigrant aliens, like Slavs and Greeks, showed the same occupational profile. Obviously, these 300,000 Italians declared that they were returning to Italy to resettle permanently there; they had been in the United States for about five years and had engaged in unskilled occupations. Their encounter with American society had been both brief and marginal. And to American officials these returnees declared that they were not returning to the United States in the foreseeable future.[33]

A number of returnees declared that they would return to the United States within a year. They were classified as nonemigrant aliens. For instance, in 1908, of the 214,000 Italian returnees, 166,000 were emigrant aliens and only 47,000 nonemigrant aliens, that is only one out of every five returnees declared that he intended to return within a year. In 1909 100,000 Italians departed from the United States: 83,000 as emigrant aliens and only 17,000 as nonemigrant aliens. In 1910 of the 59,000 Italians returning, only 6,000, that is 10 percent, were nonemigrant aliens. The percentage of nonemigrant aliens was decreasing over the years. These data are important. They show that most returnees intended to resettle permanently in Italy; yet, we know that second and third departures from Italy to the United States were quite common. This leads us to the conclusion that second and third emigrations must have occurred either because the resettlement in Italy was unsatisfactory and a second emigration became imperative, or because returnees set for themselves new goals that could be achieved only through another emigration. It is clear, however, that Italians departing from the United States for Italy already contemplating a return to the United States within a year were one out of five or ten, according to the year.[34]

It is virtually impossible to compare Italian and American statistics. The reason is that yearly American indicators span from July 1 to June 30 of the following year, while Italian indicators go from January 1 to December 31. Regardless of this difference, Italian indicators document that return migration from the United States was a vast phenomenon. From 1902 to 1910, 1,058,000 Italians returned from the United States; the departures were 2,200,000, that is 48 returns for every 100 departures. Return migration reached the peak in 1908, when 240,000 returned and only 131,000 departed. From 1911 to 1920 returnees dropped to 811,000, mostly because emigration and immigration came to a virtual halt from 1916 to 1920 on account of World War I. Departures too declined to less than one and a half million from 1911 to 1920, although 1913 was the peak year of emigration with 326,000 departures for the United States. In each year from 1911 to 1914, from 100,000 to 150,000 Italians returned from the United States. Although emigration and returns declined in absolute numbers, return migration increased in percentages from 1911 to 1920: for every 100 Italians heading for the United States 54 returned. Finally, from 1921 to 1930, returns and departures almost canceled each other out. Almost 385,000 individuals reached the United States and 365,000 returned, that is 95 returns for every 100 departures.[35] The National Origins Act of 1924 and the worldwide recession of 1929 brought to an end the unprecedented emigration and return migration of Italians to and from the United States.

Return migration of Italians from the United States was not the exception; it was the rule. It occurred from Brazil and Argentina, as well as from central and northern Europe. For instance, from 1902 to 1910, 670,000 Italians left for Argentina and 270,000 returned, 40 returns for every 100 departures. The peak years of return migration were 1907 and 1908. Departures declined to 310,000 in the following decade, but returns climbed to 291,000, 94 returns for 100 departures, a higher percentage than the United States. From 1921 to 1930 over half a million Italians reached Argentina and 170,000 returned, 32 returns for 100 departures. As for Brazil, 300,000 headed for that nation from 1902 to 1910, and 165,000 returned, 54 returns for 100 departures. From 1911 to 1920, 125,000 headed for Brazil and 68,000 returned, a considerable drop in absolute numbers, but the rate of returns over departures remained virtually unaltered. In the following decade, emigration to Brazil dropped to 76,000 people and returns were 12,000, 16 returns for 100 departures.[36] Although the rate of returns over departures fluctuated more erratically for Brazil and Argentina than for the United States, it is obvious that return migration was as intense and at times more intense from Brazil and Argentina than from the United States.

Detailed data available for 1905–6 provide a better insight into the dynamics of return migration.[37] In 1905, 135,000 individuals arrived at the four ports of Genoa, Naples, Messina, and Palermo: 14 percent were foreigners, 86 percent Italians. In 1906, 176,000 disembarked, the percentage of foreigners over Italians virtually unchanged. Three out of four foreigners were United States citizens either by birth or naturalization, the balance Brazilians and Argentinians. Most Italians traveled third class; only 5 percent of them arrived on first or second class. Foreigners were much more likely to travel first and second class, the U.S. citizens being the most likely candidates for this mode of travel. As for Italian returnees, those from Brazil and Argentina were more likely to travel first and second class (10 percent did so) than returnees from the United States (3 percent did so). This difference seems to indicate that Italians returning from the United States had less money or that they were more concerned about keeping their savings than returnees from Latin America.[38]

For the two years under consideration, about half of the returnees, 43 percent, arrived on Italian ships, while 46 percent left on Italian ships. British ships carried 26 percent, German 16 percent, French 10 percent and Austro-Hungarian 2 percent.[39] The time of arrival showed an additional difference between returnees from North and South America. In general emigrants from South America departed in October, which was the beginning of the farming season in South America. And they returned in April, the beginning of the season in Italy. Emigrants to the United States departed in February and returned in November or December, on account of the rigorous weather. This difference affected also the ports of arrival. Returnees from South America landed generally in Genoa, which was busiest in April-July. Returnees from the United States generally landed in Naples in the November-December period. The port of arrival was of course chosen according to the final destination: returnees from North America landed in Naples, because most of them were from the south; those from South America arrived in Genoa, because the north of Italy was their final destination.[40]

American and Italian statistics concur in outlining the sex and age profile of returnees. In addition, Italian data show a vast difference between returnees from North and South America. In the aggregate, four out of five returnees were males. But returnees from Brazil were the exception, with one woman for every two men. This corroborates accounts of prefects from the Veneto region that in general emigrants to Brazil took their families along, remained in Brazil for a longer period than other Italians did in the United States, and in the end returned with their families. Emigrants to the United States and Argentina, on the other hand, were more likely to be males, unmarried or with families in Italy. Three of every four returnees were between the age of 16 and 45, returnees from Brazil being generally older than those from the United States. This corroborates other evidence we have that many individuals going to the United States were either single males intending to save money to start a family in Italy or recently married males eager to improve their economic condition before having children.[41] Emigrants to Brazil, on the other hand, were likely to have wives and children along. As for women, they were less likely to return than men. These data too corroborate other evidence showing that many departing women were individuals joining their husbands in America, after the husbands had decided in favor of a permanent resettlement overseas.[42]

Returnees arrived either alone or in family groups. Of the 36,221 returnees from Brazil in the two years under investigation, 27 percent traveled alone and 73 percent in family groups, the average group having 4.2 people, quite close to the size of the northern Italian household at the turn of the century. As for returnees from the United States, three of four traveled alone, the size of the average family group being 2.7 people.[43] We know that most returnees from the United States were southerners; those from Brazil northerners. The difference in group sizes reflects the difference in family sizes in the north and south: throughout the period of mass emigration, southern families were considerably smaller than northern families, the larger southern families being a rather recent phenomenon beginning in the mid-1930s.[44] Another explanation of the difference between family groups arriving from Brazil and the United States is that family groups arriving from Brazil were in general whole families, while those from the United States were generally fathers with one or two sons.

### Regional differences

Our concern here is mostly with return migration to southern Italy. A comparison between return migration to the north and to the south, however, will be useful to emphasize the unique character of return migration to the south. About 70 percent of the returnees in 1905–6 headed for the south; of all emigrants from Italy in the 1901–5 period, 73 percent were southerners. Returnees, of course, headed in general for their home communities. By and large, returnees from the U.S. headed south, with a percentage of 87; returnees from South America generally headed north. For the period under consideration, in the north returns outnumbered departures. This was the result of disastrous economic conditions in Brazil, which forced many Italians to leave. As for Argentina, return migration had been a long tradition since the beginning of mass emigration, notwithstanding the long distances. Conversely, in the south, departures outnumbered returns, as the North American market increased its demand for labor.[45]

A variety of factors seem to have determined patterns of return migration to each province or region. It is not uncommon to find differences within provinces of the same region to the point that return migration affected one province deeply but left untouched the neighboring province. Some generalizations, however, seem to be in order. First, for the period 1905–6, return migration was most intense in those provinces where outmigrations had started earlier. For example, the provinces of Alexandria, Turin, Parma, Milan, and Lucca reported high rates of returns. Emigration from these provinces had started earlier than from other provinces. In the south, return migration was most intense in the provinces of Caserta and Cosenza, which had witnessed the earliest emigration in the south. Second, contrary to a common belief, rates of return migration of southerners from Argentina were higher than those from the United States. For example, the province of Chieti reported the highest rates of return from Argentina. Most individuals from that province headed for, and returned from, Argentina. A similar phenomenon occurred also in some towns in the province of Cosenza. Third, returns were higher in provinces with better economies. For instance, return migrations to the provinces of Potenza and Matera in Basilicata were among the lowest in the south. The two provinces were among the poorest in the south. In Calabria, return migration was intense in Cosenza, followed by Catanzaro and Reggio Calabria, the former province having a better economy than the latter two. Obviously these generalizations do not apply in all cases. But they provide an indication as to the vastly varied dynamics of return migration.

A further comparison between return migration and the countries from which Italians returned shows a variety of patterns and emphasizes regional differences. By the early twentieth century four streams of return migrations were clearly noticeable. The first was directed to the Italian northwest, regions of Piedmont, Liguria, and Lombardy, with most returnees from Argentina. The second headed for the Veneto region, where about 70 percent of the returnees were from Brazil. The third, embracing the central northern regions of Emilia, Tuscany, Marche, and Latium, encompassed almost equal numbers of returnees from North and South America. And the fourth stream affected the whole south, where returnees came almost exclusively from the United States. The regional differences were noticeable also in family patterns. For instance, almost 75 percent of the returnees directed to the southern region of Calabria traveled without families; an equal percentage of returnees to Veneto traveled with families. With Veneto and Calabria at the opposite end of the spectrum, returnees to the north were more likely to have families along than returnees to the south. Finally returnees to the south arrived after three to four years in the United States; returnees to the north from Brazil had been in South America for about ten years. And returnees from Argentina were a mixed group: some had been there for as long as fifteen years, while others crossed the Atlantic just about every year.

Surprisingly return migration was more intense in the north than in the south for the 1905–6 period. There are three explanations for the difference. First, more people returned to the north because emigration from the north had started earlier, and obviously was affecting a larger number of people by 1905–6 than in the south, where mass emigration started later. Second, the rates of return to the north for the period 1905–6 were perhaps exceptional, since both the Argentinian and Brazilian economies were undergoing a period of decline.[46] A combination of statistical indicators and of other evidence, however, shows that emigration and return migration developed differently in the north than in the south. Third, Italians who emigrated seasonally to central and northern European countries were almost exclusively northerners. For example, in 1912, of the 298,000 northerners who left the country, 75 percent headed for European or Mediterranean destinations. In contrast, of the 278,000 southerners who emigrated outside Italy, 90 percent headed for North and South America. Obviously, return migration from European countries to northern Italy was easier and less expensive than return migration to southern Italy from the Americas.[47]

These indicators show that north and south experienced emigration differently. Contrary to common assumption, for the 1875–1925 period, more people emigrated from the north of Italy than from the south, although most northerners were likely to emigrate to neighboring European countries than to the Americas. Northern Italian emigration developed in a more erratic way than the southern counterpart. Northern emigration started in the early 1870s, became a mass phenomenon in the late 1880s and early 1890s, declined drastically at the turn of the century, picked up momentum in 1904, declined again in 1908, and resumed after World War I. Southern emigration started in the mid-1880s and picked up momentum at a steady pace, reaching its peak in the 1910–14 period and after World War I. Return migration from central and northern European countries was also the result of governmental policies that discouraged foreigners not only from becoming citizens but also from permanent residence. Although emigration and return migration were more intense in the north than in the south, historians have concentrated almost exclusively on the south for an obvious reason. Northern emigration was, perhaps, the result of dislocations brought about by the process of modernization.

Eventually it ended. In the south, contrary to expectations, emigration became a permanent fixture of that society to this very day.

*Some typologies of returnees*

Why did so many return? And, can we reconstruct some typologies of returnees? The return migration of northern Italians from European countries does not need explanation. It was simply an extension of the internal migrations that had occurred in northern Italy since the eighteenth century. And because these internal migrations had traditionally been seasonal, the new European migrations too remained seasonal. Overseas emigrations, however, were long distance movements, especially for people who had never traveled even within Italy. Moreover, southerners who engaged in transatlantic emigrations had a limited previous experience of internal migrations and accordingly of return migrations. Yet, they returned. What did they return to? The lives they had left behind when departing for America were filled with poverty and dejection. Pasquale Villari, who lived for a number of days with a group of southern peasants, commented that he could not think of anything that could be added to those lives to make them more miserable. Yet, they returned en masse. Was it nostalgia, as somebody suggested? Perhaps. But we should not forget that even southern peasants, although illiterate, knew how to assess costs and benefits. Evidence presented in previous chapters and to be discussed in future chapters shows that emigrants were also calculating individuals led by interests as much as by emotions. Returnees were individuals with clear economic goals, although we can argue that those goals were perhaps outdated and, at least to a degree, self-destructive.

Obviously, the transportation network available in Italy and elsewhere at the turn of the century made the return of Italians and other groups easier and cheaper than the return of immigrants like Germans and Irish who had arrived in the United States in the first part of the nineteenth century. For instance, faster ships and cheaper fares made return migration accessible even to unskilled immigrants. It was possible to return to Italy from New York or one of the North Atlantic states in a week or ten days. And by the turn of the century, competition among shipping companies had driven fares so low that even a laborer could pay for his way back with two to three weeks' worth of wages. Besides, there was an added financial reason to return to Italy for the winter: it was cheaper to return to Italy in November and go back to New York in early February than to stay in New York for two months without working. Many New York Italians, for instance, and the argument can be extended for many other Italians throughout the United States, were engaged in construction jobs or other outside jobs, which had to stop during the winter. It was cheaper for an individual to return to Italy, live with his family, and return in the spring, than to stay in the United States for the winter, with no income, but with the expenses of room and board.[48]

Some scholars have argued that the changing economy of the United States explains why return migration became a mass phenomenon at the turn of the century. Throughout most of the nineteenth century, farming and food processing provided jobs for most immigrants. With the passing of the farming frontier and the rising demand of manpower by urban industries, immigrants flocked to cities from abroad and from American farms. Immigrants going into farming were less likely to return to Europe, especially when they purchased land. Immigrants in industries, on the other hand, were more likely to change jobs and to abandon them altogether, especially during the winter, to return to Europe. Even among Italians, return migration among immigrants in farming was less common than among immigrants in industries. And this was equally true in North and South America. For instance, repatriation from the states of Rio Grande and Santa Catarina in Brazil was the exception, because most Italians became small landowners in the two states. Return was quite common among Italians from São Paulo, where immigrants engaged in small trade or menial jobs in industries. Italians in the United States behaved likewise. Those who engaged in truck farming in California, New Jersey, Wisconsin, and some southern states were less likely to return than those in cities with industrial jobs. And because more industrial jobs were available in the United States than in South America, the United States became the preferred destination. In addition Italians intended not to commit themselves to jobs tying them to the New World. Those who did seek permanent relocation overseas went to South America, Canada, and Australia.

A few years ago, D. J. Gould advanced the argument of long-range planning to explain the increased return migration, especially among Italians and other southern Europeans at the turn of the century.[49] Immigrants are attracted to a country, Gould argues, either by wage differences between home countries and countries of immigration or by a wide range of opportunities to be achieved over a long period of time. The former are likely to become temporary immigrants, and the latter permanent. To permanent immigrants, the wage difference is not likely to be the central reason for leaving; rather, they seek better jobs, career advancements over a long period of time, better

working conditions, social stability, political freedom, and especially
better opportunities for their children. These goals, Gould shows,
seem to have determined the emigration and immigration of British
and Germans throughout the nineteenth century. Temporary immigrants, on the other hand, are exclusively concerned with wage differences, which have to be wide enough to justify the financial costs
of transportation and relocation, as well as the psychological costs of
breaking up families and of precarious living conditions. Seemingly,
Gould concludes, very few Italians embraced emigration with the
long-term goals of permanent immigrants; rather, most of them were
attracted by wage differences. A popular refrain common in southern
Italy stated that one could make more money in one day in New York
than in one week in southern Italy. And that certainly was the major
argument in favor of emigration.[50]

Gould's argument about Italians in the United States can be expanded to Italian emigration in general. With few exceptions, most
Italians who emigrated overseas and even to Europe were propelled
by the wage difference between intended destinations and home villages. We can reasonably ask why Italians did not contemplate the
benefits inherent in permanent emigration, like many other groups
did. Seemingly Italians heading for international destinations at the
turn of the century were propelled by the same needs and nourished
the same goals of their fathers and forefathers who had emigrated
within Italy in the eighteenth and nineteenth centuries. Traditional
internal migrations in Italy had been fueled by elementary economic
dynamics: individuals emigrated from one region to another to balance the family budget. When internal destinations became less attractive and the number of individuals seeking to balance the family
budget increased, Italians headed for international destinations. General goals and strategies did not change; only the distances became
longer. Italians, however, were not the only group to embrace international emigrations as extensions of traditional internal migrations.
Poles, for example, followed a similar route. Large numbers of them
emigrated to France and Germany, as well as to some industrial areas
of Russia temporarily to achieve the same goals Italians had set for
themselves through temporary emigration. When these European
destinations did not suffice any longer, Poles crossed the Atlantic.
But they too were attracted more by wage differences than long-term
goals. And the Poles too returned in large numbers.[51]

But why were Italians in general unable or unwilling to contemplate
and eventually embrace the long-term goals of permanent emigration?
After all, other immigrant groups did emigrate permanently. Gould
offers a cultural explanation. He argues that geography, history and

the general climate of opinion in Italy at the time of mass emigration made it virtually impossible for Italians to embrace the long-term goals of permanent emigration. Their attachment to the land was so strong that they never seriously contemplated the advantages of permanent relocation elsewhere, according to Gould. The attachment to the land had two components: the desire to return to the ancestral home and the determination to buy land properties in home villages as a way to economic security and social status. Gould's argument is so broad that it needs some further elucidation.

Let us begin by asking why other groups embraced permanent immigration without second thoughts. Some, like the Jews, had no alternatives. Returning was simply out of the question. Others, like the Irish, longed for the ancestral villages, as Kerby Miller has shown, but were quite aware that the available economic resources in home villages were so scarce that a permanent resettlement in Ireland was impossible. Others, like the Germans who emigrated in the mid-nineteenth century, simply could not return because the crossing of the Atlantic at that time was too expensive. Finally, other immigrants reached America through a series of intermediate stops in other nations. By the time they reached the United States, they had lost the original attachment to home communities and therefore had no desire to return. One could argue, however, that immigrants in general did not return also either because returning was impossible or because it was very difficult and expensive. For many immigrants, either in the nineteenth or twentieth centuries, a permanent resettlement was perhaps not so much a question of a choice as a necessity. Italians, on the other hand, embraced emigration at a time when return emigration was a reasonable alternative for several reasons: transportation was cheap, land was being made available in home villages, and the American labor market was organized in such a way as to encourage seasonal migrations. From this point of view, Italians were not, perhaps, so different from other immigrants. Simply, their emigration occurred at a time when return migration was reasonable and profitable.

This negative argument, however, does not go far enough. It seems to me that the ability of an individual to embrace permanent or temporary emigration was determined or conditioned by the degree of change affecting home communities at the time emigration occurred. More specifically, societies undergoing a significant process of modernization were likely to give rise to permanent emigration. Conversely, traditional societies only marginally affected by such processes were likely to choose temporary emigrations. Crucial to the process is the experience of change by prospective emigrants within their own communities. Let us take the example of German emigration in the nineteenth century. In Germany emigration was mostly the result of the crisis of the old order. But it was also one outcome of the rise of the new industrial order. In general, German emigrants were, at least to a degree, aware that the new industrial order was coming about. This led them to consider emigration as a permanent alternative in the range of choices or impositions mandated by the new order. In Italy, on the other hand, emigration was prompted by the crisis of the old order brought about, as we have seen, by economic dynamics originating outside Italy. Unfortunately the crisis of the old order in Italy was not followed by the emergence of the new order, with very limited exceptions. Prospective emigrants were aware that the old order was in crisis. But they were unaware of the new order, and especially of its dynamics. Their reaction was to salvage the old order with the cosmetic changes mandated by the circumstances. In the end, emigration was an economic and social dynamic national groups embraced differently, the difference being determined by the specific conditions of each society.

*Some types of returnees*

Although each returnee cherished and pursued personal goals de-termined by individual and family circumstances, it is possible to categorize returnees by the degree of success and failure and by goals they wanted to pursue. Available evidence indicates that returnees could be divided into four broad categories: returnees of failure, re-turnees of retirement, returnees of investment, and ambivalent returnees.

The returnees of failure were either emigrants rejected by immi-gration officials or forced back to Italy by a catastrophic illness after being admitted to the U.S. At the turn of the century, a criminal record or a contagious disease were the two reasons for exclusion from the United States. Seemingly immigrants rejected by immigra-tion officials were few. In 1907 1,508 returnees disembarked in Italy, after having being rejected at Ellis Island. However, these numbers were deceptive. Most Italians rejected at Ellis Island went to other countries in South America, which had less stringent entrance re-quirements. Available statistics indicate that from 1 to 2 percent of arriving Italians were rejected by immigration officials, that is from 2,500 to 5,000 individuals every year. In absolute terms, they were very few; in reality, they were the source of constant recrimination between immigration officials and shipping companies. Virtually all these rejected individuals had no money to pay their way back and

shipping companies were unwilling to shoulder the burden of transportation. In addition, the immigrants rejected because of potentially
contagious diseases had to face also the rejection of their townsfolk
once they arrived in Italy.[52]

Among the returnees of failure we count also those individuals
who were repatriated because of catastrophic illness or a serious industrial accident. Their tickets were generally paid by Italian consuls,
American charitable organizations, Italian mutual aid societies, and,
more rarely, friends. In 1907, for instance, 6,270 Italians landed in
Italy with charity tickets: 2,474 from the United States, 1,722 from
Argentina, and 2,074 from Brazil.[53] Most of them were immigrants
without families or without close relatives willing to take up the burden of their care. Reports from Italian consuls abound with descriptions of immigrants in extreme poverty, abandoned by relatives and
friends, with no alternative left but to return to Italy.[54] Health officials
in Italy became concerned because many of these returnees were
bringing back contagious diseases. Syphilis and tuberculosis were the
two most common diseases among returnees from the United States.
Trachoma was the prevalent disease among returnees from Brazil and
Argentina.[55] To prevent contagion, the Italian government opened
three hospitals at the ports of Genoa, Naples and Palermo. But, as a
visitor reported in 1912, "the three hospitals take care only of a fraction
of the returnees in need of medical care; most returnees, even if
seriously ill, are sent back to their communities, where they become
a public menace."[56] From 1903 to 1909 over 16,000 Italians returned
from the United States in ship infirmaries, but only one-tenth of them
were treated at the three hospitals. The others were sent home for
lack of space.[57] Health officials from all over Italy complained; but the
central government had neither the political ability nor the economic
resources to address the problem.[58]

The largest number of returnees of failure were healthy individuals
with broken dreams. They returned dejected, either because they had
been unable to adjust to life in America or because they had failed
financially. To save face, those who had been unable to adjust to life
in America spread the rumor that doctors advised them to return,
because the American climate was dangerous to their health. Those
who had failed financially tried to keep a low profile, some of them
living for a number of months or relocating permanently with relatives
in another town. Reports by prefects document that such returnees
were many. That of Cosenza, for instance, wrote: "The poor and
disillusioned returnees are many. Relatives in America and sometimes
friends in Italy pay for their return, to avoid further public embarrassment."[59] From Palermo, the prefect wrote: "Public opinion ig-

nored those who fail. And they themselves have no desire to be singled out. But they are many. Some have joined socialist organizations and spread discontent."[60] Friedrich Vochting, who wrote a penetrating analysis of the impact of return migration on southern agriculture, concludes that returnees who came back with money and were able to settle permanently and profitably in Italy were only a handful.[61] This statement seems to imply that most returnees should be classified as returnees of failure. Perhaps Vochting's criterion to establish the success or failure of return migration was too strict. But, unquestionably, return migration was a painful experience for more than a handful of individuals.

Returnees of retirement and returnees of investment shared a common characteristic: they had money. The former, however, planned to live on their savings; the latter planned to invest them. Observers left various assessments of the sums the average returnee had at the end of his migration. Luigi Rossi, for instance, wrote in 1910 that in the south returnees had "from 1,000 to 1,500 lire," that is from 400 to 600 dollars.[62] An American observer was more generous. "Returnees," he wrote, "are in much improved economic conditions, the average savings varying from 250 to 1,000 dollars."[63] Prefects generally agreed that the average returnee had from 500 to 1,000 lire. We have few testimonies from returnees. They were generally unwilling to share the secret of their success with anybody, their families included in many cases. When the interviewers for the 1907–9 survey asked returnees in the south how much money they had brought back, they received evasive answers, like "enough" or "not enough," while some got so concerned as to run to the post office where savings were kept and withdraw them. Of course, it is virtually impossible to provide accurate sums, because individual savings varied with the length of emigration, the type of job an emigrant had had and the ability to save.

I will deal later with the aggregate savings of returnees and how they were used. At this point it is important to assess how returnees compared their savings with the prevalent wages in their region. During the time of mass emigration there was little fluctuation in wages, especially for peasants. Inflation in wages, as well as in all areas of Italian economic life, occurred during World War I. In 1878–9 a southern laborer was paid 1.25 lire a day, for a total of 275 lire per year, because the working days were about 200. In the north yearly wages ranged from 400 to 450 lire, with noticeable variations from region to region.[64] Contrary to complaints common among landowners, mass emigration did not push wages up substantially. In 1905, for instance, a laborer made 1.60 lire a day in Sicily, for a total of 350 to 450 lire a year. It was only during and after World War I that wages were affected by the general spiral of inflation; by 1921 a laborer, even in the south, was making 12 to 20 lire a day.[65] General surveys conducted at several intervals document that most laborers could not make ends meet on such wages and at the end of the year they were in the red. Industrial workers, still a minority at the turn of the century, were better off. Daily wages were 2.48 lire a day in 1908, 3.26 in 1910, and 14.27 in 1920.[66] But, in the end, they were not much better off than agricultural laborers. Rents were higher in cities and underemployment was endemic in many occupations.

Under the circumstances, a returnee with 1,000 lire considered himself and was considered by others a successful individual. At the turn of the century, 500 lire was considered a very generous yearly wage for a laborer, even in the best region. Vochting observed that in general savings from 1,000 to 3,000 lire were considered "extraordinary by peasants who had never owned anything."[67] Returnees themselves expressed their satisfaction, although they carefully avoided revealing how much money they had saved. Southerners voiced their enthusiasm with a popular saying: "America has become the paradise these god-forsaken regions have never known in the past." Authorities too joined the chorus of those praising the wonderful results of overseas migrations. The perfect of Cosenza reported: "If the local economy has not collapsed altogether, it is because of the generous savings from America."[68] And his colleague from Palermo added: "We can only be hopeful for the new generation and its future, since never before has so much money been available in this province."[69] Writing almost at the end of mass emigration, the prefect of Lucca commented: "Emigration and remittances have become the most important industry in this province. American savings have reached unprecedented proportions."[70] The successful returnees were many.

Thousands of returnees came home to retire. They were not necessarily old individuals. Rather, they had saved enough money to live comfortably for the rest of their lives. Incidentally, time was to show that many of them had overcalculated their fortune. Some of them owned land before departing. When they returned, they did not go back to the land. They rented it out. They kept their savings in local post offices or in savings institutions in the provincial capital, miles away from the home village to prevent neighbors and especially relatives from knowing how much money they had made. Returnees were obsessed by secrecy about their money; their relatives who had never migrated nourished often the conviction that they were entitled to enjoy in some way the fortune made by relatives in America. Although secretive about the sums brought back, returnees were compelled to let everybody know that they "had made it in America." And they displayed their success in their clothes, in their houses, and in a life of leisure. Luigi Capuana, a popular writer, for instance, described the returnee of retirement as the man who showed up in town at the time of the yearly fair with "a fine hat, a new suit, shining shoes: the perfect image of the gentleman who savors the envy mixed with adoration of his neighbors."[71] And a British traveler who personally observed a returnee arrive in a small northern Italian town wrote: "When he came back from America, he had a dark blue suit and the most wonderful yellow boots Campià had ever seen."[72] If they stayed in old houses, they renovated them; if their success had been spectacular, they built a new house. And they spent the balance of their days visiting relatives and playing cards at the local coffeehouse, reminiscing about America with other returnees.

Returnees of retirement did not enjoy a good press. Their success, of course, did not ingratiate them to those who had not migrated and were forced to work hard just to exist. But there was more than envy in the negative reaction. Observers commented that many returnees boasted incessantly about their success, while being secretive about their savings. Some prefects reported quarrels between returnees who expected to be addressed as gentlemen and locals who refused to take off their hats in their presence.[73] They were critical of the backward ways of their home villages and compared Italy unfavorably to the United States. Yet they were unwilling to get involved in community projects. As a villager in Calabria commented: "Returnees are the worst parasites I have ever encountered." And they were generally reluctant to associate with those who had never emigrated, whom they considered uncultured. Reports by southern prefects voiced all too frequently the general displeasure with these returnees. "Although they bring back money," the prefect of Cosenza commented, "they seem to create unnecessary tensions within communities. My greatest frustration is that I am unable to get their support for any project. Anything we try to do here is wrong in their eyes." And Francesco Coletti remarked that in general returnees of retirement were lazy and "a drawback in the south, where the work ethic has never been granted citizenship. The common aspiration is to go to America to make some money in order to return and enjoy the traditional dolce far niente."

Seemingly Italians who returned to invest their savings in Italy were less flashy in their first appearance in town. They intended to let their investments speak for themselves. Almost invariably, their goal was to buy land. As soon as one of these returnees showed up in town, the general gossip was how many acres of land will he be able to buy. Luigi Capuana, who observed many such returnees, reported that as soon as a deal was made and became public, it was widely commented upon. And the size of the acquired property established the reputation of the returnee.[74] Returnees themselves commented on their goals. One of them said that land was the only aspiration he had had in mind since he was a child. He concluded: "I worked in construction in New York for five years. It was a backbreaking job. But every day I dreamed of the land I would one day buy with my savings. Land anywhere else has no value to me."[75] Prefects too regularly reported on the number of returnees buying land and how the increased demand inflated prices.[76] It was a process capable of rejuvenating the stagnant agrarian communities of the south. New capital was coming in; new landowners, perhaps more willing to experiment, were replacing the unimaginative landowners of the past; an unprecedented level of competition seemed to awaken communities where tradition and stagnation had reigned for centuries. The expectations were high. A popular saying in the south generated by return migration was: "Nothing is impossible to the man who has seen the Brooklyn Bridge."[77] But some observers had misgivings. Coletti, for instance, lamented that in many cases returnees did not buy land to farm it, but to rent it out. Perhaps many returnees of investment were not that different, Coletti added, from returnees of retirement. Return migration was not, as many observers wrote, the great success that popular opinion was making it out to be.

Then, there were the ambivalent returnees: they embraced emigration without clear goals as to whether to stay in America or return, or they eventually changed their minds. Emigrants about to depart generally stated that they intended to return. But some kept their options open. One of them commented to an emigration official: "Of course I think I will be back. But I have never been in America and perhaps I will change my mind. Others have done exactly that."[78] Some intended to settle in America permanently; but the process of adjustment and the nostalgia for the home community proved to be too strong. And they returned. One such returnee said: "When I was in Brooklyn, this town of mine, so old and so dear, became like a paradise to me in my imagination. And in the end I had to return." But his contentment proved to be short-lived. After four months in Verbicaro, he confessed to a visitor: "For some inexplicable reason, I did not like the town I found at my return. I was unable to adjust in Italy. And, totally unexpected to me, Brooklyn now seems like the promised land. And I know it will be only a question of time before I leave for New York again."[79] Stories abound of individuals crossing the Atlantic several times. The individuals engaged in these serial migrations were unable to forget either country, yet unwilling to commit themselves totally to one. In many instances, external circumstances forced ambivalent emigrants to make up their minds. For instance, children born in America forced parents to remain there permanently. Antonio Mangano quoted a story that seems to have been quite typical. An immigrant returned from New York to Toritto in southern Italy with a fourteen-year-old son, born in Italy but raised in Brooklyn. In Toritto the returnee opened a barber shop. The son objected all along to returning and when he reached the age of sixteen he took off for the United States. Reluctantly, the father joined him in America in order not to be separated from his son. It is perhaps safe to state that many ambivalent emigrants finally settled in the United States by default: family circumstances, in most cases, made it impossible for them to return.

Returnees were individuals with different agendas. They shared the assumption that emigration was a temporary device to solve problems at home. They were attracted to America by high wages. But they were either unwilling or unable to see emigration as an end in itself. Permanent emigration demanded a break from the past and a new start for which many Italians were not prepared. Italian returnees were by and large creatures of traditional societies where drastic changes were never contemplated and much less welcome. Consequently, the goals returnees tried to pursue fell within the boundaries of what was considered a decent life in traditional societies: land, a house, enough money to live on, and the simple enjoyments of life southerners had known for centuries. Emigration was a change. But southerners did not intend to make it a radical change.

# 6    *American remittances*

As returnees pursued their private goals by crossing the Atlantic in both directions, their quest did not go unnoticed. And the savings they carried with them or channeled home before their final return stimulated debates and interests that were to last a long time. Italian villagers were mesmerized by remittances. In many small towns nobody had ever heard of so much money. Adolfo Rossi, an Italian commissioner of emigration, for instance, reported that in Sanfili, a a town of 5,000 people in the province of Cosenza, five brothers emigrated to the United States in the late 1890s and returned after eight years with 200,000 lire. With that money they bought a large property and two houses.[1] Savings and returnees became the strongest argument in favor of leaving even for those who had rejected emigration initially. Social scientists interested in the economic development of Italy saw the tremendous potential of remittances. Individual savings were small, they remarked, but their aggregate was substantial. How could the national economy take advantage of this capital? Could remittances be channeled toward larger goals than the private ones pursued by returnees?

Politicians too took an interest in remittances. How could the state facilitate the flow of remittances into Italy, prevent immigrants from investing abroad, and use remittances as a way to accumulate hard currency? The arrival of increasingly strong American dollars was a particularly enticing occurrence, as Italy was joining the most developed Western nations in international markets. Bankers and individuals contemplating personal profits in the business of transmitting remittances from America to Italy took a great interest in immigrant savings too. American commercial banks were reluctant to handle the small savings of immigrants. Shrewd immigrants, popularly known in America as *banchisti*, stepped in to provide a much needed service to fellow immigrants who wanted to save and send money home. Of course the service was provided for a fee. The questionable activities of the banchisti attracted wide attention both in the United States and in Italy. The American government and a sector of the American banking community eventually got involved in the business of remittances. When it became obvious that millions of dollars were leaving the United States heading for Italy every year, the argument was made that government and banks should get involved in the business of immigrant savings to keep them in the United States, if possible. This chapter deals with all these questions. In addition it offers an estimate of how much money arrived in Italy from 1870 to the 1920s.

## The economic integration of immigrants

American remittances created a lot of converts to the soundness of emigration, even among those who had originally opposed it on the grounds of social disruption, loss of manpower, and threat to traditional values. The first convert was the average Italian. Remittances became a household name. New York, Rio de Janeiro, and Buenos Aires were closer to the heart of the average Italian than Rome or Florence. *Fare l'America* turned into the main goal for young people, almost a sign of manhood. Egisto Rossi reported that in some southern towns young men who had never crossed the Atlantic had a hard time finding a bride. Simply, it was almost a prerequisite for adulthood. Mangano, who traveled the south extensively, reported that the most common topic of conversation everywhere was America. He was asked for advice as to the most profitable jobs and most favorable destinations. When a small group left a town, the whole village turned out to see them off, those who stayed behind openly expressing a sense of envy and the determination to follow them as soon as possible. American letters became almost common property: their content was widely discussed in towns. The arrival of savings through international money orders or by other means became a common occurrence for families, almost as the daily wages had been in the old days. America and its promise of abundant savings generated an unprecedented and, unfortunately, unfounded sense of optimism. Everything was possible, as a popular saying put it, to the man who dared to cross the Atlantic.

Educated observers, of course, were more cautious. But, eventually they came to share in the optimism of everybody else. For some time, observers of mass emigration had debated how to integrate the phenomenon within the national purpose. How could Italy profit from emigration and return migration? Initially the debate had centered on whether emigration was good or bad for the country. But when it turned into a mass phenomenon, the debate switched to the potential advantage for the national economy. Jacopo Virgilio and Vittorio Ellena, for instance, argued that Italians abroad, and especially those in Brazil and Argentina, could become customers of the national market. They could spend part of their savings in buying national products, which Italian shipping companies would transport to South America.[2] But the reality was quite different. Most emigrants were not prosperous and certainly could not afford on a regular basis to buy Italian products with the markup mandated by such long distances.[3] Moreover, it was quite questionable whether Italian shipping companies had the resources to supply Italians scattered over such vast territories of South America. The limitations of the marketing abilities of Italians became painfully obvious in 1888, when, after a commercial break with France, Prime Minister Francesco Crispi found the necessity of opening new markets in Europe and South America. Crispi's overture to Italians in South America got nowhere.[4] Notwithstanding these failures, the idea of supplying immigrants with national products to increase national trade was voiced at various times throughout the period of mass emigration.[5]

Others argued that emigration could be profitable to the nation if emigrants would band together to establish agricultural colonies, especially in South America, where land was still available at reasonable prices at the turn of the century. A cluster of such colonies, with exclusively Italian settlers and capital, could in time become almost a geographical extension of Italy. These colonies were to send their produce to Italy and buy manufactures from Italy to stimulate the national economy. More ardent nationalists suggested that at some point in the development of Italian agrarian colonies in South America Italy would be entitled to claim political control over those geographical extensions of Italy. The promoters of agricultural colonies pointed out that such enterprises would be less costly than military imperialism and more effective than the trade arrangement recommended by Virgilio, Ellena, and Crispi. But these promoters overlooked some basic realities. First, neither the public nor the private sectors in Italy had enough money to purchase extensive tracts of land needed for agricultural colonies. Second, because most immigrants intended to return to Italy within a number of years, few were interested in purchasing land and settling permanently in the Americas.[6] Attempts were made – modest in the United States and more vigorous in South America – to establish agricultural colonies with Italian capital and manpower. But the rate of success was poor. In the United States, for instance, New Palermo in Alabama and Sunnyside in Arkansas were abysmal failures. In Brazil the rate of success was higher, but the achievements hardly extensive enough to make these colonies an asset for the Italian economy.[7]

Nationalists dismissed the trade arrangements and the farming colonies as unworkable ways to make emigration profitable for Italy. For them, the only realistic solution was the military occupation of foreign territories to be converted into destinations for Italian emigrants. After all, that had been the course followed by France and Great Britain. Italy had an additional right to such a takeover: it had a big population surplus in need of an outlet. This argument that overpopulation at home created rights abroad was used to obtain popular support for the military expedition to Eritrea in 1884–6, Libya in 1911, and Ethiopia in 1935. Emigrants were to follow the armies. And an eminent person like Francesco Coletti suggested in 1912 that American returnees should be redirected to Libya to purchase African land with American money.[8] But potential emigrants and returnees remained skeptical. The government resurrected the old argument that every peasant was entitled to a plot of land. Unfortunately, not everybody could have land in Italy. But now the government was making it available in Africa. Potential emigrants and actual returnees remained unconverted. Nationalists insisted that Italians had a civilizing mission in Africa and that peasants too had to share that responsibility by relocating there instead of going to the Americas. Still, peasants remained unmoved. The government then engaged in a publicity campaign to persuade emigrants that going to Africa was the patriotic and religious thing to do. Prominent senators and eminent bishops showed up in Genoa to give their commendation or blessing to the few who left for Africa. But senators and bishops were unable to convince a skeptical peasantry. By 1905, there were sixty-five farmers in Eritrea protected by 531 military officers.[9] In looking back to the African fiasco, Antonio Gramsci, certainly not a friend of the Italian government, argued that the African adventure represented the peak of the Italian political folly.[10]

The history of the Italian farming colonies shows that educated Italians who hoped that such colonies would become a national asset – the names of Florenzano, Carpi Nitti, and Marcone come to mind – were unrealistic both about the available Italian resources to be mobilized for such enterprises and about opportunities for farming in countries of destination. Italy not only lacked capital but did not have farmers capable of competing, with few exceptions, with Germans and other northern Europeans. Both in North and South America farming required capital so large that Italians were unable to join commercial farmers. In the United States, for instance, Italians engaged not in the profitable cotton or wheat farming, but in truck farming around cities like New Orleans and San Francisco. In South America, where more Italians engaged in farming, capital-intensive coffee growing was out of reach for most Italians. Instead, immigrants farmed a variety of products for the local market.[11] Searching for the reasons of the marginality of Italians in farming in the United States, the Dillingham Commission concluded that Italians lacked "self-reliance, initiative, resourcefulness, and self-sufficing individualism" needed for commercial farming.[12] The observation had some truth; although lack of capital and the determination to return were even more detrimental than psychological handicaps.[13]

## The integration through remittances

Events progressively convinced these social planners and nationalists that emigration could not be made into a national asset by influencing or controlling the phenomenon in America or in European destinations. The poverty of most immigrants and their determination to save for return excluded any chance of having them become purchasers of national products while living overseas. The establishments of clusters of agricultural colonies was even more unrealistic, because of lack of capital and the determination of most immigrants to avoid farming, because returning was the common goal. The creation of Italian colonies abroad where emigrants could be channeled was attempted but in the end proved to be an abysmal failure.

Eventually observers came to realize that emigration could be turned into a national asset by the intelligent use of remittances. From the very beginning of the movement, immigrants had been sending back part of their earnings to their families, either to satisfy some immediate needs or to be set aside for future investments. The largest sums were ordinarily brought back by returnees themselves. The impact on local economies was immediately apparent. Potential emigrants learned quickly by word of mouth and by comparison the destinations with the best opportunities to save. A saying common in the south spelled out that the "yield" from the United States was 1,000 lire a year, while a season in Germany could net from 300 to 500 lire.[14] Savings reoriented the destinations of emigrants. South America, with lower remittances, progressively turned into a less desirable destination, while the United States became the preferred destination on account of the wage differential. In addition, emigrants were attracted to the United States by the increasingly favorable rates of exchange of American dollars in Italian markets.[15] By the mid-1880s it was obvious that international migration was replacing the traditional internal and seasonal migrations within Italy. Seasonal migrations had made possible modest savings, ordinarily used to survive from year to year. The new international migrations were generating sums that allowed the unprecedented luxury of making plans about one's future.

Of course, returnees had their own personal agendas, as everybody could see. But educated observers began to discuss the long-term impact of remittances. Remittances were a national asset of great magnitude, they remarked, certainly more effective than all other plans tried by the government to modernize the south. Remittances were to solve the chronic problem of the Italian economy, especially in the south: shortage of capital. Remittances were to affect every Italian town, because return was a universal phenomenon. The housing industry would be affected first, because the immediate goal of returnees was to remodel the old house or, if their success had been spectacular, to build a new one. Trade would expand as the demand for consumer goods increased. The land market would be affected in important ways. Unpropertied peasants would join the class of landowners, as many medium and small landowners would be forced to sell and emigrate. The new capital was going to be handled by new men, the returnees. Some of them, aware that the future was going to be in industrial investments, would eventually engage in activities other than farming. Some observers optimistically concluded in the 1890s that Italian mass emigration would last only two decades, enough time to accumulate the capital the country needed to be economically self-sufficient.[16] At that point, the government would declare emigration no longer necessary and the country would erect a memorial to the millions who had made possible the economic independence of Italy.

Because remittances were perhaps the most important national asset at the turn of the century, the government had to protect them – so the argument went – from the time they left the United States to the time they reached families in Italy. To ensure the orderly flow of money, the government had to help solve problems all along the way. First, consuls and other government representatives had to discourage immigrants from taking naturalization papers and from settling permanently in the Americas. Second, immigrants in remote areas had to be offered the opportunity to send their savings back to Italy. Similarly, immigrants with language problems had to be helped in the transaction. Third, foreign governments had to be reminded to expedite the process, because families in Italy depended on the regular arrival of remittances. Fourth, once in Italy, the post office had to channel the money orders to every individual town as safely and expeditiously as possible. Fifth, if the money got lost in the process, the government had to set in place measures for the reimbursement of the money. Sixth, the government had to provide a safe place for returnees to keep the money until such time they were ready to use it. Moreover, the government was to provide guidelines as to how savings should be invested. Finally if a plan for investment was to be made, the government should have some ideas as to how much money was arriving in Italy.

In a process so long and complicated, the potential for error was everywhere. Immigrants could be deceived on pay day or at the exchange office. Dealing with post offices or American banks was a monumental problem for immigrants because of the language problem. The language problem was increased by the fact that immigrants were unwilling to ask for help, even from friends, because they did not want to share with anybody their financial deals. In addition, post office clerks could not always be trusted, especially in South America. Regardless of warnings to the contrary, many immigrants sent cash or coins, which prevented immigrants from being reimbursed in cases of loss. Experienced immigrants who engaged in the process of transmitting remittances to Italy proved to be less than reliable and capable. Cases of embezzlements were frequent. In Italy the postal service was rather poor, especially in remote communities. Returnees were so protective of their savings that they did not tolerate any inquiry about them.[17] Even when in Italy, remittances were far from safe. Cases of spouses and parents spending profligately savings arriving from America and intended for deposit were fairly common, according to the judicial records of several communities.[18]

### Channeling the savings

Of all the hurdles remittances had to overcome to arrive safely in Italy, the most difficult was at the assembly point in America, when immigrants surrendered the savings to an individual or an institution for safe transmission to Italy. Repeated abuses and loud complaints forced the Italian government to look into the matter. The controversy continued for years, the government achieving only limited results in correcting abuses. Immigrants could send their savings to Italy in three ways: through returning friends, through the mail, and through a banchista. The banchista was generally an experienced immigrant who had made a modest fortune in America and enjoyed some reputation. The banchista engaged in the business of transmitting savings to Italy. Some banchisti had been labor agents, who in time realized that there was more money to be made in the remittances business than in running employment agencies.[19] In most cases a banchista was an individual offering this services in connection with other services, like travel tickets, money exchange, legal and referral services.

Unfortunately, few of these individuals were philanthropists and many immigrants became the victims of their innocence and of the banchisti's frauds. As for returning friends, immigrants had two problems. First, very few people returned to Italy during the working season, that is March to October. Yet, families who depended on savings for survival could not wait until the end of the season. Second, southerners had problems in entrusting their savings even to friends. Lack of familiarity with the English language prevented Italians from using the United States postal service. Besides, postal clerks were generally annoyed at the small sums Italians used to send to Italy. The easiest way to send savings was, of course, the banchista.

Few Italians availed themselves of consular money orders. This service was restricted to immigrants in cities with consuls. And there were few such cities. For instance, in the entire southeast of the United States, there was only one consul in New Orleans serving Louisiana, Texas, Alabama, Mississippi, Florida, Tennessee, and Arkansas. In Argentina and Brazil poor roads and railroads made it virtually impossible for immigrants to use consular services. In addition, political differences and regional animosities kept immigrants and consuls apart. Politically, consuls represented the king of Italy. Many immigrants were republicans. Consuls were likely to be from the north, at least initially; in the United States most immigrants were from the south.[20] Many immigrants sent Italian currency. They purchased Italian lire at a premium in American countries, put the cash in an envelope and sent it to Italy by registered mail. Others sent gold coins, using a piece of cardboard with as many holes as the coins to be sent. The card was stuffed into an envelope carrying the label "pictures" to avoid postal inspection. Notwithstanding losses that obviously could not be reimbursed and warnings from the government not to send cash or coins, this system was quite popular and unfortunately it gave origin to many regrets. The major advantage of sending currency was that families in Italy did not need to go to an exchange office, a procedure that could jeopardize secrecy.[21]

The bulk of the remittances was handled by the banchisti.[22] Because of his previous experience and social prestige, the banchista was the natural choice by immigrants who needed to send their savings to Italy. Many banchisti were travel agents who owned the only safe in the neighborhood. Immigrants deposited their savings with them until savings would be large enough to warrant being sent to Italy. It did not take long before an agent had a "nucleus of banking business and adopted some banking functions." To immigrants, the banchista was preferable to American banks, as the Immigration Commission discovered in 1910. American banks fared poorly with immigrants for several reasons: ignorance of immigrant ways, lack of sensitivity, and especially the "ability and willingness of immigrant bankers to perform for their countrymen services that it would be impossible to obtain otherwise."[23] Immigrants trusted the banchisti. They provided a number of services. Banchisti spoke English, they knew local politicians, they controlled jobs, or knew of available jobs, and especially they were familiar with American ways. Banchisti were willing to go and talk to judges and school principals. In desperate cases, they were expected to help out of their pocket. If they obliged, they had the unlimited trust of immigrants. With bosses and *padroni*, banchisti were leaders in Italian communities.[24]

Banchisti transmitted savings to families through Italian banks. Typically, a banchista secured accreditation with a specific Italian bank by posting a sizable security. The most respectable banchisti did business with accredited banks, like the Banca Commerciale, the Credito Italiano, the Banco di Sicilia, and the Banco di Napoli. But most banchisti dealt with private banks to avoid controls. The largest such bank was the Meurikoffe and Co. in Naples, handling from 30 to 50 million lire a year in savings by the end of the century.[25] Several hundred banchisti from North and South America did business with it. Small private banks in Naples, like the Casa Bancaria Ferolla, the Banca Italo-Americana, the Banca Tocci, the Casa di Francesco Zanolini, and the Vincenzo De Luca and Brothers serviced from 30 to 50 banchisti each. Some private banks operated also in Genoa, like the Casa Passadore. A few banks were to be found in Palermo, Lucca, and Milan. These banks were generally more efficient and provided faster services than the Italian postal system. Once banks received the money from the American banchista, they issued a money order to the name of the payee and sent it by registered mail, with a receipt to be signed by the payee. The receipt was returned to the Italian bank, which transmitted it to the banchista in America, to be presented to the original payer as proof that the transaction had occurred.[26]

The efficiency and reliability of the services available to transmit savings to Italy varied from nation to nation. Immigrants in cities could count on better and faster services than those in remote areas. For instance, Italians in Buenos Aires enjoyed perhaps the most effective and safest service, since their savings were handled by "eight solid Italian banks" established by Genoese merchants since the first half of the nineteenth century. Besides, regular shipping services between Buenos Aires and Genoa kept the transmission of savings in Italian hands. But Italians outside Buenos Aires ordinarily sent their savings through the mail, with obvious losses. Notwithstanding pressures from Italian consuls, the Buenos Aires Italian banks refused to open branches in smaller cities to handle immigrant savings.[27] Italians in Brazil were not well served. The international money order service was not available to them. Italian banks in Rio and São Paulo were generally unwilling to handle immigrant savings. Besides, they did not enjoy the trust of Italians. Most savings from Brazil were sent in Italian currency by registered mail. But the Brazilian postal service refused to refund, even in cases of loss. Consuls in Brazil called for the establishment of exchange offices to avoid the exorbitant rates charged by Brazilian banks. But the Italian government had no funds to underwrite the project. Immigrants in remote areas of Brazil faced insurmountable problems created by distances and the unreliability of the Brazilian postal service.[28]

Italians in the United States relied on a variety of services. Money orders were safe and efficient. But language was a major problem because postal clerks rightly expected to be addressed in English. American banks refused to handle immigrant savings because they were too modest to make a profit. Under the circumstances, the banchisti handled the bulk of the remittances. An 1897 survey by the Department of Labor counted 150 immigrant banks in New York, mostly on the West Side and on Mulberry, Mott, Elizabeth, and Spring streets, with so-called branches in other parts of town. A banchista needed no capital to open a bank; neither did banchisti seek legal incorporation or comply with governmental regulations.[29] The banchisti's main concern was to impress illiterate immigrants by giving their operations impressive names like Banca Roma, Banca Italiana, and Banca Abbruzzese and by displaying in their offices a sample of European and American currencies. Banchisti offered a variety of services, like notarization of documents, legal assistance, steam and railroad tickets, mailing of packages to Italy, and confidential investigations both in New York and in Italy, an important service for immigrants with wives in Italy. Gambling and prostitution too were not beyond the control of several banchisti.[30] Manhattan was not the exclusive area of operation. Brooklyn, with the second largest Italian community in the United States, hosted about sixty immigrant banks. Philadelphia had twenty-five, some operating with false accreditation. Boston had about fifteen. New Orleans, St. Louis, Chicago, and Providence, to quote only the most important cities, had several banks. San Francisco was the exception. Italians in that city enjoyed banking services comparable to those of Italians in Buenos Aires.[31] According to a United States estimate, 2,625 immigrant banks operated in the United States at the beginning of the century: 684, one in four, were Italian. They were located in 146 cities and serviced a population of 1,328,000 Italians.[32]

*The abuses of the banchisti*

On both sides of the Atlantic, public opinion became increasingly concerned over immigrant banks. In the United States the alarm was triggered apparently by blatant abuses. In reality there was also a growing concern over the millions of dollars leaving the country every year, and perplexities over the refusal of American banks to handle immigrant savings. In Italy the concern was generated by countless complaints by immigrants defrauded by banchisti and by the realization that the orderly flow of remittances from America to Italy was vital to the national economy. Protracted abuses by the banchisti, some argued, could undermine the immigrants' trust and perhaps force them to invest their savings in the United States, a result to be avoided at any cost.

In the United States, the abuses of banchisti, often by embezzlement, were initially guarded as secrets within Italian communities. Immigrants, although badly hurt, were reluctant to admit that they had been taken advantage of.[33] Eventually some rumors reached both Italian and American presses. Investigations by reporters revealed that some banchisti had failed through reckless investments, others through circumstances beyond their control. In early 1900, for instance, an average banchista handled from 10,000 to 20,000 dollars in cash every three months. Immigrants deposited with him their savings at the end of every week, until they were large enough to be sent to Italy. Banchisti realized that they could use the cash at hand for their investments, with the expectation of a quick return. If the investment was unsound, savings were lost and the banchista took off in a hurry to avoid legal prosecution. Some banchisti left the country even without failing. They simply ran off with the cash at hand, ordinarily heading for South America.

Immigrants were generally unable to substantiate their claims. Banchisti did not volunteer receipts for every deposit. And immigrants were reluctant to ask for a receipt they could not read. Besides, prosecution was almost impossible, once the banchisti left the country. In 1894, for example, four banchisti embezzled about 200,000 lire (or 50,000 dollars) by leaving Boston for unknown destinations. In 1895 eight banchisti vanished from New York, and four others failed. The following year twelve banchisti took off. In 1908 a respected banchista in New York escaped to Brazil. At that moment he was handling 315 accounts worth 35,000 dollars. He was arrested in Brazil and extradited. But the prosecution had a difficult time in proving the charges. Depositors were reluctant to press charges, either because they had no passbook or because they were embarrassed by their error in judgment. Finally the banchista was convicted on the testimony of a woman who had deposited 120 dollars to be sent to the Banco di Napoli. She still had the receipt for the money, which never reached Naples, as it should have.[34]

State legislatures tried to stop the abuses by passing legislation to regulate private banks. Massachusetts opened the way in 1905. In 1910 New York followed suit. Banks, even private banks, had to be approved after posting as security at least 10 percent of the regular deposits, for no less than 5,000 dollars. Agents of foreign banks were not allowed to keep for over a month the savings of patrons with permanent residence in the United States.[35] The New York law directly disciplined immigrant banks and indirectly favored American banks. Italians in Italy praised the efforts to protect immigrant savings against abuses. But they reacted negatively to the enhanced position of American bankers, as a possible threat to the flow of remittances and a first step to convince immigrants to invest in the United States. American bankers, finally aware of the aggregate potential of immigrant savings, were not the only group supporting the legislation. Even some prominent Italian bankers, like A. P. Giannini in San Francisco, founder of the Bank of Italy, now the Bank of America, supported the idea that Italians should invest in the United States Giannini argued that by investing their savings in America, immigrants would finally settle permanently in the United States, an outcome he openly favored. Of course, Giannini was aware that a stable Italian population in San Francisco was the greatest blessing for his bank, already skillfully marketed as the bank of the small saver.[36]

Nationalists in the United States, traditionally opposed to temporary Italian immigration, not only supported state banking laws, but lobbied for an additional postal savings federal law to create American postal savings banks, quite common in Europe since the mid-nineteenth century. Their goal was to entice immigrants to keep their savings in the United States "in order to direct them into the active channels of American industries," as an American document put it.[37] The implementation of the federal Postal Savings Law, passed in 1910, was greatly helped by the nationalism stirred up by the outbreak of World War I. Investing in America, immigrants were told, was the patriotic way.[38] Some indicators show the impact of the federal law. In 1913 the Postal Savings system handled 33 million dollars, in 1919 167 million; 70 percent was deposited by immigrants, who numbered 50 percent of all the depositors.[39] Seemingly, the Postal Savings Law altered, to a degree, the temporary nature of Italian immigration, as

Giannini had hoped. Rates of returns declined drastically after 1911. Progressively, Italians, instead of channeling all their savings to Italy every few weeks, began to deposit them in American post offices and in time invested them in real estate or in a family business in the United States.

Complaints filed by Italian consuls in the United States and interrogations to the government by families in Italy made the Italian public aware that the transmission of remittances was plagued by serious abuses. Eventually the Italian press made available in Italian translation articles published in the United States. For instance, in 1897, *La Riforma Sociale* carried an article by John Karen, originally published in the "Bulletin of the Department of Labor."[40] Beginning in 1902, the yearly reports of the Banco di Napoli to the Italian legislature never failed to mention the shady activities of the banchisti, especially in the United States.[41] Similarly, beginning in 1901, the Commissariato dell'Emigrazione published occasional reports on the activities of the banchisti in the *Bollettino dell'Emigrazione*.[42] And the prefects corroborated these findings by reporting that increasing numbers of families had suffered because of the banchisti's frauds.[43]

Interrogations in the Italian Parliament and editorials in the national press urged the government to take action. The U.S. government too asked the Italian government to discipline the activities of the banchisti. Respectable Italian banks in the United States advised the Italian government that the banchisti were undermining the confidence of all immigrants in the banking system. To deal with this increasing problem, in 1894 the New York Italian banker Cesare Conti made the proposal of a convention between his bank and the Italian postal service to guarantee the safe transmission of immigrant savings. To insure a reliable service, Conti was willing to post as security whatever amount the Italian government would deem necessary. Two years later, professor Enrico Ambauer suggested the creation of a new Banca Coloniale with central offices in Rome and branches in the countries of mass Italian emigration, with the dual purpose of accepting savings from immigrants and transmitting remittances to Italy. In the same year the Banco Italia-Brasile volunteered to become the Brazilian correspondent of the Banca d'Italia, in case the central Italian bank would open overseas branches to serve immigrant needs.[44]

## Protecting the immigrant savings

In Italy the public discourse centered on the most effective plan to protect immigrant savings. One of the earliest plans was presented to the Italian Minister of the Treasury in 1896 by Francesco Saverio

Nitti, a long-time observer of Italian emigration.[45] Nitti proposed the foundation of a new bank, the Banca Italo-Americana, with central offices in Italy and branches in the countries of immigration. He was aware that the proposal of a new bank would encounter opposition, because bank failures in Italy had been almost a regular occurrence. Several banks had failed in 1888, for instance, when Italy and France had engaged in a tariff war. Others folded in 1892–3 because of the international recession and reckless speculation in real estates by some bankers. But, Nitti argued, the new bank was destined to succeed for the very same reasons others had failed. The protracted economic downturn in Italy was forcing large numbers out of the country. They were to become the depositors in the new bank. There were two reasons why the bank was destined to have a long life. First, population increases and limited economic resources would force Italians to emigrate for decades. Perhaps some American countries would close the doors to Italians. But Italians had shown resilience in creating new destinations when previous destinations had closed. Second, Italians were determined to return, and that determination was not likely to change in the near future. The bank would be a necessity as long as that determination continued. Nitti was aware that the average immigrant had only small savings; but he was cognizant that their aggregate was impressive. In his computations, in 1895 alone 70 million lire had entered the country from the United States.[46]

Nitti's plan was quite specific as to the economic potential of Italians in America. Obviously, the main branch of the new bank was to be located in New York to force the banchisti out of business. In the first year the New York branch could handle as much as 20 million lire in remittances and 30 million lire in savings. In addition, branches had to be opened in cities with large Italian communities, like Philadelphia, Boston, Chicago, and perhaps Kansas City. As for Brazil, a branch had to be opened in Rio de Janeiro or "even in São Paulo, the focus of Italian emigration to Brazil," with the dual purpose of undermining the power of the local banchisti and generating about 30 million lire in business every year. Argentina was not to be forgotten, although its economy was undergoing a recession. Nitti lamented that although Italians in Buenos Aires had some respectable banks, banchisti with questionable credentials handled a disproportionate volume of remittances. In this specific case Nitti suggested not to open a branch but to work out an agreement with one of the existing Italian banks. Branches were to be provided for Italians in Uruguay and Paraguay.[47] But what about Italians in other cities? And they were the majority. Nitti suggested that the new bank select one or more correspondents in every locality with a sizable Italian community.

Certainly, he concluded "there will be some honest people among Italians, whom immigrants will trust more than the banchisti."[48]

The bank could provide additional services to immigrants and returnees. For instance, it could offer life and property insurance to returnees. This service was badly needed, especially after the shipwreck of the *Utopia* and *Maria Pia* with no survivors. The main office and branches of the bank would accept savings, which, of course, needed to be invested. On this score, Nitti sensed a potential conflict. The bank could extend loans to Italians in America, but that was hazardous on two accounts. Those investments were financially risky, considering the temporary nature of Italian emigration. And they could also provide an incentive to Italians not to return, an outcome Nitti did not favor at all. To offset these two negative possibilities, Nitti suggested that two-thirds of the loans be made in Italy. The Italian economy would be the beneficiary. As for remittances, Nitti insisted on having them transferred to Italy as quickly as possible. Efficiency would increase the confidence in the bank both among immigrants and among their families. Remittances in dollars would be purchased by the Italian government in need of 15 million lire a year to buy American tobacco. Remittances from Latin America would be converted into francs and pounds to be used in trading with France and Great Britain.[49]

Although Luigi Luzzatti, minister of the treasury, received other proposals, Nitti's was the most comprehensive. Luzzatti used it as the outline for a bill he presented to the Chamber of Deputies in 1896. But there was a major change: instead of a new bank, the bill recommended that the service be provided by the Banco di Napoli, the largest and oldest southern Italian bank. The Banco had not been spared difficult moments during the critical years 1888–94, Luzzatti admitted to his colleagues. But the institution was now on a sound financial basis, Luzzatti added, because Nicola Miraglia, former director general of the Ministry of Agriculture, had been elected chairman of the board. The guidelines were strict. The bank could not make loans to immigrants in America. Two-thirds of the profits made by the bank in handling remittances had to be disbursed to the government to pay for other services to emigrants. The bank would open a handful of branches in major American cities and reach the other Italians through correspondents. And, once in Italy, remittances would be sent to families through the postal service.[50]

It took several years before the bill became law. The strongest opposition was mounted by the New York banchisti who resented the negative characterization and disliked the termination of a profitable business. But some Italian banks too expressed strong opposition to

the selection of the Banco di Napoli as the only bank to handle remittances. The traditional vagaries of Italian politics, with resignations
of prime ministers and anticipated elections, compounded this time
by the assassination of King Humbert I in 1900, contributed to the
delay. But public opinion eventually forced the government to act.
Reports from the United States were depicting an increasingly dete-
riorating situation. In late 1898, for instance, Ugo Oietti, during a visit
to the United States to report on the Spanish-American War, denounced banchisti as scoundrels in two letters published by the *Cor-
riere della Sera*.[51] Giuseppe Giacosa, Puccini's librettist, in another visit
to the United States denounced the sordid activities of banchisti and
deplored the ignorance of immigrants exposed to exploitation by their
credulity and suspicion. Unfortunately, Giacosa commented, the government was the major culprit because it showed no concern.[52] Ferruccio Macola, a visitor to South America, denounced the banchisti
in São Paulo as no less corrupt than those in New York.[53] All these
reports were topped by the news published by the *Bollettino della Sera*
on Sept. 18, 1889 that the New York banchista F. Paura had taken off
with the savings of several hundred immigrants. His whereabouts
were unknown, but was believed to be in Latin America.[54]

### A heated debate

Official Italy and New York banchisti went to war over the issue of
the bank. The attack from New York was swift. Alessandro Bolognesi,
a leading banchista and an agent for the Navigazione Generale Italiana, dismissed the allegations of Oietti, Macola, and Giacosa on the
ground that Italians visiting the United States for a few days were in
no position to pass judgment on a complicated subject. The banchisti,
Bolognesi argued, were the best friends immigrants had. There was
a problem, Bolognesi admitted, and that was the immigrants' ignorance. The government's responsibility was to foster public education
in Italy so that immigrants would be able to discriminate between
trustworthy and corrupted banchisti. The government, Bolognesi concluded, was overstepping its jurisdiction by centralizing the remittances service in one bank, simply because some bankers were
corrupted.[55] The controversy became so heated that it was picked up
by the New York press. Some newspapers, like *The New York Journal*
and the *Journal of Commerce*, supported the banchisti. They argued
that the Banco di Napoli wanted the monopoly of the remittances to
solve its cash flow problem.[56] Luzzatti's highly inflammatory language
against the banchisti was but a smokescreen to arouse public support
for the bill, as a New York newspaper added.[57] Other American news-

papers applauded the measure for integrity and efficiency. As one newspaper put it, the bill provided both the way to weed out corrupted banchisti and the structure to integrate all services into a chartered bank operating under governmental control.[58] Another newspaper called for the simultaneous approval of the bill under discussion in Italy and the Weeks bill under study by the New York legislature, to make all private bankers accountable under New York state banking laws.[59]

New York Italian newspapers generally rejected the accusation of dishonesty and the call for reform.[60] For instance, a newspaper featured an article written by "one of the most intelligent and trustworthy bankers in the city," as the newspaper itself put it. The writer argued that the accusations did a disservice to New York Italians by fostering among Americans prejudice and discrimination. The Italian government, the banker concluded, had the right to regulate savings in Italy; but the intrusion into the lives of immigrants outside the national territory was unlawful and unwelcome. After all, why should the Italian government, unable to provide jobs in Italy, claim jurisdiction over poor people at the time they began to make some money?[61] But the New York banchisti did not limit themselves to attack the bill in the press. They organized to defeat the government plan. At a preliminary meeting on March 22, 1900, fifty banchisti issued a declaration condemning the inflammatory rhetoric of Luzzatti and the pending bill. Some banchisti proposed the establishment of a trust to undermine any changes in the status quo. The proposal of a trust among banchisti was obviously a utopia, as a newspaper put it, because no banchista was willing to give up his autonomy.[62] The New York Italian press widely commented on the meeting and rejected Luzzatti's bill. The argument was that the banchisti were perfectly capable of policing themselves, as the meeting had shown.[63] The immediate result of the meeting was a telegram to Luzzatti, protesting the attacks and announcing a forthcoming position paper.[64] The telegram did not impress either Luzzatti or the Italian legislature. Nor did it alter the perceptions of banchisti by Italians in Italy.[65]

Although in the Americas, and especially in New York, the banchisti argued that the bill was not needed and indeed counterproductive, the common wisdom in Italy was that the bill did not go far enough. Nationalism was on the rise in Italy at the turn of the century. Nationalists pointed out that the issue of immigrant savings had to be more cogently integrated into the project of a colonial bank. After all, if Germany, France, and Great Britain, and even the Netherlands, had been so successful in setting up colonial banks, why should not Italy follow the example? Nationalists maintained that Italy needed a bank handling immigrant savings to promote the industrial, commercial, and financial expansion of Italy overseas.[66] More sober minds pointed out that a colonial bank was wishful thinking. Italy did not have enough capital even to take care of the most pressing domestic problems. There was no money available to be invested in colonial adventures. A colonial bank was out of the question, and the issue of remittances had to be dealt with separately.[67] Private bankers in Italy too, traditionally the correspondents of American banchisti, opposed the bill. They argued that the problem was in the Americas, not in Italy. The solution was to request the banchisti to post a security as demanded by American law and to require every banchista to be approved by the Italian government.[68] This counterproposal did not encounter more sympathies than the previous ones. In the end, the Italian Chamber of Deputies voted the bill into law on Dec. 11, 1900, followed by the approval of the Senate on Jan. 31, 1901.[69]

### The role of the Banco di Napoli

The implementation of the new law encountered great obstacles and its effectiveness was limited. In 1907, for instance, the first International Congress of Italian Immigrants lamented the poor performance of the Banco di Napoli, a remark reiterated in 1911 by the Second Congress, with the recommendation that the government take additional steps to protect immigrant savings. According to a survey conducted in 1910, only one-fourth of the remittances reached Italy through the Banco, a poor performance in the light of the earlier expectations that the bank would handle from the beginning of its operations at least 50 percent of the remittances for overseas.[70] But those expectations were unrealistic, because the Banco had to face insurmountable problems.

The first problem was the geographical dispersion of Italians in North and South America. The second problem was the high cost of the service. According to the 1901 law, the Banco was to provide the service either by opening branches in large American cities or by nominating correspondents approved by the Italian Department of the Treasury. But to open a branch of the Banco in New York, Chicago, Rio de Janeiro, or any other city was expensive. Besides, American governments did not welcome the idea of a foreign bank in their territories which had the purpose of channeling immigrant savings to Italy.[71] On paper, the use of correspondents was to be less expensive and more effective. But the selection proved to be difficult, because each individual or institution could be approved only after a thorough investigation. Besides, every correspondent was requested to post a security with the Banco, an unacceptable demand to many foreign banks, otherwise willing to act as correspondents. The third limitation was the opposition of the banchisti. The Italian government was powerless in enforcing the law outside the national territory. In addition, most immigrants trusted the personalized help of the banchista more readily than the impersonal services of the Banco or one of its correspondents. Foreign governments too were obviously unwilling to assist in this endeavor, because its purpose ran contrary to their interests. And finally there was no legal way to stop the banchisti from sending remittances to Italy, either through private or chartered banks in Italy or through the mail.[72]

It would be wrong, however, to conclude that the efforts of the Banco were an exercise in futility. Certainly the events surrounding the whole episode show that immigrants were more willing to entrust their savings to dishonest but personally known banchisti than to safer but impersonal institutions. Besides, agents for the Banco soon found out that it was virtually impossible to provide the services mandated by law, because immigrants were scattered virtually all over America. After all, we should not forget that a united Italy was only four decades old in 1900 and its organizational apparatus was still in its infancy. In the final analysis, the control of banchisti over savings and immigrants indicates that Italian emigration and return migration occurred by and large as a premodern, almost tribal phenomenon, outside the bureaucratic and institutional channels of the modern state. The 1901 law and the Banco's operations were first steps toward introducing bureaucratic and rationalized services. If legislators and the Italian public at large were disappointed with the results, it was because of their limited understanding of traditional peasant culture. From our understanding of those years, the Banco's success in handling 25 percent of the remittances was an impressive achievement, and certainly an indicator of the modernization of Italian mass emigration.

The controversy surrounding the passage of the 1901 law brought about an indirect result, which, in the end, was more important than the actual service it provided. It focused the awareness of many Italians on the huge sums entering the country every year, and it originated a national debate over the use of remittances. The debate became more intense after 1910, as events signaled that a large percentage of the immigrants' savings were deposited in American postal savings banks, although the sums entering Italy were larger than ever. American governments were actively pursuing a policy of encouraging immigrants to invest their savings in America. And a number of Italians began to send for their families instead of returning every few years or every winter for a visit. It was obvious that for a number of Italians the American experience was changing from a temporary stage to a resettlement of indefinite duration.[73]

*Remittances: 1860–1925*

It is difficult to assess how much money immigrants sent or brought back to Italy, both because savings returning with immigrants went unreported and because Italian data on remittances are unsatisfactory, at least until 1921.[74] Notwithstanding these shortcomings, we should try to assess how much money entered the country. This research is important for several reasons. It shows the steady growth, at least until the mid-1920s, of remittances. It documents yearly fluctuations determined by the expansions or contractions of American economies. It points out how changes in destinations were results of variations in economic opportunities available in Europe and in the Americas.[75] Eventually remittances became one of the major entries in the Italian balance of international payments, together with revenues from tourism. By the early 1900s, emigration had become one of the major "Italian industries."[76]

During the 1860s a large share of the remittances came from France. For example, in 1861 remittances amounted to 13 million lire, one-third of them from France, then the main destination of Italians.[77] The following year they declined to about 10 million lire. Emigration to France declined as the process of political unification fueled hopes of economic prosperity in Italy. Three years later, in 1865, remittances increased to 41 million lire. Emigration had picked up momentum since late in 1863, when it became apparent that political unification was not bringing about the much waited economic renaissance. In addition, better political relations between France and Italy, after the disagreements of the early 1860s over the wars for independence, had paved the way to increased emigration to France.[78] The outbreak of the Franco-Prussian War in 1870 slowed down emigration to France. Remittances accordingly declined.[79] During the decade of the 1860s, remittances had grown substantially. In the first five years the yearly average was 21 million lire; in the second five years it was 52 million lire, a growth of over 100 percent. The growth was only partially the result of increasing numbers of emigrants and higher wages. It was also due to the devaluation of the lira. Although still relatively modest, remittances already made up 3 percent of the Italian balance of payments in the period 1861–5 and 5.5 percent in the following five years.[80]

Remittances from the United States were negligible at that time.

The largest savings came from France, with South America second, Northern African and Levantine countries came in third, and the United States a distant fourth. In 1870, for instance, 6 million lire entered Italy from non-European countries through consular money orders. Of these, over 2.5 million arrived from Buenos Aires, 1.5 million from Montevideo. Rio de Janeiro was the third largest contributor with over 700,000 lire. The largest savings from the United States arrived, of course, from New York – 340,000 lire – followed by San Francisco with 320,000 lire. But the remittances from the United States were smaller than those from Tunis, half a million, and Constantinople with over 350,000 lire. Naturally, Leone Carpi, who gathered these figures, predicted that the economic future of Italian emigration was in South America, especially in Brazil and Argentina.[81]

Remittances increased substantially in the 1870s, the yearly fluctuations caused by internal and international events. In 1871, for instance, remittances declined to 52 million lire from the 63 million of the previous year. The major cause was declining emigration to France after the defeat by Prussia and the unfavorable exchange of the franc in Italian markets.[82] But the downturn was only temporary. In 1873, 73 million lire were sent to Italy, an increase of 10 million over 1870. As emigration to France kept declining, Italians were discovering new opportunities in Germany. The German victory over France and the ensuing war indemnities paid by France created confidence in the future of Germany and expanded investments there, followed by a substantial increase in wages. Even Italian exports to Germany increased substantially in 1873 and 1874.[83] The German boom was short-lived, however. By 1874–5 the German economy was in a recession, an unfortunate downturn that affected also other European nations and the United States as well. Accordingly, Italian emigration to Germany declined. Notwithstanding these fluctuations, more Italians were leaving in absolute numbers and remittances were increasing.[84] The European economic recovery, which started in 1876, had a positive impact on Italian emigration and remittances, which reached the 108 million mark in 1876. Emigration declined in 1877, when the Italian government required every individual applying for a passport to show proof that he had the money for travel and some additional funds to get started.[85] Eventually Italians adjusted to or evaded the new law, and emigration picked up momentum in 1878 and 1879, with a consequent increase in remittances: 115 million lire in each of the two years 1878 and 1879, and 127 million in 1880. In the 1876–9 period the average yearly remittances totaled 114 million lire, over 100 percent increase over the previous decade.[86]

This rapid increase leveled off during the following five years. In

1881, for instance, remittances totaled 144 million lire, and in 1885, 145 million. The general improvement of the Italian economy, which started in 1870, had opened up opportunities at home, and emigration had declined. Imports of raw material as well as exports of wine and cattle increased. Tariffs set in place in 1878, highly protective of Italian textile industries, both created new jobs and increased state revenues. The optimistic outlook of Italian entrepreneurs led to speculative investments in urban real estate, especially in Rome, Florence, and Naples, mostly subsidized by major Italian banks backed by foreign capital. Unemployment decreased and emigration slowed down. The program of national improvements, and especially the construction of railroads, created additional jobs, further reducing emigration rates. The grand total of yearly remittances from abroad, however, did not decline. Although fewer people emigrated, higher wages abroad and a favorable exchange of German and French currencies contributed to keeping remittances to the level of 1880.[87]

The economic recovery was short-lived. The speculative boom in urban real estate collapsed. Several banks, including some of the strongest, failed. The Italian textile industry, notwithstanding prohibitive tariffs, could not compete with American and British imports. American farm products progressively invaded Italian markets and set in motion a long and painful economic downturn. Economic indicators showed that the new nation was ill equipped to compete with more advanced European nations and with the United States. The years 1883–1913 witnessed the largest mass emigration of Italians. Average yearly departures climbed from 260,000 in the 1886–1900 period to 623,000 in 1901–13. The unprecedented and unexpected growth of the American economy, with its need for manpower and high wages, exercised the strongest attraction. Southern Italian emigration to the U.S. progressively outnumbered northern Italian migration to Europe. Even in Europe, major changes took place. In 1886, for instance, France was still the main destination of Italians, followed by Austria, Germany, and Switzerland. By 1913 Switzerland had replaced France as the main destination, with Germany second, and France third. The change in sex and age distribution of emigrants heading for European countries indicates that, at least from 1900 to 1910, Italian emigration was becoming almost exclusively seasonal, and the percentage of women and young people under fourteen declined.[88]

Remittances registered unprecedented yearly increases, especially from 1895 to 1913. The yearly average for the 1891–5 period was 254 million lire. In the following five years the yearly average climbed to 347 million. In the 1901–5 period, the yearly average was 691 million, and 846 in the 1906–10 period. Four major factors explain the unprecedented growth. More people engaged in emigration than before. Wages were substantially higher in the United States – then by far the preferred destination – than in South America or Europe. Southern Italians in the United States lived extremely frugal lives to set aside money as quickly as possible. And emigrants with some skills, better equipped for higher paying jobs, increased over the years.[89]

If the aggregate figures show a constant growth in remittances, yearly indicators point out that domestic and international events adversely affected the flow in some years. For instance, the increase in remittances in the 1886–8 period was the result of a larger number of emigrants, but also of a further devaluation of the lira. In 1889 remittances slightly decreased, both because large numbers of potential emigrants were drafted to fight the Abyssinian war, and because the United States discouraged immigration when its economy took a downturn and railroad construction slowed down. Emigration and remittances rose in 1890 and 1891. In 1889 remittances were 191 million lire, rose to 214 million in 1890 and 286 in 1891, a total that was unsurpassed until 1897. The decline in the 1892–5 period was caused by an economic recession in the United States brought about by high tariffs, inflation, and high rates charged by railroads. Departures for the United States declined from about 50,000 in 1893 to slightly over 31,000 the following year. Remittances likewise dropped from 246 million in 1893 to 216 in 1894. Two circumstances prevented a possibly bigger drop in remittances. New commercial treaties with Germany and with the Austro-Hungarian Empire opened up other destinations for Italians. And the increasing strength of foreign currencies against the Italian lira worked in favor of immigrants. By 1895 remittances covered about 15 percent of the Italian balance of payments.[90]

Renewed confidence in the future of the American economy affected departures, which rose from 38,000 in 1895 to over 53,000 in 1896. Remittances likewise increased from 240 million lire in 1895 to 273 in 1896. But the expansion was short-lived. On the one hand, the Spanish–American War discouraged further emigration to the U.S. On the other hand, the drastic drop in coffee prices together with widely publicized stories of exploitation of Italians in Brazil reduced both remittances from and emigration to Brazil. But the impact of the Brazilian recession was not as severe and long lasting as anticipated. In addition, savings from Brazil had been traditionally modest. Savings from the United States, although smaller than before, were still substantial, on account of a further devaluation of the Italian currency. In 1898, 333 million lire arrived in Italy, while the previous year remittances had amounted to 294 million.[91]

The concern over the Spanish-American War was dispelled by the quick American victory. Accordingly, Italian emigration to the United States increased to 63,000 in 1899 from the 56,000 of the previous year, 87,000 in 1900, and 121,000 in 1901. Remittances likewise jumped from 436 million in 1900 to 663 in 1901, the largest increase in a one-year period in the history of Italian emigration. Both emigration and savings remained high in 1902 and 1903. The following year there was a decline in the number of departures and savings. Emigration to France decreased because of a falling economy and reduced wages. The Italian government stopped emigration to Brazil both because of the economic downturn in that economy and because of some horror stories of abuses of Italians in coffee plantations. From the United States, over 150,000 Italians returned home, alarmed by the unstable economy and political uncertainties. Remittances were likewise affected. They declined from 634 million in 1903 to 589 in 1904. Notwithstanding the unprecedented emigration rates, the 1898–1904 period was relatively prosperous in Italy. Increased domestic production and stipulation of commercial treaties with the United States, Brazil, and France enhanced the Italian standing in the international economy. Remittances were a great help for the national economy. In 1897 they covered 16 percent of the international balance of payments, 27 percent in 1901, and 22 percent in 1904.[92]

Because the previous indicators are aggregate for the whole nation, it is impossible to determine how much money arrived from each country and when it was sent to Italy. For the years 1902–5, however, data collected by the Banco di Napoli and the Italian Post Office allow us a break down by country of origin and region of destination. The computation is based on international money orders arriving from the Americas through the Banco. Most of them were directed to the south. In addition, the computation is also based on money orders issued by European post offices, mostly directed to northern Italian regions. In 1904, for instance, when 589 million lire in remittances arrived in Italy, about 150 million (25.4 percent) were sent in money orders through the Banco or international money orders through the mail.[93] Of those, 150 million, 43 percent, came from the United States, 14 from Germany, 13 from France, 8 from Switzerland, and only 2.3 from Brazil and 1.78 from Argentina. As for the regions of destination, aggregate data for the 1907–25 period show that 17.9 percent arrived in the north, 8.6 percent in central Italy, and 73.5 percent in the south, Sicily and Sardinia included. In the north, Piedmont claimed the largest share, followed by Lombardy and Veneto; remittances in Liguria and Emilia were negligible. As for central Italy, the regional standing in declining order was Marche, Tuscany, Latium, and Umbria. In the south, Sicily was the leading region, followed by Campania, Abbruzzi, and Calabria. Puglie, Basilicata, and Sardinia had negligible remittances, Puglia and Sardinia being regions of very low emigration, and Basilicata a comparatively very poor region.[94]

These figures could be misleading, because they seem to suggest that almost three-fourths of all remittances arrived in the south. A partial explanation is that the United States paid higher wages than any other nation, and southerners were the overwhelming majority of Italians in the United States. Moreover, it was generally recognized that southerners abroad saved more than northerners. In addition, the low percentage of remittances arriving in the north is to be explained by the fact that northern Italians were less likely to use international money orders. They stayed abroad for one season and brought their savings back with them. Besides, the Banco di Napoli was virtually unknown in northern Italy. Southerners in the United States, on the other hand, were likely to be away from home from three to five years. Savings had to be sent back at regular intervals both to support families and to accomplish other goals. In addition, banks in the United States refused to handle the savings of immigrants because they were too small.[95] Finally, after the turn of the century, northern emigration progressively declined to the point that the industrializing northwest – the so called industrial triangle bounded by Milan, Turin, and Genoa – progressively turned into another destination for southern emigrants.

After these qualifications, it is safe to state that after 1900, remittances from the United States were larger than those from any other nation. According to an estimate by Francesco Coletti, for instance, remittances from the United States amounted to 465 million lira in 1907, with an average of 800 lire per immigrant; those from Europe totaled 85 million, or only 15 percent of the total. In the two years 1907–8, 420 million lire arrived in Italy through international money orders. Of these, 194 million were sent from the United States (46 percent), Germany came in second with 77 million (18.3 percent), France third with 57 million (13.5 percent), and Switzerland fourth with 46 million (10 percent). Not surprisingly, Italian emigration to the United States, the remittances from that nation, and the immigration policies of the United States became an increasing concern among Italians.[96]

After 1905 the bulk of the remittances came from the United States. The American economic expansion of 1905–7 attracted unprecedented numbers of Italians. In 1906, remittances peaked at 981 million lire, an all-time high, if we adjust the remittances of the following years for inflation. The 1907 depression slowed down emigration to and remittances from the United States. Emigration to Brazil too declined, while more Italians left for Germany, Switzerland, and France. In 1910, emigration to the United States picked up again and remittances increased from 736 million lire in 1909 to 899 in 1910. Remittances fell in the two following years: young men were drafted into the Italian army to fight in Libya. In addition, the economic growth of the United States slowed down. Italy discontinued emigration to Argentina be- cause of poor sanitary conditions aboard ships directed to that nation. The year 1913 marked the all-time high of departures with 873,000 Italians leaving. The American economy was expanding again and the Italian government had lifted the embargo on emigration to Argentina. Remittances totaled over one billion lire, 25 percent of the Italian balance of international payments.[97]

The outbreak of World War I substantially altered the flow of emigration and savings. Chronic unemployment disappeared in Italy. Young men were drafted into the army. Women, children, and old people took over the family farm. Able-bodied adults found jobs in industries. Accordingly, emigration to the United States declined. The lack of safety in wartime on the Atlantic was an overriding concern too. There was an increase in the number of women and children departing to join husbands and fathers in the United States, a safer place than Italy. Savings declined, but not proportionally to declining emigration rates. In fact, the American economy expanded at an unprecedented rate, first to provide help to the Allies, then to engage in war directly. Wages rose accordingly: the average Italian saved 18 to 30 dollars a month before the war; by 1917 he could save from 30 to 60 a month. Remittances increased from 624 million dollars in 1916 to 865 in 1917, and to 898 in 1918. But these figures were deceptive to a degree. High wages and larger savings did not keep pace with galloping inflation in Italy and Europe. Accordingly, the purchasing power of remittances declined by over 38 percent from 1914 to 1915.[98]

As soon as the war ended, Italian emigration resumed. Males outnumbered females four to one, young people below the age of fourteen were but a negligible percentage, and individuals departing with families were a small minority. Emigration was still a temporary phenomenon engaging young and middle-age men. But there was something new in the old pattern: more emigrants with skills. Remittances grew from 2.7 billion dollars in 1919 to 4.9 billion in 1920. Increased emigration and higher wages explained only partially the increase in remittances. Another reason was the increasing strength of the dollar, which rose from 6.33 lire in March 1919 to 13.21 by the end of the year, to 28.22 in December 1920.[99] In 1921 the economies of most Western nations entered a period of recession, mostly the result of the transition from war to peace production, social tensions fueled by the breakdown of the prewar social order and by unrealistic expectations of social reforms and of economic growth raised by the war. Departures from Italy declined and remittances dropped by 2.5 percent over 1920. When the recovery started in the second half of 1922, Italian emigration to Europe and the United States resumed. Remittances climbed from 4 billion dollars in 1922 to 4.3 billion in 1923.[100]

But the economic liberalism of the nineteenth century with its corollary of free flow of manpower was coming to an end. One by one immigration countries closed the gates. Canada excluded illiterate newcomers and immigrants with less than 50 dollars. The United States virtually put an end to Italian immigration with the National Origins Act in 1924. In Germany, entrepreneurs before hiring foreigners had to prove that native labor was not available. Switzerland devised an ingenious way of expanding and contracting the supply of foreign labor according to the demands of the national market. In addition, Switzerland made it virtually impossible for foreigners, children of immigrants born in Switzerland included, to obtain Swiss citizenship. South American countries had no need to establish quotas. Their declining economies discouraged further emigration. The fascist government, which took power in 1922, topped the restriction movement with a program of demographic growth. Leaving Italy became increasingly difficult. The world-wide depression that began in 1929 made all these restrictions almost irrelevant. Unemployment rose to unprecedented percentages even in the United States, a country traditionally suffering for shortage of manpower. Remittances accordingly declined from 4.6 billion dollars in 1926 to 2.9 in 1927, and from 2.3 in 1930 to an all-time low of 532 million in 1935.[101]

Undoubtedly remittances were one of the most important dynamics in the Italian economy and society during the half century 1875–1925. Remittances affected millions of individuals and hundreds of thousands of families. They raised high expectations and fueled a national debate on how to protect savings and channel them into a national purpose. Remittances became the most valid argument in favor of emigration among those who had nourished doubts about leaving. They generated the hope that the chronic shortage of capital, most noticeable in the small communities of the south, could be finally solved. They created a new industry in the immigrant bank, with an ambivalent record. They taxed the inventiveness of Italian politicians as to the best way to protect them. In the end, they were a national event of major proportions. Among Italians who had never been in America, remittances prompted a popular opinion still common in Italy that in America money grows on trees. America became a fantasy land, where getting rich was not a hazardous task, but a pleasant and relaxed pastime. But regardless of how difficult or easy it was to make money in America, returnees faced new and unexpected challenges in home communities. How were they to invest their savings?

# 7 Investing American savings

Senator Eugenio Faina wrote the final report of the Inchiesta Parliament, 1907–9. The Italian legislature had mandated the Inchiesta as a preliminary step toward a substantial revision and homogenization of land contracts in the south. Since the time of national unification, in fact, a number of economists and legislators had made the argument that any land reform in the south had to start with a revision of land contracts. Of course, southern landowners had strongly opposed the revision and had been able to kill any legislative effort to revise the contracts for over four decades. And even this time they were powerful enough not only to force the government to set aside any plan for the revision of land contracts, but to convince the members of the Inchiesta Faina that no revision was needed. The south was already on its way to substantial changes, landowners argued, thanks to emigration and return migration. The best course of action the government could take, landowners concluded, was to allow return migration and remittances to work their way into southern society.[1]

This chapter discusses the use of remittances by immigrants and returnees. Obviously this is a topic of great interest, which economists and political scientists are still exploring. There is no consensus as to the ultimate economic potential of return migration and remittances. In the specific case of Italian returnees, the profits from emigration were first used to subsidize emigration itself. Perhaps as many as one-third of all Italian emigrants borrowed the money for their first journey. Transportation costs and living expenses while abroad were carefully weighed by prospective emigrants. Profits were used to pay debts and to support families in Italy, as well as to maintain a small reserve of cash for family emergencies and a possible second emigration. Returnees were determined not to fall prey to moneylenders. But the great and ultimate goal was the purchase of land. The achievement of land ownership was like the passage through a golden door. In the mind of returnees, it spelled financial security and social status.

150

Of course returnees made their decisions within the range of economic and social opportunities available in their towns and the country at large. Investment opportunities were almost exclusively limited to land, especially in the south. And even those opportunities were poor in many southern regions. World War I and the social turmoil it generated opened up unprecedented opportunities for many returnees to become landowners. And returnees skillfully exploited those opportunities. Unfortunately the 1929 depression dashed the great dreams of most post–World War I returnees.

### Emigration: The great hope for the south

Observers like Faina, who applauded the positive impact that remittances had already had on the south and envisioned further improvements shared a major concern. American governments encouraged permanent immigration and naturalization. Italians were not immune to these seductions. Immigrants in cities were likely to be seduced by urban life. Immigrants engaged in farming, if successful, were tempted to buy land, a step toward permanent settlement and eventual citizenship. The role of the Italian government was to see to it that Italian emigration remain temporary. Faina concluded: "Emigration without return will be the ruin of Italy. Return migration and American savings will be the powerful levers the south needs for modernization. And no other region of Italy needs to join the modern world more desperately than the south. Government should make the goal of protecting emigration and return migration its priority, since the future of the south depends on them."[2]

To keep emigration temporary, Faina suggested the revision of the naturalization process for returnees and of military draft laws. Italians who became citizens of other countries lost Italian citizenship. It they returned and reapplied for citizenship, the process was lengthy and costly. Current legislation should be revised, Faina suggested, and double citizenship considered. As for the draft, young Italians living abroad had either to return to Italy for the service or to report to the Italian consul in their jurisdiction. Failure to do so resulted in a warrant of arrest effective as soon as the delinquent person set foot on Italian soil. Ignorance of the requirements of the law and distrust for consular officers prevented many young Italians from reporting. Their return became impossible, even after many years. Draft evaders were afraid of arrest upon arriving in Italy. Faina suggested that young Italians living abroad replace military service with some community service, preferably on behalf of other immigrants.[3]

Faina's conclusion that return migration was changing the south and that the Italian government should leave the south alone sounds surprising to us today, if we keep in mind that the report was written in 1909. By that time the generally shared political wisdom was that classical economic liberalism had to be corrected with some form of governmental intervention in economic and social matters. Instead, Faina and his team insisted that the government had failed in the south. The social and economic recovery of the region was going to be the result of the free market, Faina argued. Southerners would accomplish the change on their own, if only the government let them alone. The role of the government was to protect and expand the freedom of movement, so that Italians could go and return without restrictions. The invisible hand of the free market was accomplishing in the south a modernization the government had been unable to set in motion.

Southern Italian historians have interpreted the Inchiesta Faina as a political document sealing the final demise of the south. Return migration and remittances provided the excuse to abandon the south to itself. And, of course, the outpouring of moral indignation among southern Italian historians is as strong as the belief that political expediency dictated the conclusion.[4] Perhaps these historians think that the writers of the Inchiesta had a deeper understanding of the situation of the south than they actually had. On the one hand, the writers of the Inchiesta realized that national resources were limited. The special legislation in favor of the south had been largely ineffective; and nobody disputed that conclusion. In addition, in international markets Italy needed to increase industrial exports produced in the north. Besides, the political support for special legislation and financial help in favor of the south had quickly eroded in the north. The south could not be helped, as the common wisdom in the north put it. Or, at least, the south could not be helped through governmental programs. On the other hand, it was apparent that return migration was having a big impact on the south. And nobody disputed that observation either. The writers of the Inchiesta were old enough to remember that only a few decades before the common wisdom was that the invisible hand of the free market was the best agent of change. It is not unlikely that these gentlemen came to the conclusion that return migration was exactly one of those circumstances where the invisible hand of the free market was in fact working. But, regardless of how they reached the conclusion, the national debate focused on return migration and savings as the best agents of social and economic change in the south. The shared wisdom was that if every returnee was in better economic condition, the whole south would, in the end, be more prosperous.[5]

*The debate over return migration*

Since the days of the Inchiesta Faina, many scholars have explored the impact of return migration and remittances. This exploration had become more pressing in recent decades because return migrations have become a worldwide phenomena.[6] If we restrict our inquiry to the last twenty-five years, we notice sharp changes in the very basic conclusions reached by scholars. Well into the 1960s economists almost took for granted that the massive outflow of workers from underdeveloped countries and the remittances they sent to their families would be beneficial to original communities. Relief from unemployment, inflow of foreign currency to be used for family consumption and personal investments, returnees with improved skills and modern attitudes are some of the benefits envisioned for the countries of origin.[7] Since 1975 this view has been challenged. Mass departures of young workers, so the new argument goes, induce additional unemployment and fuel further emigration. Remittances provide private gains to individuals; but they also generate inflation, which ordinarily affects adversely those who do not emigrate. Returnees contribute little to the development of sending communities. Rather, they become social and economic burdens, as their reinsertion in the labor market proves quite often difficult. The conclusion is that emigrants in the long run are detrimental to the development of sending countries.[8] Today, the common wisdom seems to be that although the personal benefits to be derived from temporary emigration are unquestionable, the social benefits are less obvious. The central question in the ongoing debate is: are temporary migrants, return migrants, and remittances positive dynamics – and if so, for whom? Other students debate as to whether sending or receiving countries derive more benefits from the phenomenon. And the final question is quite broad: does return migration in the end retard indigenous economic development?[9]

Regardless of the conclusions reached, most economists today agree that "the maximization of individual private objectives is not necessarily consistent with the maximization of the broader objectives of society."[10] In personal terms, unless information about conditions in the prospective country is incorrect, incomplete, or uncertain immigration results in individual improvement measured in more money. The cost might be high, especially for emigrants with families, but individual emigrants feel that perceived benefits exceed perceived costs. In structural terms, however, there is no reassurance that individual benefits, even when substantial, will become social benefits. Returnees might pursue goals generally detrimental to the larger wel-

fare of society. Scholars call this variance between personal and structural components "externality," that is, the divergence between
private and social costs and benefits.[11]

Let us illustrate this concept of externality with a specific case. In
an analysis of return migration to the countries of the Mediterranean
basin today, W. H. Bohning concludes that, although temporary emigration solves individual problems, there are few indications that
remittances and returnees are positive dynamics for developing countries. For instance, the departure of the most able-bodied people from
rural societies, although relieving unemployment, has some adverse
consequences: productivity declines, wages increase, savings channeled into farming are used unintelligently, inflation rises, and the
introduction of new consumption patterns fails to replace old habits
inhibiting development. In addition, return migrants as bearers of
development and modernization prove to be a myth. While working
abroad, emigrants are generally marginal and certainly unable to absorb the culture of the host country. Once back, they are reabsorbed
into the old culture with no desire or ability to change it. Bohning
discards even the argument that returnees with better skills are an
economic resource for urban labor markets. In most cases, he argues,
the skills acquired abroad are minimal and for a specific production
technique. In the home country, techniques are likely to be different
and the training acquired in the countries of immigration proves to
be irrelevant. Bohning does not deny the personal benefits to be
derived from temporary emigration and savings as desirable dynamics
for developing countries. But he concludes that only governmental
regulations from sending and receiving countries can correct the "ex-
ternalities" inherent in emigration, return migration, and remittances.

Of course, most of the literature put out by economists and political
scientists is prescriptive. The goal of these scholars is to find a general
model to integrate the dynamics created by return migration and
savings with the general dynamics of the countries of emigration and
to recommend specific political and economic courses of action. Historians do not share this goal. The past cannot be changed. But the
task of the historian is equally challenging. He must analyze how
returnees with their savings had an impact on the larger social and
economic dynamics of the original communities. In this specific study
the ultimate purpose is not to assess why return migration failed to
bring about a spectacular modernization of the south, as Faina and
many others had hoped. Rather, it is to analyze the larger parameters
within which emigrants and returnees made their choices. Emigration
and return migration were not isolated phenomena. Rather, they were
components of larger social and economic dynamics at work in Italy

at the turn of the century. In the end, returnees with their savings were shaped by their social and economic environment and, to a degree, they reshaped it through their American experience and the savings they brought back.

Five parameters should be taken into account in the analysis of the use of the money generated by emigration. The first is the cost of the process itself. Emigration and return migration had costs attached to them, and emigrants and returnees made a variety of decisions about the costs of their emigration. The second is the demographic and socioeconomic position of the household from which emigrants departed. Emigration occurred often at the peak period of family building, when consumption costs were increasing. The immediate needs of the family overrode any consideration or plan to invest for old age or for future generations. In other instances emigration occurred before marriage, with the goal of temporary savings without long-term plans. Finally in some cases, especially among children of returnees, emigration occurred with the clear idea of long-term savings to avoid another generational trauma. The third parameter is the nature and the maturity of the migratory process itself. Within a few years emigration from Italy became a mass phenomenon, with its set of unwritten rules and expectations. Once emigration acquired a momentum of its own, individuals joined it and accepted the benefits it provided and the costs it demanded without much questioning of the validity of the premises. Initially, for instance, each community selected two or more destinations and worked out its priorities, which later emigrants accepted without critically assessing their validity. The fourth parameter is the place of each community within the regional economy. Of course, returnees with savings had no choice but to make their decisions within the range of economic opportunities available in their towns. In most cases such opportunities were severely limited, as we shall see. Finally, the fifth parameter is the historical and cultural factors affecting returnees. Although emigration exposed Italians to other cultures, at least in very limited ways, most returnees made their choices within the frame of reference of the culture of the south.

## The costs of emigration

Emigration had several costs attached to it: transportation from original towns to ports of embarkation, the crossing of the Atlantic or the railroad journey for those going to Europe, living expenses while abroad, and the cost of returning. In addition, there was the loss of potential wages to be made in Italy. Obviously, those who in fact departed considered all those costs acceptable in the light of the high wages to be had abroad and the savings to be set aside in a number of years. But in the assessment of costs and benefits, the learning process was slow and the false starts many. In the end, however, most Italians had broader ideas about international labor markets, manifest and hidden costs of emigration, international fluctuations in wages, and decision-making processes. Of course, the psychological cost of emigration was carefully weighed before reaching a decision, and in many cases it discouraged prospective emigrants. Here, however, I am dealing with those individuals who, after accepting the psychological burdens of emigration, compared costs and benefits, and in the end concluded that benefits overrode costs.

Early emigrants did not enjoy the wealth of information made available to those who followed them. Some early emigrants were adventurers, propelled more by curiosity and restlessness than by clear knowledge about opportunities available in intended destinations. Others were individuals acting on impulse, with the scant information provided by the network of itinerant workers, like chimney sweepers or merchants of statuettes. Finally others left because no other choice was available to them at home. In time, however, savings started arriving and their appearance initiated a process of calculation and decision-making. Remittances from overseas had definitely a different impact than savings generated by traditional seasonal emigrations. Seasonal emigrations had been common in most regions for a long time. But those engaging in them could save barely enough to survive from year to year. Remittances from overseas, substantially larger, allowed individuals and families to make plans. It was that realization that transformed the selective emigration of the 1870s into a mass phenomenon within a decade.

Obviously the first task of prospective emigrants was to compare wages at home with those abroad. According to long-established peasant traditions, the new knowledge was codified in refrains. In Calabria, for instance, a popular refrain of the early 1900s was that a year in the United States yielded 1,000 lire, 600 in France, and 500 in Germany.[12] Letters from friends and relatives, of course, were the best source of knowledge about wages abroad. Southern prefects, for instance, reported that when letters arrived from overseas and were read by relatives in the public square, the question asked by bystanders was whether wages were going up or down.[13] The *Bollettino dell'Emigrazione* regularly reported monthly wages made by Italians abroad, the figures being provided usually by Italian consuls.[14] In the computation of wages prospective emigrants also took into account the number of working days per year. For instance, the initial preference for South America seems to have been prompted, among other things, by the realization that work was available in Brazil and Argentina for more days per year than in any Italian village. The United States, on the other hand, was less desirable from this point of view, because rigorous winters interrupted public works for as long as three months, especially in northern states. Eventually, however, southerners learned that more money could be made in nine months in New York than in twelve months in Rio de Janeiro or Buenos Aires. Accordingly, the southern American connection became less desirable, and emigration to the United States turned into a mass phenomenon.[15]

Transportation costs were a major concern for emigrants. Systematic abuses by Italian and other shipping companies and by emigration agents in the first years of mass emigration and complaints by individuals and public authorities forced the Italian government to set up a regulatory commission to monitor transatlantic fares. In 1903, for instance, the highest allowed fare from any Italian port to New York was 198 lire (about 60 dollars) and the lowest 150 (about 50 dollars). The highest fare for Brazil was 180 lire and the lowest 165, the highest for Argentina was 200 and the lowest 175. Over the years, through competition, fares came down by about 10 percent by 1906 on the New York route and 5 percent on the South American routes.[16] Obviously, the differences between the two routes were not substantial. But some historians have argued that southerners chose the United States because the North Atlantic fares were cheaper than the South Atlantic fares. That was not the case. The choice of the United States by southerners occurred for two interrelated reasons: the decline of the economies of Brazil and Argentina at the turn of the century and the prodigious expansion of the U.S. economy, with its substantially higher wages, than any other nation. Transportation costs, however, prevented southerners from heading for central and northern Europe. The ticket Palermo-Paris was more expensive than Palermo-New York. In addition, the profits to be made in France did not compare favorably with those to be made in New York. In the end, the United States became the preferred destination because of high wages, the cost of crossing the Atlantic being about the same, whether to North or South America.

Another cost of emigration was rent while abroad. Prospective emigrants were likely to pay little attention to this at the initial stage of mass emigration, concerned as they were with putting together the money for the crossing. But returnees invariably commented on the shock they experienced when they went hunting for a place to stay. Generally speaking, at the turn of the century, rents in the United

States were four times higher than those in large southern Italian towns. For instance, in New York in 1901 a single male could room and board with a family or in a boarding house for 3 to 4 dollars a week. Rent for a small three-room apartment was at least 7 dollars a month. Most Italians who rented a house or a larger flat paid from 15 to 20 dollars a month. To Italians these were astronomical costs, because in large and medium towns in southern Italy the average rent for a three-room house was 5 to 6 dollars a month.[17] In South America rents were more reasonable. Even there rents were substantially higher than in Italy. To offset these costs prospective emigrants secured addresses of relatives and friends to stay with initially. The overcrowding in Italian enclaves lamented by many Americans was the result of the immigrants' efforts to save on rents. This determination to save explains also the formation of Italian enclaves in American cities, generally located in areas with the most rundown real estate and the cheapest rents.[18] The same concern over high rents explains the frequency of return migration among Italians in the U.S. during the winter months as well as the rates of home ownership among Italians in the United States, when the flow back and forth began to subside. By 1930, for instance, in most American cities the percentage of Italian homeowners was higher than that of the general population.[19]

Food and clothing were less of a concern. And prospective emigrants were aware of what was in store for them. The Commissariato dell'Emigrazione regularly printed in the *Bollettino dell'Emigrazione* lists of food prices in the largest American cities. For instance, a report dated October 1901 from New York specified that a pound of beef sold for 10 to 12 cents, a pound of veal from 15 to 25, of lamb 14 to 16, of bread 5 to 6 cents, of fish 7 to 10 cents. Of course, the report could not omit to report the prices of some home items like wine and macaroni. F. Pratt, the New York consul who prepared the report, warned prospective emigrants in Italy that one pound of imported macaroni sold for 10 cents and a gallon of California wine for from 40 to 50 cents. With the exception of imported items and wine, other food prices were only slightly higher than those in Italy. The comparison of prices of clothing was more difficult, because most emigrants had never bought a suit in home villages, their clothing being homespun. Without giving specific figures, however, Italian government reports indicated that clothing in the United States was slightly less expensive than in Italy. Of course, reports concluded, these were the costs of food and clothing for the working class. For the person with money to spend, the U.S. market offered a much larger assortment than Italy did.[20]

Prospective emigrants added up all these costs and came up with some sense of how expensive emigration would be. New York was, of course, not only the preferred destination but also the city to be carefully monitored by those contemplating emigration. In a way, it set the trend for variations in costs and benefits. In the early 1900s, a single immigrant willing to live frugally by taking up room and board with a family or in a boarding house could live on 20 dollars a month. Individuals with families needed a small apartment, of course, either by themselves or to be shared with another family. And this was the rule among New York Italians. In the case of a four-member family, rent, food, and medical expenses would range from a minimum of 40 to a maximum of 60 dollars a month. If two families roomed together, the total for any single family would be, of course, less. Over a period of twelve months, the individual paying for room and board would spend 250 dollars; the expenses of a family would range from 480 to 780 dollars a year. Of course, there were several intermediate arrangements; but we can take the figure of 250 to 780 dollars a year as maximum and minimum for living expenses in New York. The cost of the crossing of the Atlantic had to be added to these expenses to have the grand total: 430 dollars for an individual and 660 for an individual with family, provided that the expenses for the crossing of the Atlantic of family members not be added to the total.

These were the economic costs of emigration prospective emigrants balanced against economic benefits. Incidentally, we should keep in mind that for most Italians the immediate economic benefit to be derived from emigration was the exclusive criterion for their decision. The economic benefits came from wages. And in this case too New York was generally used as the sample for American wages in general. In 1901, for instance, at the lowest end of the spectrum was the shoeshiner who made from 15 to 28 dollars a month, for a yearly total of 180 to 360 dollars. Above him was the ditchdigger with an income of 45 to 55 dollars a month, for a yearly total ranging from 540 to 780 dollars. At the high end of the spectrum were masons, woodworkers, and stone cutters, with wages ranging from 120 to 175 a month, 1,440 to 2,100 a year. In between there was a wide variety of semiskilled jobs, mostly in construction and food industries, jobs that paid more than digging ditches and far less than building houses; their average was from 70 to 95 dollars a month for a yearly total from 850 to 1,140. Because many Italians worked in construction in New York, they could count only on ten months of work, because of the harsh winters. Accordingly, the yearly wages of immigrants working in the open had to be adjusted downward.[21]

With these data, we can figure out how much money an unskilled

Italian working in New York was likely to save in 1901. Most Italians were single men, likely to board with a family or in a boarding house. Room and board was about 250 dollars a year. We can add some extra expenses of 50 dollars, although the evidence indicates that southerners in the U.S. lived so frugally that Americans found it hard to believe that anybody could survive on so little. The income of immigrants engaged in unskilled occupations (like ditch digging) and semiskilled (like construction laborers) ranged from 540 to 1,000 dollars a year. In the end, the lowest paid immigrant, provided he be employed constantly, could save 250 to 300 dollars, and the semiskilled could save as much as 700 dollars. Wages in southern Italy at that same time ranged from 400 to 600 lire a year, or 130 to 200 dollars. Prospective emigrants did not need to be schooled in economics to draw conclusions. First, an individual could earn three to seven times more in New York as an unskilled or semiskilled worker than as a field hand in southern Italy. Second, after paying for personal expenses, the same immigrants could save from 700 to 2,000 lire, an amount two to six times the total yearly wages of a southern peasant. Rounding up these figures, southerners expressed their newly acquired knowledge of economics in the refrain: "One year in America can net 1,000 lire." Prospective emigrants, as they assessed the economic costs of emigration, concluded without hesitation that emigration paid well. The fervor that conclusion created was documented by visitors, who reported that the determination to go to America had become like a fever or an obsession.

*Mandatory costs*

Before exploring what to do with American savings, prospective emigrants, immigrants, and returnees had to deal with the unpleasant reality of paying their debts, an unfortunate condition affecting most emigrants. A representative survey of Italian family budgets taken in the 1870s shows that over 50 percent of all small landowners were in debt, with higher percentages for day laborers. By the early 1900s, as another survey pointed out, the budget condition of the average Italian had not changed. Families were in debt to the grocery store, local merchants and money lenders. Local grocers extended credit to families, especially from March to August, when families ran out of cash and the new harvest was still a few months away. Local merchants loaned money only to landowners, with the stipulation that landowners would pay back at harvest time or lose the property. Families borrowed from moneylenders to cope with a family emergency, like a death or a protracted illness, or to celebrate in style a happy occasion like a wedding or a baptism. In addition, many emigrants had to pay back for the ticket to America. As many as 50 percent of the emigrants borrowed the money to buy the ticket, especially during the first years of mass emigration, when few emigrants could rely on prepaid tickets sent from relatives already in America. Historians have called this first mandatory use of remittances "to arrest the fall." There is no evidence of individuals escaping these obligations by going into hiding in the vast Americas. To meet these obligations was a question of honor that emigrants and returnees took very seriously. After all, everybody contemplating return knew that he would face social ostracism in town had he defaulted on these obligations.[22]

Other costs had to be met to prevent a second possible fall. Returnees were determined to avoid getting into debt again. Returnees with land, if wise, set aside some money to pay taxes, because repossession for tax delinquency was increasing all over the south at the turn of the century. The loss of one's farm was not only a financial disaster; it was also a personal embarrassment implying the demotion from the rank of gentleman to that of peasant. Moreover, several returnees set aside money for a possible second crossing of the Atlantic. Ample evidence indicates that even returnees determined to resettle in Italy had not escaped the seduction of America and cherished the idea of a second stage. To avoid the high interest rates to be paid on borrowed money to buy a ticket, they set aside some money for that eventuality. In addition, savings were set aside to avoid having to borrow money for family emergencies or family celebrations. For instance, returnees with children about to get married set aside money for the wedding, an expensive event in southern towns, because the amount of money spent established social rank and was the source of popular comments for a long time. Finally a small amount was set aside for the yearly celebration of the feast of the local patron saint. And this was done both by returnees in Italy and immigrants still in America. It was considered in bad taste not to send a donation to the local priest for the occasion. During the celebration, the statue of the local saint was carried in a procession. Devotees approached the statue and pinned cash on ribbons streaming down the head of the saint. Because the individual offering occurred in front of the whole town and ordinarily near the house of the person making the offering, the amount of the offering – ordinarily spelled out by the local band, which used different tunes for different amounts – was a way to establish social rank.

The determination of returnees to avoid falling into the hands of moneylenders requires some additional explanations. It played an important role in the overall planning of how to use remittances. Moneylenders were powerful individuals in southern towns, because the only two southern banks in existence at the time when mass emigration started – the Banco di Napoli and the Banco di Sicilia – restricted their operations almost exclusively to the cities of Naples and Palermo. Peasants and small landowners with little or no cash who fell on hard times had nowhere to turn but to moneylenders. Families planning special celebrations could have cash only through them. Individuals contemplating emigration could not make any plan until they got assurance from a moneylender that he would lend the money. Of course, this economic control of the cash situation in a community gave moneylenders incredible social and political power. Moneylenders were generally given all the proper signs of respect, because people without cash did not know when necessity might strike. In addition, moneylenders were likely to use the deference they commanded to be elected to political office. And through political power they further increased their economic control. The rates charged by moneylenders were high.[23] As late as 1905, when the flow of remittances was already substantial, the mayor of Monteleone in Calabria reported that rates ranged from 40 to 100 percent for the period of one year and 6 percent a month for short-term loans. Of course, many borrowers defaulted, an unfortunate occurrence which moneylenders used to increase their control. Perhaps as many as 50 percent of the southern emigrants were in debt to moneylenders at first departure.[24]

Returnees were determined to avoid moneylenders at any cost. Most returnees set aside some money for those emergencies for which they had been forced to go to moneylenders before. Ironically, some returnees did not stop there, but became moneylenders themselves. Aware that one of the fastest ways to get rich in a southern town was by lending money, some returnees became moneylenders in their own right. The prefects of Palermo and Cosenza reported that when this happened, the newly arrived moneylenders were likely to charge higher interest rates and be harsher about repayments than old moneylenders.[25] When the Inchiesta Jacini was taken, the issue of moneylenders, interest rates and political control of southern communities by moneylenders was widely explored. Interviewers were puzzled that remittances had not yet put moneylenders out of business. There were towns with savings ranging from half a million to one million lire. Returnees and their families could have established a savings institution where people in need of cash could go and borrow. Returnees resisted the suggestion. The explanation for the refusal, given by the mayor of Monteleone, was echoed by many other mayors:

"Why do people refuse to pull together to force moneylenders out of business? Because there is no social solidarity here. Everyone is convinced that he will solve his financial problems better by doing things independently." Perhaps the mayor was pointing out the strongest weakness of southern culture.[26]

To arrest the fall and to prevent a second fall were goals that many returnees were able to achieve. In fact, returnees of failure, although conspicuous, were only a handful. The average immigrant had to work for a year to a year and a half to achieve the goals described above. Then, emigrants could choose – an unprecedented luxury – what to do with the savings. Seemingly a better house was a common goal, although there were differences determined by location and age. Home ownership was a rather uncommon condition for southern peasants at the beginning of mass emigration. Younger returnees were more likely to invest in land, deferring to a later date the problem of the house. Older returnees, more likely to see their return as a retirement, invested in a new house and kept enough savings to suffice until their natural death. The goal of a house was more common in regions where rents were high, like Campania and Sicily, than in Basilicata and Puglie. Obviously rents in Italy were not as high as in the United States. But returnees were puzzled by the escalation in rents even in Italy, and seemingly determined to avoid the high costs they had been paying in the United States. For instance, between 1890 and 1910 rents in Augusta, Sicily, increased by almost 100 percent. Immigrants who showed up in Italy every few years for a visit were afraid that Italy too might go the way of the United States. To avoid unpleasant surprises, they purchased a house.[27]

Visitors invariably described how the houses built by the *Americani* – the name given to returnees – had changed the southern landscape. The traditional southern town was characterized by a densely nucleated pattern. Houses were built next to each other in one location, ordinarily on a high elevation. Houses in the countryside or in small hamlets detached from the center of town were the exception. Returnees selected an alternative place, only a few hundred yards from the old town. Although not far from each other, the new houses were built according to modern criteria. Each house was detached from the others, with land around. Some returnees also enclosed the property with modern fences. The new houses were easily identifiable: they were painted white, with blue trimmings. Visitors reported that many of them had running water – in towns where such facilities existed – and toilets, as well as some luxury items, the obvious sign that the owner had seen the larger world. Some observers voiced their disappointment at the ostentatiousness of some of these houses. But to

returnees the new house was to them and to others the outward sign
of the American success they wished to celebrate. After all, returnees
who could afford a house had been abroad for at least ten years.
Visitors invariably reported that when they entered the houses of the
Americani they noticed a portrait of President Theodore Roosevelt,
often flanked by a framed American dollar. As a returnee put it: "Our
capital is New York, not Rome and our king is Roosevelt, not the
monarch of Savoy."[28]

## The purchase of land

Younger returnees, who did not equate returning with retiring, used
their savings to get established. The choices, however, were limited.
The southern economy was almost exclusively agricultural, and virtually every opportunity one could think of had to do with land. The
acquisition of land properties became the paramount goal of many
returnees. A refrain put it succinctly: "Fare l'America è cumprare lu
campu." (To make it in America is to buy the field). The purchase of
land was a complicated task. In some areas there was little or no land
for sale. In other areas prices escalated so rapidly that returnees could
no longer afford it by the time they returned. Moreover, there were
few assurances that the purchase of land would automatically bring
prosperity. Competition from well-established and experienced landowners, lack of familiarity with farming techniques, and changes in
the economic and social structures of the south were only the most
obvious obstacles to a new career in farming. To understand the
dynamics surrounding the purchase of land by returnees we must
outline briefly the economic structures of southern agriculture and
the main changes that affected the south from 1875 to 1925.

Notwithstanding the termination of feudalism in the early nineteenth century and the changes promised during the wars for independence, the south joined the new nation with a land system that
was basically feudal. A small number of families owned most of the
land. These families enjoyed noble status and lived off rents. Medium
landowners, called borghesi, were few, their properties ranging from
20 to 200 hectares. Small properties, called particellari (small properties) ranging from half a hectare to 10 hectares were rare in several
regions, like Sicily, Sardinia, Puglie, and the Po valley. But in the
areas of the Alps and the Apennines they were the rule. Three main
events affected the south from 1875 to 1925: the sale of government
land in the 1870s and 1880s, the drop in commodity prices at the end
of the century, and the ungluing of the traditional social order during

and immediately after World War I. The cumulative effect of the three events was that the traditional order, although surviving, was shaken and significant changes were introduced. Returnees with their savings took advantage of the changes and tried, sometimes successfully, sometimes unsuccessfully, to become part of the process of change.

The sale of land by the government created several thousand new landowners and increased the determination to fight for land among those who were excluded. Immediately after unification, the Italian government placed on the market about 30,000 land properties from estates previously owned by the church, the Italian states, and municipalities. Financial and political considerations prompted the sale. The new nation needed the cash the sale of land could provide. Besides, the common wisdom of the time indicated that the new state would be stronger through the creation of a large number of small landowners. As several commentators put it, Italy was going to be a rural democracy, with small landowners as the main supporters. The sale was marked by corruption and mismanagement, with large landowners often purchasing the best properties. But, even under optimal circumstances, 30,000 small properties were hardly enough to satisfy the demand. Many peasants were unable to purchase for lack of funds, inability to secure credit and, often, shortage of land. But in the end, the sale increased the determination to buy. Because money was needed for the purchase, many peasants concluded, they would emigrate for a time to save the money they needed.

The drop in commodity prices created unexpected problems for the Italian economy, especially in the south. An increase in worldwide production and the internationalization of markets through cheaper and better transportation caused prices to drop. Rents and sharecropping agreements were affected. Large landowners saw their profits decline. In addition, increased expectations and declining wages among peasants spread discontent, which exploded in open rebellions, especially in Emilia-Romagna, Puglie, Tuscany, and Sicily. Large landowners sensed that the traditional deferential society was coming to an end and that neither their social status nor their economic security were safe. Finally foreign economic operators who had invested in Italy pressed the government to introduce some changes in the agrarian economy as the only way to stabilize a precarious social situation. Landowners developed a variety of strategies to cope with these pressures and control change. In some regions like the Po valley and Puglie, landowners learned modern techniques: direct management of the land, introduction of machinery, hiring of experts, formation of market cooperatives, and opposition to peasant demands for higher wages and better working conditions. Of course, they opposed emigration. Some were so hard pressed that they decided to sell.[29] Returnees did not let the opportunity go by. Medium landowners were even more adversely affected by the economic challenge and the social protest. Shortage of cash, inability to compete with large landowners, lack of social status and political power to cope with peasant unrest forced them into unpalatable choices. Some undersold. Some made a profit by selling to returnees. Others crossed the Atlantic to save money in order to preserve their properties. Medium landowners were perhaps the hardest hit in the process. In fact, northern landowners in trouble were given the alternative of moving to cities and looking for jobs in manufacturing. That alternative was not available to southern landowners.[30]

Small properties were adversely affected too, for different reasons. And owners developed strategies to deal with the challenge. Most such properties were located in the Alps and Apennines, although they were not unknown in the flatlands, especially around cities. The reason for their presence in mountain areas was that in previous centuries feudal lords had shown little interest for unproductive mountain properties. Family ownership had become the norm. But, throughout the nineteenth century, through partible inheritance such properties had been subdivided into small entities of little economic value. Testimonies abound of individuals going to court over the inheritance of one olive tree or two vines. Peasant unrest did not affect these properties. Declining commodity prices did. But the owners of such properties had been in trouble even before the changes I describe here. Even in the early nineteenth century, for most of these landowners, temporary migration was the only way to make ends meet. Declining commodity prices, in addition to declining opportunities in temporary migrations, forced changes. Some owners, especially those with the most unproductive land, abandoned their properties. Others, especially northerners, replaced their seasonal migrations to Europe with seasonal migrations to Argentina, where wages were higher. Finally a number of them decided to purchase additional land to increase production. If prices were declining, they argued, increased production would offset the loss. At that juncture, overseas migration and the profit it made possible were embraced as means to purchase additional land.[31]

And then there were the peasants. The 1911 census counted 10 million of them, out of a population of 32 million. Their abysmal existence had been documented even before the social and economic changes of the late nineteenth century. And it got progressively worse. Declining commodity prices depressed wages, notwithstanding mass emigration. The expectation of land ownership became a reality only for a handful. Most peasants were caught between rising expectations induced by the promises made during the wars for independence and a declining economy. Of course, most of them could not understand the dynamics of international change. But they were aware that they were becoming poorer and more marginal. Violent upheavals followed, especially in the areas of large estates. The Italian government, which had previously pressed landowners to introduce reforms, promptly stepped in to oppose peasant demands and in defense of private property. And the peasants were made aware that there was no free land and no benefit for anybody without payment. The lofty promises of the past had just been promises, peasants finally realized. Any alternative interpretation of the promises of the government was labeled as naive. The army moved in and the peasants retreated, pondering what other alternative they had, if they wanted land.[32]

The economic downturn and peasant unrest brought about a number of changes. Some owners lost their properties either for nonpayment of taxes or for inability to make a living. Some owners introduced changes and survived. And the peasants vented their frustrations through strikes. But the changes were, at best, marginal, as the government came to realize in the early twentieth century, when it commissioned the Inchiesta Jacini for the south. The key issue to be explored by the commission was the agrarian contracts in the south. Because landowners had total control over contracts, no change would ever occur in the south, so the argument went, until landowners would be forced to written contracts with legal enforcement. Southern landowners reacted violently, threatening political reprisal. And the results of the survey were exactly in line with what the government wanted to hear. There was no need to reform land contracts. Return migration was bringing about spectacular changes. Southerners were solving the problem on their own. Government intervention was not needed. Obviously, the change was less spectacular than the survey led the Italian public to believe. Emigration, return migration, and remittances were having in reality only a cosmetic impact. But both government and public opinion were satisfied. And the south was back to business as usual.

World War I became a turning point, not in the military annals of Italy, but in the changes it brought about and the opportunities it offered peasants. The war provided legitimacy to their demands for land. It made available savings to purchase it. It unglued the old social order, by curtailing the power of large landowners and offering peasants some form of control over their destiny. Unfortunately the monumental changes made possible by the war were short-lived. By the mid-1920s, Fascism had restored law and order. But the 1915–25 decade was an eventful one. More land transactions occurred in that decade than in any other. More money entered the country in form of remittances than in any other decade. For a brief moment return migration and remittances seemed to play the determinant role in the modernization of Italy, especially in the south.

## The ungluing of the traditional society

War politics precipitated a sequence of events which enhanced the bargaining power of peasants. It all started in 1914, with the national debate whether Italy should enter the war or remain neutral. Supporters of intervention argued that the war would enhance national integration, do away with regionalisms, and make Italy an international power. Supporters of neutrality rebutted that Italy was unprepared for war and the loyalty of the peasants was in doubt. Peasants could hardly relate to the debate. But they knew that, in case of war, the burden of fighting would fall on them. The socialist slogan "Rich people cause wars and poor people fight them" found wide acceptance among peasants. Besides, even before Italy entered the war in 1915, Italians were adversely affected by the outbreak of hostilities in Central Europe in 1914. In that year half a million Italian immigrants had been forced out of belligerent Germany and the Austro-Hungarian Empire. Most of these returnees were unable to find jobs in Italy.[33] After nine months of debate, Italy declared war. The initial response of Italians was enthusiastic. They were promised a short war, a certain victory and a better economy. The reality was different. The war lasted four years; the humiliating defeat at Caporetto showed that Italy could in fact lose the war; and inflation coupled with increased taxation were the bitter legacies of the conflict. The opposition of the peasants mounted, prompted also by the realization that as peasants-soldiers were dying in the trenches, industry operators in the north were making handsome profits through war contracts.

To turn war events around, the government needed the loyalty and support of peasants. To this effect, the government used a strategy that had proven effective in previous times. Peasants were promised land in exchange for war services. "Land to the peasants" was the slogan. And peasants believed it once again. Peasants willingly shouldered the cost of the war; 100,000 killed in action, 200,000 dead from illnesses contracted in the trenches, 900,000 wounded, and 600,000 victims of the 1918 summer epidemics, 100,000 of whom died. Northerners put up with the ravages of the war in their territory. Southerners endured the forced arrest of emigration and the decline of remittances. In both sections, women and children replaced in the fields seven million men fighting the war. Italy, with the help of the Allies, won the war. As the end approached, peasants serving in the army prepared a bill to be presented to the government as compensation for war sacrifices.[34] Land opened the list of requests. Political parties promptly stepped in to support the request and drafted platforms on land redistribution. The Democratic Constitutional Party and the recently formed Popular Party joined the socialists in drafting a bill for land expropriation and redistribution.[35]

Veterans had cash to back their demands. Although inflation and increased taxation were the bitter fruit of the war, some groups benefited from the conflict. From 1913 to 1918 inflation rose by over 100 percent. A quintal of wheat, for instance, jumped from 30 lire in 1915 to 64 in 1919; a hectoliter of wine from 27 to 172, and olive oil from 150 to 450. Large and medium landowners living on rents were adversely affected notwithstanding the escalating prices of farm commodities. In fact, because the government did not allow rents to adjust for inflation, landowners with rental agreements of several years lost money. Wages escalated even more rapidly than inflation, however, because all able-bodied men were recruited for the war. Landowners who worked their properties through hired labor were adversely affected too. Moreover, taxes were more onerous for people with property than for landless peasants. In the end, many large and medium landowners were in financial trouble. Besides, they had to face a negative press, which indicted them for having caused the war. The military victory seemed to have generated little national elation. Of course, the distress of landowners was exploited by those whose image had been enhanced by the war. And the veterans were among them.

They were laborers, renters, and sharecroppers. Of course, many of them suffered because emigration stopped and remittances declined during the war. In addition, inflation hurt them badly. But these losses were compensated by government subsidies to soldiers and their families. Until March 1917 the yearly subsidy was 338 lire per soldier; after that date 565 lire.[36] Small landholders, sharecroppers, and renters were the individuals who benefited the most from the government subsidies. As men fought and their families saved the subsidies, women and children, in addition to old men, farmed the land with the help of soldiers on leave during the planting and harvesting seasons. Accordingly, the output of those family operations did not decline significantly during the war. Moreover, family consumption decreased because men were away and fewer goods were available.[37] Deposits in post offices and people's banks increased rapidly. For instance, from 1909 to 1913 deposits increased by 22 percent. The increase from 1915 to 1919 was 115 percent.[39] By the end of the war these small savers not only had more money than before the war, they were also claiming that they were entitled to preferential treatment because they had shouldered the heaviest burden of the war.

Enhanced economic power and improved social status provided these groups with the ammunition they needed to press for major changes. They demanded a new social order, based on property redistribution according to war efforts and the social function of each group. To make their point, peasants, renters, sharecroppers, and small landowners carried red flags in marches celebrating the victory. In some regions socialism became a cherished word and the Russian Revolution a social experiment to be seriously considered, even for Italy. The government was powerless in checking the revolt against the old social order. The transition from war to peace production, the financing of the national debt caused by the war, and the resumption of international trade seemed to be more pressing items than the demands of the veterans. But veterans disagreed with the priorities and timetables for reform the government was proposing. Socialists played a major role in this transition. They abandoned the original revolutionary stand and supported a new economic order based on individual land ownership, but with production and marketing cooperatives controlled by landowners and workers. With the support of the Socialist party, the most militant veterans rejected the governmental recommendation to rely on the legislative process for reform and took over hundreds of properties, especially in the Po flatlands and in the southern regions of Sicily and Puglie.[39]

Moderate parties stepped in to contain or end local violence that might threaten to erupt into a national civil war. The newly formed Partito Popolare of Catholic inspiration, for instance, rejected the unqualified redistribution of land but supported specific cases of land expropriation, especially of *latifondi*, and espoused a joint management of land properties by owners and laborers. A bill to this effect was presented in May 1920 to the Chamber of Deputies. But impatient peasants did not wait for the outcome. In the summer of 1920 violence erupted. Members of the White Leagues of Catholic affiliation took over properties in the heavily Catholic regions of Veneto and Lombardy, while members of Red Leagues of socialist affiliation engaged in even bloodier confrontations in Emilia-Romagna, Sicily, and Puglie.[40] Landowners asked for protection. But, seemingly, the central government was either unwilling or unable to maintain law and order. At the local level, authorities and police often publicly supported the violent takeovers. In some instances, local police provided protection to peasants as they marched from the town square, where they had assembled, to the properties they "repossessed" in the name of the people.[41]

The breakdown of law and order and the economic dislocations caused by the war forced many large and medium landowners to consider alternative ways to make a living. A very small number had their properties taken over by peasants, but later restored to them. A considerable number put their properties on the market in a hurry to avoid violent expropriation and probably bloodshed. In several instances, these owners undersold. More calculating individuals weathered the storm but concluded that times had changed and that the prewar social and economic order would never be restored. Accordingly, some made plans to sell as soon as the turmoil subsided. Others accepted the fact that they would be operating in a different social and economic environment. Landowners willing to sell had no problems in finding takers. Of course, very few individuals had enough cash to buy large properties. But there were many individuals with enough cash to make a substantial down payment on a small property. These buyers had accumulated money in two ways: part were remittances from America or Europe, part were savings from war subsidies. Immigrants who had kept their savings in the United States during the war promptly sent them to Italy, to take advantage of the favorable exchange of the dollar. In fact, the rate escalated from 8 lire in 1909 to 18 in 1920 and 24 in 1921. International money orders from the United States through the Banco di Napoli swelled from 249 million lire in 1918 to 498 in 1919 and 728 in 1920.[42] As the prefetto of Cosenza put it: "American savings are taking over our properties."[43]

The breakdown of law and order was short-lived. But the impact of the war had a lasting impact on Italian society. More land was placed on the market in Italy in the 1920s than in any other decade. And, seemingly, there were many good reasons to buy. Remittances and savings for war subsidies had to be invested to cope with galloping inflation. Rising commodity prices allured individuals into farming to make a quick profit. Banks were willing to lend money to individuals able to make a substantial down payment. Rapidly escalating land prices suggested both that land investments would be profitable and that one had to enter the land market as soon as possible to avoid higher prices. Of course, all these arguments proved devastatingly erroneous by the end of the decade. New landowners were caught in the spiral of declining prices, high mortgages, and the despair induced by a depression of unprecedented length and severity. The number of new properties defaulting was extremely high. For many, the overseas experience with its many years of sacrifice and saving concluded in personal and family tragedy.

Returnees with remittances took advantage of the opportunities created by three major changes affecting Italy from 1875 to 1925: the sale of state and church land, the agrarian depression and ensuing social unrest, and the social dislocations caused by the war. The end result of the three occurrences was that more land was placed on the market during those fifty years than at any other time in Italian history. And returnees were eager to buy. Of course, one could argue that returnees should have been, perhaps, more discriminating in assessing whether the purchase of small properties was the way to get established. In reality land was the only way to invest returnees were familiar with. Those who tried alternative ways of investing, such as real estate or retailing, were only a handful, as the Inchiesta Iacini pointed out. And their rate of success was disappointing. Lack of familiarity with alternative ways and the persistence of the old belief that the only lasting investment was land properties prevented most returnees from considering alternative investments. Returnees with remittances acted within the limited options available in a traditional peasant society undergoing minor adjustments. Of course, time was to show that these land investments had all the liabilities of traditional economies. When they were forced to face the competition of modern economies, they collapsed.

*Community dynamics*

Individual returnees invested their savings in home communities. Those who relocated to other towns with better investment opportunities were only a handful, as the Inchiesta Jacini revealed. Investment opportunities varied from town to town and from region to region. And those differences will be dealt with in the next chapter. Here I outline briefly some general patterns of investment at the town level. Land was the overall goal for younger returnees. But not all returnees had enough money to buy land. Besides, not every town had land for sale. Returnees with modest savings, generally individuals forced to return by family circumstances, became renters or sharecroppers. They purchased farming equipment and a donkey or a mule, which were prerequisites for moving up from the condition of laborer. In towns with no land for sale, several returnees with enough savings to buy land temporarily rented a plot, in the hope that land would be placed on the market at a later date. Some returnees headed for coastal towns where fishing had been a traditional way to make a living, often combined with farming. These returnees purchased a boat to be independent fishermen, whereas before they had worked as hired hands. Some returnees moved into food processing, like making pasta or producing olive oil. But they were only a few and generally unsuccessful.[44]

Returnees successful or lucky enough to find land had to confront a sequence of challenges for which they were poorly prepared. Ample evidence documents that many returnees spent all their savings in purchasing land. As they embarked on their new careers as independent farmers, they discovered they needed additional money to buy farming equipment and to make improvements on the land. Many rented the recently purchased property and crossed the Atlantic a second time to save more money. Inflation was perhaps the biggest challenge. Increased demand for land coupled with the unprecedented availability of cash pushed land prices up. After five or more years in America, a typical returnee discovered with dismay that he could not achieve what he had planned to achieve at first departure. During his absence, in fact, land prices had escalated. Letters from family and friends as well as recent immigrants had brought to America news of escalating prices in the land market in Italy. Thus returnees could not claim that they were totally unaware of the changes at home. Yet, as prefects reported, many returnees had not fully grasped while in America the magnitude of the changes. In some regions land prices doubled over a five-year period. In the end, for many returnees the resettlement in home communities turned into a big disappointment.

Lack of experience created another challenge. For most returnees, the purchase of a plot of land was the first substantial financial transaction of their lives. And they were dealing with landowners quite informed about the local market and the psychology of returnees. Impatient, most returnees hurried to conclude a deal as soon as possible after their return, with little or no advice from relatives and friends, as prefects reported.[45] Landowners skillfully took advantage of the returnees' impatience and placed on the market land of poor quality for a price that seemed quite reasonable. Often land transactions were concluded in a matter of days, especially in the early fall, before the planting season started. It was only the following year, at harvest time, that many returnees, now glorious landowners, discovered that the land they had purchased was perhaps the worst in the area.[46] In other cases landowners of a given town commonly agreed not to sell land for a time to force prices up. And indeed the increased demand pushed prices up. By the time these astute landowners placed their properties on the market the demand was so high that owners were offered more money than they had asked, because several returnees outbid each other. The highest prices paid on land were called *prezzi d'affezione* (affection prices). They were based not on land value but on personal preference or affection. The purchasers were generally returnees who wanted to own the same plot they had worked as laborers or renters before emigration. To have that property, they were willing to pay any price. Several prefects marveled at the phenomenon, because such transactions made little financial sense. But the purchase was very important for returnees who through that acquisition established a link between a difficult past and an allegedly more prosperous present.[47]

Financing was another challenge that created ambivalence among returnees. The goal, of course, was to pay cash. But many returnees had to settle for less, either because of inflation or because they had not been abroad long enough to save all the cash needed. Of course, borrowing was unpalatable to southerners for a couple of reasons. Traditionally, borrowing from moneylenders was linked to exploitation and even oppression. In addition, there was a negative moral connotation attached to the act of borrowing, a perception that has not totally disappeared to this day. However, several returnees had to borrow to achieve their goal. By the late nineteenth century many towns had some lending institutions of their own. They were small operations, often limited to a town or a province. In many cases these institutions had been promoted by the local clergy to make small and short-term loans available to farmers and individuals in particular distress. Although reluctantly, returnees applied for loans from these institutions, the security being the very plot they purchased.

The challenges that returnees had to face did not end the day they signed the purchase agreement. Rather, the new challenges were even more taxing. Returnees who purchased land before World War I were puzzled by the contrast between escalating land prices and declining farm commodity prices. Somehow, even in their rudimentary knowledge of economics, returnees perceived that there should have been a direct correlation between the two sets of prices. But that was not the case. Increased production in the Americas and northern Europe, coupled with cheaper transportation, were the main causes for the decline in farm commodity prices. Wheat, wine, and olive oil, the three main cash crops of Italian agriculture, were deeply affected. For instance, in 1873 a quintal of wheat sold for 38 lire; three decades later it had dropped to 19, notwithstanding substantial protective tariffs. Olive oil sold for 159 lire per hectoliter in 1873, but 104 in 1894. Wine prices fell from 83 to 34 lire. The United States caused the drop in the price of wheat, Spain that of olive oil, and France that of wine.

As this was occurring, the prices of small properties in southern Italy were rapidly escalating.[48]

The response of small landowners – and among them we include returnees who had purchased land – was to produce more to offset declining prices. Of course, in the end, that decision was self-defeating. But small landowners did not know that. In several cases, to increase production owners bought more land, if available. To this end, a number of returnees crossed the Atlantic another time to save money to buy more land; and in the end, they were totally baffled by the process of decline to which they themselves contributed and increased.

Independent farming was a challenge that few had anticipated. In the old days, before emigration, peasants had envied landowners who commanded deference, had political power, and a relatively good life. Now returnees who had finally joined the ranks of landowners were forced to acquire also the taste for the responsibility connected with land ownership. Independent farming required making decisions about crops, rotation of crops, wages of hired labor, farming techniques, and marketing the produce. Unfortunately most returnees were poorly prepared for all this. Visitors to the south observed that returnees displayed an abysmal ignorance about farming, a particularly damaging fault for a region where agriculture was the only viable economic activity. Cooperation in farming and especially in marketing was out of the question in most cases. Although some enlightened southerners tried to educate small farmers on the advantages of co-operation, fierce individualism prevented most southerners from embracing cooperative ventures. For instance, small farmers refused to borrow and to lend even the most expensive farming equipment to be used only a few times a year. Thus even small owners were forced to make large expenditures that could have been avoided through cooperation. Cooperation in marketing could have provided several advantages, including keeping prices up. Unfortunately, even small farmers sold the produce individually; and the competition drove prices down. Guidance both in production and marketing could have helped greatly. But the farming agencies established by the government in each province were by and large inactive. When members of such agencies moved to offer advice or help to farmers, they were rejected on the ground that government representatives could not be trusted. In the end, returnees discovered that the American experience had not been the most difficult part in their effort to get established financially. Managing the land in Italy was perhaps more taxing than finding a job in New York.[49]

In time observers began to notice a vast variance between the seemingly spectacular impact of remittances and the real and lasting changes occurring in the south. On the surface the south was being transformed: new houses were being built, more money and more goods were available, the land market was booming, and post offices reported record high deposits. Antonio Mangano, who toured the south at the peak of return migration, noticed that America was the most discussed topic and the origin of the greatest changes in the south. Even the Inchiesta Jacini corroborated these observations for the whole south, province by province. In reality there were reasons to be alarmed about the changes. Or, if we want to be more optimistic, the changes were not profound enough to align the economy of the south with those of northern Italy and north-central Europe. Properties changed hands, but there was little real change in farming techniques in the south. In fact, the new owners were hardly better off or more imaginative than the old ones. The basic structure of the southern economy had not changed. The large estate survived. Large landowners kept control of the economy and politics in southern communities. Producing and marketing techniques continued along the lines of the old individualism of southerners. And increased consumption seemingly showed that the south only acquired a more voracious appetite for goods and services. But one could hardly find any product or service labeled "made in the south."

# 8 Regional differences

The preceding chapter conveys the picture of a rather homogeneous south. In reality the south was far from homogeneous. Differences among regions and even within provinces were profound. In some regions and provinces the dynamics described did not even take place. In others those dynamics occurred in different ways. This chapter discusses regional differences in return migration and investments of savings in the south.[1]

The study of regional differences in return migration and investment of remittances within the south raises an important historical question that goes beyond the study of emigration and immigration history. How should we define the unit or units of historical investigation when we discuss social and economic events, like southern Italian emigration, before World War I? In this book I have discussed Italy and the differences between north and south. At this point, perhaps, the reader assumes that there was a south, sharing common social and economic characteristics. And to an extent that was the case. Yet a detailed study of regional differences in patterns of return migration and investments reveals that, seemingly, the south was only a mental construction. In reality the responses of towns and regions to opportunities provided by emigration and return migration were so varied as to call into question the very idea of a south. This chapter will indicate that regions, provinces, and probably individual towns should be studied one by one for the period we are investigating. But the reader should not be surprised by the differences within the south. Today we live in a society that has achieved a high degree of integration. It was World War I, in my opinion, that greatly expedited this process of social and economic integration, which had started in the nineteenth century. In the United States, the New Deal and World War II increased the tempo of the process. But the world of our fathers was vastly different, especially in the Italian south, as Chapter 3, on the southern ethos, indicated.

Fortunately, we can rely on three major and detailed surveys to study regional differences. And they were taken at most appropriate times to document variations over the years. The first survey, popularly known as Inchiesta Jacini was conducted immediately before the beginning of mass emigration and a few years after political unification.[2] The second, generally known as Inchiesta Faina, was taken in the early twentieth century, when return migration and the great hopes it generated were in full swing.[3] The third, the Inchiesta Lorenzoni, was taken in the late 1920s and early 1930s, when the impact of the Great Depression on land properties was already apparent in all its devastating force.[4] The Inchiesta Jacini documents the regional differences in Italy immediately after political unification. The findings were interpreted within a conservative frame of reference. Tradition was upheld, social change was rejected, and emigration was considered a danger to social and economic stability.[5] The Inchiesta Faina is limited to the south, Sardinia and Sicily included, and documents all the great hopes of economic and social modernization raised by return migration and American savings. The Inchiesta Lorenzoni describes the demise of the great hopes when the 1929 depression set in. This survey too covers all Italian regions, and is by far the most accurate, because it relies on indicators gathered for the first national census of agriculture taken in 1930.

### Puglie: The atypical region

Puglie differed more than any other region from the pattern described above.[6] The first difference was that emigration from Puglie became a mass phenomenon only immediately before World War I. For instance, in 1890, only 823 individuals left Puglie, while 22,766 departed from neighboring Campania. In 1900, 5,000 left, while 50,000 emigrated from Campania. In 1908, a local observer questioned whether emigration would ever affect Puglie as it had other southern regions for a couple of decades.[7] But by 1910 it became obvious that mass emigration was taking off from Puglie too: 30,000 individuals departed.[8] The second difference was that Puglie had a higher percentage of farm laborers than any other southern region. In the 1920s, for instance, people engaged in farming in one of the provinces of Puglie and Foggia were thus grouped: 50 percent laborers, 27 owners, and the balance renters and sharecroppers.[9] The not distant province of Salerno in Campania posted the following percentages: 43 percent owners, 20 laborers, and the balance renters and sharecroppers.[10] Obviously, the Puglie region had a large number of farmhands who, surprisingly, did not join the mass emigration from the south until well into the twentieth century. The third difference was within the region itself. When mass emigration started, it affected only the province of Bari and spared the neighboring provinces of Lecce and Foggia. For instance, in 1910 about 30,000 people departed from Puglie, then a region with six provinces: 67 percent of all emigrants were from Bari and only 15 percent from Foggia and Lecce combined. By 1920, 72 percent of all the emigrants from the region departed from Bari. In reality mass emigration affected only the province of Bari.

History provides at least a partial explanation as to why emigration from Puglie started so late and why it affected only one province. In medieval times, the region of Puglie was rich, as the mandatory route to the Orient. When international trade shifted from the Mediterranean to the Atlantic and Naples became the capital of the south, the Puglie declined. Malaria and pirates forced populations to relocate in a handful of large and safe towns. After the Spanish occupation of the south, most of the region was in the hands of a few barons who converted the area to grazing land. Farming was disallowed and the whole of Puglie became almost unfit for human habitation. In the early eighteenth century, feudal lords embarked on a project of conversion from grazing land to farmland in the provinces of Bari and Lecce. To make a more effective use of labor, they created a number of small settlements, so that the peasants would be close to the land. The conversion from grazing to farming land in the province of Foggia occurred in the late eighteenth century. But this time peasants resisted landowners in their attempt to resettle them in small communities. Accordingly, in the province of Foggia peasants kept living in large towns of 10,000 to 30,000 people and had to walk for hours to reach the outermost properties in town.[11] By the mid-nineteenth century, the region was characterized by large estates, farmed by laborers living in relatively small towns in Bari and Lecce, and in large towns in Foggia. Small properties were not totally unknown. Individuals who had provided special services to barons were rewarded with small properties, ordinarily adjacent to towns. A larger number of small properties was to be found in Bari and Lecce than in Foggia.

The sale of state land in the 1870s and 1880s created additional small properties in the provinces of Lecce and Bari. But properties for sale were scarce in the province of Foggia. The major reason was that more state and church land was available in Bari and Lecce than in Foggia. Moreover, the few new properties available in the province of Foggia were located a long distance from towns. Accordingly, many such properties remained unsold, until local authorities agreed to sell them to large landowners. Finally, in the province of Foggia, large landowners, more aggressive in claiming the right to bid on small properties and in corrupting officials handling the sale, ended up purchasing most of the small properties available.

As the land sale came to a close, the differences among the three provinces had increased. The province of Foggia was characterized by large estates with a handful of small properties. The provinces of Lecce and Bari, on the other hand, had substantially larger numbers of small properties.[12] The province of Foggia was different on another account. Large landowners engaged almost exclusively in wheat farming with modern techniques. They managed their properties directly. They introduced machines. They rationalized labor assignments. By the 1880s, the Foggia agrarian economy had created two solid and antagonistic groups: a small number of energetic entrepreneurs at the top and an army of laborers at the bottom. Few people emigrated from the province of Foggia. The major reason seems to have been that early returnees to Foggia were unable to buy land. When they arrived from the Americas and approached landowners with the request of buying land, they were turned down.[13] Deprived of the opportunity of becoming landholders through emigration and return migration, peasants from the province of Foggia took the alternative route of organizing and staging strikes to obtain more favorable contracts and better working conditions. Seemingly, peasants from Foggia were exceptional individuals among southerners, who were often described as servile and fatalistic. But, perhaps, organization and militancy among peasants from Foggia was simply a different way of expressing the same dynamics set in motion by emigration among peasants from other provinces.

The provinces of Bari and Lecce, although sharing many similarities, showed great differences that, in the end, explain why emigration affected only the province of Bari. To start with, the soil in the Bari province was ideally suited for wine production. Traditionally, the strong wines produced in Bari were exported to northern Italy and France to be mixed with weak local wines. The opening of the Bari-Ancona-Bologna railroad, with connections to France, further promoted the export of wines from Bari. In addition, when the phyloxera ravaged French vines in the 1870s, the French demand for wines from Bari increased. To satisfy the demand, local producers converted as many properties as possible to wine production. Locally available manpower had to be supplemented with seasonal immigrants from neighboring provinces. In the early 1890s, for instance, about 40,000 people immigrated from other provinces from two weeks to six months to Bari province to work in the vineyards. By 1905 internal immigration had increased to 54,000 individuals a year. But why did so many people emigrate from the province of Bari, if the province had to recruit labor from outside? What compelling reasons explain this singular case of mass emigration from and return migration to a province that was also the destination of thousands of internal migrants? Because medium and small properties were better suited for wine production than large estates, large landowners in the province of Bari divided the estates into smaller units, keeping the better properties for themselves and renting or selling the others. Accordingly, individuals emigrated from the province of Bari not because they could not find jobs at home, but because they wanted to generate the savings needed to buy the small properties available.[14]

Poverty was so common and endemic in Lecce province that, seemingly, local populations did not see any hope of a better future, not even through international emigration. Of the three provinces, Lecce was the most primitive. The soil was of poor quality. Olive oil, the main cash crop in the province, was the least marketable in Italy. Because of its geographical location, the province was poorly connected with the other provinces and with the rest of the nation. The shortage of cash was perhaps worse in Lecce than in any other southern province. Few families could balance their budgets. Fortunately, the nearby province of Bari provided job opportunities in the wine industry. And individuals from Lecce took advantage of that opportunity to balance the family budget. Surprisingly, these seasonal migrants going from Lecce to Bari every year, although aware of better job opportunities in the United States through returnees to Bari, never joined the transatlantic movement in significant numbers. The main reason seems to have been that peasants from Lecce had little interest in purchasing land in home communities, because the land was of poor quality. To deal with their financial problems, they engaged in seasonal migrations. Among southerners, the populations of Lecce were almost unique in this apparent detachment from the land. And they were unique also in how they faced their poverty. They did not react by embracing emigration, like the populations from Bari, or with labor organization and militancy, like those from Foggia. Acutely aware of the poverty of their province, they were seemingly contented with the limited opportunities offered by seasonal migrations to the Bari vineyards. Survival more than economic betterment seems to have been the goal. In the end, the population of these three provinces, stretching for no more than one hundred kilometers in length, behaved quite differently. In Foggia they chose organization and militancy, in Bari transatlantic emigration to buy land at home, and in Lecce, seasonal migration in order to survive.

Remittances and returnees affected the economy in the province of

Bari. In 1907 local mayors reported that most returnees had improved economically, especially returnees to coastal towns where emigration had started earlier than elsewhere. Initially savings were used to build new houses or renovate old ones. Then returnees turned their attention to land. Remittances affected properties in different ways. Large properties were adversely affected both because they were not ideally suited for wine production and because the decline in the labor supply caused by mass emigration pushed wages up and increased production costs. Consequently, the value of large properties declined. The high demand for land by returnees, on the other hand, pushed up the value of small and medium properties. Initially owners of large properties tried to make the best of a bad situation by refusing to divide their properties and selling to returnees. In some towns owners informally agreed among themselves to delay selling until the increased demand would push prices even higher. Returnees responded in kind by withdrawing their demand and deposited their savings in post offices.[15] More astute returnees realized that there were big profits to be made by speculating in real estate. Some joined forces and entered into partnerships to buy large properties to be later subdivided and placed on the market as the demand increased and prices soared. Others borrowed money from local rural banks to achieve their goals. These borrowers were confident that increasing commodity prices and increased demand for land would make them enough to pay back their mortgages and enjoy handsome profits. For instance, in Reno di Puglie, five returnees put together their savings and borrowed a large sum to buy an estate in the early 1920s, with the stipulation that the estate would be divided and sold only after the death of the original owner. Contrary to expectations, the original owner lived well into the 1930s. By this time land prices had dropped so drastically that the five investors lost their money and the bank most of its loan.[16]

Land transactions increased after World War I, because large savings became available through remittances and war subsidies and because wine production became increasingly profitable. In fact, before the war several towns had been adversely affected by the phyloxera, which destroyed vineyards. A number of owners had been forced to sell at a loss. Others had had their properties repossessed by lending institutions. The elimination of the phyloxera after the war through chemical treatment of vines, the availability of money, and increasing confidence that good profits could be made in wine production increased the demand for land. By the end of the 1920s, about 40,000 hectares of land had changed hands in the province of Bari, and that was about 10 percent of the farmland in the province. Most of the properties for sale ranged in size from three to six hectares or were plots carved out from large estates. In the other two provinces, Foggia and Lecce, land transactions were fewer in numbers. In Foggia, for instance, only 3 percent of the farmland changed hands and 4.5 percent in Lecce. In the province of Lecce the capital available for land purchases was not from remittances, but from war subsidies and the small savings accumulated through seasonal migrations to Bari. These indicators show that there were few land transactions, even in the province of Bari. So it seems to us today. In reality contemporaries regarded these transactions as a substantial change from the past. The writer of the Inchiesta Lorenzoni thus reported the common reaction in those days: "This has been a monumental change in our province, since in previous decades it was almost unheard of that an individual would sell or buy land."[17]

Land transactions came to an abrupt end in 1929. Credit was no longer available. Lending institutions recalled the loans. Commodity prices dropped. Small rural banks failed with an estimated loss of 500 million lire, mostly savings by returnees. Properties were variously affected. Small properties purchased before or immediately after the war at reasonable prices survived, because most owners had already paid off the mortgage by the time of the depression. Small properties bought at high prices in the mid-1920s or after did not, and were repossessed by lending institutions. Vincenzo Ricchioni sadly noted: "What a slaughter of small properties in the province. Court bulletins are filled with foreclosures and repossessions." But some individuals profited from the depression. Old landowners who had profited by selling to returnees stepped in and bought back properties at deflated prices. For instance, in the town of Martina a landowner had sold 16 hectares of land in the early 1920s at 25,000 lire per hectare. In the early 1930s he bought them back at 7,000 lire per hectare. Some local observers remarked that small owners could have coped with the depression more successfully by forming production and marketing cooperatives. But individualistic returnees could not even entertain that idea. Efforts by some local leaders to promote cooperatives failed. In 1930 Ricchioni counted only a handful of olive oil, wine, and dairy cooperatives in the province of Bari, and a few fruit and vegetable marketing associations. In addition, there was strong resistance to cooperatives among local moneylenders and merchants, afraid as they were that they would be unable to collect their loans if their clients joined cooperative enterprises. But, perhaps, the new landowners were their worst enemies. Their emigration had been a strictly personal venture and they embraced independent farming with the same fierce commitment to finding an individual solution to their economic problems.[18]

### Calabria: The true south?

Of all regions, Calabria perhaps best fits the profile outlined in the previous chapter.[19] Initially mass emigration was directed to Brazil and Argentina. But by the end of the century, emigrants avoided Brazil, which had turned into a nightmare for a number of emigrants who had returned to Calabria poorer than they were at departure. Argentina was considered a desirable destination until the end of the nineteenth century, when Argentina suffered an economic decline. By 1900 the United States had become the preferred destination. Returning from the United States was the rule, the rate of returnees over emigrants being 75 percent in the province of Cosenza, 72 in Catanzaro, and 71 in Reggio. The dynamics of investments followed a predictable pattern: first a house then land.[20] But there were noticeable differences between towns located on the Joinian and Tyrrhenian coasts. The differences were determined by natural and historical circumstances. The Jonian coast, traditionally the target of pirate raids, with poorer soil and malaria, was the area of large estates, farmed by laborers who lived in towns located on the hills. These laborers relocated to estates on the flatlands for a number of days when their services were needed. These populations did not embrace either emigration or militancy. Rather, like the populations in Lecce, they were resigned to their poverty. The Tyrrhenian coast, on the other hand, had more fertile land, was better protected from raids, had less malaria, and was characterized by small and medium properties producing olive oil, fruits, and vegetables. Emigration from towns located along the coast was a mass phenomenon, with coastal towns like Scalea, Diamante, and Belvedere Marittimo reporting that half of the population was abroad in the early twentieth century. Return was the norm. Between the two coasts was the Sila, a mountain range with a variety of land-tenure systems. Originally a royal domain, by 1900 it was characterized by large estates used as pasture land at high altitudes, and a mixture of large estates rented out in small plots and small properties at lower altitudes. Most small properties had been carved out by clearing forests. Emigration was more intense from the region of the Sila than from the Ionian coast but less than from the Tyrrhenian coast.[21]

Within this general pattern were differences within each of the three provinces of Cosenza, Catanzaro, and Reggio. The discriminating factor seems to have been land tenure. Emigration was high from areas with small and medium properties and low from areas with large estates. For instance, in the province of Cosenza emigration was high from the *circondario* of Cosenza and Castrovillari with small properties, and low in the circondario of Rossano characterized by large estates. In the province of Catanzaro, emigration was intense from the circondario of Crotone on the Ionian coast and low from the circondario of Catanzaro, Monteleone, and Nicastro on the opposite coast. The prefetto of Cosenza explained that peasants from the Ionian coast could not leave because landowners refused to lend the money to go overseas.[22] But Coletti, a more astute observer, remarked years later that emigration from the Ionian coast started only in the early 1900s when local landowners, who had traditionally refused to sell land to returnees, relented and placed sections of their properties on the market. It was the availability of land, Coletti concluded, that started mass emigration.[23]

Savings arriving in the region from overseas grew rapidly, especially in the 1890s: 61,000 lire arrived in 1876, 5 million in 1888, 14 in 1897, and 50 in 1906.[24] Savings helped turn around a disastrous sequence of events that had affected land properties in Calabria from 1870 to 1900. The most ominous sign had been that the number of landowners had been declining. For instance, 16 percent of the population in the province of Cosenza were landowners in 1882; by 1901 the percentage had declined to 12 percent. Catanzaro and Reggio reported slightly higher percentages of landowners, but the decline ranged from 5 to 6 percent in each province. Several dynamics had contributed to this result. Soon after political unification the Banco di Napoli and the Banca Nazionale made some money available in the three provinces, in Reggio especially, for land purchases. With confidence running high, both large and small owners borrowed to buy additional properties. But the expected profits did not materialize. Wine and olive oil production declined because of the devastation brought about by the phyloxera and the olive fly. Fruit and vegetable prices declined because of international competition. Foreclosures followed at a rapid rate, and by 1905 the Banca Nazionale and the Banco di Napoli became, although reluctantly, the two largest landowners in Calabria, their properties valued at 6 million lire. Many small landowners who had borrowed from local moneylenders to purchase government land were equally forced to surrender their properties to their lenders. A small number of landowners had their properties repossessed by the government when they failed to pay taxes. Finally, a number of landowners abandoned their properties altogether and emigrated permanently overseas.[25]

Under the circumstances, one would expect that few individuals would be willing to consider land properties a safe investment in Calabria at the turn of the century. Yet, mayors unanimously reported with surprise that returnees were determined to buy land. The mayor of Falconara Albanese, for instance, could not suppress his surprise:

> Commodities prices decline and land values go up, because of the increased demand for land. Landowners are delighted. They make substantial profits by selling properties they purchased at very low prices only a few years ago. What is happening is hardly believable: some returnees seeking land are the same individuals who sold their properties at low prices ten years ago. Now they buy them back at highly inflated prices.

The mayor of Sauro marveled at the fact that some returnees outbid each other and paid more than the asked price. The mayor of Colosimi remarked: "Returnees buy at astronomically high prices." Sellers could not ask for a better market as prices, the mayor of Melito di Porto Salvo added, "are out of sight."[26] By 1909 Ernesto Marenghi observed, the land market in Calabria was economically unsound, since "asking prices far surpass the real value of the land."[27] Coletti marveled that because rents were declining substantially, returnees were not interested in renting land. He regarded the determination of returnees to buy an obsession that made little economic sense: "Returnees are exclusively interested in buying. Nobody rents, although renting would be financially more profitable." By 1910 the agrarian economy of the region was affected by two contrasting dynamics: profits in farming were declining as land prices were moving up. The outcome was disastrous for a number of returnees. Some were forced into a second emigration to make improvements on the land they had purchased. Others emigrated a second and a third time to buy additional land, on the assumption that with larger properties they could offset in quantity what they lost in price. And some, after years of effort, either undersold the land or abandoned it altogether when they could not find a buyer. The most surprising feature of the whole process was that notwithstanding so many failures, new returnees were determined to repeat the cycle.[28]

Prospects for good profits in farming increased after World War I. By this time the phyloxera and the olive fly had been defeated. Land prices kept escalating; but there was money to buy, mostly through remittances. Almost 90 percent of the land purchases after the war were made possible through remittances from the United States. Generally, returnees paid cash and dealt directly with landowners. Very few returnees borrowed from moneylenders or from institutions of credit. Returnees intended to avoid the pitfalls of the 1880s and 1890s, when some returnees found themselves in the predicament of being unable to pay the mortgage. Moreover, in the mind of returnees, only total payment established legitimate ownership. Returnees wanted the land *franca e libera* (free and clear) because, as the prefetto of Cosenza put it, "a property with a mortgage is not considered genuine property," a sentiment still common in Calabria to this day. Obviously, because land prices were so high, returnees could afford only very small properties, ranging from half to three hectares. Accordingly, many returnees, besides buying small properties, rented additional land to make ends meet. Their ultimate goal, however, was to buy some more land eventually, their hope fueled by the good profits to be made in farming after the war. The postwar years witnessed some land transactions on the Jonian coast too. But this was a marginal phenomenon, confined to small properties at the fringes of the large estates.[29]

The depression of 1929 arrested this flurry of activity. In retrospect, substantial sums had been invested in land in Calabria, perhaps more money than in any other region per capita. Yet, the achievements had been meager and in most cases almost irrelevant. Large estates still dominated the local economy. There were 285 of them in 1930, with a combined extension of 345,000 hectares. Ironically, the largest number, 137, was in the province of Cosenza, where emigration, return migration, and savings had been higher than elsewhere. The 1930 census reported 40,000 families of small owners in Calabria, many of them returnees. But their conditions were hardly enviable. Most of them owned properties smaller than three hectares and many as small as half a hectare. For instance, in Reggio, of the 73,900 properties, 82 percent were smaller than 3 hectares; only 635 ranged from 20 to 40 hectares and 184 from 50 to 100 hectares. In Catanzaro 75 percent of the properties were smaller than 3 hectares, and 68 percent in Cosenza. These small owners were hardly better off than hired laborers, who were still a high percentage: 40 percent of the entire farming population in the whole region.[30] Obviously return migration and remittances had created large numbers of small farmers. But many of them could hardly make a living off the land.

## Basilicata: The poorest south

Basilicata was perhaps the poorest southern region and, together with Sardinia, the least affected by return migration and remittances. About 70 percent of the region was mountains and the farmland was poor because of insufficient rains and lack of perennial streams. In addition, the region was cut off from the main lines of communication to the point that most Italians were virtually unaware of the existence of this region. The land tenure system at the time of political unification was a mixture of large estates and very small properties. The number of small properties eventually increased through deforestation, an unfortunate process in many ways, because it increased the frequency of landslides. Emigration, initially to Brazil and Argentina, later to the United States, started in the early 1880s. But few returned. And, surprisingly, returnees showed little interest in buying land, as Eugenio Azimonti remarked, notwithstanding the number of small properties for sale. Contrary to what happened in other regions, land prices declined in Basilicata at the turn of the century by as much as 50 percent.

Several circumstances explain the disenchantment with the land among returnees to Basilicata. The first was that farming was very unattractive. In the early 1900s the phyloxera and olive fly had caused major devastations in the region. The demand for fruits and vegetables, the main cash crops in the region, sharply declined in the early 1900s, mostly because of competition from Greece and Spain. The properties reclaimed through deforestation proved to be less fertile than expected. Under the circumstances, few returnees engaged in independent farming, although there were exceptions in some towns, like Sartriano, Viggianello, Castelluccio, and Castelgrande.[31] The second circumstance had to do with culture. The populations of the region had traditionally shared an uncommon lack of attachment to the land, as Azimonti and other observers reported with surprise. Seemingly, the disengagement from the land was the result of poor harvests, lack of communications with the outside world, and extreme poverty. Giustino Fortunato, a representative from the region, used to tell his colleagues in Rome that he was the representative of nothingness. The infamous caves of Matera, used for human habitations for lack of housing, were a national embarrassment. The third circumstance was that temporary emigration to America from this region turned into permanent relocation faster than that from any other Italian region. Initially several emigrants from Basilicata returned, like emigrants from other regions. Azimonti reported that very few showed any interest in the land. Rather, they came to consider their temporary return as a vacation and squandered their savings in a few months to impress their peers. Eventually, they stopped coming back. Seemingly, there were very few ties keeping these populations attached to the land.[32]

The events surrounding emigration from Basilicata prompt two questions that help us understand Italian emigration in general. Why did emigrants return to such a poor region, especially if they did not intend to buy land? And why did they eventually relocate overseas permanently? Cultural attitudes provide the answer to the first question. Initially every emigrant, whether internal or international, embraced emigration as a temporary device to balance the family budget. In time experience led these temporary emigrants to realize that serial emigrations and returns provided no lasting solution. And they settled in the Americas, although reluctantly, as one of them put it: "My life is here; but the bread is in America. Perhaps we are a cursed race, since we are forced to go elsewhere just to survive."[33]

As World War I came to an end, the land market registered an unprecedented flurry of activity. The largest percentage of buyers were returnees with American savings and war subsidies. The unexpected change was prompted by three interrelated events. Returnees and veterans were confident that the government would finally introduce those social and economic changes that could make farming profitable, even in Basilicata. Moreover, the properties on the market were of better quality than those available at the turn of the century. In many cases the new properties were subdivisions of large estates with good harvest records. Owners were willing to sell to avoid potential violence. Peasant upheavals did not affect Basilicata. But landowners were alarmed by news coming from other regions. Finally, rising farm commodity prices convinced returnees and veterans to try their luck in farming. Seemingly the chronically most depressed southern region was changing, and for the better, as the prefetto of Matera reported.[34]

Savings from emigration and war subsidies affected properties located on flatlands differently from properties on high elevations. The 80,000 hectares in the flatland were mostly estates managed by entrepreneurs, with hired laborers. This was the best land in a poor region. And initially these entrepreneurs strongly resisted pressures by returnees to sell. It was only after World War I that some owners decided to sell to avoid violence. Unfortunately, the sale of these properties occurred mostly in the mid-1920s, when land prices were high. By the time the 1929 depression set in and commodity prices collapsed, the new owners were still saddled with mortgages they were unable to pay. Original owners stepped in and bought back at half price properties sold to returnees only a few years before. Properties located on the foothills or higher altitudes experienced the impact of peasant organizations and a certain degree of militancy. Owners of large properties generally managed properties located on foothills and mountains through middlemen, whose main task was to hire laborers daily. The social upheaval unleashed by the war suggested that a different course of action should be taken. Landowners divided their properties in plots and rented them out. Accordingly, the services of the middlemen were no longer needed. Seemingly individual renters, although anxious to buy the land they rented, could not come up with the cash they needed to buy. To compensate for the lack of cash, several renters and returnees joined forces and resources, and asked large landowners to sell. When landowners refused, renters and returnees intimidated them and forced them to sell, although at no point did local peasants embrace the principle of expropriation without compensation. From October 1919 to March 1921, peasants took over 3,000 hectares of land in Lavallo, Rapolla, and Melfi. But these efforts failed. Lack of funds, poor farming techniques, inability to compromise, and rejection of any advice coming from outside killed the cooperative effort. By 1921, by governmental order these properties were returned to the original owners, and the region settled down to business as usual. Large property owners were in control once again. And as in the old days they managed their properties through middlemen who used the services of laborers.[35]

At the end of this process, the land-tenure system in Basilicata strongly resembled that of other southern regions, with the significant exception that Basilicata had a higher percentage of medium properties. Large estates, however, were the rule. There were 134 of them larger than 500 hectares each. But of the 55,000 properties in the province of Potenza, 10 percent ranged in size from 10 to 100 hectares. Of the 24,000 properties in Matera 12 percent fell in the same category. In comparison, only 4 percent of the properties in Calabria fell in that category. Of course, most properties were very small, as in other regions. In general, as Azimonti noted, Basilicata was, together with Sardinia, the region least affected by return migration and savings. Well into the twentieth century visitors reported that Basilicata was a south within the south. In 1907, for instance, the prefetto of Matera observed: "Most of my colleagues tell me that emigration and savings are changing their provinces. This is not occurring in Matera."[36]

*Campania: Ambivalent success*

Campania, the region around Naples praised since classical times for its beauty and fertile soil, felt the impact of returnees and remittances more profoundly than any other southern region. But the results were mixed. On the one hand, remittances to the region were substantial and families benefited because of them. On the other hand, returnees, by pursuing the goal of land ownership, increased the pace of an irrational and economically unsound partition of land properties. Perhaps Campania was the best showcase of the variance between personal and social goals. In no other region, observers remarked, remittances and returnees created a better life for individuals and families than in Campania. Yet observers reported also that remittances and returnees had a negative impact on local economies. A combination of natural and historical circumstances explains why returnees to Campania were more determined than returnees to other regions to buy land. The land around Naples had been since Roman times and still was in the late nineteenth century the most fertile in the south. Accordingly, the purchase of land was considered a sound investment. Moreover, historically the regional land-tenure system had been a combination of large estates with many medium and small properties and a sustained degree of land transactions. Thus land transactions had a long history in the territory.

Remittances were not the only dynamics affecting land in Campania. The region was affected also by other forces not to be found in other regions: the control of land policies by the government in Naples until 1860, the availability of cash through the Banco di Napoli, and the easy access to the port of Naples as a gateway to the rest of Italy and to the world. The control of land policies by the government started in 1806, when Joseph Bonaparte, after abrogating feudalism in the region allowed local barons to keep most of their former estates as private properties in compensation for lost feudal rights and assigned the balance of the feudal estates to the towns for the care of the poor. The restoration of the Bourbon dynasty after the fall of Napoleon did not bring back feudalism. But the Bourbon king successfully undermined the power of the barons by making land management less desirable and by alluring barons to live at the court. Under the circumstances, barons were willing to sell at least part of their properties to support their expensive life-style in Naples. For energetic entrepreneurs willing to try their luck in farming, there was credit available through the Banco di Napoli, provided the borrower be a *civile* with proper connections.

The new purchasers, ordinarily bourgeois professionals with access to credit and ambition to join the local nobility one day, were unsuccessful in their endeavors. Eventually some of them were forced to sell part of the properties they had acquired. Thus they contributed to the further subdivision of the land. By the 1880s most of the new purchasers were returnees with American savings and with access to some credit from the Banco di Napoli which in 1893, for instance, lent 170 million lire for land purchases. But returnees were no better managers than bourgeois professionals. So many returnees defaulted that the Banco was on the verge of collapse. New lending policies set in place by Nicola Miraglia, the general director of the Banco, saved the bank and tightened credit. By the early twentieth century loans and defaults had decreased in numbers, as Oreste Bordiga observed, and concluded: "Most land purchases are now made with American savings and little help from the Banco di Napoli."[37]

Policies set in place by towns and by the central government in Rome after 1860 accelerated the process of land partitions. Joseph Napoleon had granted towns substantial land holdings in the early nineteenth century. After 1860 towns confronted with the high costs of services mandated by the central government, like schools and hospitals, divided the public domain and placed properties on the market to generate the needed funds. According to an estimate made by Antonio Brizi, over 100,000 new properties were carved out in the region from the public domain between 1800 and 1904. Most purchases occurred after 1895 with American money.[38] The central government too put on the market a number of properties after 1860. These new properties were originally church land taken over by the government and subdivided into small holdings of three hectares each. The reason for making these holdings so small was prompted by the desire of offering as many unpropertied peasants as possible the opportunity of becoming small owners. Moreover, the common wisdom was that because most land in the region was very good, a property of three hectares could suffice for a family of four. In this case too, properties were purchased with cash from remittances and loans from the Banco di Napoli. This occurred until the early 1890s. After that date the Banco revised its lending policies and made it more difficult for returnees to secure loans. Accordingly, purchasers relied almost exclusively on American savings.[39] But this process of increasing land partition was not universal in the region. In some areas the reverse process occurred, as small properties were consolidated into large estates. At Vico di Pantano, for instance, when the government placed on the market fifty small properties, peasants bought them. But, unable to make a living off them, the new owners sold them to a local large landowner. Similarly, at Piana di Eboli, a count purchased several hundred small properties and introduced extensive farming. Similar processes were under way in Mondragone, Castel Volturo, and the Ofanto valley.[40]

Seemingly American savings were greater in Campania than elsewhere, because a larger percentage of people emigrated from that region than from any other in the south. The closeness of the port of Naples was the major reason. Moreover, mass emigration started earlier in Campania than elsewhere. For instance, as early as 1883 one-fifth of all Italian emigrants were from Campania. Throughout the 1890s and 1900s Campania remained the leading southern region in emigration rates. The initial destinations to Brazil and Argentina were replaced by the United States at the end of the century. For instance, of the 10,958 emigrants from the province of Salerno in 1895, 40 percent went to Brazil, 40 to the United States and the balance to Argentina. By 1905, however, of the 16,713 emigrants from the same province, 85 percent reached the United States. Returning was the rule, the rate ranging from 65 to 85 percent of the departures. Second- and third-time emigrations were common.[41] Although Oreste Bordiga lamented that emigration had caused many social ills, like family instability and diseases brought back by returnees, the positive impact of remittances on local economies, he admitted, overrode every negative impact. As elsewhere, the first goal was a house, as Brizi put it: "A new house, not land, is the first goal." Later, land, of course, was the preferred investment, although, as Bordiga noted, returnees showed poor marketing and farming abilities. Most properties were purchased at highly inflated prices and many returnees displayed a shocking lack of skills at running farms. "In America," Bordiga concluded "they made some money, but unfortunately returnees come back as ignorant as when they left. Or perhaps even worse."[42]

Returnees and remittances affected properties for sale and for rent differently. Because of increased demand, land properties increased in price by 35 percent from 1880 to 1900. Rents, on the other hand, declined by 30 to 40 percent, both because of declining demand for rented properties on account of mass emigration and because returnees showed little interest in renting. Demand, not the quality of the land, determined the asking price. For instance, land prices were high in the province of Avellino, where land was rather poor. Emigration from and return migration to Avellino was the highest in the region. Benevento, on the other hand, had very good land. But because emigration from Benevento started later and many returnees to that province preferred to deposit their savings in post office banks rather than to invest in land, land prices declined steadily. In the province of Caserta, the land was good, emigration and return migration were high, and prices extremely high. Bordiga reported some "incredible" land prices in Caserta in 1908: 7,000 lire per hectare, with properties as high as 10,000 lire per hectare if they had irrigation facilities. The escalation in demand for land properties, prices, and land transactions further accelerated after World War I, a pattern, as we have seen, common throughout the south.

Seemingly Campania was the success story of return migration and remittances. And in reality it was. But only to a degree. The apparent success hid serious problems. In reviewing the record of returns and investments in 1930, Brizi admitted that in Campania returnees and savings had brought rents down, forced wages up, decreased the number of defaults and repossessions, made possible many new houses, and given many former peasants the pride of becoming land-owners. But that was exactly the problem. These new landowners were unable to make ends meet because the properties they had bought were too small. For instance, in 1929, of the 106,000 properties in the province of Naples, 86 percent were smaller than three hectares. Less than 1 percent ranged in size from 20 to 100 hectares and only a handful were larger than 500. In Salerno properties smaller than three hectares were 76 percent and only 86 properties were larger than 100 hectares. Brizi suggested that, for all its positive impact emigration and return migration had created many properties too small to be of any use. He suggested the passage of legislation to the effect of forcing the consolidation of small properties into larger hold-ings. But he recognized that in Campania "where land is wanted more for social status than for economic reasons the chances of success are very slim." Brizi's remark could be made for any southern region. Obviously emigration generated a lot of cash but did very little to replace traditional southern individualism.[43]

### Sicily: A case apart

At the turn of the century, Sicily was the showcase of all the ills of the south: large estates run as feudal domains by barons, large num-bers of small and unprofitable properties, and vast cohorts of impov-erished laborers. For instance, in the province of Agrigento 65 percent of the 32,000 properties were smaller than three hectares, twenty estates were larger than 1,500 hectares, and 45 percent of the popu-lation engaged in farming were laborers. In the province of Catania, 50 percent of the farming population were laborers, and 80 percent of all properties were smaller than three hectares, of which 30 percent were smaller than half a hectare each; twenty-two estates had a com-bined acreage of 50,000.[44] The very small properties were generally located along the coast, the large estates in the hinterland. Moreover, small properties were to be found adjacent to towns.

Visitors commented widely on the uniqueness of the geographical and human landscape to be observed on the island. People lived in large and isolated communities, the distance between them ranging from five to twenty-five kilometers. Concern for personal security discouraged families from living anywhere else but in densely nu-cleated and large towns, mostly located either along the coast or on mountaintops. Many landowners, especially those with properties smaller than three hectares, had to hire themselves out regularly to make ends meet. For all practical purposes they were not different from laborers, who were over 50 percent of the farming population in Sicily, the highest such percentage in the south. Large estates were worked by hired hands. These individuals lived in large towns, and relocated in the estates for a number of days during the planting and harvesting seasons. Most estates owners lived in Palermo, and visited their properties once a year, ordinarily in September and October. For all practical purposes, the Sicilian agrarian economy was still a medieval operation.

Even the struggle Sicilian peasants waged in order to have some form of control over the land was fiercer on the island than anywhere else in the south. In earlier days barons governed their estates with almost total autonomy from the central government, which had been traditionally weak on the island. No ruling family had been able to stay in power for very long in Sicily. The island, in fact, was one of the most strategic and coveted pieces of real estate before the discovery of America. And virtually all nations around the Mediterranean, and some from the north too, fought to occupy Sicily. Small properties began to appear in Sicily in the sixteenth century, when some barons granted small properties to individuals with special merits or to families willing to relocate in small and new communities created to shorten the distance between human habitations and farmland. These properties were called *chiuse* (enclosures) and were granted with long lease agreements. Beginning in 1787, the government of the Bourbons too encouraged the creation of small properties carved out of state-owned land to undermine the excessive power of the barons. In some cases, the government confiscated large estates from the barons and placed them on the market in small holdings. Seemingly, this agrarian reform worked and productivity increased. For instance, the *latifundium* Gulpa, in the province of Palermo, "barren and unproductive" in 1700 had become "fertile, inhabited and pleasant to see" only a couple of decades later, after the government took it over and offered it in small plots to farmers.[45]

The struggle over land ownership became more intense in the nineteenth century as more individuals competed to purchase land. In the early part of the century pressures from the British government to introduce more liberal land policies pitted the Bourbons against the barons, as the Bourbons supported the British recommendation of centralizing power by taking away prerogatives from the barons and by introducing much needed land reform. In the end, however, the crown was unsuccessful in implementing land reforms, as the barons neutralized through the Sicilian parliament they controlled every piece of legislation introduced by the crown. Later in the century peasants were more successful in achieving their goal, when several thousands new properties were placed on the market. That occurred as a result of the wars for independence, when the government promised peasants land in exchange for political support. The ensuing sale of church and state land in small plots in the 1880s and 1890s satisfied, at least to a degree, the demand for land and increased the determination of those who could not buy to find new ways to purchase land. Finally, a revolt of unprecedented proportions generally known as the upheaval of the *Fasci Siciliani* forced owners of large estates to reconsider their opposition to the sale of land. They finally agreed, at least in part, to satisfy the demand for land by American returnees.[46]

By that time – the late 1890s – emigration had become the common strategy to generate the cash needed to buy land. Initially Sicilians had emigrated to Tunis, Africa. Some had even resettled in Tunis and bought land at the incredible low price of 150 lire per acre in 1875. Eventually the French government disallowed foreigners from purchasing land in Tunis. At that point Sicilians began to emigrate to the United States. But virtually no one bought land in the United States. Sicilians could buy land in Tunis, because Tunis could be considered an extension of Sicily. But the United States could not. The goal of these temporary emigrants to the United States was to save enough money to buy land at home, as Giovanni Lorenzoni wrote: "The dream of all Sicilians going to the Americas is to buy land in Sicily. Sicilians pursue this goal with incredible determination, since they equate land ownership with liberty and independence." Remittances grew rapidly: from 4.5 million lire in 1901 to 55 million in 1907, the coastal towns being the largest beneficiaries. Among the provinces, Palermo received the largest savings because emigration was higher from this than from any other province.[47]

Return migration and returnees had a different impact on large estates and small properties. In the areas of large estates emigration was uncommon, remittances poor, and return migration the exception, mostly because owners adamantly refused to sell. As a peasant put it:

> We are imprisoned by the *latifundium* as by an iron cell. We cannot do anything but experience our powerlessness. There is plenty of rich and inviting land all around us. But we cannot buy it. The latifundium cannot be broken. It is like an unassailable wall. The government itself, unfortunately, instead of helping us to break the latifundium, has made it stronger by allowing large owners to purchase the small plots originally put on the market for peasants. In addition, many new landholders have lost their properties for inability to pay taxes.[48]

Peasants also did not emigrate from the areas of large estates because landowners refused to lend the money for the crossing. A peasant from Caltagirone noted: "We do not go because we are unable to borrow the money for the trip. But as soon as we will secure it, we will go." In the areas of small properties, on the other hand, emigration was intense, both because peasants were able to borrow the money they needed and because there was land for sale. Two additional dynamics fueled the selling and buying of land at the turn of the century. On the one hand, increasing wages due to mass emigration and declining prices of farm commodities made farming less profitable. On the other hand, the increasing demand for land by returnees made it profitable for medium and small landowners to sell land.[49]

In no other southern region did land prices escalate as rapidly as they did in Sicily. The first reason was that the number of returnees was higher on the island than elsewhere in the south. The second reason was that owners of large estates and even small owners in trouble were reluctant to part from their properties, regardless of how pressed they were to sell. The link between land ownership and personal honor was stronger among Sicilians than among other southerners. The limited supply of land coupled with the high demand for land properties doubled land prices on the island from 1890 to 1905. Returnees were adversely affected by the rapidity of the escalation in land prices. Many returnees had to settle for smaller properties than those they had envisioned at first departure. Others had to emigrate a second or even a third time to reach the goal. And finally some were so disenchanted at their first harvest that they eventually abandoned the plots and relocated permanently in the United States. The Inchiesta Jacini provides ample evidence of increasing prices, high demand, and the disappointment of so many returnees. Prices escalated even more rapidly after World War I, as savings from America and from war subsidies increased the demand. From 1919 to 1925, 150,000 hectares of land changed hands in Sicily. Even some powerful barons from the interior relented, perhaps afraid of a new wave of violence like the one unleashed by the *Fasci Siciliani*, and placed at least part of their holdings on the market.

The increased demand for land by returnees triggered several marketing mechanisms which generated additional profits for energetic entrepreneurs and further pushed land values up. Large estates were generally sold through *gabellotti*, middlemen who had originally managed estates for barons. Because a number of barons were unwilling to deal directly with ignorant returnees, gabellotti acted as brokers. They advanced to the owner one-fifth of the stipulated price, then subdivided the estate in plots, and negotiated with several buyers a collective act of purchase. At the act of sale, the full price was paid and the gabellotto kept for himself one-third of the estate. Not only did gabellotti end up with the lion's share of the land, but they kept for themselves also the best holdings. Eventually many of these land transactions ended up in court, many returnees complaining that they had been cheated. Other owners of large estates conducted the sale of their estates directly, using the services of surveyors and other agents to divide the land. Finally some estates were purchased by a number of returnees joined in cooperatives. These cooperatives came about after World War I. They were promoted by veteran organizations with the backing of the Banco di Sicilia. Cooperatives bought estates at going prices, divided them into small plots, and sold them to peasants at cost. All these transactions, of course, came to an end in 1929. But notwithstanding this intense buying and selling of real estate, Sicily was like the rest of the south by 1929: properties smaller than three hectares ranged from 60 percent of all land properties in the province of Palermo to 40 percent in Catania, the other provinces falling somewhere in between. Large estates were still the rule, especially in the hinterland, and an army of peasants provided the labor the *latifundia* needed, their number ranging from 50 to 70 percent of the farming population in each province.[50]

### Sardinia: The forgotten south

Sardinia is geographically removed and socially different from the rest of the south. Often the island is not included in studies of the south. Yet in the traditional three-tier division of Italy – north, center, and south – Sardinia resembles more closely the south than the other two areas. Here I introduce Sardinia as an interesting counterpoint in the study of emigration, remittances, and the buying and selling of land stimulated by return migration and American savings. Emigration from Sardinia never became a mass phenomenon, not even after World War I. Only after World War II did Sardinians find their way to central and northern Europe. Consequently, remittances had virtually no impact on the island's economy until recent times. The local economy was, and still is, mostly pastoral, with large owners of estates and armies of laborers. But, contrary to what happened in Puglie, organization and militancy never took roots on the island. By 1929 Sardinia was hardly different from what it was in 1870. The island remained an outstanding example of social and economic stagnation.

At no point did emigration from Sardinia affect more than a few thousand people per year. In 1893, for instance, only 43 people left the island. In 1903 18 people departed and 4,000 in 1913. Seasonal migrations to central Italy, Tunisia, Southern France, and Spain were common throughout the nineteenth century and well into the twen- tieth century. In 1903, for instance, 2,500 Sardinians left for the above destinations for a season. The war did not change this pattern. In 1920 only 4,000 people left for overseas destinations, while 5,000 mi- grated seasonally to Tunisia and central and northern Europe. Per- haps we are led to suspect that Sardinians did not reach the United States, the most common destination of southerners, because they were unaware of opportunities available there. Prefetti testified that such was not the case. Seemingly not only were Sardinians, even in small and remote communities, aware of opportunities in the United States, but they had also access to the cash they needed to buy the ticket. Probably the main reasons why the populations of Sardinia did not emigrate were the pastoral economy of the island and the consequent uselessness for Sardinians to buy land.[51]

Land tenure had a history of its own in Sardinia. Collective own- ership, common in Sardinia in the tenth and eleventh centuries, was progressively tempered by the introduction of private property during the dominations of the republics of Pisa and Genoa. Feudal entail was introduced in 1421, a measure that initiated a long economic decline. Feudal lords converted their estates to pasture land and disallowed the so-called common rights to peasants, rights common almost every- where else in Medieval Europe. Contrary to what had happened in all other regions of Italy, Sardinians were not given the opportunity to buy land from the government after political unification. Lack of land to be placed on the market and opposition from large landowners were the two reasons. By 1930 the land-tenure system of the island had been affected by very few changes. The island was still the domain of large properties with a very few small landholdings. In the province of Cagliari, for instance, there were fifty-nine estates larger than 1,000 hectares. Nuoro and Sassari shared the same predicament. The few emigrants who eventually returned did not seek to buy land. They either deposited their savings in post offices or invested in houses.[52]

Sardinians in general not only avoided emigration but also showed no inclination for organization and militancy. By 1930 65 percent of the working population in Sardinia were propertyless laborers. The reason for this apathy was the very nature of the Sardinian pastoral economy. Seven of ten laborers were shepherds working for owners of large flocks. Because shepherds followed the flocks through hills and mountains for months, returning to town only a couple of times a year, they seldom interacted with other shepherds. This isolation of each individual shepherd prevented the development of social consciousness and cooperation. Purchasing land was not a desirable goal. After all, in a pastoral economy, small tracts of land are virtually useless. A more desirable goal among many Sardinians was the ownership of a few sheep. But then the owner of the sheep had to negotiate with landowners the terms for the use of grazing land. Seemingly the very nature of the Sardinian economy explains why neither emigration nor militancy developed. Emigration was discarded since, as the prefetto of Cagliari wrote, land was neither available nor desirable.[53] Cooperation and militancy could not take roots among shepherds who seldom crossed each other's path. The shepherds' lives were characterized by solitude and the island by isolation from the rest of the country. Sardinia was and still remains to a large degree a world unto itself.

The discussion of regional differences suggests two concluding remarks. The first and most specific is that it is rather difficult to generalize about southern Italian emigration, return migration, and investments of remittances, because every southern region and seemingly every province reacted to those dynamics in unique ways. The second and more general remark is that the longer we go back in time the more difficult it becomes to make general statements about social and economic events. Today we live in societies that share many similarities, regardless of how large these societies are. Accordingly, we can analyze social and economic events on a national scale. But things were different one hundred years ago. Then there were very few social and economic dynamics affecting large groups. Most social and economic dynamics were confined within a region, a group, a limited environment. A dialect, a mountain range, a religious ritual, a historical tradition determined the horizons of one's life. As stated at the beginning of this chapter, it was World War I that changed drastically this world of our fathers. And the change has continued, and even accelerated its course, since then. But we should be aware that the world of our fathers was different, not exclusively smaller than our own. They lived in self-contained social and economic environments. And those environments have to be given individual attention if we want to achieve some historical accuracy.

# 9    *Return and retirement*

Land ownership was the goal of most returnees. But it was not universal. Returnees to some regions, like Basilicata and Sardinia, for instance, showed very little interest in land. In both regions land was considered a poor investment. The prefetto of Matera, for instance, reported that although land prices were escalating in other regions, they were declining in his province.[1] Other returnees, aware that many of those who had preceded them had failed as independent farmers, sought alternative ways of investing. But in the agrarian south, alternatives to farming, even in related food processing, were limited. Moreover, few returnees had the entrepreneurial abilities and the courage to break the traditional opposition to economic innovation. Finally a number of returnees, and they were many, did not seek land or alternative ways of investing. They simply deposited their savings with local post offices or other savings institutions and planned to live the rest of their lives on the savings they had accumulated and the modest interest they generated. Some were even willing to take part-time jobs to supplement American savings with occasional income at home.

This chapter discusses returnees who did not invest in land. It will show that the returnees who became disenchanted with land investments were more than a few, especially in some regions, and after 1900. In addition this chapter will point out that opportunities for alternative ways of investing were few, by discussing in some detail the economy of a typical southern province, that of Cosenza in Calabria. The core of this chapter will be dedicated to those returnees who deposited their savings in post offices or other institutions in the hope of having accumulated enough to live comfortably for the rest of their lives. Of course, these returnees were quite different from those who invested in land. Generally speaking, they did not enjoy either the affection of their fellow citizens or a good press. This chapter deals also with another issue related to returnees and savings. Italian historians have debated for decades how the government used the savings these returnees deposited in post offices. The traditional argument has been that the government siphoned off those funds through the Cassa Depositi e Prestiti to subsidize industrial expansion in the north. A careful reading of the investments record of the Cassa will call into question that conclusion. The discussion of the investment policies of the Cassa, the traditional interpretations of historians of such policies and the evidence which seems to contradict those interpretations are quite important. They allow us to sever rhetoric from reality in the study of Italian return migration and assess both shortcomings and strengths in the process itself. Both the study of how remittances were deposited in post offices by returnees and of the investments of the Cassa Depositi e Presitit show how individual returnees and society at large tried to integrate return migration with local and regional dynamics.

## Alternative investments

Over the years the search for alternative investments increased, even in regions where early returnees had shown an almost exclusive interest in purchasing land. The search for alternatives was prompted by a number of reasons. Some returnees looked for other investments because of the failure of previous returnees who had bought land. Others sought alternative ways of investing because of their American experience, which had taught them that there were ways to make a living other than farming. Other returnees, especially those who returned after World War I, took advantage of the increasing economic diversification occurring even in the backward south at that time. Finally a small number of returnees invested their savings in the very business of emigration by opening up hospices in the ports of embarkation, exchange offices, information and labor agencies both in the United States and Italy. The reader, however, should keep in mind that here we are talking about a small percentage of returnees, the overwhelming majority of them pursuing the goal of landownership or the cherished dream of a worry-free retirement.

Seemingly the major reason returnees searched for alternative investments was the failure of earlier returnees as independent small farmers. Few returnees, in fact, had anticipated the problems stemming from running small properties independently and with making a living in a subsistence economy. As returnees basked in the newly acquired social status of landowners and gentlemen, they progressively learned the painful lessons of inflation, poor harvest, taxation, declining commodity prices, and inadequate services from credit institutions and agrarian organizations. The most painful problem for returness arose from the fact that they were ill-prepared to deal with all the challenges of independent farming. Lack of managerial skills, ignorance of farming techniques, and problems of budgeting turned the excitement of land ownership into the nightmare of ever-increasing debts, forced sales or, in the most fortunate cases, an embarrassing second or third departure to make additional savings to salvage threatened properties. Repeated failures by returnees slowed down the demand for land in those regions, like Calabria, where poor harvests, lack of support services, and distances from regional markets made farming a difficult endeavor.[2]

Surprisingly the failure of earlier or later returnees had a slighter impact than we would expect. A number of earlier returnees, besieged by problems stemming from independent farming, sold out or had their properties repossessed by the government for failure to pay taxes. Ironically, new returnees stepped in and bought properties placed on the market by previous returnees. In many cases the new returnees repeated the old cycle and eventually sold to other returnees. Other disappointed returnees simply abandoned properties purchased with American money or donated them to relatives and left for overseas permanently. There were also cases of returnees taking off for America at nighttime to escape creditors and avoid public embarrassment. To all these returnees, letting go of the land was most painful. The pain stemmed from the unexpected realization that the traditional faith that land was invariably the best source of financial security and social status was no longer valid. The disappointment of returnees over land ownership eventually expanded into a larger bitterness toward the social and political order in Italy in general. Searching for a scapegoat, returnees began to blame the government for their failure. The Italian government had encouraged return migration and land investments, they argued. But returnees felt that the nation was unwilling to give them the support they needed in their new endeavors as small farmers.[3]

Returnees seeking to invest in nonfarming activities because of the failure of earlier returnees were joined by those who had never considered land as the best investment in the first place. Although the two groups combined made up perhaps no more than 30 percent of all returnees, we should follow their activities to have a more complete picture of how returnees and savings affected southern Italy. Unfortunately the evidence we have on the topic of investments outside farming is more limited than the evidence for land investments, because both the Inchiesta Jacini and the Inchiesta Faina focused on agriculture and dealt with emigration and returnees only insofar as they affected local agrarian economies. The sparse evidence on alternative investments to be derived from the two surveys, however, can be expanded through reports from prefetti, interviews with returnees, and governmental reports on industrial investments.

Where could returnees not interested in land properties invest their money? Of course, returnees were conditioned by the economies of the towns and provinces to which they returned. What opportunities were available to them at the turn of the century? To illustrate this, I have chosen the region of Calabria, and within the region the province of Cosenza, which can be considered an average southern province. The provinces of Campania were generally better off, those of Basilicata worse off. This portrait is offered so that the reader might have an idea of the investment opportunities available in a southern province. In 1891 half a million people lived in each of the three provinces of Calabria: Cosenza, Reggio, and Catanzaro. Eighty-six percent of the males were illiterate, although schooling had been made mandatory since the early 1870s. The few males who attended school stopped at the third grade. At that time they joined their fathers in the fields. The education of girls was still considered morally unacceptable. Individuals pursuing an education beyond the third grade were a minute percentage in the early 1890s. The only place open to them was vocational schools; there were six in the region, with 300 students in 1890. The few individuals with resources, family connections, and the will to pursue a high school education or to enter a university had to relocate to Naples.

Farming was the almost exclusive occupation, with 97 percent of the population in the Cosenza province engaged in it. Only 3 percent of the population was employed in food processing, textile, or other forms of manufacturing. Mechanization was still unknown. The list of industries in the province was very short. The great pride of the province of Cosenza was the rock salt quarry in Castrovillari, with 272 workers and, as the government report noted with pride, one steam engine bought in 1884. Five iron workshops producing agricultural implements with a total of eighteen employees met the needs of the whole province. The city of Cosenza boasted a gas company with three employees and an electric company with four. An 1891 report proudly stressed that the city was lit by 200 lamps during special nights. About 166 people were employed in twenty-one small quarries for the excavation of travertine to be used in construction, as an alternative to the very expensive bricks. An undetermined number of lime and iron foundries employed 260 adult males and 242 boys. Of course, food processing was the largest industry: 742 mills employed 866 males. Three establishments, open only three months a year, took care of hulling the rice harvest. Thirty-two people worked in the processing of pasta. Olive oil was the main cash crop in the province: 664 presses driven by animal power processed the local harvest of olives. Cosenza had its touch of modernity and a foreign market. The province produced licorice – 200 people worked at it – exported to faraway places like Germany, Belgium, and England. Thirty-three silk-processing shops, nine wool shops, a few rope-making establishments, a handful of tanneries, twelve printing presses, and an undetermined number of wood and meat-processing establishments completed the list. Clothing was still produced at home: in 1891 there were 6,089 home looms in the province of Cosenza.[4]

This small-scale economy did not need credit for improvements and expansion. Neither was there a demand to expand. The profits generated were very small, if we are to rely on records of savings institutions. In 1893, for instance, one savings institution with 5,033 depositors serviced the whole province. In 1893 about 4 million lire were deposited and 3 million withdrawn. During the 1880s, following intense efforts by the government and northern promoters to introduce cooperatives among farmers in the south, some people's banks sprang up in the province of Cosenza. These banks catered to small savers and to individuals in need of small and short-term loans, ordinarily not available through the only two commercial banks in the south, the Banco di Napoli and the Banco di Sicilia. By 1893 four cooperative banks were operating in the province of Cosenza. The Banca Popolare Cosentina founded in 1883 and the Banca Agricola Cosentina established in 1889 – both located in the city of Cosenza – had 660 and 773 depositors, respectively. The Banca Popolare Cooperativa Umberto I in Cassano Ionio, started in 1886, had 462 depositors and total assets of 50,000 lire. The Banca Popolare Cooperativa in Mormanno, founded in 1886, had seventy-four depositors and assets of 7,925 lire.[5]

For several reasons returnees to the province of Cosenza avoided the people's banks and deposited their savings with local post offices. The commercial bank in Cosenza refused the small accounts of returnees. Returnees avoided the other savings institutions because they were unfamiliar to them. Post offices were the safest places to deposit savings, because deposits were guaranteed by the government. By 1892 the ninety-nine post offices in the province handled 24,080 accounts, 5,691 of them opened in 1891.[6] These accounts were generally small, ranging from 150 to 800 lire (50 to 260 dollars). As the prefetto of Cosenza reported, most of those accounts had been opened with American savings.[7] Returnees felt more confident with the post offices than with other savings institutions.

As elsewhere, return migration to Cosenza raised great expectations of new investments and business expansion.[8] The traditional resignation to poverty and backwardness seemed to be replaced, almost overnight, by a new sense of optimism. Emigration was no longer a curse, but an opportunity, and the province was about to see an economic renaissance, as the prefetto reported.[9] Old debts were being paid, people had money to spend, commerce was expanding, new houses were being built, and some people even began to travel from small towns to Cosenza to buy better quality goods.[10] The prefetto was not the only person to notice the new spirit of optimism and the increased opportunities. Educated people and local politicians joined the band wagon. If lack of capital had been the major reason for the economic backwardness of the province, remittances would bring about the long-awaited economic recovery.[11]

But that optimism was short-lived. Remittances increased consumption, but investments in economic activities outside farming were but a handful. In 1907, for instance, the prefetto reported that returnees investing in small businesses or even in food processing were but a few. And their rate of success was even more limited than among those who purchased land. The rate of failure was higher in small towns, where the demand for services and goods was necessarily limited: "A few among the most successful returnees," the prefetto of Cosenza wrote, "started construction companies, since the demand for new houses and remodeling of old constructions is high. But most failed for lack of expertise. The only successful returnees seem to be barbers and coffeeshop owners who purchase businesses from other people and use skills developed in America."[12] Savings institutions too eventually witnessed the absence of the expected entrepreneurial spirit. By 1910 most local savings institutions, with the exception of the post offices, of course, were refusing new deposits because there was no demand for loans. "Seemingly," the prefetto concluded, "we have more money than we can use or that we are able to invest." And that trend was common everywhere throughout the south. Under the circumstances deposits in post offices swelled because by law every citizen was entitled to open an account insured by the government to 10,000 lire.[13]

Some astute returnees joined forces with local landowners to profit from the availability of cash through remittances. By offering interest rates higher than post offices, landowners convinced a number of returnees to place their deposits with them; they added that they could offer higher interest rates because they had connections outside the province to invest the money in profitable enterprises. For instance, using this approach, a prominent landowner in San Pietro Apostolo in the region of Calabria opened his private bank in 1904 and in two years he was handling 113,000 lire in deposits from returnees. Unfortunately these operators were hardly more honest than the American banchisti discussed in Chapter 6. Some operators absconded with savings of returnees, heading for South America. This happened on a small scale, even in the province of Cosenza; however the two most celebrated cases that made the national press occurred in the city of Avellino and the town of Rionero in Volture in the early 1900s.[14] These two occurrences and lesser scandals corroborated the returnees' perception that the only safe place to save money was the post office. As the prefetto of Cosenza commented: "Our people are not exactly the best friends the government has. But returnees have come to realize that the government through post offices is more reliable than any banker."[15]

Returnees who did not place their savings either in land or investments, but instead put them in a post office or savings institution, generally received a bad press. They were regarded as lazy, uncooperative, antisocial, and a burden to home communities, notwithstanding the money they brought back.[16] Returnees to Cosenza too were not spared critical comments. Contrary to what many contemporaries concluded, many returnees refused to invest not exclusively because they lacked entrepreneurial spirit, but also because opportunities to invest were few. True, emigration did not change the cultural habits of southerners, tenaciously committed to individualism, fatalism, tradition, and lack of social solidarity. But as noted by Agostino Caputo, a writer from Cosenza, the failure of returnees to invest was also the result of lack of opportunities at home. Opportunities to invest in other activities but farming were virtually nonexistent in many small communities. With the exception of the city of Cosenza, 97 percent of the population farmed the land in one way or another. The few food-processing establishments and a handful of other services were all that most southern towns needed; therefore little room was left for other investments. Of course one could argue that returnees should have tried to create a more diversified economy. In reality the burden of tradition, lack of entrepreneurial abilities, and poverty of infrastructures made such an alternative very unlikely. Caputo, otherwise a great admirer of return migration and its positive influence on the province, concluded: "Return migration and American savings have started big changes in the province. Or so most of us have been led to believe. In reality, everything is still the same. Will things ever change for real in the south?"[17]

*Postal savings*

A large number of returnees seemingly did not share Caputo's concern over the absence of change in the south. They liked the traditional south they had grown up with. And that was one of the the reasons, perhaps the most important, why they were returning in such large numbers; although, once back, they were haunted by the ambivalence between staying in Italy or returning to the United States. The ultimate goal of these returnees was not to do anything upon returning but to have enough money to retire and live the life they had been accustomed to before going to the United States. Return and retirement became identical. Savings, of course, had to be deposited somewhere, although many returnees kept savings in cash at home.[18] Returnees to large cities could avail themselves of the Banco di Napoli or the Banco di Sicilia. A few others used the people's banks. But most deposited their savings in post offices.

The use of post offices as savings institutions was introduced in most European nations in the second half of the nineteenth century. France, Germany, and Great Britain led the way. In the new market economy and wage-labor system of the nineteenth century, it was important to promote savings habits among the population at large. Individuals would benefit from it, and society at large would have an advantage as well, so the argument went. Individuals could use savings for personal and family emergencies as well as for possible investments, and institutions could lend them out to businesses. Both individuals and society would, in the end, benefit. Responding to this philosophy, the Italian government passed a piece of legislation on May 27, 1875, giving every post office in the country the authority to accept deposits beginning on Jan. 1, 1876. Deposits were not to exceed 10,000 lire each, and post offices were to issue certificates of deposits backed by the national government. The interest rate was to be determined every six months by the national legislature. In principle, deposits in the post offices of a given region had to be invested within the region itself, according to guidelines provided by the Cassa Depositi e Prestiti.[19]

The Cassa Depositi e Prestiti was a large umbrella organization. The management of the postal savings banks, as they were called, was one of the several tasks assigned to the Cassa Depositi e Prestiti by the government. The Cassa was in fact a national bank, established on May 17, 1862, which superseded and merged several banks operating in Italian states before political unification. Through the 1860s and 1870s this national bank was assigned the management of several national funds and financial services, like the management of the fund for charities in the city of Rome, the retirement fund for elementary school teachers, the pension fund for military and civilian personnel, and, beginning in 1876, the control and investments of the funds collected through postal savings banks. Although a fraction of the Cassa's liquid assets could be invested by law in treasury bonds, the legislature disallowed the Cassa from making loans to commercial and industrial operations. The Italian legislature assigned the Cassa the primary function of extending loans at below market interest rates to cities and towns in need of money to undertake public works, especially the construction of roads and schools. Because the Cassa managed funds collected through the postal savings banks – and a large part of them were remittances – the lending policies of the Cassa have been scrutinized by historians to this day.[20]

Postal savings banks played an important role in the history of return migration, remittances, and investments in the south. In fact, when mass emigration started, southerners, with the exception of a handful of wealthy people in Naples and Palermo, had no access to savings institutions. Most emigrants were unaware that such institutions existed elsewhere in the country. In the north, for instance, savings institutions, banks and people's banks were quite common by the early 1880s. The people's banks, for instance, in existence since 1864, accepted savings from small savers and made loans to small borrowers, mostly farmers, ordinarily turned down by commercial banks. The people's banks were to be found mostly in small and rural communities.[21] Efforts to establish people's banks in the south encountered only limited success. Unwilling to engage in cooperative efforts, southerners gave limited support to people's banks, as the above narrative about Cosenza illustrates.[22] By the early 1880s, when mass emigration started in the south, the north counted on a network of private and public financial institutions, while such institutions were still the exception in the south. For instance, in 1882, of the fifteen largest savings institutions in the country, only two were in the south: the Cassa di Risparmio Vittorio Emmanuele in Sicily and the Cassa di Risparmio in Cagliari in Sardinia. By comparison, however, these two southern banks were quite small. The Vittorio Emmanuele had an operating capital of 18 million lire and the Cassa di Risparmio in Cagliari 11.6 million. On the contrary, the Cassa di Risparmio delle Provincie Lombarde in Milan had a capital of 320 million lires, which increased to 491 by 1889. At that time the Vittorio Emmanuele had 22 million lire and the Cassa di Risparmio 12 million. As for the people's banks, both in 1882 and 1892 no southern bank figured in the list of the top fifteen in the country. Similarly, in 1882 only the Banca Tiberina in Rome and the Banca Napoletana in Naples ranked among the top fifteen in the country.[23] Under the circumstances, most southerners had no choice but to deposit their savings in post offices.

A qualification is in order here. Returnees were not the only customers of the postal savings banks. Obviously, they were open to all citizens. Since 1851, in fact, when the government of tke Kingdom of Sardinia created the Cassa di Risparmio in Turin, Camillo Benso di Cavour, the chief architect of Italian unification, had promoted the idea that economic growth required capital. And capital could be accumulated only through the savings of many individuals. The conclusion was obvious. People had to be instructed that saving money was a civic duty as well as a personal advantage. Individuals who had traditionally kept their savings under a mattress or buried in a safe place under the house slowly overcame their distrust and brought their cash to the local post office or other savings institution. But the conversion was slow, especially among southerners, who had been raised to regard every governmental operation as suspicious and perhaps inimical to them. Returnees seemingly were less reluctant to trust post offices than individuals who had never emigrated. In America emigrants had learned through necessity the painful lesson that they needed to trust somebody with their money. And the American experience made them more willing to entrust their savings to a post office clerk in Italy. But, regardless of what influenced the attitudes of returnees toward post offices, the arrival of American remittances and their deposit in post offices have to be placed in the larger context of the increased awareness and practice of saving money among the Italian population at large.

Undoubtedly, however, among Italians returnees were the largest savers, as a number of observers reported. The Inchiesta Faina, for instance, discussed in detail remittances, deposits, and investments in the south. And the unanimous observation of the several reporters was that returnees were the largest depositors in post offices. In Calabria savings from returnees increased from 61,000 lire in 1876 to 32 million in 1905. A team of writers of another survey in Calabria conducted in the early twentieth century commented: "Most of the money comes from America. The two provinces with higher emigration, Cosenza and Catanzaro, post larger savings than the province of Reggio where emigration is still proportionally smaller." In fact, savings in Reggio amounted to 4.4 million lire, while in Catanzaro they were at the 10 million level and 17 million in Cosenza.[24] Over 100,000 lire in remittances were deposited in the post office of Santa Caterina Vallermosa, in the province of Caltanisetta, Sicily, for instance, within a two-month period in late 1907. A family of four in

Castrogiovanni, in the same province, deposited 30,000 lire upon returning from the United States. In Licodia Eraclea the 1907 deposits reached the 250,000 lire mark.[25] Commenting on these figures, the prefetto of Palermo reported: "Savings in post offices are almost exclusively of American origin. As a matter of fact, most of the cash available in this province comes from the United States."[26] And the prefetto of Cosenza echoed in 1911: "The communities with the highest emigration rates enjoy the largest savings."[27]

Indicators published yearly by the Postmaster General show the rapid growth of postal savings accounts, with breakdowns for regions and provinces. For instance, in 1881, deposits from remittances totaled 340,000 lire; ten years later they reached 20 million. In 1900 28 million lire were deposited, 662 million in 1904, and in 1913, the peak year of overseas emigration, deposits reached 100 million, a sum topped only in 1920, when 134 million in remittances were deposited.[28] Deposits were larger in provinces and regions with high emigration rates. In Campania, for instance, the second largest southern region with high emigration rates, deposits increased from 21 million lire in 1892 to 50 million ten years later. In 1910 deposits totaled 107 million lire. By 1920 the total for Campania was 339 million and half a billion in 1925. In Sicily, another region with high emigration, 30 million were in deposits in 1892, 50 million in 1902, 120 million in 1910, and 369 million in 1911. In Sardinia, on the other hand, a region of low-population density and virtually no emigration, the increase was more modest from 10 million in 1892, 20 million in 1902, 50 million in 1910, and 225 million in 1925. And in Basilicata, a region very similar to Sardinia, savings rose from 5 million in 1892, to 9 million in 1902, to 22 million in 1910, and 96 million in 1925.[29]

Not surprisingly there were differences also among provinces in the same region. Provinces with high emigration reported larger deposits than provinces with low emigration. In Puglie, for instance, in 1902 13 million lire were deposited in the post offices of the province of Bari, a large province with high emigration, as we have seen. The neighboring province of Lecce, on the other hand, posted only 6 million lire. The province of Lecce was smaller than Bari and with low emigration rates. Foggia, with virtually no emigration, posted only 4 million lire in savings. Similarly, in the region of Calabria, the province of Cosenza, with high emigration rates, posted almost 12 million lire in savings, while Reggio, with low emigration, reported 5 million.[30] The prefetto of Cosenza commented: "From the savings deposited in post offices one can readily determine emigration patterns. Towns with large savings have high emigration rates; towns with small savings have little or no emigration. But, in this province, towns with small or no savings are the exception."[31] And the prefetto of Palermo concluded: "Returnees are not the exclusive depositors; but they certainly deposit more money than individuals who do not emigrate."[32] Obviously, by the turn of the century, a number of Italians were saving part of their earnings. And the largest savers were returnees from the Americas.

Naturally, prefetti, politicians, and all observers of the snowballing phenomenon of emigration and return migration could only sing the praises of remittances and deposits. In addition, they predicted marvelous results for the southern economy. The argument was that the backwardness of the south had been mostly the result of lack of capital. Now capital was entering the south in large quantities. The economic development of the region was only a question of time. In the end, the south would join the most advanced northern and central European nations. But American observers too became progressively aware of the millions of dollars leaving the United States every year as remittances. And they reacted negatively. If Americans were disappointed, Italians in Italy applauded the arrival of the American savings. The expectations were boundless. As a peasant from Calabria put it: "I never envisioned that this would occur. But it did. Now people with relatives in America can afford to buy things that only the very wealthy could afford in the past."[33]

Returnees were most secretive about their savings, mostly with outsiders. Some returnees kept even their families in the dark as to the sums they had deposited in post offices. When some American observers from Chicago showed up in southern Italy to interview returnees about their American experience and their lives in Italy after their return, most returnees stated that they had left their savings in the United States. Of course, they added, they intended to be back in the United States in a short period of time. But that was not the case. Those returnees were simply suspicious that the visitors might have been sent by the Italian government to inquire about their savings in order to tax them. In another instance, when interviewers for the Inchiesta Faina arrived in Calabria, returnees suspected that the intruders were American officials with a good command of the Italian language. Their task was to find out where returnees had deposited their savings. Even local mayors were suspicious of the intruders, although they had been informed by local prefetti that the interviewers had been sent by the Italian government with the sole purpose of studying land contracts in the south and reporting about social and economic changes in the region. In the province of Cosenza the concern turned into panic. A number of returnees withdrew their deposits from post offices until the suspicious characters left town.[34]

Initially savings institutions welcomed the rapidly growing accounts of returnees. Soon enough, savings institutions were unable to invest the savings because there was no demand for loans. Incidentally, this did not happen for the post offices because by law every citizen was entitled to deposit up to 10,000 lire. Borrowing to expand an existing business or to start a new activity was virtually unknown in the south, especially in small towns. Traditionally, rural southerners had borrowed money from local moneylenders at exorbitant rates to cope with personal or family emergencies and to "save face." The operation was shrouded in secrecy and often kept hidden, even from family members. Nobody borrowed for other purposes. Incidentally, few returnees borrowed money to buy land, especially before World War I. They paid the whole amount in cash at the act of sale. Only after World War I did an increasing number of returnees supplement their savings with money borrowed from financial institutions to buy larger tracts of land. But apart from the traditional opposition of southerners to borrowing money, the local economy was so stagnant and traditional that individuals with entrepreneurial spirit were an exception in the south.[35]

## Differences between north and south

The focus of this research is the Italian south. However, a comparison between the north and the south will be useful to assess how American savings affected the economic development of the two regions. In general, regions affected by a variety of economic dynamics benefited from American savings proportionally more than regions with stagnant economies. This remark seemingly states the obvious. However, it is a first important step to assess when return migration is likely to be beneficial and when it is likely to retard economic development. The first difference between the north and the south was that southerners preferred to put their savings in post offices, whereas northerners chose other savings institutions. For instance, in 1906 in Lombardy, 12 percent of the savings were in post offices and 88 percent in other institutions. In Emilia 12.5 percent were in post offices and 87.5 elsewhere. On the contrary, 72 percent of the savings in Sicily, 64 in Calabria, 65 in Puglie, 97 in Basilicata, and 95 in Sardinia were in post offices, with the respective balances in other institutions. Among southern regions, only Campania did not follow the southern pattern. In Campania, in fact, savings were almost equally divided between postal banks and other savings institutions.[36]

Over the years savings increased in all Italian regions. But the difference between the north and the south as to the preferred institutions of deposit persisted. For instance, in 1915 82 percent of all the savings in Lombardy, 76 in Veneto, and 82 in Tuscany were in a variety of savings institutions, with the respective balances in post offices. In the south, on the other hand, 63 percent of the savings in Campania, 89 in Sardinia, 94 in Basilicata were in post offices.[37] Apparently the regions with the lowest per capita savings showed the strongest preference for postal savings. World War I and the social dislocations that followed did not alter the preferences of northerners and southerners. In 1924, for instance, only 16 percent of the savings in Lombardy, 27 percent in Veneto, and 13 in Emilia were in post offices. Tuscany, Marche, and Umbria reported similar percentages. In the south, however, 94 percent of the savings in Basilicata, 91 in Sardinia, 84 in Calabria, and 73 in Puglie were in post offices. It appears that a major change had occurred in Sicily, where only 44 percent of the savings were in postal banks, the balance in other institutions. A breakdown of these figures for Sicily, however, shows that the change had occurred only in the province of Palermo which, by itself, posted larger savings than the remaining six provinces combined.[38]

A caveat is in order here. These indicators are cumulative of all savings, whether from emigration or from other sources. And because substantial savings were brought back personally by returnees or friends of returnees – and thus went unrecorded – it is impossible to assess the size of remittances in comparison to savings from other activities. At this stage, however, the important point to be stressed is that southerners preferred postal savings banks, where deposits were safer. Northerners, on the other hand, chose commercial savings institutions which invested in a variety of economic activities. For northerners, interest was high, but so was the risk. Apparently, the overriding concern of southerners was the safety of their savings more than a good return on their money. Northerners, on the other hand, were more willing to take risks for the sake of higher returns.[39]

The second difference between north and south was that the process of savings formation occurred differently in the two regions. In the north it was the result of a variety of economic dynamics. In the south, remittances seemingly were the almost exclusive source of savings. Moreover, although the north started out with a clear advantage over the south, the south (or at least some southern regions) eventually caught up with, and in some cases surpassed, the north. Notwithstanding the fact that savings accumulated in southern post offices and other institutions grew rapidly and in some cases more spectacularly than in the north, total investments in the south lagged far behind those in the north. Some indicators illustrate these points. In 1866, at the time of political unification, northern regions posted larger per capita savings than southern counterparts: 64 lire per person in Lombardy, 26 in Tuscany, 25 in Emilia, 11 in Liguria, 8 in Piedmont with Veneto lagging behind with 6.5 lire per person. In the south, Sicily and Campania reported 3.5 lire in savings per person, the other regions posting virtually no savings.[40] Over the years, although the overall performance in the north was better than in the south, some southern regions did better than some weaker northern counterparts. By 1891, for instance, even the poorest northern region of Veneto posted per capita savings of 40 lire, a clear advantage over Sicily, the richest southern region, with 15 lire per person. By 1905, however, the difference had narrowed. Veneto posted per capita savings of 62 lire, but Campania had advanced to 57, Basilicata to 54, and Sicily to 41.[41] By 1916 some southern regions posted savings larger than Veneto: 94 in Basilicata, 92 in Campania, 83 in Calabria, while Veneto lagged behind with 81. And Veneto was not alone in this predicament. Emilia-Romagna followed a similar pattern of relative stagnation.[42] The proportionally faster increase of savings in some southern regions than some northern counterparts came to an end in 1924. The passage of the National Origins Act in the United States left many southerners uncertain as to whether they would be able to return to the United States after visiting Italy, as they were in the habit of doing. Accordingly, many sent for their families who reached them across the Atlantic. Obviously, remittances from overseas declined and the growth of savings in southern post offices slowed down. Indicators seemingly show that the growth of southern savings was mostly the result of remittances.[43]

We can corroborate this last statement with indicators of regional differences within the south. Regions with larger savings had higher emigration rates. Regions with smaller savings had lower emigration rates. The largest savings were to be found in Campania, Calabria, and Sicily, three regions of high emigration. The lowest savings were in Puglie and Sardinia, which had the lowest emigration rates. For instance, in 1906 Calabria reported 45 million lire in savings, Campania 56 million and Sicily 40 million. In 1924 Calabria had 84 million, Campania 92 million, and Sicily 70 million. On the other hand, Sardinia had 20 million and Puglie 8 million in 1906, and in 1924 Sardinia had 48 million and Puglie 47 million. Prefetture too reported a direct correlation between emigration and savings. In 1912 the prefetto of Cosenza wrote: "The bulk of the money available in this province, especially in post offices, is of American origin." And the prefetto of

Palermo corroborated: "An unprecedented amount of money is now available. Most of it comes from America either through the mail or directly through returnees."[44]

In the north the process of savings formation through remittances and domestic economic activities was more complex. It appears that in some regions savings from remittances had a negligible impact. In other regions remittances, combined with other economic activities, contributed to the transformation of local economies. Veneto typifies the former pattern: high emigration rates, substantial remittances, and yet slow economic growth. Several reasons explain why remittances failed to modernize the Veneto region. The emigration of the Veneti to South America and central Europe generated smaller savings than the emigration to the United States from other regions. Fewer Veneti sent their savings home, because many of them took their families along to Brazil and Argentina. Veneti, while abroad, saved less than southerners in general. Finally the Veneto economy was almost exclusively agrarian. Remittances were the almost exclusive source of savings. Venice, once a leading trading center of the Mediterranean basin, had turned into a tourist attraction by the turn of the century.

The region of Liguria typifies the other model: remittances combined with other dynamics transformed the region. Liguria started out at the time of political unification with disadvantages similar to Veneto. Per capita savings in Liguria were 25 lire and 19 in Veneto in 1881. But the differences in savings increased dramatically. In 1905 Liguria reported per capita savings of 182 lire and Veneto 80; in 1924 Liguria had 607 and Veneto 286.[45] By the early 1920s Liguria had become part of the industrial triangle, including Piedmont and Lombardy. The reasons for the spectacular growth of Liguria were given by the prefetto of Genoa in 1913. Family emigration had been less common in Liguria than in Veneto, return migration more frequent, and remittances found profitable investments in an economy that was becoming increasingly diversified. In fact, the port of Genoa, the busiest in the nation, had generated a host of ancillary economic activities in the city and the province. "Land sales have declined," the prefetto wrote in 1913. "And most returnees invest in small businesses, especially in cities and large towns along the coast."[46] Seemingly the discriminating element between Liguria and Veneto was that remittances and savings found investment opportunities in a diversified economy in Liguria. Such opportunities were lacking or very limited in Veneto.

The comparison between north and south provides a clue as to how remittances affected the economies of the north and the south. In the north a variety of economic dynamics, including emigration, return migration and remittances, fueled the process of savings formation and investments. Industrial development and the modernization of farming were the two leading dynamics in the most advanced regions, like Piedmont and Lombardy, where remittances played only a minor role. In Liguria and Veneto remittances were more substantial, although the final outcome in the two regions was rather different, the discriminating element being the diversification of the local economy in Liguria and the lack of such diversification in Veneto. In the south the process of savings formation was fueled almost exclusively by remittances. Although substantial, remittances played a minor role in the transformation of the local economy, mostly because the lack of a diversified economy limited the range of investment opportunities for returnees. Obviously, by themselves, remittances were impotent to bring about substantial changes. But in regions with a variety of economic dynamics remittances were a great help.

The goals of returnees were strictly personal. One cannot avoid being surprised by the absence of long-term family goals. To interviewers, returnees stated over and over again that they hoped to have saved enough to live comfortably for the rest of their lives. In many cases, however, savings were so modest that returnees could not rely exclusively on them. But returnees were confident that savings from America supplemented with income from temporary jobs during the planting and harvesting seasons would suffice. Several returnees eventually realized that they had overestimated how far they could go on their American savings. Even in Italy inflation was becoming a fact of life at the turn of the century. Besides, the availability of money increased the general expectations of southerners. Accordingly, living became more expensive for the average family. To cope with the new situation, many returnees crossed the Atlantic a second or a third time to save additional money. A returnee from Amantea in Calabria confessed that "my American savings and some income from odd jobs are now enough to live comfortably. But I do not know how long all this will last." And in Termini Imerese, in Sicily, another returnee argued that he had thought that ten years in the United States would suffice to retire in style in Sicily. But, he concluded: "I was wrong. I will have to leave for New York in March." This was in 1907. Surprisingly of all returnees interviewed for Inchiesta Faina, nobody mentioned the future of the children. Seemingly returnees were so consumed by their personal situation that they did not concern themselves with a future that seemed so distant. Perhaps, they thought that the children would have to find a solution of their own.

### The Cassa Depositi e Prestiti

Within the general topic of remittances and investments, Italian historians have focused for a long time on the investment policies of the Cassa Depositi e Prestiti, a financial institution that handled the remittances deposited in postal savings banks. The Cassa was a national bank, whose policies were mandated by the central government. In the end, the government determined how remittances deposited in post offices were to be invested. The consensus among Italian historians, especially those from the south, has been, for a number of decades, that remittances deposited in southern post offices were not invested in the south. Rather, they were used to subsidize industrial growth in the north, especially during and immediately after World War I. During the war, so the argument goes, the government used funds from the Cassa to subsidize war industries. After the war, to save from bankruptcy some northern industries during the difficult process of reconversion from war to peace production, the government subsidized them with money from the Cassa. Francesco Balletta, an economic historian at the University of Naples, best summarizes the traditional argument: "It was in the north that most savings of southerners were invested. Southern savings subsidized the growth of northern industries, especially during the war, through government bonds. After the war, some major northern Italian industries, like Ilva and Ansaldo, avoided bankruptcy only because the central government borrowed from southerners – and returnees were the only southerners with savings – to bail out northern industries. Northern banks drained to the north most of the savings southerners deposited in southern banks. Most of the loans made by the Cassa Depositi e Prestiti benefited northern provinces and municipalities, although southerners contributed the larger share of the savings in the Cassa. In the end, the gap between the industrial north and the agrarian underdeveloped south had widened: southern savings not only failed to modernize the southern economy, they also accelerated the process of modernization in the north. Once again, the south was exploited like a colony, to the exclusive advantage of the north."[47]

Southern Italian historians have made this argument for over half a century now. The purpose was to show that the ultimate failure of emigration, return migration, and remittances to modernize the south was not the fault of southerners, but the government's. Mass emigration, these historians have argued, was a social and economic dislocation of major proportions, with countless personal hardships, including the disruption of family life. Yet, southerners endured the ordeal for the sake of a better future. Unfortunately, that day never came because northerners drained whatever cash became available in the south for the industrial growth of the north. Guido Dorso and Antonio Gramsci were the first to make this argument in the 1920s. The purpose was clearly political. Dorso wrote:

> The dollars sent home by southern emigrants follow the same route of the cash which became available in the south under the Bourbon. Southern savings end up in northern banks by an inexplicable process. Southerners were led to believe for a brief shining moment that the dream of Sonnino and Franchetti was about to become a reality. Remittances would give the south the opportunity of joining developing nations. Instead, southern remittances subsidized northern industries through policies devised by the Italian government and implemented by the Cassa Depositi e Prestiti.[48]

Gramsci, in a widely debated Marxist analysis of the south, placed the blame of the failed economic renaissance in the south at the doorstep of the government:

> The silent social and economic revolution in the south, which the government allegedly supported and seemingly protected by encouraging emigration, remittances and return to Italy as a way to generate capital and transform the south, was killed at birth by the government itself. Every attempt by returnees to create some capital in the south failed because the Italian government deliberately prevented those regions from achieving their goals.[49]

The obvious conclusion of the whole argument is that if the south had been left alone, remittances would have accomplished the economic transformation of the region. Remittances and return migration failed not because of the inability of returnees and a backward southern culture. Governmental policies caused that failure.

Today this is the standard explanation southern Italian historians offer, when discussing why remittances and return migration failed to fulfill the expectations they had generated. If the argument made by these historians is true, then the implications are important. Return migration and remittances could have had a substantial impact in the south, according to this argument, notwithstanding its traditional and undiversified economy, had the government supported the process. The failure was political. Accordingly one should not fault southerners, their economy, or culture for the failed economic renaissance. On a larger scale, if this has been the case in the Italian south, then other regions or nations with substantial remittances and savings should be analyzed accordingly. The hypothesis in this case is that when remittances and return migration fail to bring about modernization, the political process perhaps is at fault. But before drawing these conclusions, at least for the Italian south, we should analyze the investment policies of the Cassa Depositi e Prestiti.

Such policies are easily documented through yearly reports made by the board of directors of the Cassa to the Italian legislature. In assigning to the Cassa the management of postal savings banks, the legislature mandated that the savings collected in post offices were not to be invested in industrial or commercial activities. Rather, the Cassa was to make loans at below market interest rates to municipalities, regions, and provinces for public works, like streets, schools, parks, and libraries. Moreover, the Cassa was empowered to renegotiate at low interest rates existing loans of municipalities and provinces. Of course, loans for public works are important in any economy, because they make possible the setting in place of infrastructures for further economic development. These loans, however, do not affect directly local industries and commerce. But, regardless of the importance one might attribute to loans for public works in the development of a given economy, the records of the Cassa show that larger loans were made to southern municipalities, provinces, and regions than to northern counterparts, with the municipalities of Rome, Naples, and Palermo the largest beneficiaries.

A random sample of the investment activities of the Cassa shows that southern municipalities and provinces, rather than northern counterparts, were the main beneficiaries of the loans. In the years 1877–9, the Cassa granted loans for over 100 million lire. Deposits increased rapidly during those three years: 7.9 million lire in 1877, 28.7 million in 1888, and 81.9 million in 1879. Unable to invest all the deposits coming in from postal savings banks, the Cassa requested the Italian legislature to lower the interest rate from 4.3 to 3.5 percent. Many depositors found the new rate too low and moved their savings elsewhere. Accordingly, in 1880 deposits declined to 67.3 million lire. Because of these substantial deposits, the Cassa granted all the loans requested by municipalities, provinces, and regions in the 1877–9 period. Only applications that did not meet the specifications of the Cassa were rejected. Most rural municipalities requested loans to build roads. Large municipalities in general requested money to build schools, because the national government had made mandatory three years of schooling for all children in the nation.

A closer analysis of the loans shows which municipalities most benefited from them. In 1878 the Cassa granted 461 loans to 290 municipalities and six provinces, for a total of 40 million lire. The largest loan of 16 million lire was made to sixty-three municipalities in Tuscany, which had borrowed heavily from commercial banks in the early 1870s and were unable to meet their obligations. But almost all the other loans were made to southern municipalities and provinces. Rome secured almost 10 million lire for public works; Naples was granted another 10 million: 4 million to pay off old debts and 6 million for public works. A total of 160 rural municipalities in the Sicilian provinces of Siracusa and Girgenti and the province of Salerno in Campania were granted 4.3 million lire for road construction.[50]

The following year the Cassa granted 282 loans to 276 municipalities and six provinces for a total of 38.5 million lire. With the exception of two loans to northern provinces, all other loans were granted to central and southern municipalities and provinces. In central Italy the three provinces of Pisa, Leghorn, and Arezzo in Tuscany secured loans for 7.3 million lire, mostly to refinance debts contracted in the early 1870s, while twenty-six municipalities in the province of Mantua were granted loans totaling 1.86 million to offset expenses incurred to repair damages caused by a major flood caused by the Po River in 1877. In the south, twenty-nine municipalities in the region of Campania were given loans for almost 8 million lire, with the city of Naples the largest beneficiary. In Sicily the province of Palermo secured loans for slightly over 2 million lire, the province of Foggia for 1.7 million, and the province of Rome for 1.2 million.[51]

In 1880 the Cassa made 497 loans, but the money allocated decreased to 27.6 million lire, with southern provinces and regions the almost exclusive beneficiaries. In Campania twenty-six municipalities, with Naples heading the list, were granted loans for 9.6 million lire; the city of Rome obtained seventy-one loans, mostly to refinance old debts. A number of municipalities in the provinces of Foggia and Cosenza were granted loans totaling 3.5 million lire. Incidentally, from 1870 to 1873 several municipalities had borrowed money from commercial banks at rates ranging from 7 to 11 percent, confident that they would be able to meet their obligations, because the economy was expanding. But in late 1873, as a severe economic recession set in, it became obvious that many municipalities would be unable to do so. When requested, the Cassa stepped in to refinance the loans at a substantially lower rate.[52]

Although the Cassa was able to accept all loan applications, with the exception of those not qualifying under the existing guidelines, millions of lire were still idle in the coffers of the Cassa. In 1879, for instance, 81.9 million lire were deposited and only 38.5 million lent to municipalities and provinces. The surplus was invested in treasury bonds at an interest rate of 4 percent, and in government-backed mortgages, as the bylaws of the Cassa mandated.[53] It is virtually impossible to trace the final investments of the treasury bonds. The purchase of treasury bonds and government-backed mortgages, how-ever, occurred only after all proper requests for loans by municipalities and provinces were met. If all the funds available in the Cassa were not invested in public works in the north and in the south, it occurred only because municipalities and provinces did not see fit to request them.

Over the years, the policies of the Cassa did not change. Southern provinces and regions, although with fewer people than northern counterparts, were granted the larger share of the loans. In 1902, for instance, in the north, only the regions of Piedmont and Emilia se-cured loans for over 1 million lire each, with Lombardy, the largest Italian region, being granted only half a million. In the south, on the other hand, Lazio – mostly the city of Rome – received 3.2 million lire, Abbruzzi and Molise 3.6 million, Campania 11 million, 9.6 million of which was for the city of Naples; Calabria received 2.5 million, and even the sparsely populated Puglie got 1.1 million.[54]

The pattern of requests for loans from southern municipalities and provinces is puzzling. Although some secured substantial loans, oth-ers showed limited borrowing activity. In 1914, for instance, Calabria borrowed over 13 million lire, and Sicily 11.5 million. But Campania, with a much larger population than Calabria, borrowed only 4.8 mil-lion, Abbruzzi e Molise 3.5 million, Puglie 2 million, and Basilicata just over half a million. However, as the report for 1914 indicates, the difference was not the result of discriminatory policies. Rather, it reflected the demands, because all applications meeting the guidelines were granted.[55] In 1914 no northern Italian region, although most of them had larger populations than Calabria and Sicily, requested loans as large as those given to Sicily and Calabria. The preponderance of investments in southern regions and provinces became even more noticeable after World War I. In 1922, for instance, total loans reached the 151 million lire mark, thus subdivided: 84.7 million to the south and 29.7 million to central regions, with the north receiving only 26.6 million. As the report for that year indicated, the larger loans to the south were justified by the greater need for public works there.[56]

These randomly selected indicators show that the lending policies of the Cassa were not biased in favor of the north. Rather, the south was the main beneficiary. This conclusion applies also to the general policies implemented by the government at the turn of the century in the two sections of the country. Historians generally agree, with the notable exception of many southern Italians, that the Italian government did not engage in conspiratorial policies to drain capital from the south to the north. Although the south paid proportionally lower provincial and municipal taxes than the north, the south received proportionally more money than the north for public works. State investments in railroads are a case in point. In 1861 only 7.2 percent of the national network was in the south. By 1875 it had increased to 32 percent. In Italy railroads were built with public money. As Shephard B. Clough and Carlo Levi conclude, the south was not exploited by the central government. Rather, it received preferential treatment from the government to bridge the gap between the north and the south in order to create an integrated and balanced national economy.[57]

All the evidence discussed in this chapter shows that most of the returnees who did not purchase land used their savings as retirement funds. Accordingly the standard of living in the south increased substantially, as local observers and visitors alike noticed. But the much anticipated and celebrated economic renaissance of the south did not occur. Remittances deposited in post offices or other savings institutions could be eventually used by returnees personally or by financial institutions for investments. Returnees, however, generally failed to invest in economic activities other than farming, because investment opportunities were extremely limited in the south and because lack of entrepreneurial skills and a culture generally opposed to economic innovations made such investments extremely unlikely and difficult. Financial institutions too progressively discovered that there was little or no demand for loans. Indeed, many such institutions, with the exception of post offices, either discouraged additional deposits or flatly rejected them. Only deposits made in post offices eventually found their way to the south through loans made by the Cassa Depositi e Prestiti to towns and regions. But those funds were invested in schools and roads, not in industrial and commercial enterprises. Obviously, remittances failed to bring about the anticipated results. But, perhaps, it was unrealistic to expect a different outcome. American remittances, certainly one of the greatest blessings for the south, from 1890 to 1929, could not by themselves bring about the economic transformation of the south. The comparison between the north and the south shows that remittances were effective in regions where other economic dynamics were at work. The south was affected by very few such dynamics. The impact of remittances and returnees – like the entire process of emigration for that matter – has to be assessed within a broader picture of larger social and economic dynamics. Emigration was not an isolated fact. It was a part of larger social and economic dynamics at work at the turn of the century.

# Conclusion: National integration and return migration

In Italy the early national experience lasted about fifty years. It started in 1870, with the occupation of Rome and the relocation of the Italian government to that city from Florence. It ended in October 1922, when Benito Mussolini marched to Rome with his black shirts. During those five decades Italy went through monumental changes. At times the nation seemed to be on the verge of collapse. For instance, during the 1870s banditry in the south threatened to expand into a full-fledged civil war, with the possible secession of some southern regions from Italy. Similarly, in the early 1890s bank failures and a protracted economic recession with consequent withdrawal of foreign investments in Italy seemed to put an end to the national experience. But the nation survived. And slowly Italy became a modern nation by engaging in the process of integrating its economy and of homogenizing its social and political functions. One can rightly question how successful Italy was in the process. After all, the half century of the national experience ushered in the fascist experiment. And Italian historians still argue as to whether fascism was an aberration of an otherwise sound national development or whether it was the logical outcome of unsound political processes started in 1870. There is no doubt, however, that by 1922 Italy was a more robust and modern nation than in 1870.

During those five decades the public discourse in Italy ranged from foreign investments to Italian military involvement in other countries. It dealt with the tormented relationship between the Vatican and Italy as well as with the role of the government in social and economic matters. Emigration eventually became one of the major topics in the national discourse. The reader of the popular and scientific literature documenting the range of the Italian political discourse of those five decades cannot but be impressed and perplexed by the attention Italians paid to the phenomenon, especially from the 1890s to the early 1920s. The topic was introduced in the 1870s through petitions in the Italian Chamber of Deputies, governmental reports from Italian consuls in the Americas, and scientific surveys. In general, the new phenomenon was regarded with suspicion because of its potential for social destabilization. By the 1880s emigration had become a mass phenomenon of such magnitude that the public discourse shifted. The new national concern was how to regulate the phenomenon to prevent social and economic destabilization. It had become obvious that no opposition would arrest the mass exodus. By the early 1890s, however, the concern over the negative impact had turned into a wholehearted endorsement for emigration. Return migration and remittances had raised great hopes of individual and social betterment, especially in the south. And from about 1895 to the beginning of World War I the national debate centered on ways to capitalize on return migration and remittances as dynamics of national integration. Of course the war introduced more pressing concerns and the interest in emigration, return migration, and remittances resumed only after the conflict. But it never regained the intensity of the prewar decades. The national interest was moving in other directions.

How are we to assess emigration and return migration? The hopes they raised were boundless. The lasting accomplishments were seemingly limited. Obviously, emigration and remittances were complex phenomena with multiple impacts both for individuals and for society at large. To start with, today we wonder how at the turn of the century Italians came to believe that return migration and remittances would almost single-handedly change the country, especially the south. The Inchiesta Faina remains the most extensive record of such boundless faith. Obviously, even the best-educated Italians of those days had a limited knowledge of the complex dynamics of modern economies. We should keep in mind, for instance, that the conventional wisdom of Italian economists in the 1870s was that the United States was ill prepared to compete with Europe and that the American economy would be able to match the performance of the European economy by the year 2000 at the earliest. The same conventional wisdom maintained that lack of capital was the exclusive reason for the economic underdevelopment in the Italian south. As American remittances began to arrive and have an impact even in the most remote villages, educated Italians argued that the capital available through remittances would almost automatically modernize the country. After all, in the Italian south, where poverty was endemic, economic dependency a fact of life, and where even hope in a better future almost impossible, the arrival of American savings was likely to be regarded as a miracle.

Some attentive observers, like Francesco Coletti, pointed out that the growth of a large-scale capitalistic economy, although based on large capital, required social and cultural attitudes which were still in short supply in the Italian south at the turn of the century. Coletti often lamented, for instance, that the peasants' resistance to change was more of an obstacle to modernization than the lack of capital. No amount of capital, Coletti concluded, could bring about modernization, as long as cultural and social attitudes would not change. But Coletti was a lonely prophet in Italy at the turn of the century. Educated Italians seemingly shared a rather simplistic faith in the transforming power of capital. Of course, events were to show that their faith was misplaced. Remittances had a marginal impact, at best, in the modernization of the Italian south. But educated Italians who shared that faith at the turn of the century should not be judged too harshly. After all, return migration and remittances affected Italy in the very early stage of its capitalistic development. And educated Italians could not rely on the national past or the history of other nations to predict and prescribe a course of action for the future. Today, after an additional eight decades of capitalistic development in Western societies, we have a much more sophisticated knowledge of the social and economic dynamics needed to bring about modernization. Yet, even today we are likely to think that availability of cash will cure poverty and set in motion economic development.

We can advance a more cynical explanation as to why Italians seemingly placed such high hopes on return migration and remittances. And there is evidence to support this explanation. The debate on remittances and the argument that return migration was changing the south provided an escape from unpleasant social and economic realities, which demanded radical reforms in the south. The best illustration for this statement is the Inchiesta Faina. As I mentioned earlier, in the early twentieth century some members of the Chamber of Deputies argued that no social and economic change would ever occur in the south without a profound reform of land contracts.[1] Of course, southern landowners opposed the suggestion and moved that the government engage in a fact-finding survey to obtain a true picture of the south. The Inchiesta Faina, after three years, concluded that the south was already on its way to major social and economic changes, thanks to return migration and remittances. Land contracts were not even mentioned. But the implication was clear. There was no need to engage in land reform. The south was changing by itself, with no outside interference. It was the conclusion southern landowners had wanted all along. The marvelous impact of return migration and remittances was emphasized in that particular instance and on many other occasions to divert the national attention from the social and economic reforms needed in the south, reforms that some interest groups strongly opposed.

These general statements, however, need qualification. Return migration and remittances affected the Italian northwest differently from the south. And even within the south, the responses varied from region to region and from province to province. The evidence indicates that return migration and remittances had a more profound impact in those regions, like the Italian northwest, where a variety of economic dynamics were at work. The impact was less profound in those regions, like the south, where very few economic dynamics were at work. Of course, it is difficult to establish such a comparison, because the variables of return migration and remittances are studied against the background of two rather different social and economic environments. But there seems to be little doubt that return migration and remittances played a great role in the development of Liguria, now one of the most developed regions in Italy. It is equally obvious that Calabria is still one of the most depressed regions in the nation, notwithstanding the great hopes generated by remittances at the turn of the century. Return migration and remittances are economic dynamics to be assessed within the larger frame of reference of the social and economic changes affecting a region. In very depressed areas, return migration and remittances seem to have a marginal impact at best. In developing areas they become one of the many dynamics at work and thus are likely to have a larger impact.

Individual returnees too showed a large variety of responses. For many, emigration provided and still provides economic security. The impact of return migration and remittances on Roccasicura can be quoted as a typical example of such response. Roccasicura is a town of 600 people in the Italian hinterland between Rome and Naples. I happened to be there the first weekend of September 1987, during the annual celebration of the local patron saint the Madonna of Vallisbona. The destinations of the emigrants from Roccasicura were manifested in the bills they pinned to the statue of the saint during the procession: Swiss francs, German marks, British pounds, French francs, and American, Canadian and Australian dollars, with a much smaller representation of Latin American currencies. In conversation with men – few women were accessible – I found out that almost everybody (four individuals excepted) had been abroad for a number of years.

Returnees from the United States were particularly interested in sharing their experiences with me. Emigrants from Roccasicura had selected three destinations in the United States: the Bronx, New Haven, and Cleveland. Most returnees were over fifty. They had returned to Roccasicura to retire. Most of them had children and grandchildren in one of the three American locations. Some returnees were making plans to return to the United States for a time to see children and grandchildren. Thanksgiving seemed to be the preferred time for family reunions; some were going to stay until after Christmas, others until Easter. Many such returnees went back to the United States every year. Before leaving, they locked the house and gave the key to a relative in town. These returnees, although eager to tell me how well they knew the place where they had lived for a number of years, and could describe it block by block, were less willing to talk about their savings. These returnees lived in comfortable houses and probably kept their savings in some financial institutions in Isernia, the provincial capital. Savings and social security from America seemed to provide enough for a comfortable retirement. None seemed to have invested in land or business. Most of the land – Roccasicura is on a high hill – was not under cultivation. The town had only the essential services it needed, like two grocery stores, a pharmacy, a meat store, and plenty of coffeehouses, where returnees spent their days. The only investment was made by a returnee from Cleveland who had opened a laundromat. But, as he told me, the business was slow and he was planning to close. As everybody agreed, the town lived on remittances from the Americas, Europe, and Australia. Most returnees seemed satisfied with their past. They had very little interest in larger events occurring in America. Italian events seemed to interest them even less. Their request was invariably whether I would visit their relatives in the three destinations. Names, addresses, and phone numbers were provided. Some had ambivalent feelings about where to live. Friends, the old house, and a strong attachment to a picturesque town kept them in Roccasicura. But children and grandchildren were in America, and they missed them. For most, the best compromise was to divide their time between Italy and the United States. Family ties, and nothing else, determined that compromise.

Of course, one is not likely to find in Italy the dissatisfied returnees. They live now – they and their children – on this side of the Atlantic. I met them over the years in New York, Washington, D.C., Chicago, San Jose, San Francisco, and New Orleans. Most old immigrants reluctantly confessed that initially they did not intend to settle permanently in the United States. And the children born or brought to the United States as infants corroborated this statement. It was after one or more returns that these individuals decided – or events prevented them from making a decision – to settle in the United States permanently. Some confessed that the major reason for staying was the children, who simply refused to return.[2] Incidentally, returnees to Roccasicura agreed that they missed their children. But they argued that perhaps they had the best of both worlds by living part of the year in Italy and part in the United States. A small number of immigrants stated that at some point they had bought property in Italy. Eventually they opened a family business in the United States. In most cases their children worked in the family business and expanded it. Some immigrants, but fewer than expected, had returned to Italy for a sentimental visit or to impress relatives and friends that "they had made it in America."

Most immigrants admitted that their final settlement in America had occurred after one or more failed attempts at relocating in home communities, with American money. Returnees who bought land were more likely to become disappointed than returnees who planned to spend the rest of their lives relying on savings. Although these events occurred several decades ago, immigrants who lived through them had no explanation as to why they had failed. In general, they argued that the original goal was to buy land in Italy. And a number of them had left with the goal of buying a specific property, after talking with the owner. But eventually they had come to realize that the dream of settling in Italy was turning into a big disappointment. When asked why, most answered that it was destiny, that it had been the government's fault, or, in some cases, that there was something wrong with what they had tried to do. In several instances, immigrants relocated in the United States without selling their land in Italy. Children of immigrants discovered after the death of their parents in the 1960s and 1970s that the parents owned property in Italy, a secret immigrants had not shared with their children, perhaps out of fear of being ridiculed. In all these accounts immigrants seemed to convey a sense of shame for something they had tried and which had gone wrong, perhaps through their own fault.

After a number of conversations with these immigrants, I realized that they shared some basic similarities. All of them were financially secure. They owned their own houses, had savings, and could afford some modest luxuries available to individuals who had worked hard all their lives and saved. They were proud of the success of their children more than of anything else. Toward home communities in Italy they had ambivalent feelings. Some wished they could have retired there. Others did not want to contemplate that option. In reality most immigrants, with rare exceptions, had never been back to Italy after the final break, nor had they intended to do so in the near future. Their memories of life in the old country were bitter sweet. Yet time and distance had created an idealized nostalgia for the old days. But there were also painful buried memories connected with life in the old country, and many immigrants were unwilling to resurrect those memories through a visit. As for America, they could sing endlessly the praises of the country that had given them a life they had not imagined in Italy. But they showed little or no interest in American society in general or even in the larger events of their own communities. Their families and relatives in America were the only world they knew. Many complained of rejection, discrimination, hard times, but with a profound sense of resignation that reminded me of the fatalism I had encountered in southern Italy. These immigrants seemed to have carved out an existence free from material want. But that was all they had achieved. The larger world apparently made little sense to them.

Yet large economic transformations affecting both Italy and the United States were the forces that shaped the lives of Italian immigrants both in Italy and the United States. Perhaps the best way to conceptualize those transformations was provided by some world-system analysts, such as Immanuel Wallerstein, who describes the formation of the capitalist world system and the market relations creating it.[3] According to this paradigm, the nature of capitalism is economic growth, which creates unequal developments. In the specific case of the Western world, the core economies of northern and western Europe created dependent economic peripheries in southern and eastern Europe and in the North American colonies through the fifteenth and sixteenth centuries. Trade linked core and periphery. Initially the periphery exported raw material and food to the core. Later the periphery became market for industrial production from the core and source of cheap labor. In the world system, Italy and especially the Italian south was a periphery, exporting wheat to central and northern Europe, as Chapter 3 describes. Although linked, through commercial agriculture, to core capitalistic nations as early as the sixteenth century the Italian south could hardly be described as a capitalistic society at that time. Rather, it was a feudal society, with peasants having virtually no control over the means of production. In time, however, the commercial ties between core and periphery disseminated capitalistic ferments, even in the Italian south. And one of the social components of capitalism is the individual drive toward some form of control over production either through direct ownership or through labor organization. In the agrarian economy of the south, that drive became the peasants' determination to buy land.

In theory, the approach was sound. Land ownership would give previously propertyless peasants some form of control over their lives. In fact, southern peasants had traditionally suffered because of two handicaps: underemployment and total lack of control over land contracts. Even in the late nineteenth century, a southern peasant could secure employment for less than two hundred days a year. In addition, if he rented land with a sharecropping or other agreement, he had no control over the contract. In a market economy these two handicaps were most debilitating. The new Italian state too was encouraging propertyless peasants to buy small properties, both to curb the power of large landowners and to create a larger pool of small landowners loyal to the new state. Temporary emigration and remittances were the most effective strategies peasants found to achieve the goal of land ownership. Unfortunately as this process was under way the trade arrangement between the core and the periphery changed. Within a matter of a few years the south turned from a supplier of wheat to central and northern Europe to an importer of American wheat first and American manufactures later. The south became a consumer of goods produced elsewhere and an exporter of men raised in the south. What southerners needed, however, was cash to buy, not land to farm. Small land properties became obsolete. But returnees were obviously unaware of the big change that had occurred in the world market. The economic protectionism and some reforms set in place by the Italian government to save small properties were of no use in the long run. The change in trade arrangements between core and periphery was of such magnitude that any political decision to arrest the economic course was bound to fail.

Returnees who bought land and eventually failed were baffled. Land properties had traditionally been the source of economic stability and social status in the south. Suddenly land became almost a liability. As they left home communities for the last time, these former returnees could not avoid the disappointing realization that they had failed. They and their ancestors had been marginal people in Italian societies for centuries. This last attempt to break the cycle of poverty and powerlessness failed. That sense of failure crossed the Atlantic with them and vastly colored their perception of American society. But these now permanent immigrants were not willing to take all the blame. They progressively developed the argument that governmental policies too were responsible for their failure. And educated southerners elaborated that argument into a full-fledged interpretation of southern dependency. The economic policies set in place after unification, educated southerners pointed out, had effectively maintained the south in a position of economic dependency. The administrative and political systems forced on the south by the north had had an adverse impact on the southern economy, which had evolved for centuries under a different system. The fiscal policies of the central government – and this was a major point – were openly biased in favor of northern industries. And even the remittances sent home by emigrants were ending up in northern coffers. Insofar as southerners equated the Italian north and the central government with the modern state, these permanent emigrants departed with a deep-seated perception that their failure was also the result of conspiratorial policies by the modern state. If a solution was to be found, emigrants concluded, it had to be worked out privately. It was useless to expect anything from the state.

Educated southerners who observed emigration, return migration, remittances, land purchases, failures, and final departures advanced a radical solution, which sounded quite similar to the one advanced by the states of the American Confederacy to explain the economic decline of the Italian south and to justify secession. Because the south was economically discriminated against by the north, educated southerners maintained, the south should secede or at least set in place substantial regional autonomies to keep remittances in the south and prevent the north from keeping the south in a dependency situation. The proposed solution found wide acceptance among many southern intellectuals. Southern historians, for instance, readily elaborated a set of data showing that north and south were about equal at the time of political unification and that the disparity had been created by governmental policies in the first few decades of national experience. Southern anthropologists added that northern Italians, by openly embracing widely accepted theories of southern inferiority, had created the cultural presuppositions for excluding the south as an equal partner in the new nation. Northern Italians felt betrayed by the negative reaction of southerners. A few northerners argued that the north had made a mistake in bringing the south into the nation, but most northerners pointed out that the nation had given preferential treatment to the south for a number of decades. Besides, some southern regions had been granted administrative and even political autonomies. Perhaps, northerners concluded, southerners should have reexamined their loyalty to the nation, instead of questioning the validity of governmental policies.

In reality the negative reaction of southerners toward Italy in general and toward the government and northerners in particular was not directed to the historical state of Italy. Rather it was the reaction against modern economic dynamics, the capitalist state, and the demands that the modern state and economy invariably make of individuals. And for a moment southerners indulged in psychological escapism by arguing that their economic problems could be solved by severing the ties with the north and establishing an independent south. Southern Italians were not unique in elaborating that response. Over the years, other regions experiencing economic decline because of inability to compete with stronger economies tried to find a political solution to economic woes through political independence, separation, or at least political autonomy. Unfortunately, in the increasingly interdependent system of world capitalism, peripheral nations are simply likely to increase their dependency on core nations when they chose political separation. After all, in the market economy of Western capitalistic societies, economic dynamics vastly overpower and condition political decisions. Any political decision vastly out of step with the dynamics of the market economy is likely to backfire. And any maverick economy is certainly dysfunctional in the interdependent system of world capitalism.

Many Italians who eventually settled in the United States embraced their new life in America with a sense of having failed in Italy. Insofar as their failure had been the result of political and economic dynamics beyond their control, they emigrated with resentment toward the modern state that had been unable to control those dynamics. In their specific case, the state was Italy. But the resentment extended to the new country as well. Accordingly, when they settled in the United States, these permanent immigrants worked hard to achieve economic independence, as they had tried to do in home communities as returnees, with a minimum of interaction with the larger forces at work in American society. Italians in the United States tried by and large to find a very private solution to their material needs. And when they encountered resistance, they overreacted either by withdrawing or by attacking. The overreaction was the result of oversensitivity developed during the previous experience as returnees in Italy. Unfortunately, return migration was a negative experience for many Italians. It made more difficult the process of adjustment to modern societies. And it certainly conditioned for a long time the Italian experience in the United States. This is why so many Italian Americans are still so ambivalent, in my opinion, toward American society. The battle that immigrants fought and lost in Italy as returnees keeps haunting them. Until Italian Americans purge themselves of that experience they will not be able to embrace American society unreservedly.

# Notes

Abbreviations used in Notes

ASB   *Archivio di Stato di Bari*
ASC   *Archivio di Stato di Cosenza*
ASF   *Archivio di Stato di Foggia*
ASG   *Archivio di Stato di Genova*
ASM   *Archivio di Stato di Matera*
ASN   *Archivio di Stato di Napoli*
ASP   *Archivio di Stato di Palermo*
ASS   *Archivio di Stato di Salerno*

## Introduction

1   Italo Musillo, *Retour et emploi des migrants dans le Mezzogiorno* (Geneva, Organisation Internationale du Travail, 1981, Mimeographed); Solon Ardittis, *Migrations internationale pour l'emploi. Document de travail* (Geneva, Bureau International du Travail, 1988), pp. 1–15.

2   W. H. Bohning, "Some Thoughts on Emigration from the Mediterranean Basin," *International Labor Review* 111 (March 1975): 251–77.

3   For a collection of essays by a team of specialists on return migration in Europe, see Daniel Kubat, ed., *The Politics of Return. International Return Migrants in Europe* (New York, 1984).

4   Rosemarie Rogers, "Return Migration in Comparative Perspective," in Daniel Kubat, ed., *The Politics of Return. International Return Migrants in Europe* (New York: 1984), pp. 288–92.

5   A. S. Oberai and H. K. Manmohan Sing, "Migration, Remittances and Rural Development," *International Labor Review* 119 (March–April 1980): 229–41; John R. Harris and Michael Todaro, "Migration, Unemployment and Development: A Two Sector Analysis," *The American Economic Review* 60 (March 1970): 126–42.

6   Luigi Favero and Graziano Tassello, "Cent'anni di emigrazione italiana: 1876–1976," in Gianfausto Rosoli, ed., *Un secolo di emigrazione italiana: 1876–1976* (Rome, 1978), pp. 21–37.

7   See, for instance, John Briggs, *An Italian Passage: Immigrants in Three*

*American Cities, 1890–1930* (New Haven, Conn., 1978); Humbert Nelli, *The Italians in Chicago, 1880–1930: A Study in Social Mobility* (New York, 1970); and Virginia Yans-McLaughlin, *Family and Community: Italian Immigrants in Buffalo, 1880–1930* (Ithaca, N.Y., 1977).

8  Richard Gambino, *Blood of My Blood* (New York, 1974); Patrick Gallo, *Old Bread, New Wine. A Portrait of the Italian-Americans* (Chicago, 1981).

9  Kerby Miller, *Emigrants and Exiles. Ireland and the Irish Exodus to North America* (New York, 1985), pp. 4, 8.

## Chapter 1. The difficult task of national integration

1  Historians have variously interpreted the economic, social, and political dynamics that led to the political integration of Italy. For a discussion of the different interpretations, see W. Maturi, *Interpretazioni del Risorgimento* (Turin, 1962); R. Romeo, *Nuove questioni di storia del Risorgimento e dell'unità d'Italia* (Milan, 1961); idem, *Il giudizio storico del Risorgimento* (Catania, 1967); R. Moscati, *Risorgimento liberale* (Catania, 1967). For a left-wing interpretation of the Italian Risorgimento, see Antonio Gramsci, *Il Risorgimento* (Turin, 1949). This is a collection of essays written by Gramsci between 1927 and 1945 while in prison. Another learned left-wing interpretation is G. Candeloro, *Storia dell'Italia moderna*, vol. 1 (Milan, 1956). For some general works on the events of the time, with particular reference to politics, see Alfredo Oriani, *La lotta politica in Italia* (Turin, 1892); P. Gobetti, *Rivoluzione liberale* (Turin, 1924); Renzo De Felice, ed., *Storia dell'Italia contemporanea*, vol. 1: *Stato e Società, 1870–1898* (Naples: 1976); G. Perticone, *L'Italia contemporanea dal 1871 al 1948* (Milan, 1962); G. Carossi, *Storia d'Italia dall'unità ad oggi* (Milan, 1975). One of the best studies in English is Dennis Mack Smith, *Italy. A Modern History* (Ann Arbor, Mich. 1959).

2  See, for instance, Eugen Weber, *Peasants into Frenchmen. The Modernization of Rural France* (Stanford, 1976). For a brief discussion of the American Civil War within the context of regionalism versus nationalism in Western societies, see David M. Potter, "The Civil War in the History of the Modern World: A Comparative View," in David Potter, ed., *The South and the Sectional Conflict* (Baton Rouge, 1968), pp. 287–99.

3  Pasquale Villari, "Sulla questione sociale dell'Italia meridionale," *Nuova Antologia* 216 (1907): 460.

4  Incidentally, only 17 percent of the Sicilian population cast their vote in the popular referendum. On this, see Francesco Guardioni, "La Sicilia nell'unità italiana," *Nuova Antologia* 22 (1909): 480.

5  Dennis Mack Smith, "Regionalism," in Edward R. Tannenbaum and Emiliana P. Noether, eds., *Modern Italy: A Topical History since 1861* (New York, 1974), pp. 125–46. See also Francesco De Sanctis, *Il Mezzogiorno e lo Stato unitario* (Bari, 1960); Rosario Villari, ed., *Il Sud nella storia d'Italia.* (Bari, 1961); Carlo Tivaroni, *Storia critica del Risorgimento italiano* (Turin, 1894).

6  Prefetto of Naples, (report, 7 May 1887), ASN.

7  Pasquale Villari, *Italian Life in Town and Country* (New York, 1902), p. 2. See also Michele Viterbo, *Il Mezzogiorno e l'accentramento statale* (Bologna, 1923); Francesco Saverio Nitti, *Napoli e la questione meridionale* (Naples, 1903); Adriana Petracchi, *Le origini dell'ordinamento comunale e provinciale italiano. Storia della legislazione piemontese sugli enti locali dalla fine dell'Antico Regime al chiudersi dell'età Cavouriana: 1770–1861* (Venice, 1962).

8  Incidentally, some of them escaped to the Americas and became the first Italian immigrants in some American cities.

9  Tullio De Marco, *Storia linguistica dell'Italia unita* (Bari, 1963), p. 41; Umberto Zanotti-Bianco, *Meridione e meridionalisti* (Rome, 1964).

10  Ettore Ciccotti, *Mezzogiorno e settentrione d'Italia* (Milan, 1898), p. 13; Marc Mormier, *Histoire du brigandage dans l'Italie meridionale* (Paris, 1860), pp. 112–25.

11  A. Caracciolo, *Il Parlamento nella formazione del Regno d'Italia* (Milan, 1960); A. Pavone, *Amministrazione centrale e amministrazione periferica da Rattazzi a Ricasoli, 1859–1866* (Milan, 1964); A. Acquarone, *L'unificazione legislativa ed i codici del 1865* (Milan, 1960).

12  A. William Salomone, "Statecraft and Ideology in the Risorgimento: The Italian National Revolution," in Edward R. Tannenbaum and Emiliana P. Noether, eds., *Modern Italy: A Topical History since 1861* (New York, 1974), pp. 3–26. See also Edgard Holt, *The Making of Italy* (New York, 1971); George Martin, *The Red Shirt and the Cross of Savoy: The Story of the Italian Risorgimento* (New York, 1969); and Rosario Romeo, *Risorgimento e capitalismo* (Bari, 1959).

13  The increase in cotton growing in the Italian south represented a major reversal after several decades of decline, which started in the 1820s, when southern Italian cotton could no longer compete against the cheaper Indian and, especially, American imports. In 1863 cotton production in Italy reached its peak, with 88,000 hectares under cultivation. But the decline was quite rapid after the American Civil War came to an end. By 1874 only 35,000 hectares of land were farmed at cotton; by 1886, they had declined further to 16,000. See Confederazione Fascista dei Lavoratori dell'Agricoltura, *Agricoltura ed autharchia economica* (Rome, 1937), p. 215. On this topic, see also *Annales internationales de statistique agricole, 1933–34* (Rome, 1934), p. 258.

14  Filippo Virgilii, *L'Italia agricola odierna* (Milan, 1930), p. 44; Giacomo Acerbo, *La economia dei cereali nell'Italia e nel mondo* (Milan, 1934), pp. 610, 742; Giustino Fortunato, *Il Mezzogiorno e lo Stato italiano. Discorsi politici, 1880–1910* (Florence, 1926), vol 2., pp. 339–46.

15  Acerbo, *La economia*, p. 424; Fortunato, *Il Mezzogiorno e lo Stato*, vol. 2, p. 340. Wine exports from Italy increased from 260,000 hectoliters in 1861 to 390,000 in 1871, to 1 million in 1879. From 1880 to 1886 the yearly exports of wine averaged almost 2 million hectoliters, with an all-time high of 3.5 million in 1887. See Virgilii, *L'Italia*, p. 79; see also Italy, *Direzione Generale della Statistica* (hereafter cited as DGS), *Annuario statistico italiano, 1887–88*, pp. 326, 1,283. For some broader studies of the Italian economy at the time of political unification, see Gino Luzzatto, *L'economia*

*italiana dal 1861 al 1914*, vol. 1: *1861–1894* (Milan, 1963); S. B. Clough and L. De Rosa, *Storia dell'economia italiana dal 1861 ad oggi* (Bologna, 1971); E. Corbino, *Annali dell'economia italiana 1861–1914*, vols. 1–5 (Città di Castello, 1931–1938). To meet the increased European demand for wine and wheat, thousands of hectares of forest land were cleared for wheat and wine production. On this, see Italy, *Annuario statistico dell'agricoltura italiana, 1936–38*, vol 1 (Rome, 1940), p. 7; and Friedrich Vochting, *La questione meridionale* (Naples, 1955), p. 57.

16  Quoted in Virgilii, *L'Italia*, p. 39.

17  Smith, "Regionalism," in Tannenbaum and Noether, eds., *Modern Italy*, p. 136. For more general studies on the south at the time of political unification, see Salvatore F. Romano, *Storia della questione meridionale* (Palermo, 1945); B. Caizzi, ed., *Antologia della questione meridionale* (Milan, 1962); Villari, ed., *Il Sud nella storia d'Italia*.

18  Fortunato, *Il Mezzogiorno e lo Stato*, vol. 2, pp. 67–70, 204.

19  Giustino Fortunato, *Pagine e ricordi parlamentari* vol. 2 (Rome, 1947), p. 225.

20  Vochting, *La questione*, p. 183.

21  As late as 1901 Antonio Salandra, then the country's prime minister, lamented that "the fatal and irresponsible illusions about the fabled riches of the south are still alive, simply because northerners did not go anywhere off the beaten track" (Smith, "Regionalism," in Tannebaum and Noether, eds., *Modern Italy*, p. 136).

22  The first survey was conducted by Leopoldo Franchetti, *Condizioni economiche ed amministrative delle province napoletane. Appunti di viaggio* (Florence, 1875). See also by Sidney Sonnino, *La Sicilia nel 1876. I contadini in Sicilia* (Florence, 1877).

23  The survey, commissioned and funded by the Italian Senate, was directed by Senator Stefano Jacini, an expert on agriculture in Lombardy. He himself had written a book on the topic, *La proprietà fondiaria e le popolazioni agricole in Lombardia* (Milan, 1854). The survey was authored by several experts on agricultural matters. The findings were published in fifteen volumes in Rome from 1883 to 1886. For two studies on that important survey, see A. Caracciolo, *L'inchiesta agraria Jacini* (Turin, 1958); and D. Novacco, *L'inchiesta Jacini* (Palermo, 1963).

24  The north was first introduced to a realistic view of the south when Pasquale Villari published the famed *Lettere meridionali* (Florence, 1878), a collection of letters previously published in *L'Opinione*, a Milan newspaper, throughout the year 1875. De Viti De Marco, Nitti, Colajanni, Ciccotti, and Fortunato were all involved in Italian national politics and expressed their points of view both on the floors of the Senate and of the Chamber of Deputies and in national magazines. Only later in life had they the leisure to write book-length analyses of their regions. Among their most important works, see A. De Viti De Marco, *Un trentennio di lotte politiche, 1894–1922* (Rome, 1929); Francesco Saverio Nitti, *La città di Napoli. Studi e ricerche* (Naples, 1902); idem, *La ricchezza d'Italia*.

*Quanto è ricca l'Italia e come è distribuita la ricchezza in Italia* (Turin, 1905); Napoleone Colajanni, *Settentrionali e meridionali. Agli italiani del Mezzogiorno* (Milan, 1898); idem, *Le condizioni economiche, demografiche, biologiche, intellettuali e morali di alcune regioni d'Italia* (Naples, 1906); Ettore Ciccotti, *Sulla questione meridionale. Scritti e discorsi* (Milan, 1904); Fortunato, *Il Mezzogiorno e lo Stato*; idem, *Pagine ricord parlamentare* (Florence, 1920) vol. 1; idem, *Pagine e ricordi parlamentari* (Rome, 1947) vol. 2

25   Alfredo Niceforo, *L'Italia barbara contemporanea* (Milan: 1898).

26   Vochting, *La questione*, pp. 3–18; See also G. Valmorani, *I terreni della Sicilia. Sguardo pedologico-agrario* (Palermo, 1948); Vincenzo Nigri, *La capitanata. Foggia ed il suo clima* (Sansevero, 1914); Vincenzo Rivera, *Il problema agronomico nel mezzogiorno d'Italia* (Rome, 1924).

27   The only exceptions in the south were the *masserie*. They were the houses of wealthy landowners ordinarily built at the very center of a large estate, especially in the Sicilian hinterland. Those buildings, however, were fortresses as well as centers of food processing, besides being residences. The 1881 Italian national census took a survey of housing. One of the purposes was to assess whether people lived in nucleated communities or on the very land they farmed. For this, see Ministero di Agricoltura, Industria e Commercio, *Censimento della popolazione del Regno d'Italia al 31 dicembre 1881*, vol.1, pt. 2: *Popolazione secondo la qualità della dimora degli abitanti dei comuni* (Rome, 1883). In future references, the Ministero di Agricoltura, Industria e Commercio will be quoted as MAIC. See also Jane Schneider and Peter Schneider, *Culture and Political Economy in Western Sicily* (New York, 1976), pp. 32–6.

28   Italy, Ministero dell'Interno, Direzione generale della sanità pubblica, *La malaria in Italia ed i risultati della lotta antimalarica* (Rome, 1924), pp. 24–35, 68; see also Vochting, *La questione*, p. 18.

29   Vochting, *La questione*, p. 19; see also Nunzio Prestianni, *L'economia agraria della Sicilia* (Palermo, 1947); Manlio Rossi-Doria, "I problemi della trasformazione fondiaria nel mezzogiorno e nelle isole," *Rivista di Economia Agraria* 3 (1946): 195–207; Schneider and Schneider, *Culture*, pp. 32–40.

30   In the province of Palermo, people lived in nucleated communities also to be safe from the Mafia.

31   Otto Maull, *Landerkunde in Südeuropa* (Leipzig, 1929), p. 246; Antonio Pompa, *Inchiesta sul latifondo: Agro di Foggia* (Foggia, 1932), p. 41; Guido Mangano and Stefano Scrofani, *Un tipico comprensorie siciliano a granicoltura estensiva* (Palermo, 1935), p. 27.

32   Prefetto of Palermo, report, 17 May 1883, ASP; and prefetto of Cosenza, report, 16 April 1893, ASC.

33   Giovanni Morso, *La Sicilia e la libertà.* (Gela, 1944), p. 4; Pasquale Villari, *Scritti sulla questione sociale in Italia* (Florence, 1902); A. Carcciolo, *La formazione dell'Italia industriale* (Bari, 1973); G. Fissore and G. Meinardi, eds., *La questione meridionale* (Turin, 1976).

34   On Sicily, see Dennis Mack Smith, *A History of Sicily: Medieval Sicily 800–*

*1713* (New York, 1968); idem, *A History of Sicily: Modern Sicily After 1713* vol. 2 (London, 1968); and for Italy in general, idem, *Italy: A Modern History* (Ann Arbor, 1959).

35 Robert Davidsohn, *Geschichte von Florenz* pt. 2 (Berlin, 1925), pp. 409–23; and also Georges Yver, *Le Commerce et les merchants dans l'Italie meridionale au XIII et XIV siècles* (Paris, 1920).

36 The Florentine Renaissance in art and literature was made possible, at least to a degree, by the money collected in the south at this time.

37 The opposition was so fierce that agents of the Florentine banks requested and obtained permission to bear arms in public.

38 Only the southern republic of Amalfi came close to compete, at least for a time, against the powerful northern rivals.

39 On this topic see Antonio Serra, "Breve trattato delle cause che possono far abbondare i regni d'oro e d'argento dove non sono miniere," in Augusto Graziani, ed., *Scrittori d'Italia: Economisti del cinque e seicento* (Bari, 1913), p. 150.

40 Alfredo Pino-Branca, *La vita economica degli stati Italiani nei secoli XVI, XVII, e XVIII* (Catania, 1936), pp. 460–5, 478–85.

41 The Spanish domination of the south lasted from 1503 to 1734, when the Kingdom of Naples became independent, but with a Bourbon king. The Bourbons ruled the south – with the brief interlude of the Napoleonic occupation – until 1860, when Giuseppe Garibaldi took over the Italian south on behalf of the king of Italy, Victor Emmanuel II. After the Congress of Vienna in 1815, the Kingdom of Naples had been renamed the Kingdom of the Two Sicilies.

42 Silk production provided jobs to thousands of people in the Naples region.

43 Luigi Dal Pane, *La questione del commercio dei grani nel settecento in Italia*, vol. 1 (Milan, 1932), p. 50–7.

44 In the late eighteenth century, there were twenty non-Italian commercial houses in Naples. But there was no Neapolitan commercial house in any northern Italian city or in any foreign city. See Gino Arias, *La questione meridionale* vol. 3 (Bologna, 1919), p. 387.

45 It is reported that tax collectors used to make good of the peasants' obligations by taking off the tiles from the roofs of the houses of peasants when peasants could not pay in any other way. See Pino-Branca, *La vita economica*, pp. 472–5. This is one of the best books on the Spanish economic policies in southern Italy.

46 Antonio Genovesi, *Lezioni di economia civile* vol. 8 (Milan, 1803), p. 219.

47 Research on sanitary conditions in the south at that time is still at the beginning stage. We know for a fact that malaria spread at that time in the flatlands around Rome. See Angelo Gelli, *Storia della malaria nell'agro romano* (Città di Castello, 1925).

48 Ernesto Pontieri, *Il riformismo borbonico nella Sicilia del sette e dell'ottocento* (Naples, 1965); idem, *Il tramonto del baronaggio siciliano* (Florence, 1943).

49 Carl Ulysses Salis-Marschlins, *Reisen in Verschirdenen Provinzen des Konigreichs Neapel* (Zurich: 1790); and Vochting, *La questione*, pp. 46–7.

50  Incidentally most agreements were verbal, owners reserving to them-
    selves the right to change the terms of the agreement at any time before
    the harvest season.
51  An industrial south did not begin to take shape until after World War
    II.
52  Pino-Branca, *La vita economica*, pp. 461–5, 495; Carl Ulysses Salis-
    Marschlins, *Beitrage zur Naturlichen und Okonomischen Kenntnis des Koni-
    greichs beider Sizilien*, vol. 1 (Zurich, 1790), pp. 139–46.
53  Leopoldo Franchetti, *Inchiesta in Sicilia* (Florence, 1876), pp. 344–63; Pino-
    Branca, *La vita economica*, pp. 461, 495; P. Villari, *Lettere Meridionali*, pp. 4,
    6; idem, *La Sicilia ed il Socialismo* (Florence, 1899), p. 65.
54  On this important topic, see Giuseppe Alongi, *La Maffia nei suoi fattori e
    nelle sue manifestazioni. Studio delle classi pericolose in Sicilia* (Turin, 1887);
    Marc Bloch, *Feudal Society* (Chicago, 1961); Enzo D'Alessandro, *Brigan-
    taggio e Mafia in Sicilia* (Florence, 1959); Gaia Filippo, *L'esercito della Lupara.
    Baroni e banditi siciliani nella guerriglia contro l'Italia* (Milan, 1962); Salvatore
    F. Romano, *Storia della Mafia* (Verona, 1966). And for a work of fiction
    on this topic, see Giuseppe Tomasi di Lampedusa, *Il Gattopardo* (Milan,
    1958).
55  M. I. Finley, Dennis Mack Smith, and C. Duggan, *A History of Sicily* (New
    York, 1987), pp. 151–7.
56  Smith, *A History of Sicily Modern: Sicily after 1713*, vol. 2 (London, 1968);
    Nicolò Genovese. *La questione agraria in Sicilia. Cause e rimedi* (Milan, 1894).
57  Franchetti, *La Sicilia*, pp. 344–7; Sidney Sonnino, *La Sicilia nel 1876. I
    contadini in Sicilia* (Florence, 1877), pp. 190, 290.
58  Prefetto of Cosenza, report, 23 October 1889, ASC; and prefetto of Pal-
    ermo, report, 6 December 1901, ASP.
59  Ciccotti, *Sulla questione meridionale*, p. 13.
60  In Calabria, for instance, a mother would express her affection for a small
    child by calling him "my darling little brigand."
61  Mormier, *Histoire du brigandage*, pp. 112–27; Alfredo Oriani, *La lotta politica
    In Italia. Origini della lotta attuale* (Florence, 1921), vol. 3, p. 142. See also
    E. J. Hobsbawm, *Primitive Rebels. Studies in Archaic Forms of Social Move-
    ment in the Nineteenth and Twentieth Centuries* (Manchester, 1959).
62  *Omertà* is connivance. People witnessing a crime were expected to say
    that they had not seen or heard anything.
63  Perhaps the best study on the origins of the Mafia is Anton Block, *The
    Mafia of a Sicilian Village, 1860–1960. A Study of Violent Peasant Entrepreneurs*
    (New York, 1974). See also Giuseppe Alongi, *La Mafia nei suoi fattori*;
    Antonio Cutrera, *La Mafia ed i mafiosi* (Palermo, 1900); Hobsbawm, *Prim-
    itive Rebels*; Giuseppe C. Marino, *L'opposizione mafiosa, 1870–1882. Baroni
    e Mafia contro lo Stato liberale* (Palermo, 1964). Ernesto Pontieri, *Il tramonto
    del baronaggio siciliano* (Florence, 1943); and Francesco S. Romano, *Storia
    della Mafia* (Verona, 1966).
64  Morso, *La Sicilia e la libertà*, pp. 16–21; P. Villari, *Lettere meridionali*, pp. 6,
    14.
65  Gaetano Mosca, "Che cos'è la Mafia?"*Giornale degli Economisti* 20 (1900):

236–63; Barrington Moore, *Social Origins of Dictatorship and Democracy. Lord and Peasant in the Making of the Modern World* (Boston, 1966).

66  C. Pavone, *Amministrazione centrale e amministrazione periferica da Rattazzi a Ricasoli* (Milan, 1964); Petracchi, *Le origini dell'ordinamento comunale e provinciale italiano;* Caracciolo, *Il Parlamento.*

67  M. D'Addio, *Politica e magistratura, 1848–1876* (Milan: 1966); A. Acquarone, *L'unificazione legislativa;* R. Ruffilli, *La questione regionale dall'unificazione alla dittatura: 1862–1942* (Milan, 1971); idem, "Problemi dell'organizzazione amministrativa nell'Italia liberale," *Quaderni Storici* 18 (1971): 699–730. On this topic, see also two reports by the prefeto of Palermo to the Minister of the Interior in Rome, 17 May 1873 and 7 October 1882, ASP, Palermo.

68  A. Plebano, *Storia della finanza italiana nei primi quarant'anni dell'unificazione,* 3 vols.(Padova, 1960); L. Jona Celesia, *Il bilancio degli stati preunitari e la loro influenza sul bilancio dello Stato italiano* (Turin, 1971).

69  Ciccotti, *Sulla questione meridionale,* pp. 16–23; G. Are, "Alla ricerca di una filosofia dell'industrializzazione nella cultura e nei programmi politici in Italia, 1861–1915," *Nuova Rivista Storica* (1969): 44–133.

70  B. Stringher, *Gli scambi con l'estero e la politica commerciale italiana dal 1860 al 1910* (Rome, 1911); Luigi Izzo, *Storia delle relazioni commerciali tra l'Italia e la Francia dal 1860 al 1875* (Naples, 1965).

71  Guido Dorso, *La Rivoluzione Meridionale,* 2d ed. (Rome, 1945), p. 111.

72  Francesco Manzotti, *La polemica sull'Emigrazione nell'Italia unita fino alla prima guerra mondiale* (Milan, 1966); Grazia Dorè, *La democrazia italiana e l'emigrazione in America* (Brescia, 1946).

## Chapter 2. A blueprint for change

1  Dennis Mack Smith, "Regionalism," in Edward R. Tannenbaum and Emiliana Noether, eds., *Modern Italy. A Topical History since 1865* (New York, 1974), p. 137.

2  Friedrick Vochting, *La questione meridionale* (Naples, 1955), p. 153.

3  On this problem, see Luigi Carbonieri, *Della regione in Italia* (Modena, 1861); Francesco De Sanctis, *Il Mezzogiorno e lo Stato unitario* (Bari, 1970); Adriana Petracchi, *Le origini dell'ordinamento comunale e provinciale italiano. Storia della legislatura piemontese sugli enti locali dalla fine dell'Antico Regime al chiudersi dell' età Cavouriana: 1770–1861* (Venice; 1962); Michele Viterbo, *Il Mezzogiorno e l'accentramento statale* (Bologna, 1923).

4  C. Ghisalberti, *Storia costituzionale d'Italia, 1849–1948* (Bari, 1971).

5  Campanilismo means loyalty to the bell tower of one's commune.

6  Vochting, *La questione,* p. 150; Smith, "Regionalism," in Tannenbaum and Noether, eds., *Modern Italy,* pp. 125–44.

7  To compound the problem, northerners had little confidence in the administrative abilities of southerners.

8  For instance, there was such a variety of land-tenure systems in the Italian states before the political unification of the country that the compilation

of a national register of land properties under uniform guidelines provided by the new Italian government took sixty years.

9 Pasquale Villari, *Il sud nella storia d'Italia* (Bari, 1961), pp. 72–3 Francesco De Stefano and Francesco L. Oddo, *Storia della Sicilia dal 1860 al 1910* (Bari, 1963), pp. 38–94; idem, "La Sicilia e lo Stato unitario," in *Giornale Officiale di Sicilia*, 26 November 1860; G. Scichilone, *Documenti sulle condizioni della Sicilia dal 1860 al 1870* (Rome, 1962). See also *Atti Parlamentari* (Camera dei Deputati) (the publication of the daily deliberations of the Italian House of Deputies), (Rome, 2 April 1861), pp. 367–9, 408, 415, 418–19; idem, (Rome, 8 December 1863), p. 2,189; idem, (Rome: 23 July 1868), pp. 7,555–6.

10 G. Raffaele, *Rivelazioni storiche* (Palermo; 1883); F. Perrone-Paladino, *Mali e rimedi* (Palermo, 1865); F. Maggiore-Perni, *Lo Stato italiano ed i beni di manomorta siciliana* (Palermo, 1864); De Stefano and Oddo, *Storia della Sicilia*, pp. 241–59.

11 Dennis Mack Smith, *Cavour* (New York, 1985), pp. 248–55. On this important promoter of the Italian Risorgimento, see also by the same author *The Making of Italy, 1796–1870* (New York, 1968); idem, *Victor Emanuel, Cavour and the Risorgimento* (New York, 1971); idem, *Cavour and Garibaldi, 1860* (Cambridge, 1964). For other biographies in English, see A. J. Whyte, *The Early Life and Letters of Cavour, 1810–1848* (Oxford, 1925); idem, *The Political Life and Letters of Cavour* (Oxford, 1930); W. R. Thayer, *The Life and Times of Cavour*, 2 vols. (Boston, 1911). For some studies in Italian, see F. Ruffini, *La giovinezza di Cavour*, 2 vols. (Turin, 1912); and idem, *Ultimi studi sul conte di Cavour* (Bari, 1936); A. Omodeo, *L'opera politica del conte di Cavour*, 2 vols. (Florence, 1940). For some general studies about the debate on the organization of the new Italian state and Cavour's role in favor of centralization, see Petracchi, *Le origini dell'ordinamento comunale e provinciale italiano*; N. Raponi, *Politica ed amministrazione in Lombardia agli esordi dell'unità* (Milan, 1967); F. Brancato, *La dittatura garibaldina nel Mezzogiorno ed in Sicilia* (Trapani: 1965) and A. Scirocco, *Governo e paese nel Mezzogiorno nella crisi dell'unificazione, 1860–61* (Milan, 1963).

12 Smith, *Cavour*, pp. 199–255; idem, "Regionalism," in Tannenbaum and Noether, eds., *Modern Italy*, pp. 125–44.

13 Vochting, *La questione*, pp. 150–1; Napoleone Colajanni, *Latini e anglosassoni* (Rome, 1906), p. 374.

14 Salomone Saladino, "Parliamentary Politics in the Liberal Era: 1861–1914," in Edward Tannenbaum and Emiliana Noether, eds., *Modern Italy: A Topical History since 1861* (New York, 1974), pp. 27–51.

15 On this topic, see Giustino Fortunato, *Il Mezzogiorno e lo Stato Italiano, Discorsi politici, 1880–1910* (Florence: 1926); Benedetto Croce, *Storia d'Italia dal 1871 al 1915*, 4th ed. (Bari, 1925); Gioacchino Volpe, *L'Italia in cammino. L'ultimo cinquantennio* (Milan, 1928); Napoleone Colajanni, *Settentrionali e meridionali Agli italiani del Mezzogiorno* (Milan, 1898); Ettore Ciccotti, *Sulla questione meridionale. Scritti e discorsi* (Milan, 1904); Eugenio Anzimonti,

*Il Mezzogiorno agrario qual'è.* (Bari, 1921); Robert Michels, *Italien von Heute* (Zurich, 1930).

16  On Italian imperialism, see B. Battaglia, *La prima guerra d'Africa* (Turin, 1958); R. Ciasca, *Storia coloniale dell'Italia contemporanea.* 2d ed. (Milan, 1940). And on the national debate on imperialism with special attention to those who opposed it, see R. Raniero, *L'anticolonialismo italiano da Assab ad Adua* (Milan, 1971).

17  Robert Michels, *L'imperialismo italiano* (Milan: 1914), pp. 136, 140; Vochting, *La questione,* p. 138.

18  On Francesco Crispi, one of the most influential Italian politicians of the nineteenth century, and on his foreign policy, see F. Ercole, *Francesco Crispi* (Rome, 1930); C. Zaghi, *L'Africa nella coscienza europea e l'imperialismo italiano* (Naples, 1973); M. Ganci, *Il caso Crispi* (Palermo, 1976); M. Ghillardi, *Francesco Crispi* (Turin: 1969); G. Salvemini, *La politica estera dell'Italia dal 1871 al 1914* (Florence, 1944).

19  On the domestic policies of the Right, see I. Bonomi, *La politica italiana da Porta Pia a Vittorio Veneto: 1870–1918* (Turin, 1944); N. Valeri, ed., *La lotta politica italiana dall'unità al 1925. Idee e documenti* (Florence, 1958); F. Cusin, *L'Italia unita: 1860–76. Saggio di una nuova sintesi storica* (Udine, 1952). On a left-wing interpretation of the conservative domestic policies of the right, besides the already quoted volume by Gramsci, see P. Alatri, *La lotta politica in Sicilia sotto il governo della Destra: 1866–74* (Turin, 1954). A different synthesis is offered by A. Capone, *L'opposizione meridionale nell'età della Destra* (Rome, 1967).

20  For some basic studies on the domestic policies of the Left see C. Morandi, *La Sinistra al potere ed altri saggi* (Florence, 1944); G. Carocci, *Agostino Depretis e la politica estera italiana dal 1876 al 1887* (Turin, 1956); C. Vallauri, *La politica liberale di G. Zanardelli* (Milan, 1967).

21  E. Beneventani, *La bonifica integrale* (Milan, 1929).

22  Prefetto of Cosenza, report, 12 March 1889, ASC.

23  Rosario Romeo, *Breve storia della grande industria in Italia: 1861–1961,* 4th ed. (Bologna, 1975); Bruno Caizzi, *Storia dell'industria italiana dal XVIII secolo ai nostri giorni* (Turin, 1965); Luigi Cafagna, *Il nord nella storia d'Italia* (Bari, 1962); Emilo Sereni, *Capitalismo e mercato nazionale* (Rome, 1966).

24  Massimo L. Salvadori, *Il mito del buongoverno. La questione meridionale da Cavour a Gramsci* (Turin, 1960); I. Bonomi, *La politica italiana da Porta Pia a Vittorio Veneto: 1870–1918* (Turin, 1944); Cusin, *L'Italia unita;* Morandi, *La Sinistra al potere.*

25  Carocci, *Agostino Depretis.*

26  Gino Luzzatto, *L'economia italiana dal 1861 al 1914,* vol. 1: *Dal 1861 al 1894* (Milan, 1963), pp. 51–2. See also A. Caracciolo, *Problemi storici dell'industrializzazione e dello sviluppo* (Urbino, 1965); L. De Rosa, *La rivoluzione industriale in Italia ed il Mezzogiorno* (Bari, 1974).

27  Luzzatto, *L'economia italiana,* p. 49; F. C. Cobbs, *Italy: Brief Acts on Politics, People and Places* (London, 1864); G. Are, *Il problema dello sviluppo industriale nell'età della Destra* (Pisa: 1965).

28  The other two thirds were funded through credit from Italian nationals.

29  A. Plebano, *Storia della finanza italiana nei primi quarant'anni dell'unificazione* 3 vols. (Padua, 1960); F. A. Repaci, *La finanza pubblica italiana nel secolo 1861–1960* (Bologna, 1962); Ragioneria Generale dello Stato, *Il bilancio del Regno d'Italia negli esercizi finanziari dal 1862 al 1912–13* (Rome, 1914); L. Jona Celesia, *Il bilancio degli stati preunitari e la loro influenza sul bilancio dello Stato italiano* (Turin, 1971).

30  Luzzatto, *L'economia italiana*, pp. 68–71; Italy, *Atti della commissione d'inchiesta sull'esercizio delle ferrovie italiane*, 7 vols. (Rome, 1879–81); G. Capodaglio, *Storia di un investimento di capitale. La Società Italiana per le Strade Ferrate Meridionali, 1862–1937* (Milan, 1939).

31  P. Dupont-Ferrier, *Le Marche français de Paris sous le Second Empire* (Paris, 1925). L. Salvatorelli, *Storia dell'Europa dal 1871 al 1914* (Milan, 1940); M. Beaumont, *L'Essor industriel 1878–1904* (Paris: 1937).

32  Quoted in Luzzatto, *L'economia italiana*, p. 17.

33  Egisto Rossi, *Gli Stati Uniti e la concorrenza americana. Studi di agricoltura, industria e commercio* (Florence, 1884).

34  *Il Diritto: Giornale della Democrazia Italiana* (Rome, 2 and 3 January 1883).

35  On this topic, see *Report Presented to Parliament by the English Commissioners Messrs. Pell and Read on the Agricultural Resources of the West* (London, 1880). For two analyses on American and European assets with recommendations on how to strengthen the European economy, see Max Wirth, *Dir Krisis in der Landwirthschaft und Mittel zur Abhulfe* (Berlin, 1881); and Heinrich Sermler, *Die Wahre Bedeutung and die Wirklichen Ursachen der Nord-Amerikanischen Concurrenz in der Landwirthschaftlichen Production* (Wismar, 1881).

36  The American opposition to a large standing army was most puzzling to European visitors, since in nineteenth-century Europe the power of a nation was assessed through the strength of its standing army. The lack of a standing army spared Americans the costs of military expenditures that European states had to shoulder and promoted American investments in agricultural and industrial productions.

37  Rossi, *Gli Stati Uniti*, chs. 1–3 passim.

38  Ibid., pp. 663, 691.

39  Italy, Direzione Generale della Statistica (hereafter cited as DGS), *Annuario statistico italiano, 1905–07* (Rome, 1908) p. 558.

40  Italy, DGS, *Annuario statistico italiano: 1895*, pp. 512–14.

41  E. Rossi, *Gli Stati Uniti*, pp. 696–8, 701, 709, 724.

42  Fortunato, *Il Mezzogiorno e lo. Stato*, Italiano vol. 2, p. 402.

43  Luzzatto, *L'economia italiana*, pp. 27–36.

44  See Italy, *Atti del Comitato dell'Inchiesta Industriale*, 7 vols. (Rome, 1872–74); V. Ellena, *Notizie statistiche sopra alcune industrie* (Rome: 1876); Ministero di Agricoltura, Industria e Commercio, *La statistica di alcune industrie italiane*, 13 vols. (Rome, 1879–80).

45  Luzzatto, *L'economia italiana*, pp. 112–16; on this topic, see also Luigi Luzzatti, *L'inchiesta industriale ed i trattati di commercio* (Rome, 1878); B. Stringer, *La politica doganale degli ultimi trent'anni* (Bologna, 1889); A. Monzilli, *Studi di politica commerciale dell'Italia* (Città di Castello, 1895); D.

Morelli, *Il protezionismo industriale in Italia dall'unificazione del Regno* (Milan, 1920).

46  Luzzatto, *L'economia italiana*, pp. 224–7. See also V. Castronuovo, *L'industria laniera in Piemonte nel secolo decimonono* (Turin, 1964); L. De Rosa, *Iniziativa e capitale straniero nell'industria metalmeccanica nel Mezzogiorno: 1840–1904* (Naples, 1968); T. Tremelloni, *L'industria tessile italiana* (Turin, 1937).

47  Italian politicians made the erroneous assumption that France simply would have to accept the Italian terms, since France could not, allegedly, afford to do without Italian wines and raw silk.

48  Italy, Ragioneria Generale dello Stato, *Il bilancio del Regno d'Italia negli esercizi finanziari dal 1862 al 1912–13* (Rome, 1914); Plebano, *Storia della finanza italiana*; Repaci, *La finanza publica italiana*.

49  T. Canovai, *Le banche di emissione* (Rome, 1912); E. Corbino, *Moneta e credito dal 1861 al 1914* (Naples, 1970).

50  On this topic, see C. Supino, *Lo sviluppo marittimo nel secolo decimonono: Il traffico marittimo* (Rome, 1907); and E. Corbino, *L'economia dei trasporti marittimi* (Città di Castello, 1926).

51  The argument has been stated initially by Guido Dorso and Antonio Gramsci and restated after them by many southerners. For one of the latest reformulations, see Francesco Paolo Cerase, *Sotto il dominio dei borghesi. Sottosviluppo ed emigrazione nell'Italia meridionale: 1860–1910* (Rome, 1975).

52  Sereni, *Capitalismo e mercato nazionale*; Are, *Il problema dello sviluppo*.

## Chapter 3. The southern ethos

1  Dino Taruffi, Leonello De Nobili, and Cesare Lori, *La questione agraria e l'emigrazione in Calabria* (Florence, 1908); Leopoldo Franchetti, *Condizioni economiche ed amministrative delle province napoletane* (Florence, 1875); Sidney Sonnino and Leopoldo Franchetti, *La Sicilia nel 1876: Condizioni economiche ed amministrative* (Florence, 1878).

2  Guistino Fortunato, *Il Mezzogiorno e lo Stato italiano* (Rome, 1911); idem, *Pagine e ricordi parlamentari* (Bari, 1920); Giuseppe Scalise, *L'emigrazione dalla Calabria* (Naples, 1905); Napoleone Colajanni, *Settentrionali e meridionali Agli italiani del Mezzogiorno* (Milano, 1898); idem, *Le condizione economiche, demografiche, biologiche, intellettuali e morali di alcune regioni d'Italia* (Naples, 1906); idem, *Latini e Anglosassoni* (Rome, 1906); Ettore Ciccotti, *Mezzogiorno e settentrione d'Italia. Scritti e discorsi* (Milan, 1904); Guido Dorso, *La rivoluzione meridionale*, 2d ed. (Turin, 1955).

3  Corrado Alvaro, *Gente d'Aspromonte* (Milan, 1955); idem, *Quasi una vita* (Milan, 1950); idem, *Mastrangelina* (Milan, 1982). For a study on Corrado Alvaro, see Francesco Besaldo, *La società meridionale di Corrado Alvaro* (Cosenza, 1983).

4  For an English translation, see Tommaso di Lampedusa, *The Leopard*, trans. A. Colquhoun (New York, 1961).

5  Carlo Levi, *Cristo si e fermato ad Eboli* (Turin, 1947).

6 Constance Cronin, *The Sting of Change. Sicilians in Sicily and Australia* (Chicago, 1970), p. 30.

7 For some important literature in English on the Italian south, see Edward Banfield, *The Moral Basis of a Backward Society* (Glencoe, Ill., 1958); Charlotte Chapman, *Milocca: A Sicilian Village* (Cambridge, Mass., 1971) is a study researched in the late 1920s but published in 1971; Sydel Silverman, *Three Bells of Civilization. The Life of an Italian Hill Town* (New York, 1975); Jane Schneider and Peter Schneider, *Culture and Political Economy in Western Sicily* (New York, 1976); Rudolph Bell, *Fate and Honor, Family and Village. Demographic and Cultural Changes in Rural Italy since 1800* (Chicago, 1979); Filippo Sabetti, *Political Authority in a Sicilian Village* (New Brunswick, 1984); Cronin, *The Sting of Change*; Joseph Lopreato, *Peasants No More. Social Classes and Social Change in an Underdeveloped Society*. San Francisco: 1967; Ann Cornelisen, *Women of the Shadow*. Boston: 1976; Dennis Mack Smith, *A History of Sicily: Medieval Sicily (800–1713)*; and idem, *A History of Sicily: Modern Sicily (after 1713*, vol. 2 (London, 1968). One of the most perceptive studies of a southern region – Calabria – was written by a team of Belgian anthropologists. See Jean Meyriat, ed., *La Calabre: Une region sousdéveloppée de l'Europe méditerrannéen.* (Paris, 1960).

8 Banfield, *The Moral Basis* (Glencoe, Ill., 1958).

9 Smith, *A History of Sicily: Modern Sicily*, pp. 475–8.

10 H. G. Koenigsberg, *The Practice of Empire* (Ithaca, N.Y., 1969).

11 Schneider and Schneider, *Culture and Political Economy*, p. 228.

12 Rosario Donati, letter to to the prefetto of Palermo. 5 November 1892, ASP.

13 Cornelisen, *Women of the Shadow*, p. 225.

14 Levi, *Cristo*, p. 71.

15 Eboli is a small town about twenty miles southeast of Salerno, on the road leading to Potenza and Matera, two of the poorest provinces in the south.

16 Levi, *Cristo*, p. 70.

17 Incidentally, every large organization, whose functions southerners are unable to comprehend, is "the state" for them.

18 Alvaro, *Gente d'Aspromonte*, pp. 86–7.

19 Napoleone Colajanni, *I partiti politici in Italia* (Rome, 1912); and idem, *Statistiche economiche, politiche, intellettuali, morali* (Naples, 1914); Ettore Ciccotti, *Sulla questione meridionale. Scritti e discorsi* (Milan, 1904); Giustino Fortunato, *Il Mezzogiorno e lo Stato italiano. Discorsi politici: 1880–1900* (Florence: 1926); and idem, *Pagine e discorsi parlamentari* vol. 1 (Florence, 1920).

20 Francesco P. Cerase, *Sotto il Dominio dei Borghesi. Sottosviluppo ed Emigrazione nell'Italia Meridionale: 1860–1910.* Rome: 1975.

21 What is said here about the south can be applied to Latin America, which was part of the Spanish Empire.

22 Schneider and Schneider, *Culture and Political Economy*, pp. 10–11.

23 Francesco Salvatore Romano, *Breve storia della Sicilia. Momenti e problemi della civiltà siciliana* (Turin, 1964), pp. 230–5; H. G. Koenigsberg, *The Prac-*

*tice of Empire*, pp. 83, 197; I. Wallerstein, *The Modern World System: Capitalist Agriculture and the Origin of the European World Economy in the Sixteenth Century* (New York, 1974), p. 188.

24  Schneider and Schneider, *Culture and Political Economy*, pp. 47–51; Koenigsberg, *The Practice of Empire*, p. 91; Paolo Balsamo, *Memorie economiche e agrarie riguardanti il Regno di Sicilia* (Palermo, 1803), pp. 59–61, 63.

25  Schneider and Schneider, *Culture and Political Economy*, pp. 51–3.

26  In comparison, northern towns averaged ten square kilometers in Lombardy and twenty in Piedmont.

27  Wallerstein, *The Modern World System*, pp. 141–3; F. Milone, *Sicilia: La natura e l'uomo* (Turin, 1960), p. 218.

28  Francesco Salvatore Romano, *Storia dei Fasci Siciliani* (Bari, 1959), pp. 99–103.

29  Giuseppe Alongi, *La Maffia nei suoi fattori e nelle sue manifestazioni* (Turin, 1886), p. 95.

30  Napoleone Colajanni, *Gli avvenimenti in Sicilia e le loro cause* (Palermo, 1894), p. 112.

31  Sidney Sonnino, *La Sicilia: I contadini* (Florence, 1875), p. 134.

32  Alongi, *La Maffia*, p. 95.

33  Salvatore Lucchesi, chief of police, letter to the prefetto of Palermo, 22 November 1893, ASP.

34  Prefetto of Cosenza, letter to the Minister of the Interior in Rome, 14 April 1889, ASC.

35  *La Sicilia Agricola*, 30 September 1883.

36  Danilo Dolci, *Conversazioni contadine* (Verona, 1962), pp. 162, 182, 192.

37  Ibid., p. 186.

38  Pasquale Villari, *Italian Life in Town and Country* (New York, 1902), p. 2.

39  Antonio Mangano, *Sons of Italy: A Social and Religious Study of the Italians in America* (New York, 1917), p. 41.

40  Cornelisen, *Women of the Shadow*, pp. 3–4.

41  Donna Gabaccia, "Neither Padrone Slaves nor Primitive Rebels: Sicilians on Two Continents," in Dirk Hoerder, ed., *Struggle a Hard Battle. Essays on Working Class Immigrants* (De Kalb, Ill., 1986), p. 113; idem, *Militants and Migrants. Rural Sicilians Become American Workers* (New Brunswick, 1988).

42  On this topic, see John S. MacDonald, "Institutional Economics and Rural Development: Two Italian Types," *Human Organization* 23 (1964): 113; Giorgio Giorgetti, "Contratti agrari e rapporti sociali nelle campagne," in Ruggiero Romano and Corrado Vivanti, eds., *Storia d'Italia*, vol 5: *I documenti* (Turin, 1973), pp. 746–58; Domenico De Marco, "Considerazioni sulle vicende della proprietà fondiaria e delle classi rurali in Calabria dopo l'unità," *Atti del Secondo Congresso Storico Calabrese* (Naples, 1961), pp. 490–1.

43  Prefetto of Palermo, report, 2 May 1889, ASP.

44  Giuseppe Medici, *I tipi di impresa nell'agricoltura italiana* (Rome, 1951), pp. 33–4; Giuseppe Luzzato, *L'economia italiana dal 1861 al 1914*, vol. 1: *Dal 1861 al 1894* (Milan, 1963), p. 139.

45  Prefetto of Palermo, letter to the Minister of the Interior, 7 May 1882, ASP.
46  Prefetto of Cosenza, report, 13 May 1994, ASC.
47  Agostino Caputo, *Di alcune questioni economiche della Calabria: L'influenza dell'emigrazione sui costumi* (Rome, 1909), pp. 6–7. For observations from an outsider, see Leonello De Nobili, "L'emigrazione in Calabria: Effetti dell'emigrazione in generale," *Rivista dell'Emigrazione* 1 (1908): 10.
48  Italy, Ministro di Agricultura, Industria e Commercio (hereafter cited as MAIC), Direzione Generale della Statistica (hereafter cited as DGS), *Statistica delle società di mutuo soccorso e delle istituzioni cooperative: Anno 1885* (Rome, 1888); and idem, *Elenco delle società di mutuo soccorso giuridicamente riconosciute al 1897* (Rome, 1900).
49  Danilo Dolci, *Conversazioni contadine*, p. 173.
50  The most obvious indication of the different goals of socialist leaders and southern peasants can be seen in the Fasci. The leaders, true to the socialist faith, preached the socialization of the land. Peasants joined the Fasci with the hope of becoming landowners.
51  Italy, (Direzione Generale della Statistica (hereafter cited as DGS) *Annuario statistico italiano: 1905–07*, pp. 262–5.
52  Meyriat, *La Calabre*, p. 197.
53  Cornelisen, *Women of the Shadow*, p. 29.
54  Vincenzo Padula, *Persone di Calabria* (Milan, 1950), p. 384. For two interesting accounts of southern popular culture, see Francesco Angarano, *Vita tradizionale dei contadini e pastori calabresi* (Florence, 1973); and Giuseppe Pitrè, *Biblioteca delle tradizioni popolari siciliane*, 25 vols. (Turin, 1910).
55  The best documentation on the southern poverty of vocabulary is in Danilo Dolci, *Conversazioni siciliane* (Milan, 1962), which reports verbatim a series of conversations among peasants from Partinico, Sicily. On the reactions of foreigners, see the book by Cornelisen, *Women of the Shadow* and Cronin, *The Sting of Change*.
56  Pitrè, *Biblioteca*; Angarano, *Vita tradizionale*.
57  Giuseppe Pitrè, *Proverbi siciliani raccolti e confrontati con quelli degli altri dialetti d'Italia* vol. 1 (Palermo, 1890), p. 83.
58  Luigi Vigo, *Raccolta amplissima dei canti siciliani* (Catania, 1878), p. 619.
59  Amabile Guastella, *La parità e le storie morali dei nostri villani* (Ragusa, 1884), pp. 19–20.
60  Ibid., pp. 92–3.
61  Bell, *Fate and Honor*, pp. 25–6.
62  Ibid., pp. 26–7.
63  Edward Banfield paraphrased it with a statement: "An adult hardly may be said to have an individuality apart from the family" (Banfield, *The Moral Basis*, p. 85).
64  Richard Gambino, *Blood of My Blood* (New York, 1974), p. 34; Banfield, *The Moral Basis*, p. 107.
65  Dolci, *Conversazioni contadine*, pp. 161–206.
66  Bell, *Fate and Honor*, pp. 2–3; Schneider and Schneider, *Culture and Political Economy*, pp. 86–102.

67  Schneider and Schneider, *Culture and Political Economy*, pp. 102–9.

68  See Phyllis Williams, *Southern Italian Folkways in Europe and in America* (New York, 1938).

69  Humbert Nelli, *The Italians in Chicago, 1880–1930. A Study in Social Mobility* (New York, 1970), pp. 5–6, 170; Virginia Yans McLaughlin, *Family and Community: Italian Immigrants in Buffalo, 1880–1930* (Ithaca, N.Y., 1977), p. 19. See also Rudolph Vecoli, "Contadini in Chicago. A Critique of the Uprooted," *Journal of American History* 51 (1964): 404–11; and Leonard Covello, *The Social Background of the Italo-American School Child. A Study of the Southern Italian Family Mores and Their Effect on the School Situation in Italy and America* (Leiden, 1967).

70  Anna Anfossi, Magda Talamo, and Francesco Indovina, *Ragusa: Comunità in transizione* (Turin, 1959), p. 200.

71  Meyriat, *La Calabre*, pp. 197–8.

72  Cornelisen, *Women of the Shadow*, p. 16.

73  Agostino Caputo, *L'abitazione in una città di provincia* (Cosenza, 1912), p. 27.

74  Robert Foerster, *The Italian Emigration of Our Times* (Cambridge, Mass., 1919), p. 441.

75  See, for instance, prefetto of Palermo, letter, 3 March 1903, ASP. Newspapers published in American cities by Italians for Italians regularly featured lists of names of immigrants who had left no trace of themselves once they left Italy, but were believed to be in that particular region of the United States where the newspaper was published.

76  Taruffi, De Nobili, and Lori, *La questione agraria*, p. 866.

77  Italy, MAIC, DSG, *Popolazione: Movimento dello stato civile, 1902* (Rome, 1903), pp. xxxiv–xxxv. Richard Gambino argues that illegitimacy rates were higher in the Italian north than in the south and quotes Phyllis Williams to corroborate his case. Unfortunately, the yearly publications by the Italian government on vital statistics disprove Gambino's assertion. Rates of illegitimacy were substantially higher in the south than in the north throughout the five decades of mass emigration.

78  Prefetto of Cosenza, report, 11 May 1894, ASP; prefetto of Naples, report, 16 September 1889, ASN.

79  Abele Damiani, *Atti della giunta per la inchiesta agraria e sulle condizioni delle classi agricole*, vol. 13: *Sicilia* (Rome, 1885), p. 358.

80  Damiani, *Atti della giunta*, vol. 13, pp. 369, 473–5.

81  Taruffi, De Nobili, and Lori, *La questione agraria*, pp. 864–6. Prefetto of Cosenza, letter to the Minister of the Interior in Rome, 7 May 1903, ASC.

82  Angarano, *Vita tradizionale*, pp. 7–14.

83  Damiani, *Atti della giunta*, vol. 13, p. 358.

84  Cornelisen, *Women of the Shadow*, p. 222.

85  Ibid., p. 207.

86  Mario Puzo, "Choosing a Dream," in Thomas Wheeler, ed., *The Immigrant Experience* (New York, 1971), p. 227.

87  Meyriat, *La Calabre*, p. 203.

88  Sidney Sonnino, "Le condizioni dei contadini in Italia: 1875," in *Scritti e*

*discorsi parlamentari* (Bari, 1972), pp. 157–8. See also Pasquale Villari, *Lettere meridionali* (Florence, 1878), p. 137.

## Chapter 4. The national debate

1   See for instance Eugen Weber, *Peasants into Frenchmen: The Modernization of Rural France: 1870–1914* (Stanford, 1976).
2   Italy, *Atti Parlamentari* (Camera dei Deputati), 30 January 1868, pp. 2,391–2.
3   Italy, *Atti Parlamentari* (Camera dei Deputati), 20 May 1872, pp. 2,117–21.
4   Italy, *Istruzioni del Ministro degli Interni, 23 gennaio 1968* (Rome, 1868).
5   Ibid. *18 gennaio 1873* (Rome, 1873).
6   Antonio Marazzi, *Emigranti*, 3 vols. (Milan, 1880).
7   Nicola Marcone, *Gli italiani al Brasile* (Rome, 1877).
8   Giacomo Zanella, "Il Lavoro," in *Poesie*, vol. 1 (Florence, 1910), pp. 65–6.
9   Edmondo De Amicis, *Poesie* (Milan, 1880), p. 41.
10  Giovanni Florenzano, *Dell'emigrazione italiana in America* (Naples, 1874), p. 135; Antonio Caccianiga, "Agenti provocatori dell'emigrazione svelati al popolo delle campagne," *Italia Agricola* 9 (1877): 171–2.
11  Francesco Ferrara, *Introduzione al corso completo d'economia politica pratica* (Turin, 1855), pp. xciv–cxvi.
12  Girolamo Boccardo, "Emigrazione," in *Dizionario universale di economia politica e di commercio*, vol. 1, (Milan, 1875), pp. 728–34.
13  Camillo Benso di Cavour, *Opere*, vol. 1, (Turin, 1865), p. 508; Marco Minghetti, *Della economia pubblica e delle sue attinenze colla morale e col diritto*, vol. 2, (Florence, 1858), p. 51.
14  Marchese di Cosentino, *Delle perdite morali e materiali cagionate all'Italia dall'emigrazione artificiale* (Rome, 1877), pp. 25–40.
15  Ibid. *L'emigrazione italiana* (Genoa, 1874), pp. 14, 16–20; idem, *Uno sguardo sull'emigrazione italiana ed estera* (Rome, 1872).
16  Leone Carpi, *Dell'emigrazione italiana nei suoi rapporti coll'agricoltura, industria e commercio* (Florence, 1871), pp. 99–105, 107–9; idem, *Delle colonie e dell'emigrazione di italiani all'estero*, vol. 3 (Milan, 1874), p. 225; idem, *Delle colonie*, vol. 4 (Milan, 1875), p. 282.
17  Jacopo Virgilio, *Delle migrazioni transatlantiche degli italiani* (Genoa, 1868), pp. 25, 35.
18  On this congress, see Luigi Luzzatti, *Memorie*, vol. 1, (Bologna, 1931), pp. 403–34; Leo Valiani, "Il primo congresso degli economisti italiani," *Criterio* 1 (1957): 524–31; Gino Luzzatto, "Economisti conservatori e illuminati di fronte al socialismo," *Critica Sociale* 53 (1961): pp. 625–7. The statistics on Italian emigration were published by the Direzione Generale della Statistica, with the title *Statistica dell'emigrazione italiana all'estero*.
19  Antonio Caccianiga, "Agenti provocatori," 171–2.
20  Antonio Mina, "Alcune considerazioni sull'emigrazione," *Giornale di Agricoltura, Industria e Commercio* 5 (1878): 240–62.

21  Giacomo Marenghi, *Atti della giunta per la inchiesta agraria e sulle condizioni delle classi agricole*, vol. 6: *Relazione per il Mantovano* (Rome, 1882), pp. 521–2.

22  Enrico Paglia, ibid., vol 6: *Relazione per il Cremonese* (Rome, 1882), pp. 877–8.

23  Agostino Bertani, ibid., vol. 6: *Province di Genova e Porto Maurizio* (Rome, 1883), pp. 427.

24  Carlo Mazzini, ibid., vol. 3: *Toscana* (Rome, 1881), p. 529.

25  Pasquale Villari, *Lettere meridionali* (Florence, 1878), p. 44. This volume was a collection of newspaper articles originally published in the Milan newspaper, *L'Opinione*, in 1877.

26  Sidney Sonnino and Leopoldo Franchetti, *La Sicilia nel 1876: Condizioni economiche ed amministrative* (Florence, 1878), p. 127.

27  Giustino Fortunato, *Pagine e ricordi parlamentari*, vol. 1 (Bari, 1920), pp. 305–6.

28  Agostino Bertani, *Atti della giunta* p. 125; Luigi A. Caputo, *L'abitazione in una città di provincia* (Cosenza, 1912), pp. 1–13; Philip Carroll, American Consul in Palermo, to the Undersecretary of State, 14 July 1886, Palermo.

29  Francesco Zanelli, "La crisi agricola e l'emigrazione dei contadini. Lettera agli amici agricoltori," *L'Italia Agricola* 9 (1877): 4–8.

30  Marchese di Cosentino, *La questione ardente* (Rome, 1879), pp. 4–5.

31  Giulio Del Vecchio, *Sulla emigrazione permanente di italiani nei paesi stanieri avvenuta nel dodicennio 1876–1888* (Bologna, 1891), pp. 205, 212, 270.

32  Francesco Coletti, "Dell'emigrazione italiana," in Regia Accademia dei Lincei, ed., *Cinquant'anni di storia italiana* (Rome, 1911), pp. 55–6; Pasquale Villari, "L'emigrazione italiana e le sue conseguenze," *Nuova Antologia* 45 (1907): p. 59.

33  Alfredo Niceforo, *Italiani de nord e italiani del sud* (Turin: 1901).

34  F. Barbagallo, *Mezzogiorno e questione meridionale: 1860–1960* (Naples, 1980), pp. 16–26.

35  Cristoforo Negri, *La grandezza dell'Italia* (Turin, 1864), pp. 179–80; idem, "L'emigrazione," *Bollettino della Società Geografica Italiana* 7 (1872): 139–41.

36  Virgilio, *Delle migrazioni*, p. 110.

37  Gerolamo Boccardo, "L'emigrazione e le colonie," *Nuova Antologia* 27 (1874); 643–4; see also Carpi, *Delle colonie e dell'emigrazione di italiani all'estero*, vol. 1 (Milan, 1874), p. 64.

38  Emilio Cerruti, "La Melanesia considerata per rapporto alla sua produttività e alla sua importanza commerciale," *Nuova Antologia* 25 (1874); p. 474; Cesare Correnti, *Scritti scelti* (Rome, 1894), pp. 490–526.

39  See the Milan newspaper *La Perseveranza*, 7 January 1875, and Florenzano, *Della emigrazione italiana*, p. 375.

40  See, for instance, *Rassegna Nazionale* 2 (1881): p. 486.

41  Francesco Manzotti, *La polemica sull'emigrazione nell'Italia unita fino alla prima guerra mondiale* (Milan, 1966), pp. 52–3.

42  Manzotti, *La polemica sull'emigrazione*, p. 58; Italy, *Atti Parlamentari* (Senato), 19 January 1883, pp. 233–41.

43  Ibid., 9 June 1883, pp. 2,946–9; see also C. Bertagnolli, "L'emigrazione dei contadini per l'America," *Rassegna Nazionale* 9 (1887): 94–122.

44  Edmondo De Amicis, *Sull'oceano* (Milan, 1889), pp. 63–4.

45  Ada Negri, *Tempesta* (Milan, 1895), pp. 16–17.

46  Mario Rapisardi, *Opere*, vol. 3, (Catania, 1896), pp. 457–60.

47  Berto Barbarani, *Tutte le poesie* (Milan, 1953), pp. 88–9.

48  See Italy, *Annali di statistica del Ministero di Agricoltura, Industria e Commercio* 4 (1873): 103–7; ibid., 9 (1877): 160–7; ibid., 6 (1875): 82–4.

49  Luigi Bodio, "Sul movimento dell'emigrazione italiana e sulle cause e caratteri del medesimo," *Bollettino della Società Geografica Italiana* 9 (1886): 927–56.

50  Italy, *Atti del Consiglio dell'Industria e del Commercio* (Rome, 1887), pp. 141–91; F. Manzotti, *La polemica sull'emigrazione*, pp. 64–5.

51  See Italy, *Italia agricola* 14 (1882): 506; Italy, *Giornale di Agricoltura, Industria e Commercio* 24 (1887): 346; "Emigrazione e agricoltura," *L'Economista* 14 (1883): 67.

52  Francesco Crispi, *Discorsi parlamentari*, vol. 3, (Rome, 1915), p. 575.

53  C. Rosmini, "Il nuovo progetto sull'europa," *Giornale degli Economisti* 3 (1888): 121–74.

54  Francesco Saverio Nitti, *L'emigrazione ed i suoi avversari* (Turin: 1888). See also F. Rizzo, *Francesco Saverio Nitti ed il Mezzogiorno* (Rome, 1960), pp. 110–28.

55  Nicola Malnate, "La tutela dell'emigrazione italiana," *La Rassegna Nazionale* 20 (1898): 163–90; idem, "Il contegno del governo dopo la legge sull'emigrazione," *L'Economista* 16 (1889): 197–8.

56  Pietro Maldotti, *Relazione sull'operato della missione del Porto di Genova dal 1894 al 1898 e sui due viaggi al Brasile del missionario Sacerdote Pietro Maldotti* (Genoa, 1898), pp. 12–13; see also idem, "Il problema dell'Emigrazione dinanzi al Parlamento," *Civiltà Cattolica* 5 (1899): 129–45.

57  Luigi Einaudi, "Un missionario apostolo degli emigrati (1898)" in *Cronache economiche e politiche di un trentennio*, vol. 1 (Turin, 1969), pp. 90–1.

58  Giovani Battista Scalabrini, *L'emigrazione italiana in America* (Piacenza, 1887), pp. 6, 8.

59  Società Geografica Italiana, *Memorie della Società Geografica Italiana*, vol. 4: *Indagini sull'emigrazione italiana all'estero fatte per conto della stessa Società, 1888–89* (Rome, 1890): and idem, "Indagini sulla nostra emigrazione all'estero fatta dall'ufficio della Società Geografica," *Bollettino della Società Geografica Italiana* 23 (1889): 619–39.

60  Società Geografica Italiana, *Memorie*, vol. 4; idem, *Atti del primo congresso geografico italiano: 1892*, vol. 2 (Rome, 1893), pp. 1–36; idem, "Indagini sulla nostra emigrazione," 619–39; E. Corbino, "Il protezionismo marittimo in Italia," *Giornale degli Economisti* 32 (1921): 1,370–89; A. Leso, "L'Associazione Marittima Commerciale Italiana," *Rivista Marittima* (1895): 509–14.

61  Italy, *Atti Parlamentari* (Senato), 19 January 1883, pp. 221–32.

62  Girolamo Boccardo, "Spontaneità ed artifizio nell'espansione coloniale," *Giornale degli Economisti* (1886): 22–36.

63  Leopoldo Franchetti, "L'Italia e le sue colonie africane," (1891) and "L'av-
    venire della nostra colonia," in *Mezzogiorno e Colonie* (Florence, 1950);
    and "La colonizzazione dell'Eritrea," *Riforma Sociale* 1 (1894): 5–24.
64  Luigi Bodio, "Della protezione degli emigrati italiani in America," *Nuova
    Antologia* 55 (1895): 630–1.
65  Manzotti, *La polemica sull'emigrazione*, p. 99.
66  Giovanni Bovio, *Discorsi Parlamentari*. Rome: 1955, p. 355; Italy, *Atti Par-
    lamentari* (Camera dei Deputati), 24 November 1900, p. 462.
67  Francesco Saverio Nitti, *La Nuova Fase dell'Emigrazione Italia*, "La Riforma
    Sociale" (Bari, 1958): p. 392.
68  Luigi Einaudi, *Un principe mercante* (Turin, 1900), p. 14. The prince mer-
    chant was a symbolic figure standing for Italians with capital willing to
    invest among Italian immigrants in Latin America.
69  Giuseppe Giacosa, "Gli italiani a New York e a Chicago," *Nuova Antologia*
    40 (1892): 619–40; idem, "Chicago e la sua colonia italiana," *Nuova An-
    tologia* 44 (1893): 15–33; and idem, *Impressioni d'America* (Milan, 1898).
70  Paolo Barbera, "Impressioni d'America," *Nuova Antologia* 83 (1900):
    pp. 456–7.
71  Manzotti, *La Polemica sull'emigrazione*, pp. 105–11; Italy, *Atti Parlamentari*
    (Camera dei Deputati, 3 March 1900, pp. 2,309–16; idem, 23 November
    1900, pp. 298–402; idem, 29 November 1900, pp. 711–14.
72  Nicola Malnate, "I provvedimenti per l'emigrazione," *Rassegna Nazionale*
    32 (1910): pp. 118–21.
73  Barbagallo, *Mezzogiorno*, pp. 34–9.
74  Ibid., pp. 43–8.
75  F. Barbagallo, *La questione meridionale* (Milan, 1948), p. 78; Giuseppe Lo
    Giudice, "L'emigrazione dalla Sicilia orientale contemporanea, 1876–
    1914," *Annali del Mezzogiorno* 14 (1974): 54.
76  F. Barbagallo, *Stato, Parlamento e lotte politico-sociali nel Mezzogiorno: 1900–
    1914* (Naples, 1976), pp. 394–5.
77  Rosario Villari, *Il sud nella storia d'Italia*, 3d ed. (Bari, 1971), p. 404; Coletti,
    "Dell'emigrazione italiana," in *Cinquant'anni*, pp. 233–4; Barbagallo,
    *Stato, Parlamento*, pp. 394–5.
78  The survey was published in eight volumes in 1909 and 1910, in Rome,
    under the general title *Inchiesta parlamentare sulle condizioni dei contadini
    nelle province meridionali e nella Sicilia*.
79  Coletti, "Dell'emigrazione italiana," in *Cinquant'anni*, pp. 233–4.
80  Italy, *Inchiesta parlamentare sulle condizioni dei contadini nelle province mer-
    idionali e nella Sicilia*, vol. 5: *Basilicata e Calabria*, pt. 2: *Relazione del delegato
    technico Ernesto Marenghi* (Rome, 1910), pp. 86–7.
81  Leopoldo Franchetti, *Mezzogiorno e colonie* (Florence, 1950), p. 230; Fran-
    cesco Saverio Nitti, "Scritti sulla questione meridionale," in Pasquale
    Villari and A. Massafra, eds., *Inchiesta sulle condizioni dei contadini nelle
    province meridionali e nella Sicilia* (Bari, 1968), p. 189.
82  Antonio Mangano, "The Effects of Emigration upon Italy. Toritto and
    San Demetrio," *Charities and the Commons* 20 (2 May 1908): 167.

83 Ibid., "The Effects of Emigration upon Italy: Threatened Depopulation of the South," *Charities and the Commons* 19 (4 January 1908): 1,333.

84 Carmelo Sanfilippo to the prefetto of Cosenza, letter, 5 February 1892, ASC.

85 Prefetto of Palermo, report, 3 May 1897, ASP; prefetto of Cosenza, report 9 November 1899. ASC.

86 Italy, *Inchiesta parlamentare*, vol. 5, pt. 2: *Calabria: Relazione del delegato technico* (Rome, 1910), p. 96.

87 Dino Cinel, *From Italy to San Francisco. The Immigrant Experience* (Stanford, 1984), pp. 86–8.

88 Agostino Caputo, "Di alcune questioni economiche della Calabria: L'emigrazione dalla provincia di Cosenza," *Giornale degli Economisti e Rivista di Statistica* 35 (1907): pp. 1,165–6.

89 Italy, Ministero di Agricoltura, Industria e Commercio, Direzione dell'Agricoltura, *Bilanci di famiglie coloniche* (Rome, 1880).

90 Italy, *Inchiesta parlamentare*, vol. 5, pt. 2, p. 2.

91 Luigi Capuana, *Gli americani di Rabbato* (Milan, 1912), p. 24.

92 Prefetto of Palermo, report, 17 May 1901. ASP.

## Chapter 5. Return migration

1 Italy, Ministro di Agricultura, Industria e Commercio (hereafter cited as MAIC), Direzione Generale della Statistica (hereafter cited as DGS), *Statistica dell'emigrazione italiana all'estero nell'anno 1876* (Rome, 1877), p. ix.

2 Walter Willcox, *International Migrations*, vol. 1, (New York, 1929), p. 206.

3 Leopoldo Corinaldi, "L'emigrazione italiana negli Stati Uniti," *Bollettino dell'Emigrazione*, 2 (1902); 5.

4 Prescott F. Hall *Immigration* (New York, 1913), p. 78.

5 F. Scardin, *Vita italiana nell'Argentina. Impressioni e note* vol. 2 (Buenos Aires, 1899), p. 108; E. Molina Nadal, *El emigrante in America* (Madrid, 1913), p. 226; Robert Foerster, *The Italian Emigration of Our Times* (Cambridge, Mass., 1919), pp. 243–4.

6 Prefetto of Cosenza, report, 17 May 1897, ASC; prefetto of Palermo, report, 11 September 1901, ASP.

7 Agostino Bertani, *Atti della giunta per la inchiesta agraria e sulle condizioni delle classi agricole*, vol. 10: *Province di Genova e Porto Maurizio* (Rome, 1883), p. 427; Carlo Mazzini, ibid., vol. 3; *Toscana* (Rome, 1881), p. 529.

8 See, for instance, Archbishop of Palermo, Michelse Celesia, letter to the Sacred Congregation for the Bishops, 9 June 1881, Archivio Segreto Vaticano, Vatican City.

9 "L'emigrato italiano," *La civiltà Cattolica* 48 (1887): 878–923.

10 Bertani, *Atti della giunta*, vol. 10, pp. vii–xii.

11 Leone Carpi, *Dell' emigrazione italiana all' estero nei suoi rapporti coll'agricoltura, coll'industria e col commercio* (Florence, 1871), pp. 108–11.

12 Italy, MAIC, DGS, *Statistica dell'emigrazione italiana all'estero nell'anno 1878*, pp. 37–8.

13   Italy, MAIC, DGS, *Statistica dell'Emigrazione italiana all'estero nell'anno 1878*, p. 39.
14   Italy, MAIC, DGS, *Statistica dell'emigrazione italiana all'estero neglianni 1880–81*, p. 51
15   Luigi Caputo, *Inchiesta sulle condizioni del lavoro agricolo e sugli effetti dell'emigrazione nella provincia di Cosenza* (Rome, 1909), pp. 12–38.
16   D. O. Fletcher, to the Secretary of State in Washington, report, 26 September 1888, Genoa, in "Reports of American Consuls in Europe," Microfilms Collection, Stanford University Libraries. See also Maria Marenco, *L'emigrazione ligure nell'economia della nazione* (San Pier d'Arena, 1923), p. 157.
17   United States, Bureau of Immigration, *Report of the Commissioner General of Immigration* (Washington, D. C.: 1910), p. 8.
18   Francesco Coletti, "Dell'Emigrazione Italiana, in Regia Accademica dei Lincei, ed., *Cinquantanni di storia italiana* (Rome, 1911), pp. 10–12; G. Cosattini, "L'emigrazione temporanea dal Friuli," *Bollettino dell'Emigrazione* 3 (1904): 7.
19   Massimo Livi Bacci, *L'immigrazione e l'assimilazione degli italiani negli Stati Uniti secondo le statistiche demografiche americane* (Milan, 1961); J. D. Gould, "European and Inter-Continental Emigration. The Road Back Home: Return Migration from the United States," *The Journal of European Economic History* 9 (Spring 1980): 41–112.
20   Italy, MAIC, DGS, *Statistica dell'emigrazione italiana all'estero neglianni 1908–09*, p. 22; idem, *Statistica dell'emigrazione italiana all'estero neglianni . . . 1911–12*, p. xxi.
21   Ibid., *Statistica dell'emigrazione italiana all'estero neglianni 1908–09*, p. xxxiii; idem, *Statistica dell'emigrazione italiana all'estero neglianni 1911–12*, p. xxi.
22   Prefetto of Naples, report, 19 May 1901, ASN.
23   Prefetto of Cosenza, report, 12 September 1895, ASC; and prefetto of Palermo, report, 18 December 1901. ASP.
24   Prefetto of Matera, report, 19 January 1894, ASM.
25   Aberto Beneduce, "Saggio di statistiche dei rimpatri dalle Americhe," *Bollettino dell'Emigrazaione* 11 (1911): 1–112.
26   U.S. Congress, Senate, *Reports of the Immigration Commission*, 61st Cong., 3d sess. (Washington, D.C., 1911), S. Doc. 747, p. 735.
27   J. D. Gould, "European Inter-Continental," 41–2.
28   U.S. Congress, Senate, *Abstract of Reports of the Immigration Commission*, 61st Cong., 3d sess. (Washington D.C., 1911), S. Doc 747, p. 735.
29   U.S. Congress, Senate, *Reports of the Immigration Commissioner*, 61st Cong., 3d sess. (Washington D.C., 1911), S. Doc. 756, p. 373.
30   Ibid., pp. 384–5. United States Senate.
31   J. S. Gould, "European Inter-Continental," 57.
32   U.S. Congress, 61 Cong. 3rd Session *Reports of the Immigration Commissioner*, S. Doc. 756, p. 383.
33   Ibid., pp. 375–84.
34   Ibid., pp. 392–4.
35   Italy, DGS, *Sommario di statistiche storiche italiane* (Rome, 1958), pp. 66–7.

36  Ibid.
37  Beneduce, "Saggio di statistiche," 2–122.
38  Ibid., 12–17.
39  Most likely, Austro-Hungarian ships carried more than 2 percent. But because such ships landed in Venice and Trieste, their activities went unrecorded.
40  Beneduce, "Saggio di statistiche," 24–31.
41  Prefetto of Palermo, report, 7 May 1904, ASP; and prefetto of Matera, report, 6 June 1901, ASM.
42  J. D. Gould, "European Inter-Continental," p. 60.
43  A family group was not necessarily a whole family, although in the case of the Veneti returning from Brazil, it usually was.
44  Beneduce, "Saggio di statistiche," 38–41; Dino Cinel, *From Italy to San Francisco. The Immigrant Experience* (Stanford, 1982), pp. 180–7, 287.
45  Beneduce, "Saggio di statistiche," 48–9.
46  Ibid., 92–4.
47  MAIC, DGS, *Statistica dell'emigrazione italiana all'estero nell'anno 1888,* pp. xxiv-xxvii; idem, *Statistica dell'emigrazione italiana all'estero negl'anni 1900–01,* p. x; idem, *Statistica dell'emigrazione italiana all'estero negl'anni 1912–13,* pp. 84–5; idem, *Statistica dell'emigrazione italiana all'estero negl'anni 1918–19–20,* pp. 118–21.
48  Prefetto of Cosenza, report, 12 March 1899, ASC.
49  Gould, "European Inter-Continental," pp. 67–8.
50  Prefetto of Palermo, report, 7 May 1899, ASP.
51  Gould, "European Inter-Continental," pp. 70–3.
52  Italian Consul in San Francisco, report, 12 June 1872, Archives of the Ministry of Foreign Affairs, Rome.
53  Commissariato Generale dell'Emigrazione, "Notizie statistiche sui movimenti migratori: Emigrazione italiana per l'estero avvenuta negli anni 1907–08," *Bollettino dell'Emigrazione* 23 (1908): 49.
54  Consular Reports: New York, 7 May 1887; San Francisco, 6 September 1892; New Orleans, 7 December 1901, Archives of the Ministry of Foreign Affairs, Rome.
55  Luigi Rossi, "Relazione sui servizi dell'emigrazione per l'anno 1909–10," *Bollettino dell'Emigrazione* 18 (1910): 402.
56  Victor Von Borosini, "Home Going Italians," *The Survey* 28 (1912): 792–3.
57  T. Orsati, "Rimpatriati dalle Americhe e salute pubblica," *Bollettino dell'Emigrazione,* 17 (1909): 3–9; L. Rossi, "Relazione sui servizi," 400–3; F. Monaco, "Sull'esercizio della Casa degli Emigranti in Napoli," *Bollettino dell'Emigrazione* 8 (1912): 146–66.
58  Coletti, "Dell'emigrazione italiana," in *Cinquant'anni,* pp. 249–51.
59  Prefetto of Cosenza, report, 2 December 1891, ASC.
60  Prefetto of Palermo, report, 3 March 1896, ASP.
61  Friedrich Vochting, *La questione meridionale* (Naples, 1955), p. 23.
62  L. Rossi, "Relazione sui servizi," 38.
63  Von Borosini, "Home Going Italians," 793.

64 Italy, MAIC, Direzione dell'Agricoltura, *Notizie sulle condizioni dell'agricoltura negli Anni 1878–79: Bilanci di famiglie coloniche* (Rome, 1880), pp. 1–185.
65 Istituto Centrale di Statistica, *I salari agricoli in Italia dal 1905 al 1933*, (Rome, 1934), pp. 8–9.
66 Cesare Vannutelli, "Occupazione e salari in Italia dal 1861 al 1961," *Rassegna di Statistica del Lavoro* 13 (July–December 1961): pp. 195–212.
67 Vochting, *La questione meridionale*, p. 236.
68 Prefetto of Cosenza, report, 9 March 1893, ASC.
69 Prefetto of Palermo, report, 5 February 1891, ASP.
70 Aldo Pasquali, *L'emigrazione ed i suoi rapporti con l'agricoltura in provincia di Lucca* (Lucca, 1922), p. 60.
71 Luigi Capuana, *Gli americani di Rabbato* (Milan, 1912), p. 24.
72 Tony Cyriax, *Among Italian Peasants* (London, 1919), pp. 78–9.
73 Prefetto of Cosenza, report, 7 May 1897, ASC.
74 Capuana, *Gli americani*, p. 24.
75 Adolfo Rossi, "Vantaggi e danni dell'emigrazione nel Mezzogiorno d'Italia," *Bollettino dell'Emigrazione* 13 (1908): pp. 36–7.
76 Prefetto of Cosenza, report, 7 May 1902, ASC.
77 Ibid., 12 March 1894, ASC.
78 Eugenio Azimonti, *Inchiesta parlamentare sulle condizioni dei contadini nelle province merdionali e nella Sicilia*, vol. 5: *Basilicata e Calabria*, pt. 3 (Rome, 1910), pp. 89–90.
79 Ibid., p. 97.

## Chapter 6. American remittances

1 Adolfo Rossi, "Vantaggi e svantaggi dell'emigrazione nel Mezzogiorno d'Italia," *Bollettino dell'Emigrazione* 13 (1908): 40.
2 Vittorio Ellena, "Le statistiche di alcune industrie italiane," *Annali di statistica* (Rome, 1880), pp. 40–1; Leone Carpi, *Dell'emigrazione italiana all'estero* (Florence, 1871), pp. 171–3.
3 Magliano di Villar San Marco, "L'emigrazione italiana nei suoi rapporti coll'economia nazionale," *Atti del Primo Congresso Geografico Italiano: 1892* (Genoa, 1894), vol. 2, pt. 2, pp. 399–400.
4 E. Del Vecchio, "L'emigrazione italiana negli Stati Uniti quale mezzo per incrementare lo sviluppo delle relazioni commerciali: 1887–1901," in Istituto di Studi Americani, ed., *Gli italiani negli Stati Uniti* (Florence, 1972), p. 144.
5 Celestino Arena, *Italiani per il mondo. Politica nazionale dell'emigrazione* (Milan, 1927), p. 152; Angiolo Cabrini, *La legislazione sociale; 1859–1893* (Rome, 1913), p. 174.
6 Gianfausto Rosoli, "La colonizzazione italiana delle Americhe tra mito e realtà," *Studi Emigrazione* 9 (October 1972): 296–347; Giovanni Florenzano, *Dell'emigrazione italiana in America comparata alle altre emigrazioni europee. Studi e proposte* (Naples, 1874); Leone Carpi, *Delle colonie e dell'emigrazione*

(Milan, 1878); Jacopo Virgilio, *Delle emigrazioni transatlantiche degli italiani e in specie dei Liguri alle regioni del Plata* (Genoa, 1868); Francesco Saverio Nitti, *L'emigrazione italiana ed i suoi avversari* (Turin, 1880); Nicola Marcone, *Gli italiani in Brasile* (Rome, 1887).

7  A. Ravaioli, "La colonizzazione agricola negli Stati Uniti in rapporto all'emigrazione italiana," *Bollettino dell'Emigrazione* 4 (1904): 3–49; Giovanni Preziosi, *Gli italiani negli Stati Uniti del nord* (Milan, 1909), pp. 87–9; Fara Forni, "Gli italiani nel distretto consolare di New Orleans," *Bollettino dell'Emigrazione* 17 (1905): 3–17; G. Rosati, "La colonizzazione negli stati del Mississippi, Luisiana e Alabama," *Bollettino dell'Emigrazione* 14 (1904): 3–30; Giovanni Capra, "La colonizzazione agricola degli Stati Uniti," *Italica Gens* 6 (October–December 1915): 222–37 and Luigi Villari, *Gli Stati Uniti d'America e l'emigrazione italiana* (Milan, 1912), pp. 255–65.

8  Francesco Coletti, "Dell'emigrazione italiana," in Regia Accademia dei Lincei, eds., *Cinquant'anni di storia italiana* (Rome, 1911), p. 245.

9  G. Carocci, *Storia d'Italia dall unità ad oggi* (Milan, 1975), p. 100; Fernando Manzotti, *La polemica sull'emigrazione nell'Italia unita.* (Città di Castello, 1969), pp. 98–104; Ercole Sori, *L'emigrazione italiana dall'unità alla seconda guerra mondiale* (Bologna, 1979). pp. 152–8.

10  Antonio Gramsci, "Il Mezzogiorno e la guerra" in *La Questione Meridionale* (Rome, 1970), p. 56.

11  Luigi Bodio, "Sulla emigrazione italiana e sul patronato degli emigranti," *Atti del Congresso Geografico Italiano in Genova* (Genoa, 1894), vol. 2, pt. 2, pp. 145–7.

12  U.S. Congress, Senate, *Senate Documents*, 61st Cong., 3d sess. (Washington, D.C., 1911), S. Doc. 747, p. 593.

13  R. Foerster, *The Italian Emigration of Our Times* (Cambridge, Mass., 1919), p. 373; Adolfo Rossi, "Per la tutela degli italiani negli Stati Uniti," *Bollettino dell'Emigrazione* 16 (1904): 74–80.

14  O. Bordiga, *Inchiesta parlamentare sulle condizioni dei contadini nelle province meridionali e nella Sicilia* vol. 4: *Campania*, pt. 1 (Rome, 1909), p. 596; Cesare Jarach, ibid., vol. 2: *Abbruzzi e Molise*, pt. 1 (Rome, 1909), p. 258.

15  Azimonti, *Inchiesta parlamentare.* vol. 5: *Basilicata e Calabria*, pt. 1, (Rome, 1909), p. 166.

16  A. Lazzarini, "L'emigrazione temporanea dalla montagna veneta nel secondo ottocento," *Ricerche di Storia Sociale e Religiosa* 10 (1976): 427; Jarach, *Inchiesta parlamentare*, pp. 253, 264; E. Presutti, ibid., vol. 3: *Puglie*, pt. 1 (Rome, 1909), p. 121.

17  Luigi A. Caputo, "Di alcune questioni economiche della Calabria," *Giornale degli Economisti* 35 (1907): 1,187–92.

18  Prefetto of Cosenza, report, 12 March 1907, ASC; prefetto of Palermo, report, 7 June 1904, ASP.

19  John Karen, "The Padrone System and the Padrone Banks," *Bulletin of the Department of Labor* (March 1897): 117.

20  Francesco Saverio Nitti, "Per una banca Italo-Americana," in Francesco Saverio Nitti, ed., *Scritti di economia e finanza*, vol. 5 (Bari, 1969), pp. 72–

3; see also Luigi De Rosa, *Emigranti, capitali e banche* (Naples, 1976), pp. 109–10; Giuseppe De Michelis, *L'emigrazione italiana all'estero dal 1910 al 1923*, 2 vols. (Rome, 1926), vol. 1, pp. 166–71.

21  Francesco Saverio Nitti, *Scritti sulla questione meridionale*, vol. 1 (Bari, 1958), p. 392; De Rosa, *Emigranti, capitali*, pp. 110–11.

22  Seemingly the largest sums went back to Italy with returnees.

23  Immigration Commission, *Senate Documents, Immigrant Banks*, 61st Cong. 2d Sess., N. 381. (Washington, D.C., 1910), pp. 22–3.

24  Ibid., pp. 21–7; De Rosa, "Nitti, le rimesse degli emigrati ed il Banco di Napoli," *Rassegna Economica* 39 (November–December 1975): pp. 1139–42.

25  The owners of the bank were the consul and vice-consul of the Netherlands and the consul of Switzerland in Naples. See E. Trevisani, *Rivista Industriale e Commerciale di Napoli e Provincia* (Naples, 1895), p. 102.

26  Nitti, "Per una banca," pp. 73–5; idem, ed., *Scritti di economia e finanza*, vol. 5, p. 75; De Rosa, "Nitti, le rimesse. 1,346.

27  De Rosa, "Nitti, le rimesse," 1,350–1, 1,357.

28  De Rosa, *Emigranti, capitali*, p. 114.

29  Koren, "The Padrone System," p. 126.

30  Ibid.; De Rosa, "Nitti, le rimesse," pp. 1,341–5.

31  John Koren explained why banchisti did not flourish in San Francisco. Most Italians, he argued, arrived in San Francisco, not directly from Italy, but from other American cities. These immigrants were generally better adjusted to American society and economically better off than most other Italians. This enabled them to find better jobs and to use the services of banks without problems. See Koren, "The Padrone System," p. 124. This explanation is not accurate. Over 90 percent of the San Francisco Italians arrived in the city directly from Italy. Perhaps the reason for the uniqueness of the San Francisco Italian experience is that some prominent Italians like Andrea Sbarboro, Marco Fontana, Amadeo P. Giannini, James Fugazi, and others established four Italian banks with proper accreditation and incorporation and conducted a public relations campaign to convince immigrants that they were most welcome to use the services of the banks. All four banks, as a matter of fact, and especially the Bank of Italy, later to become the Bank of America, actively pursued the immigrants' small accounts and provided the service of sending savings back to Italy. For this, see D. Cinel, *From Italy to San Francisco: The Immigrant Experience* (Stanford, 1982), pp. 101–33, 233–40.

32  Immigration Commission, *Senate Documents, Immigrant Banks*, p. 17; Koren, "The Padrone System," pp. 126–8.

33  The first long exposé of the banchisti's disappearances with savings of immigrants was made in 1892 by Ida Van Etten in the *New York Herald*, 8 September 1892.

34  Italy, *Atti Parlamentari* (Camera dei Deputati), 20th legislature, 1st sess., 1887, Doc. 204, pp. 6–7; Immigration Commission, *Senate Documents. Immigrant Banks*, pp. 115–16, 145–57; De Rosa, "Nitti, le rimesse," pp. 1,343–5; idem, *Emigranti, capitali*, pp. 118–19.

35  Commissariato Generale dell'Emigrazione (hereafter cited as CGE), "Leggi contro le frodi dei banchisti nello stato del Massachusetts," *Bollettino dell'Emigrazione* 7 (1908): 57–76; Celestino Arena, *Il risparmio degli italiani all'estero* (Rome, 1923), pp. 26–7.

36  Joseph Giovinco, "Democracy in Banking: The Bank of Italy and California Italians," *California Historical Society Quarterly* 47 (1968): 195–218.

37  State Department, *Reports on the Postal Savings Banks in Foreign Countries* (Washington, D.C., 1907); Post Office Department, *Postal Savings Banks. Do We Want the Postal Savings Banks?* (Washington, D.C., 1909).

38  United States, *Senate Documents*, 61st Cong., 2d term, N. 268: *Postal Savings Banks. S. 5876 To Establish Postal Savings Depositories for Depositing Savings at Interest with Securities of Government for Repayment thereof* (Washington, D.C., 1910); and Postal Savings System, *Regulation for Guidance of Banks Qualifying as Depositories of Postal Savings Funds under Act of June 25, 1910* (Washington, D.C., 1911).

39  Arena, *Il risparmio*, pp. 14–16, 27–9. United States, *Report of the Post Master General* (Washington, D.C., 1920), p. 91.

40  John Karen, "Lo sfruttamento degli italiani a New York. Le frodi dei bosses e dei banchisti," *La Riforma Sociale* 7 (15 July 1897): pp. 695–711.

41  From 1902 the Direzione Generale of the Banco di Napoli published a yearly report for the Italian legislature on the remittances sent to Italy from North and South America, under the title: *Servizio di raccolta, tutela, impegno e trasmissione nel Regno dei risparmi degli emigrati italiani*. The place of publication was Naples, where the bank's central offices were located.

42  See the following issues of *Bollettino dell'Emigrazione*: 7 (1908): 57–61; ibid., 11 (1907): 145–50; ibid., 18 (1910): 374–96.

43  Prefetto of Cosenza, report, 17 March 1899, ASC; prefetto of Palermo, report, 7 June 1902, ASP.

44  De Rosa, *Emigranti, capitali*, p. 119; idem, "Nitti, le rimesse," pp. 1,346–7; Nitti, *Scritti sulla questione meridionale*, vol. 1, p. 392.

45  Nitti submitted his proposal at the request of the government itself. His was one of the several proposals submitted to the government.

46  Nitti, ed., *Scritti di economia e finanza*, pp. 53, 55; De Rosa, "Nitti, le rimesse," pp. 1,348–9.

47  Nitti, ed., *Scritti di economia e finanza*, pp. 67–8.

48  Events were to prove that Nitti, for all his knowledge of emigration, knew little of the psychology of immigrants.

49  Nitti, ed., *Scritti di economia e finanza*, p. 93.

50  Italy, *Atti Parlamentari* (Camera dei Deputati), 20th legislature, 1st sess., N. 204, 1897, pp. 7–9.

51  See the *Bollettino della Sera*, 18 and 19 September 1899. See also *L'Italia* (San Francisco), 10 January 1900.

52  Giuseppe Giacosa, *Impressioni d'America* (Milan, 1899), pp. 185–6, 225–6.

53  Ferruccio Macola, *L'Europa alla conquista dell'America Latina* (Verona, 1894), pp. 28–9.

54  *Bollettino della Sera*, 18 September 1899.

55  "L'emigrazione italiana negli Stati Uniti," *Bollettino della Sera* (New York), 23 and 24 January 1900.

56  *Sun*, 4 March 1900; *New York Journal*, 7 March 1900; *Journal of Commerce*, 7 March 1900.

57  *L'Araldo Italiano*, 8 March 1900.

58  *Financial Age*, 10 March 1900.

59  *The Mail and Express*, 10 March 1900.

60  *L'Araldo Italiano*, 11 March 1900; *La Sedia Elettrica*, 11 March 1900; *L'Italia in America*, 11 March 1900.

61  *Bollettino della Sera*, 21 and 22 March 1900.

62  *L'Araldo Italiano*, 24 March 1900; *Bollettino della Sera*, 23 and 24 March 1900.

63  *Bollettino della Sera*, 26 and 27 March 1900.

64  *La Tribuna* (Rome newspaper), 26 March 1900.

65  On this, see *Il Pungolo Parlamentare*, (Naples), 27 and 28 March 1900; and *La Tribuna* (Rome), 26 March 1900.

66  "Per le rimesse degli emigrati," *La Tribuna*, 26 March 1900; F. Fabbri, "Il Credito Coloniale," *Rivista Politica e Letteraria* 2 (1898): p. 109.

67  De Rosa, "Nitti, le rimesse," pp. 1,335–66; idem, "Il Banco di Napoli e la crisi economica del 1888–94," *Rassegna Economica* 1 (1965): pp. 53–7.

68  *L'Araldo Italiano*, 24 April 1900; De Rosa, *Emigranti, capitali*, pp. 150–1.

69  Italy, *Atti Parlamentari* (Camera dei Deputati), 21st legislature, 1st sess., 11 December 1900, p. 1,358; Senate, *Atti Parlamentari*, 21st legislature, 1st sess., 31 January 1901, p. 1,092; De Rosa, *Emigranti, capitali*, pp. 155–66; For the text of the law, see *Bollettino dell'Emigrazione* 1 (1902): 40–65; and Domenico Lo Presti, *Codice dell'emigrazione* (Rome, 1917), pp. 70–5.

70  Arena, *Il Risparmio*, p. 29; De Michelis, *L'emigrazione italiana*, vol. 1, p. 152.

71  "Il Console Branchi contro l'istituzione del Banco di Napoli a New York," *L'Araldo Italiano*, 16 July 1901; see also *Bollettino della Sera*, 16 and 17 July 1901. For the reaction in Brazil, see the newspaper of São Paulo, *Fanfulla*, 14 August 1901.

72  G. Vicario, "Le rimesse degli emigranti ed il Banco di Napoli," *L'Araldo Italiano*, 9 September 1901; Vittorio Soldaini, "La raccolta delle rimesse degli emigrati italiani e l'opera del Banco di Napoli, 1902–13," *Revue Internationale d'Histoire de la Banque* 2 (1969): 150–3.

73  Giovanni Preziosi, "Il problema economico dell'emigrazione italiana," *Giornale degli Economisti e Rivista di Statistica* 43 (November 1911): pp. 531–49; idem, *Gli italiani negli Stati Uniti*; Henry Dor, *The Protection of the Emigrants' Savings* (Milan, 1924); Arena, *Il Risparmio*; De Michelis, *L'emigrazione italiana all'estero*, pp. 146–91; Juan Schillizzi, *La tutela del risparmio degli emigranti* (Milan, 1924); Gino Caccianiga, *Propaganda del risparmio specialmente tra le classi operaie e medie* (Milan, 1924); G. Carano-Donvito, "Emigrazione e finanza," *La Riforma Sociale* 18 (15 August 1907): 711–24; Gino Borgatta, "Rimesse degli emigranti e turismo," *Rassegna Economica del Banco di Napoli* 3 (June 1933): pp. 310–22; Coletti, "Dell'emigrazione italiana," in *Cinquant'anni*, pp. 238–48; Bonaldo

Stringher, "Gli scambi con l'estero e la politica commerciale italiana dal 1860 al 1910," in Regia Accademia dei Lincei, ed., *Cinquant'anni di storia italiana*, vol. 3 (Milan, 1911), pp. 117–35; Gino Borgatta, *La stabilizzazione dei cambi e la bilancia italiana dei pagamenti* (Rome, 1927); G. Mortara, *Prospettive economiche* (Città di Castello, 1921); The best study on savings and remittances is Francesco Balletta, *Il Banco di Napoli e le rimesse degli emigrati, 1914–25*. Naples: 1972, and by the same author, "Le rimesse degli emigrati italiani: 1861–1975," in Franca Assante, ed., *Il movimento emigratorio italiano dall'unità nazionale ai nostri giorni*, vol. 1 (Geneva, 1976), pp. 207–86. For a synthesis, see Ercole Sori, *L'emigrazione italiana*, pp. 119–88.

74    The Italian Bureau of Statistics made an effort in 1957 to come up with a complete study of the gross national product from 1861 to 1956, including the revenues generated by Italians working abroad. For this, see the Istituto Centrale di Statistica (hereafter cited as ISTAT), "Indagine statistica sullo sviluppo del reddito nazionale dell'Italia dal 1861 al 1956," *Annali di Statistica*, vol. 9 (Rome, 1957), pp. 162–6.

75    The rate of exchange, at least until World War I, was about three Italian lire per one dollar.

76    For the impact of the remittances on the balance of payments see Stringher, "Gli scambi con l'estero," pp. 1–153.

77    The amount of the remittances is given in lire of the time. On this, see ISTAT, *Indagine Statistica*, p. 258.

78    Corbino, *Annali dell'economia italiana*, 4 vols. (Città di Castello, 1931), vol. 1, p. 18; and Gino Luzzatto, *L'economia italiana dal 1861 al 1914*, vol. 1: *1861–1894* (Milan, 1963), p. 17.

79    CGE, *Annuario statistico dell'emigrazione italiana dal 1876 al 1925* (Rome, 1926), pp. 1,706–11.

80    Corbino, *Annali*, vol. 1, pp. 308–10; Balletta, "Le rimesse," p. 214.

81    Leone Carpi, *Delle colonie e dell'emigrazione di italiani all'estero sotto l'aspetto dell'industria, commercio e agricoltura*, vol. 2 (Rome, 1874), pp. 50–4.

82    Corbino. *Annali*, vol. 2, pp. 361–2; Italy, Direzione Generale della Statistica, *Annuario statistico italiano: 1905–07*, p. 740; Stringher, "Gli scambi con Estero," p. 16.

83    ISTAT, *Sommario di statistiche storiche*. pp. 65–6; Gino Luzzatto, *Storia economica dell'età moderna e contemporanea* (Padua, 1960), pt. 2, pp. 340–1.

84    CGE, *Annuario statistico dell'emigrazione italiana*, p. 65; ISTAT, *Indagini statistiche*, p. 258.

85    Corbino, *Annali*, vol. 2, pp. 19–20.

86    ISTAT, *Sommario di statistiche storiche*, pp. 65; CGE, *Annuario statistico dell'emigrazione italiana*, p. 8.

87    Stringher, "Gli scambi con l'estero," pp. 17–18, 20–2; ISTAT, "Indagini statistiche," pp. 253, 258; Luzzatto, *L'economia italiana*, pp. 206–10; Corbino, *Annali*, vol. 3, pp. 439–42.

88    ISTAT, "Indagine statistica," p. 258; CGE, *Annuario statistico dell'emigrazione italiana*, pp. 8–11, 86–91, 195, 239. The decline in the percentage of women and children after 1900 was mostly the result of decreased emigration from Veneto to Brazil. The Veneti generally went to

Brazil with their families for an unspecified period of time, although not necessarily with the intention of settling there permanently.

89  ISTAT, "Indagine statistica," pp. 258–9; CGE, *Annuario statistico dell'emigrazione italiana*, pp. 167, 195, 239.

90  ISTAT, "Indagine statistica," pp. 65, 258; Villari, *Gli Stati Uniti*, pp. 33, 141–2; CGE, *Annuario statistico dell'emigrazione italiana*, p. 8; ISTAT, *Sommario di statistiche storiche*, p. 65; Stringher, "Gli scambi con l'estero," pp. 40–7.

91  ISTAT, *Sommario di statistiche storiche*, pp. 65–6; Villari, *Gli Stati Uniti*, pp. 34–5; A. Franceschini, *L'emigrazione italiana nell'America del Sud* (Rome, 1908), pp. 469–70; C. Supino, *Storia della circolazione cartacea in Italia dal 1860 al 1928* (Milan, 1929), p. 169; Corbino, *Annali*, vol. 4, p. 379.

92  ISTAT, "Indagine statistica," p. 258; CGE, *Annuario statistico dell'emigrazione italiana*, pp. 8, 88; Banco di Napoli, Direzione Generale (in following footnotes it will be quoted as BN-DG), *Relazione 1904* (Naples, 1905), p. 48; Stringher, "Gli Scambi con l'estero," pp. 40–71.

93  The combined total of remittances handled by the Banco di Napoli and international money orders was only 25 percent of all remittances in 1904, because the Banco was only in its third year of operations. In the following year the combined total grew to 35 percent. See Balletta, "Le rimesse," pp. 272–9.

94  CGE, *Annuario statistico dell'emigrazione italiana*, pp. 1649–51, 1699–1700; De Michelis, *L'emigrazione italiana*, pp. 921–2; Ministero delle Comunicazioni, Direzione Generale delle Poste e dei Telegrafi, *Relazione sul servizio delle casse di risparmio postali: 1931* (Rome, 1935), pp. 54–7; BN-DG, *Relazione*, for every year from 1908 to 1925.

95  Italians in European countries did not encounter the same problem.

96  Coletti, "Dell'emigrazione italiana," in *Cinquant'anni*, pp. 240–2; Borgatta, "Rimesse degli emigranti," pp. 310–22; Luigi Rossi, "Relazione sui servizi dell'emigrazione per l'anno 1909–10," *Bollettino dell'Emigrazione* 8 (1910): pp. 374–96; Bonaldo Stringher, *Sulla bilancia italiana dei pagamenti fra l'Italia e l'estero* (Turin, 1912); P. Jannaccone, *La bilancia dei debiti e dei crediti fra l'Italia e l'estero nell'anno 1923* (Rome, 1925).

97  De Michelis, *L'emigrazione italiana*, vol. 2, pp. 208–9; 652–3; ISTAT, "Indagine statistica," pp. 258–9; idem, *Sommario di statistiche*, pp. 65–6; BN-DG, *Relazione 1912* (Naples, 1913), p. 8.

98  De Michelis, *L'emigrazione italiana*, vol. 1, pp. 289, 392; CGE, *Annuario statistico dell'emigrazione italiana*, pp. 1,647–8, 1,657–60; idem, "Indagine statistica," p. 259.

99  BN-DG, *Relazione 1919* (Naples, 1920), p. 32; CGE, "Mercato del lavoro ed emigrazione nel consolato di New York, 1919," *Bollettino dell'Emigrazione*, 4 (July–August 1919): 47; idem, "Argentina: Condizioni del mercato del lavoro," *Bollettino dell'Emigrazione* 1–3 (January–March 1920): 73.

100  ISTAT, "Indagine statistica," pp. 253–9; CGE, *Annuario statistico*

*dell'emigrazione italiana*, pp. 1,647–8, 1,657–60; De Michelis, *L'emigrazione italiana*, vol. 1, pp. 69–73.

101 Balletta, "Le rimesse," pp. 273–4; Giuseppe De Michelis, *L'emigrazione italiana negli anni 1924 e 1925* (Rome, 1927), pp. 540–4; F. Peviani, *Due milioni di italiani in Brasile. L'Attualità del problema Italo-Brasiliano* (Rome, 1922), pp. 49–50; ISTAT, *Sommario di statistiche storiche*, p. 65.

## Chapter 7. Diverting American savings

1 Eugenio Faina, *Inchiesta parlamentare sulle condizioni dei contadini nelle province meridionali e nella Sicilia*, vol. 8: *Relazione Finale* (Rome, 1911), p. 73.
2 Ibid., p. 97.
3 Ibid., pp. 96–8.
4 Francesco Paolo Cerase, *Sotto il dominio dei borghesi. Sottosviluppo ed emigrazione nell'Italia meridionale: 1860–1910* (Rome, 1975).
5 Francesco Ballerini, *Di una legge per l'emigrazione* (Rome, 1878); Leone Carpi, *Delle colonie e dell'emigrazione di italiani all'estero sotto l'aspetto dell'industria, commercio ed agricoltura* (Milan, 1874); Marchese di Cosentino, *Delle perdite materiali e morali cagionate all'Italia dall'emigrazione nazionale artificiale* (Rome, 1874).
6 John R. Harris and Michael Todaro, "Migration, Unemployment and Development: A Two-Sector Analysis," *The American Economic Review* 60 (March 1970): 126–42; Michael Todaro, "A Model of Labor Migration and Urban Unemployment in Less Developed Countries," *The American Economic Review* 59 (March 1969): 138–48; A. Albert Berry and Ronald Soligo, "Some Welfare Aspects of International Migrations," *Journal of Political Economy* 77 (September–October 1969): pp. 778–94.
7 W. H. Bohning, "Some Thoughts on Emigration from the Mediterranean Basin," *International Labor Review* 111 (March 1975): 251–77.
8 X. Zolotas, *International Labor Migration and Economic Development* (Athens, 1966), pp. 7–12.
9 Bohning," Some Thoughts on Emigration," 251–77.
10 C. W. Stahl, *International Labor Migration and International Development* (Geneva, Bureau International du Travail, 1982), pp. 4–5.
11 Ibid., p. 5.
12 Cesare Jarach, *Inchiesta parlamentare sulle condizioni dei contadini nelle province meridionali e nella Sicilia*, vol. 2: *Abbruzzi e Molise*, p. 1 (Rome, 1909), p. 258, and Luigi Izzo, *La popolazione Calabrese nel secolo decimonono* (Naples, 1965), p. 180.
13 Prefetto of Cosenza, report, 3 March 1904, ASC, Cosenza.
14 F. Prat, "Gli italiani negli Stati Uniti e specialmente nello stato di New York," *Bollettino dell'Emigrazione* 2 (1902): 24–6.
15 "Relazione sui servizi dell'emigrazione per l'anno 1909–1910," *Bollettino dell'Emigrazione* 18 (1910): 2–5.

16  A. Reynaudi, "Relazione sui servizi dell'emigrazione per il periodo Aprile 1905–Aprile 1906," *Bollettino dell'Emigrazione* 7 (1906): 469.

17  Prat, "Gli italiani negli Stati Uniti," 25.

18  Giuseppe Galasso, *Lo sviluppo demografico nel Mezzogiorno prima e dopo l'unità* (Turin, 1965), p. 369.

19  United States, Bureau of the Census, *Population: Special Report on Foreign Born White Families by Countries of Birth of the Head* (Washington, D.C., 1933).

20  Prat, "Gli italiani negli Stati Uniti," 24–5.

21  Ibid., pp. 24–6.

22  Eugenio Azimonti, *Inchiesta parlamentare sulle condizioni dei contadini nelle province meridionali e nella Sicilia,* vol. 5: *Basilicata e Calabria,* p. 1 (Rome, 1909), p. 83. Francesco Balletta, *Il Banco di Napoli e le rimesse degli emigranti: 1914–25* (Naples, 1972), p. 27; Jarach, *Inchiesta parlamentare,* vol. 2 p. 254.

23  Adolfo Rossi, "Vantaggi e svantaggi dell'emigrazione dal Mezzogiorno d'Italia," *Bollettino dell'Emigrazione* 13 (1908): 87.

24  Ernesto Marenghi, *Inchiesta parlamentare sulle condizioni dei contadini nelle province meridionali e nella Sicilia,* vol. 5: *Basilicata e Calabria,* p. 3: *Relazione della sotto giunta parlamentare* (Rome, 1910), pp. 154–5.

25  Prefetto of Cosenza, report, 7 March 1902, ASC; and the prefetto of Palermo, report, 28 June 1905, ASP.

26  Marenghi, *Inchiesta parlamentare,* vol. 5, pt. 3, p. 155.

27  A. Cefaly, Francesco Saverio Nitti, and G. Ranieri, ibid., vol. 5, p. 115; Eugenio Azimonti, ibid., vol. 4: *Campania,* p. 621.

28  Giovanni Lorenzoni, ibid., vol. 6: *Sicilia,* p. 1 (Rome, 1909), p. 832; Bordiga, ibid., vol. 4, *Campania,* p. 621.

29  Arrigo Serpieri, *La politica agraria in Italia ed i recenti provvedimenti legislativi* (Piacenza, 1925), pp. 10–63.

30  A. Serpieri, *Le strutture sociali e le classi rurali italiane* (Bari, 1930), pp. 6–15; Emilio Sereni, *Il capitalismo nelle campagne: 1860–1900* (Turin, 1947), pp. 135–369; prefetto of Cosenza, report, 24 September 1907.

31  A. Rossi, "Vantaggi e svantaggi," pp. 18–27.

32  M. Ciuffoletti, M. Degli Innocenti, and G. Sapelli, *Movimento cooperativo in Italia. Storia e problemi* (Turin, 1981), pp. 3–50.

33  A. Serpieri, *La guerra e le classi rurali Italiane* (Bari, 1930): pp. 29–36.

34  Maffeo Pantaleoni, *La fine provvisoria di un'epopea* (Bari, 1919), pp. 3–17.

35  Partito democratico constituzionale, *La questione agraria e la funzionalità sociale della terra* (Rome, 1917).

36  Initially subsidies were given to wives and children under twelve years of age. Beginning in Sept. 2, 1917, subsidies were extended to grandparents, brothers, and sisters under age or unable to work. Soldiers with large families were entitled to larger subsidies.

37  Serpieri, *La guerra e le classi,* pp. 122–38.

38  Ibid., p. 150.

39  Ibid., pp. 161–76.

40  Ibid., pp. 177–84.

41  Lorenzoni, *Inchiesta sulla piccola proprietà coltivatrice formatasi nel primo dopoguerra*, Vol. 14: *Relazione finale* (Rome, 1938), pp. 201–5.

42  Banco di Napoli, Direzione Generale, *Relazione sul servizio di raccolta, tutela, impiego e trasmissione nel regno dei risparmi degli emigranti. Gestione 1918* (Naples, 1919), pp. 15–20; idem, *Gestione 1919* (Naples, 1920), pp. 15–21; idem, *Gestione 1920* (Naples, 1921), pp. 17–23.

43  Prefetto of Cosenza, report, 7 March 1921, ASC.

44  Azimonti, *Inchiesta parlamentare*, vol. 5, p. 83; Antonio Corbino, *L'emigrazione in Augusta* (Catania, 1914), p. 48; Balletta, *Il Banco di Napoli*, p. 160.

45  Prefetto of Matera, report, 11 May 1901, ASM; and report by the prefetto of Palermo, report, 6 June 1904, ASP.

46  A. Rossi, "Vantaggi e svantaggi," p. 78.

47  Prefetto of Salerno, report, (Salerno, May 21, 1902), ASS.

48  Italy, DGS, *Annuario statistico italiano, 1895*, pp. 511–12; idem, *Annuario statistico italiano: 1905–07*. p. 558; Giuseppe Felloni, *I prezzi sul mercato di Genova dal 1815 al 1890* (Rome, 1957), pp. 15–25; Pietro Bandettini, *I Prezzi sul mercato di Firenze dal 1800 al 1890* (Rome, 1957), pp. 12–24; Antonio Petino, *I prezzi di alcuni prodotti agricoli sul mercato di Palermo e Catania dal 1801 al 1890* (Rome, 1959), appendix.

49  Prefetto of Palermo, report, 13 June 1904, ASP; the prefetto of Cosenza, report, 7 March, 1896, ASC.

### Chapter 8. Regional differences

1  J. D. Gould, "European Inter-Continental Emigration. The Road Back Home: Return Migration from the United States," *The Journal of European Economic History* 9 (Spring 1980): 79.

2  For a summary of the findings, see the report of the president, Senator Stefano Jacini, *Atti della giunta per la inchiesta agraria e sulle condizioni delle classi agricole*, vol. 13: *Relazione finale* (Rome, 1885).

3  This survey was published in eight volumes. For a summary of the findings, see the volume by Senator Eugenio Faina, *Inchiesta parlamentare sulle condizioni dei contadini nelle province meridionali e nella Sicilia*, vol. 8: *Relazione finale* (Rome, 1911).

4  For a summation of the findings, see Giovanni Lorenzoni, *Inchiesta sulla piccola proprietà coltivatrice formatasi nel primo dopoguerra*, vol. 14: *Relazione finale* (Rome, 1938).

5  Incidentally, this survey covered all of the regions of Italy.

6  For a general study of the region, see Franca Assante, *Città e campagna nelle Puglie nel secolo decimonono. L'evoluzione demografica* (Geneva, 1974).

7  Errico Presutti, *Inchiesta parlamentare sulle condizioni dei contadini nelle province meridionali e nella Sicilia*, vol. 3. *Puglie*, pt. 1: *Relazione* (Rome, 1909), pp. 634–5.

8  Ministro di Agricultura, Industria e Commercio (hereafter cited as MAIC), Direzione Generale della Statistica (hereafter cited as DGS), *Statistica*

268     Notes to pages 178–90

*dell'emigrazione italiana all'estero nell'anno 1890.* (Rome, 1891), p. x; ibid.,
*1910.* (Rome, 1911), p. 85.

9  Istituto Centrale di Statistica, *Catasto agrario 1929. Compartimento delle Puglie,* pt. 73: *Provincia di Foggia* (Rome, 1936), p. 7.
10  Ibid., *Catasto agrario 1929. Compartimento della Campania,* pt. 70: *Provincia di Salerno* (Rome, 1935), table 2 and p. 7.
11  Presutti, *Inchiesta parlamentare,* vol. 3, pt. 1, pp. 4–7; prefetto of Foggia, report, 11 March 1903, ASF.
12  Presutti, *Inchiesta parlamentare,* vol. 3, pt. 1, pp. 4–7.
13  Prefetto of Foggia, report, 4 November 1889, ASF.
14  Presutti, *Inchiesta parlamentare,* vol. 3, pt. 1, pp. 6–9, 634–5, 646–75.
15  Ibid., pp. 686–7; prefetto of Bari, report, 2 May 1903, ASB.
16  Vincenzo Ricchioni, *Inchiesta sulla piccola proprietà coltivatrice formatasi nel dopoguerra,* vol. 3: *Puglie* (Rome, 1933), pp. 72–3.
17  Ibid., pp. 69–87.
18  Ibid., p. 97.
19  Luigi Izzo, *Agricoltura e clasi rurali in Calabria dall'unità al fascismo* (Geneva, 1974); see especially chapter 3. nn. 75–148 on mass emigration and its impact on society and economy.
20  Ernesto Marenghi, *Inchiesta parlamentare sulle condizioni dei contadini nelle province meridionali e nella Sicilia,* vol. 5: *Basilicata e Calabria,* pt. 2: *Calabria* (Rome, 1909), pp. 250–2, 737–41.
21  Ibid., pp. 25–36.
22  Prefetto of Cosenza, report, 7 May 1894, ASC.
23  F. Coletti, *Inchiesta parlamentare sulle condizioni dei contadini nelle province meridional: e nella Sicilia,* vol. 5: *Basilicata e Calabria,* pt. 3: *Relazione della sottogiunta parlamentare* (Rome, 1910), pp. 86–7.
24  Marenghi, *Inchiesta Parlamentare,* vol. 5, p. 252.
25  Ibid., pp. 234–5.
26  Ibid., pp. 253–4.
27  Ibid., p. 259.
28  Prefetto of Cosenza, report, 1 September, 1904, ASC.
29  Ettore Blandini, *Inchiesta sulla piccola proprietà coltivatrice formatas: nel dopoguerra,* vol. 2: *Calabria* (Rome, 1931), pp. 1–6.
30  Istituto Centrale di Statistica, *Catasto agrario 1929. Compartimento della Calabria,* pt. 80: *Provincia di Reggio Calabria,* (Rome, 1935), table 2; ibid., pt. 78: *Provincia di Catanzaro* (Rome, 1936), table 2; ibid., pt. 79: *Provincia di Cosenza* (Rome, 1936), table 2.
31  Azimonti, *Inchiesta parlamentare,* vol. 5, pt. 1, pp. 29–84.
32  Ibid., pp. 79–84.
33  Prefetto of Matera, report, 7 March 1907, ASM.
34  A. Scoyni, *Inchiesta sulla piccola proprietà coltivatrice formatasi nel primo dopoguerra,* vol. 8: *Basilicata* (Rome, 1932), pp. 7–9; Prefetto of Matera, report, 11 May 1921, ASM.
35  Scoyni, *Inchiesta sulla piccola proprietà,* vol. 8, pp. 52–6.
36  Istituto Centrale di Statistica, *Catasto Agrario 1929. Compartimento della Lucania,* pt. 76: *Provincia di Matera* (Rome, 1933), table 2; ibid., pt. 77:

*Provincia di Potenza* (Rome, 1934), table 2; prefetto of Matera, report, 17 March 1907, ASM.

37 Oreste Bordiga, *Inchiesta parlamentare sulle condizioni nelle province meridionali e nella Sicilia*, vol. 4: *Campania* pt. 1: *Relazione* (Rome, 1909), pp. 224–7.

38 Antonio Brizi, *Inchiesta sulla piccola proprietà coltivatrice formatasi nel primo dopoguerra*, vol. 9: *Campania* (Rome, 1933), pp. 12–13.

39 A. Brizi, *Inchiesta sulla piccola proprietà*, vol. 9, pp. 13–14.

40 Bordiga, *Inchiesta parlamentare*, vol. 4, p. 235.

41 Ibid., pp. 595–602.

42 Brizi, *Inchiesta sulla piccola proprietà*, vol. 9, p. 14; Bordiga, *Inchiesta parlamentare*, vol. 4, p. 613.

43 Brizi, *Inchiesta sulla piccola proprietà*, vol. 9, pp. 25–34.

44 Istituto Centrale di Statistica, *Catasto agrario 1929. Compartimento della Sicilia*, pt. 81: *Provincia di Agrigento* (Rome, 1935), table 2; ibid. pt. 83: *Provincia di Catania* (Rome, 1935), table 2.

45 Paolo Balsamo, *Giornale del viaggio fatto in Sicilia: Maggio–Giugno 1808* (Palermo, 1810), p. 27.

46 Nunzio Prestianni, *Inchiesta sulla piccola proprietà coltivatrice formatasi nel dopoguerra*, vol. 4. *Sicilia* (Rome, 1931), p. 4.

47 Giovanni Lorenzoni, *Inchiesta parlamentare sulle condizioni dei contadini nelle province meridionali e nella Sicilia* vol. 6: *Sicilia*, pt. 1, sections 1, 2, 3. (Rome, 1910), p. 833.

48 Ibid., pp. 760–1.

49 Ibid., pp. 816–17.

50 Prestianni, *Inchiesta sulla piccola proprietà*, vol. 4, pp. 12–52.

51 MAIC, DGS, *Statistica dell'Emigrazione italiana all'estero nell'anno 1893* (Rome, 1894), p. 65; ibid., *1902–03* (Rome, 1904), p. 65; ibid., *1912–13* (Rome, 1914), p. xi; ibid., *1918–19–20* (Rome, 1921), p. 101.

52 Istituto Centrale di Statitstica, *Catasto Agrario 1929. Compartimento della Sardegna*, pt. 90: *Provincia di Cagliari* (Rome, 1934), table 2; ibid., pt. 91: *Provincia di Nuoro* (Rome, 1935), table 2; ibid., pt. 92: *Provincia di Sassari* (Rome, 1936), table 2; E. Passino and G. Sirotti, *Inchiesta sulla piccola proprietà coltivatrice formatasi nel dopoguerra*, vol. 12: *Sardegna* (Rome, 1935), pp. 10–17; Lorenzoni, *Inchiesta sulla piccola proprietà*, vol. 14, pp. 120–4.

53 Prefetto of Cagliari, report, 11 May 1904, ASC.

## Chapter 9. Return and retirement

1 Prefetto of Matera, report, 7 May 1906, ASM.

2 In Verbicaro, for instance, small farmers had to travel two days through several mountain ranges to go to a regional market to sell their produce.

3 Eugenio Azimonti, *Inchiesta parlamentare sulle condizioni dei contadini nelle province meridionali e nella Sicilia*, vol. 5: *Basilicata e Calabria*, pt. 1 (Rome, 1909), pp. 83, 206. Errico Presutti, ibid., vol. 3: *Puglie*, pt. 1 (Rome, 1909), p. 668.

4 Italy, Ministro di Agricultura, Industria e Commercio (hereafter cited as

MAIC), Direzione Generale della Statistica (hereafter cited as DGS), "Notizie sulle condizioni industriali delle province di Catanzaro, Cosenza e Reggio," *Annali di Statistica* (Rome, 1894), pp. 60–81.

5   Ibid., p. 65.
6   Ibid.
7   Prefetto of Cosenza,. report, 13 May 1894, ASC.
8   Robert Michels, *L'imperialismo italiano* (Milan, 1914), p. 78.
9   Prefetto of Cosenza, report, 15 November 1892, ASC.
10  Ibid., 24 January 1899. Friedrich Vochting, *La questione meridionale* (Naples: 1955), pp. 236–8.
11  Giustino Fortunato, *Il Mezzogiorno e lo stato italiano. Discorsi politici: 1880–1910* (Florence: 1926), vol. 2, p. 500; Gino Arias, *La questione meridionale* (Bologna, 1919), vol. 1, p. 399; Giovanni Lorenzoni, *Inchiesta sulla piccola proprietà coltivatrice formatasi nel primo dopoguerra* vol. 1: *Relazione finale* (Rome, 1938), pp. 179–84.
12  Prefetto of Cosenza, report, 11 March 1899, ASC.
13  Francesco Paolo Cerase, *Sotto il dominio dei borghesi. Sottosviluppo ed emigrazione nell'Italia meridionale: 1860–1910* (Rome, 1975), p. 115; Ercole Sori, *L'emigrazione italiana dall'unità alla seconda guerra mondiale* (Bologna, 1979), p. 164.
14  A. Cefaly, Francesco Saverio Nitti, and G. Ranieri, *Inchiesta parlamentare, sulle condizioni dei contadini nelle province meridionali e nella Sicilia*, vol. 5. *Basilicata e Calabria*, pt. 3: *Relazione del delegato technico Ernesto Marenghi*, (Rome, 1910), p. 104; Oresta Bordiga, ibid., *Inchiesta parlamentare*, vol. 4: *Campania*, pt. 1 (Rome, 1909), p. 616.
15  Prefetto of Cosenza, report, 27 March 1906, ASC.
16  George Gilkey, "The United States and Italy: Migration and Reemigration," *Journal of Developing Areas* 2 (1967): 32.
17  Agostino Caputo, *Di alcune questioni economiche della Calabria. L'influenza dell' emigrazione sui costumi* (Rome 1909), p. 13.
18  Prefetto of Cosenza, report, 3 May 1901, ASC.
19  Italy, *Atti Parlamentari* (Camera dei Deputati), *Relazione della Commissione di Vigilanza sulla Cassa dei Depositi e Prestiti per il triennio 1878–80* (Rome, 1881), pp. 8–13.
20  Ibid., pp. 5–8.
21  Italy, MAIC, DGS, *Banche popolari: Anno 1893* (Rome, 1895), pp. 3–43.
22  Italy, MAIC, DGS, *Statitica della società di mutuo soccorso e delle istituzioni cooperative annesse alle medesime. Anno 1885* (Rome, 1888), pp. v-xlxii.
23  Antonio Confalonieri, *Banca ed industrie in Italia: 1894–1906*, vol. 1: *Le premesse: Dall'abolizione del Corso Forzoso alla caduta del Credito Mobiliare* (Milan, 1874), pp. 231, 244, 274.
24  Dino Taruffi, Leonello De Nobili and Cesare Lori, *La questione agraria e l'emigrazione in Calabria* (Florence, 1908), p. 853.
25  Giovanni Lorenzoni, *Inchiesta parlamentare sulle condizioni dei contadini nelle province meridionali e nella Sicilia*, vol. 6: *Sicily* (Rome, 1910) pt. 1, sections pp. 829–32.
26  Prefetto of Palermo, report, 22 May 1907, ASP, Palermo.

27  Prefetto of Cosenza, report, 12 December 1911, ASC.
28  Italy, Ministero delle Comunicazioni, Direzione Generale delle Poste e dei Telegrafi, *Relazione sul servizio delle casse di risparmio postali* (Rome, 1940), p. 24.
29  Ibid., pp. 14–24.
30  Italy, Ministero delle Poste e dei Telegrafi, *Relazione intorno ai servizi postali, telegrafici, telefonici e marittimi per gli anni 1904–05 e 1905–06 e al servizio delle casse di risparmio postali per gli anni 1902, 1903, 1904 e 1905* (Rome, 1908), pp. 318–23.
31  Prefetto of Cosenza, report, 17 March 1904, ASC.
32  Prefetto of Palermo, report, 21 June 1902, ASP.
33  Prefetto of Cosenza, report, 7 March 1904, ASC.
34  Caputo, *Di alcune questioni economiche*, pp. 1,187–92.
35  Prefetto of Cosenza, report, 3 March 1912, ASC; Prefetto of Palermo, report, 17 October 1909, ASP.
36  Italy, DGS, *Annuario statistico italiano, 1905–07*, p. 784.
37  Ibid., *1916*, pp. 305–6.
38  Ibid., *1922–26*, pp. 300–3.
39  Prefetto of Genoa, report, 11 March 1913, ASG.
40  Italy, DGS, *Annuario statistico italiano, 1905–7*, p. 784.
41  Ibid., p. 784.
42  Ibid., *1916*, pp. 305–6.
43  Ibid., *1922–25*, pp. 300–3.
44  Prefetto of Cosenza, report, 14 May 1912, ASC; and prefetto of Palermo, report, 24 September 1913, ASP.
45  Italy, DGS, *Annuario statistico italiano, 1905–7*, p. 784.
46  Prefetto of Genoa, report, 21 March 1913, ASG.
47  F. Balletta, *Il Banco di Napoli e le rimesse degli emigranti, 1914–25* (Naples, 1972), p. 171.
48  Guido Dorso, "La classe dirigente" (1925), in Bruno Caizzi, ed., *Nuova antologia della questione meridionale* (Milan, 1962), pp. 425–6.
49  Antonio Gramsci, "Alcuni temi sulla questione meridionale," in Bruno Caizzi, ed., *Nuova antologia della questione meridionale* (Milan, 1962), p. 330.
50  Italy, *Atti Parlamentari* (Camera dei Deputati), *Relazione della Commissione di Vigilanza della Cassa Depositi e Prestiti pel triennio 1878–79–80* (Rome, 1881), pp. 15–16.
51  Ibid., pp. 16–17.
52  Ibid., pp. 17–19.
53  Ibid., pp. 21–3.
54  Italy, *Atti Parlamentari* (Camera dei Deputati), *Relazione . . . , Esercizio 1902* (Rome, 1903), pp. 128–32.
55  Ibid., *Relazione . . . Esercizio 1914* (Rome 1915), pp. 163–73.
56  Ibid. *Esercizio 1922* (Rome, 1923), pp. 46–9.
57  Shephard B. Clough and Carlo Levi, "Il divario tra nord e sud e lo sviluppo economico italiano," in Giorgio Mori, ed., *L'industrializzazione in Italia: 1861–1900* (Bologna, 1977), pp. 210, 219.

### Conclusion: National integration and return migration

1 Incidentally, most such contracts were verbal. In addition, landowners vindicated the right to change the terms of the contract at any time until harvest. Under the circumstances, contracts could not be enforced in a court of law. Neither did the government have any real control over landowners who operated, as if it were, outside the law.

2 There are stories of immigrants forcing children to go back to Italy with them. But in many cases, the children returned to the United States on their own as soon as they reached the age of sixteen. Parents, reluctantly, returned to the United States to be with them.

3 Immanuel Wallerstein, *The Modern World System: Capitalistic Agriculture and the Origin of the European World Economy in the Sixteenth Century* (New York, 1976); idem, *The Modern World System II: Mercantilism and the Consolidation of the European World Economy, 1600–1750* (New York, 1980).

# Index

Printed in the United Kingdom
by Lightning Source UK Ltd.
9562400001B